STRATEGIC
MANAGEMENT
CONCEPTS

FOURTH EDITION

STRATEGIC MANAGEMENT

CONCEPTS

Peter Wright

The University of Memphis

Mark J. Kroll

University of Texas at Tyler

John A. Parnell

Texas A & M University Commerce

 Prentice Hall, Upper Saddle River, NJ 07458

Acquisitions Editor: David Shafer
Associate Editor: Lisamarie Brassini
Editorial Assistant: Chris Stogdill
Editor-in-Chief: Natalie E. Anderson
Marketing Manager: Tammy Wederbrand
Senior Production Editor: Cynthia Regan
Production Coordinator: Carol Samet
Managing Editor: Dee Josephson
Manufacturing Supervisor: Arnold Vila
Manufacturing Manager: Vincent Scelta
Senior Designer: Ann France
Design Director: Patricia Smythe
Interior Design: Suzanne Behnke
Cover Design: Amanda Kavanaugh
Illustrator (Interior): TSI Graphics
Composition: TSI Graphics
Cover Art/Photo: Letraset Phototone

Copyright (c) 1998, 1996 by Prentice Hall, Inc.
A Simon and Schuster Company
Upper Saddle River, New Jersey 07458

The Library of Congress has cataloged the Combined Volume as follows:
Wright, Peter
   Strategic management : concepts and cases / Peter Wright, Mark J.
Kroll, John A. Parnell. — 4th ed.
      p.   cm.
   Includes bibliographical references and index.
   ISBN 0-13-681750-5
   1. Strategic planning.   2. Strategic planning—Case studies.
I. Kroll, Mark J.   II. Parnell, John A. (John Alan)
III. Title.
HD30.28.W75   1998
658.4′012—dc21   97-36699
                                                           CIP

Printed in the United States of America
10 9 8 7 6 5 4 3 2

ISBN: 0-13-631623-9 (Concepts)
ISBN: 0-13-628801-4 (Cases)

Prentice-Hall International (UK) Limited, *London*
Prentice-Hall of Australia Pty. Limited, *Sydney*
Prentice-Hall Canada Inc., *Toronto*
Prentice-Hall Hispanoamericana, S. A., *Mexico*
Prentice-Hall of India Private Limited, *New Delhi*
Prentice-Hall of Japan, Inc., *Tokyo*
Simon & Schuster Asia Pte. Ltd., *Singapore*
Editoria Prentice-Hall do Brazil, Ltda., *Rio de Janeiro*

Contents

Preface

This fourth edition reflects the truth of one of our book's basic tenets: environmental change is inevitable. In fact, changes in the business environment and developments in the academic field of strategic management drove us to begin revising *Strategic Management Concepts* less than a year after the third edition first appeared on the market. This new edition not only contains those changes, but it also benefits significantly from the perceptive feedback of our reviewers and the adopters of the first, second, and third editions.

The text portion synthesizes and builds upon the most recent strategy-related literature from numerous fields. And virtually every concept, theory, or idea is illustrated with examples from real organizations. The cases represent the works of knowledgeable and discerning authors who have provided highly readable information on enterprises ranging from small, local businesses to huge, global corporations.

GOALS OF THE TEXT

Our purpose in writing this text was twofold: to provide students with the most current, comprehensive, state-of-the-art analysis of the field of strategic management, and to promote student understanding of the material with applied, innovative learning features.

To accomplish our first goal, we incorporated the most up-to-date coverage of the strategic management literature into the text in a clear, easy-to-read style. The coverage includes the most relevant and exciting multidisciplinary contributions to the field. Strategic management is a relatively young discipline that has borrowed from, built upon, and contributed to such business fields as economics, management, marketing, finance, operations management, and accounting, among others. In recent years, however, exciting developments from such diverse fields as psychology, sociology, and anthropology have also broadened and enriched the knowledge base of strategic management. Students will gain new insights from these cutting-edge, integrative developments.

The strategic management and business policy course is designed to help students integrate and apply what they have learned in their separate functional business courses and to help them gain experience in using the tools of strategic analysis. To facilitate this process and promote student learning—the second major goal of this text—we have developed a number of innovative learning tools. You will find this book rich with applied material—realistic business examples carefully woven throughout the text, provocative discussions of strategic management conducted by well-known companies, and experiential exercises to help students think strategically. Since the core of the course is case analysis, our text provides an excellent, diverse collection of up-to-date cases depicting meaningful decision situations.

STATE-OF-THE-ART COVERAGE

Along with traditional coverage, this text incorporates a number of innovative topics and provides several unique chapters that give it a distinct competitive advantage over other textbooks in strategic management. Some of that coverage includes the following material:

- Diverse theories that have influenced our approach to strategic management are briefly presented in Chapter 1. These include biological and Schumpeterian theories of evolution and revolution; theories based upon the fields of industrial organization and Chamberlinian economics; and contingency and resource-based theories.

- Chapter 3 presents not only the traditional viewpoint that a firm's strategy should be shareholder-driven, but also the competing perspectives that strategy should be customer-driven or, more broadly, stakeholder-driven. Resource-based theory is used to analyze a firm's strengths and weaknesses.
- Our S.W.O.T. portfolio framework is introduced in Chapter 5, along with more traditional approaches. New material analyzing corporate strategies and returns is also included in Chapter 5.
- Chapter 6, a unique chapter on business unit strategies, relates generic strategies to such concepts as total quality management (TQM), product/process innovations, leverage through organizational expertise and image, market share, industry life cycle stages, value analysis, and strategic groups.
- Unique coverage of how functional activities can be integrated to help a business attain superior product design, customer service, speed, and product/service guarantees is contained in Chapter 7.
- A framework is presented in Chapter 8 for helping top management assess the effectiveness of the organization's structure.
- Chapter 9 offers innovative discussion of how strategy is implemented through managerial leadership, the appropriate use of power, and the molding of organizational culture.
- A unique approach to strategic control in Chapter 10 presents multiple control standards and several different and useful ways of exerting strategic control.
- Global issues are not only integrated throughout the text but are comprehensively covered in Chapter 11. This unique chapter revisits the strategic management processes covered in Chapters 2 through 10 in the context of the world marketplace.
- Chapter 12 is devoted exclusively to strategic management in not-for-profit organizations.
- Differences in strategic management processes in large and small companies are examined in separate sections throughout the chapter portions of the text.

NEW TO THIS EDITION

New to the Fourth Edition is the coverage of the following material:

- Although the traditional industry analysis is presented in Chapter 2, it is also argued in this chapter that the pressure for enhanced firm efficiency and innovation during the last two decades has increased to such an extent that analyzing any one industry may not fully reflect what impacts an enterprise's performance. Rather, the performance of a firm may be determined by its competitive and cooperative interactions with other firms across different industries. Thus, what is newly examined are exchanges among an assemblage of firms across various industries.
- Updated "Strategic Insight" boxes and examples.
- In Chapter 6, value chain analysis is presented as a series of internal and external agency relationships. An agency relationship exists when one party (an agent) acts on behalf of another party (a principal) to increase the value of the principal's resources or activities.
- In Chapter 7, an expanded coverage of cross functional teams and process management takes place.
- In Chapter 8, an expanded coverage of the assessment of organizational structure is presented.
- In Chapter 9, leadership, power, and culture are depicted with a focus on each as components of strategy implementation.
- In Chapter 10, more recent developments on strategic control are covered.

SPECIAL LEARNING FEATURES OF THIS TEXT

We have consistently integrated theory with practice throughout the chapter portion of the book. You will find that strategic management concepts are liberally illustrated with examples from actual, well-known organizations.

To promote student learning further, we built into the text a number of special features to help students understand and apply the concepts presented. Each chapter of the text provides the following learning features:

- *A strategic management* model helps to portray visually the important stages in the strategic management process. This model is introduced and explained in Chapter 1, then reappears at the beginning of each chapter, with the portion to be discussed in a given chapter highlighted. The model serves as a student's road map throughout each chapter.
- *Key concepts* are boldfaced in the text when first introduced and are immediately defined. A list of key concepts with definitions appears at the end of each chapter.
- *Strategic Insight* boxes throughout the chapter portion of the book illustrate successful and unsuccessful applications of strategic management concepts in such companies as Southwest Airlines, IBM, Coca-Cola, and Sears, Roebuck and Company. Each of the boxes illustrates a major point in the text.
- A *chapter summary* helps reinforce the major concepts that the student has learned in the chapter.
- End-of-chapter *discussion questions* test the student's retention and understanding of important chapter material and can be used as a tool for review and classroom discussion.
- *Strategic Management Exercises* unique to this text appear at the end of each chapter. These experiential exercises offer students the opportunity to apply their knowledge of the chapter material to realistic strategic business situations.

SUPPLEMENTS

Internet Support Site—**http://www.prehall.com/ wrightsm**—features book specific, student-based exercises illustrating how to use the WWW as a strategic resource.

StratPlus—a generic *Strategic Management* web site featuring additional information on alternative methodologies, an annotated "How to Do a Case", Internet Resources, and Bi-Monthly News updates.

Instructor's Resource Manual—includes test items and extensive case notes containing a synopsis, a mini-S.W.O.T. analysis, and transparency masters for each case.

Computerized Instructor's Resource Manual—offers all the features of the IRM on a 3.5" disk.

Overhead Transparencies—covering the major concepts for the first 12 chapters.

PowerPoint Transparencies—Electronic version of the Overhead Transparency program available on 3.5" disk.

Prentice Hall Video Library—contains clips from companies discussed in the "Strategic Insight" boxes of the Concepts section of the text and selected industries within the Case section of the text.

Prentice Hall Custom Cases—allows professors to select only the Cases they want to use in their classroom. Contact your local sales representative for ordering details or visit our web site at **http://www.prenhall.com/phbusiness**.

ACKNOWLEDGMENTS

We are deeply indebted to many individuals for their assistance and support in this project. We especially wish to thank our manuscript reviewers for the first, second, third, and fourth editions. These colleagues were particularly able and deserve considerable credit for their helpful and extensive suggestions. They include:

William P. Anthony, *Florida State University*
B.R. Baliga, *Wake Forest University*
Robert B. Brown, *University of Virginia*
William J. Carner, *University of Texas at Austin*
Peng Chan, *California State University, Fullerton*
Edward J. Conlon, *University of Notre Dame*
Halil Copur, *Rhode Island College*
George B. Davis, *Cleveland State University*
Louis R. Desfosses, *State University of New York, Brockport*
Pierre E. Du Jardin, *Bentley College*
Kamal Fatchi, *Witchita State University*
Lawrence K. Finley, *Western Kentucky University*
Philip C. Fisher, *University of South Dakota*
Len Frey, *Nicolls State University*
Joseph J. Geiger, *University of Idaho*
Manolete V. Gonzalez, *Oregon State University*
Donald Harvey, *California State University, Bakersfield*
Marilyn M. Helms, *University of Tennessee at Chattanooga*
Stevan R. Holmberg, *The American University*
Tammy G. Hunt, *University of North Carolina at Wilmington*
William Jackson, *Stephen F. Austin State University*

Michael J. Keeffe, *Southwest Texas State University*
Daniel G. Kopp, *Southwest Missouri State University*
Augustine Lado, *Cleveland State University*
Don Lester, *Crichton University*
William Litzinger, *University of Texas, San Antonio*
James Logan, *University of New Orleans*
Michael Lubatkin, *University of Connecticut*
John E. Merchant, *California State University, Sacramento*
Omid Nodoushani, *University of New Haven*
Tim Pett, *University of Memphis*
Bevalee Pray, *Union University*
Elizabeth Rozell, *Missouri Southern State College*
Hael Y. Sammour, *East Texas State*
Daniel A. Sauers, *Louisiana Tech University*
Charles W. Schilling, *University of Wisconsin, Platteville*
Louise Sellaro, *Youngstown State University*
Jeffery C. Shuman, *Bentley College*
Carl L. Swanson, *University of North Texas*
James B. Thurman, Ph.D., *George Washington University*
Howard Tu, *University of Memphis*
Philip M. Van Auken, *Baylor University*
Robert P. Vichas, *Florida Atlantic University*

Richard J. Ward, *Bowling Green State University*
Marion White, *James Madison University*
Carolyn Y. Woo, *Purdue University*
David C. Wyld, *Southeastern Louisiana University*

Special thanks are due to our editor, David Shafer, and our production editor, Cynthia Regan, for overseeing this project from inception to completion. We are deeply indebted to Professor Charles "Hemingway" Pringle for the quality he imputed to the development of the first two editions of this text. His brilliance will live on and carry us through the subsequent revisions.

Administrators at each of our universities have been most supportive of our work. We particularly wish to thank Dean Donna Randall and Management Chairman Robert Taylor, University of Memphis; and President George F. Hamm, Vice President of Academic Affairs Bill Baker, and Dean Jim Tarter of the University of Texas at Tyler.

Finally, but certainly not least, the support, patience, and understanding of special family members—William, Mahin, and Teresa Wright; Nghi Kroll; and Denise Parnell—were not only helpful but essential in making this book a reality.

About the Authors

Peter Wright is a Professor of Management who holds the University of Memphis Endowed Chair of Excellence in Free Enterprise Management. He received his M.B.A. and his Ph.D. in management from Louisiana State University. He has acted as a consultant to many business organizations and was president/owner of an international industrial trading firm. Professor Wright is widely published in journals such as the *Harvard Business Review, Strategic Management Journal, Academy of Management Journal, Journal of Management, Journal of Business Research, Journal of Banking and Finance, Long Range Planning, British Journal of Management, Journal of the Academy of Marketing Science, Business Horizons, Planning Review,* and *Managerial Planning,* among others. Some of his academic publications have been reported in the media such as *The CBS Television Evening News, The Washington Post, Business Week, The Economist,* the *Wall Street Journal,* and *Smart Money.*

Mark J. Kroll is Professor Chair of the Management and Marketing Department at the University of Texas at Tyler. He received his M.B.A. from Sam Houston State University and his D.B.A. in management from Mississippi State University. His articles on strategic management topics have ap-

peared in many journals including the *Academy of Management Journal, Academy of Management Review, Journal of Business Research, and Journal of the Academy of Marketing Science.* He has also authored a number of cases, which have appeared in various strategic management textbooks and in the *Case Research Journal.* Professor Kroll consults for a wide variety of business organizations and teaches the capstone strategic management course at both the undergraduate and graduate levels.

John A. Parnell is Professor and Head of the Marketing and Management Department at Texas A & M University Commerce. He received his M.B.A. from East Carolina University, his Ed.D. from Campbell University, and his Ph.D. from The University of Memphis. He served three years as president/owner of a direct-mail firm and is the author of over 100 journal articles, published cases, and conference proceedings. His works appear in such leading journals as *Administration and Society, British Journal of Management, Human Resource Management Review, International Journal of Organizational Analysis, and International Journal of Value-Based Management.* Professor Parnell teaches the capstone strategic management course at the undergraduate and graduate levels.

STRATEGIC MANAGEMENT

CONCEPTS

I THE CONCEPTS AND TECHNIQUES OF STRATEGIC MANAGEMENT

STRATEGIC MANAGEMENT MODEL

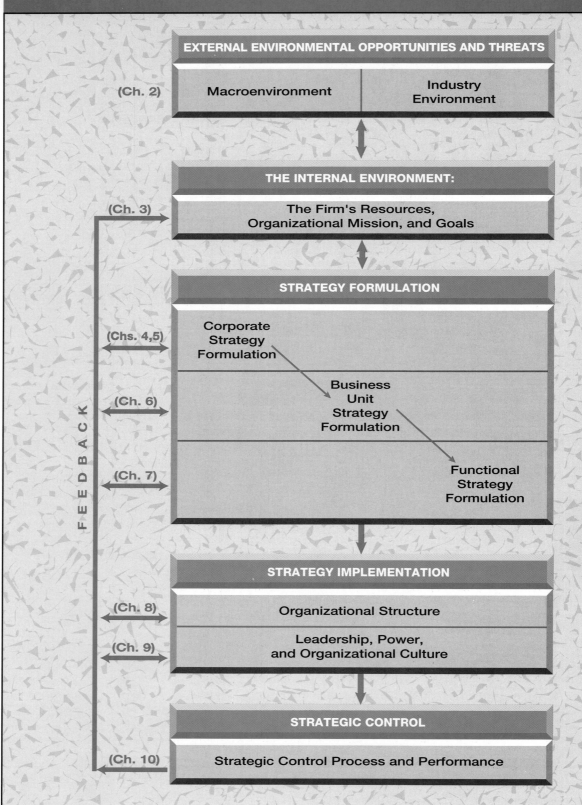

EXTERNAL ENVIRONMENTAL OPPORTUNITIES AND THREATS

(Ch. 2) | Macroenvironment | Industry Environment

THE INTERNAL ENVIRONMENT:

(Ch. 3) | The Firm's Resources, Organizational Mission, and Goals

STRATEGY FORMULATION

(Chs. 4,5) | Corporate Strategy Formulation

(Ch. 6) | Business Unit Strategy Formulation

(Ch. 7) | Functional Strategy Formulation

STRATEGY IMPLEMENTATION

(Ch. 8) | Organizational Structure

(Ch. 9) | Leadership, Power, and Organizational Culture

STRATEGIC CONTROL

(Ch. 10) | Strategic Control Process and Performance

FEEDBACK

1 Introduction to Strategic Management

Managers face no greater challenge than that of strategic management. Guiding a complex organization through a dynamic, rapidly changing environment requires the best of judgment. Strategic management issues are invariably ambiguous and unstructured, and the way in which management responds to them determines whether an organization will succeed or fail.

Strategic management is challenging because it is far more than simply setting goals and then ordering organization members to attain those goals. An organization's strategic direction depends upon a variety of considerations. Among them are top management's assessment of the external environment's opportunities and threats, and management's analysis of the firm's internal strengths and weaknesses. Senior executives are authorized to determine the mission and goals of the firm in the context of external opportunities or threats and internal strengths or weaknesses. Simultaneously, the top management team must take into account the competing desires and needs of the organization's various stakeholders (or interested parties) because their support is essential to successful strategy implementation. Stakeholders include not only the organization's managers and employees but also the firm's owners (stockholders), suppliers, customers, creditors, and community members.

This text focuses on strategic management. The issues and processes discussed are real ones that are directly relevant to all types of organizations—large or small, international or domestic, diversified or single-product, and profit or nonprofit. The material contained herein should provide keen insight into strategic management and an appreciation of its vital role in enhancing organizational effectiveness.

WHAT IS STRATEGIC MANAGEMENT?

■ Strategic Management Defined

Because the word *strategy* or some variation of it is used throughout the text, its definition should be clear. **Strategy** refers to top management's plans to attain outcomes consistent with the organization's mission and goals. One can look at strategy from three vantage points: (1) strategy formulation (developing the strategy), (2) strategy implementation (putting the strategy into action), and (3) strategic control (modifying either the strategy or its implementation to ensure that the desired outcomes are attained).

Strategic management is a broader term that encompasses managing not only the stages already identified but also the earlier stages of determining the mission and goals of an organization within the context of its external and internal environments. Hence, strategic management can be viewed as a series of steps in which top management should accomplish the following tasks:

1. Analyze the opportunities and threats or constraints that exist in the external environment.
2. Analyze the organization's strengths and weaknesses in its internal environment.
3. Establish the organization's mission and develop its goals.
4. Formulate strategies (at the corporate level, the business unit level, and the functional level) that will match the organization's strengths and weaknesses with the environment's opportunities and threats.
5. Implement the strategies.
6. Engage in strategic control activities to ensure that the organization's goals are attained.

Although the various steps in this process are discussed sequentially in this book, in reality they are highly related. Any single stage in the strategic management process must be considered in conjunction with the other stages because a change at any given point will affect other stages in the process.[1] These stages are discussed sequentially throughout the text only to make them more understandable.

In its broadest sense, strategic management consists of managerial decisions and actions that help to ensure that the organization formulates and maintains a beneficial fit with its environment. Thus, strategic managers evaluate their company's evolving strengths and weaknesses. Maintaining a compatible fit between the business and its environment is necessary for competitive viability. Because both the environment and the organization change with the passage of time, this process is an ongoing concern for management.

■ Strategic Management Model

To help one envision the strategic management process, a schematic model is presented in Figure 1.1. At the top, the model begins with an analysis of external environmental opportunities and threats. In the next stage, the organization's internal environment (firm resources, mission, and goals) is linked to the external environment by a dual arrow. This arrow means that the mission and goals are set in the context of external environmental opportunities and threats as well as of the internal strengths and weaknesses of the firm (its resources).

Figure 1.1   **Strategic Management Model**

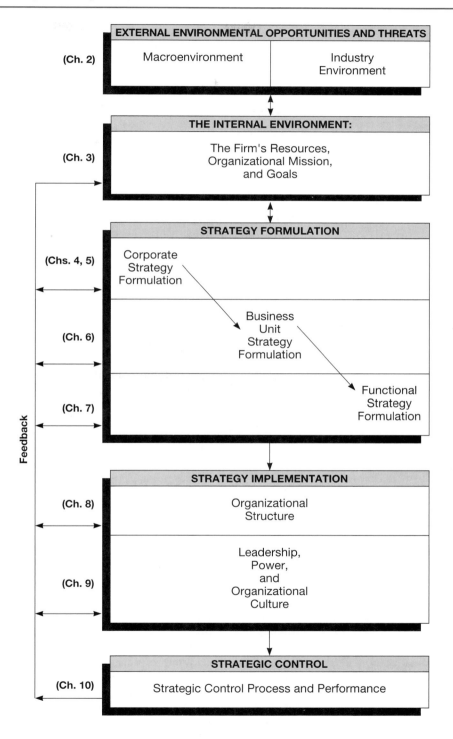

The organization is affected by external environmental forces. But the organization can also have an impact upon its external environment.[2]

> Federal legislation, for instance, can be influenced by lobbying activities; the ecological environment can be improved through corporate social responsibility actions; customer behavior can be swayed through advertising and sales promotion; large, economically powerful retailers can affect the actions of suppliers; and pricing strategy and product improvements certainly influence the activities of competitors.[3]

The mission and goals of the acquisitions drive strategy formulation at the corporate, business unit, and functional levels. However, the present and potential strengths and weaknesses of the organization (firm resources at corporate, business unit, and functional levels) also influence the mission and goals of the firm. This is demonstrated by the two-way arrow between the internal environment and strategy formulation. At the corporate level, the decision makers are the chief executive officer (CEO), other top managers, and the board of directors. Most of the strategic decisions at the business unit level are made by the top manager of the business unit and his or her key executives, and the decision makers at the functional level are the heads of the functional areas (the managers of such departments as production, finance, marketing, and research and development). In some organizations, instead of functional departments, there are core process centers (such as materials handling center rather than purchasing and manufacturing functional departments).

The next arrow depicts the idea that strategy formulation sets strategy implementation in motion. Specifically, strategy is implemented through the organization's structure, its leadership, its distribution of power, and its culture. Then, the final downward arrow indicates that the actual strategic performance of the organization is evaluated. To the extent that performance fails to meet the organization's goals, strategic control is exerted to modify some or all of the stages in the model in order to improve performance. The control stage is demonstrated by the feedback line that connects strategic control to the other parts of the model.

More details on the strategic management model are provided in the next nine chapters. At the beginning of each chapter, the part of the model that is to be featured is highlighted. In chapters 11 and 12, the entire model is revisited through a focus, respectively, on international and not-for-profit organizations.

■ Importance of Strategic Management

Current events covered in such business publications as *Fortune*, *Business Week*, and the *Wall Street Journal* involve strategic management concepts. Hence, an understanding of the business world requires familiarity with the strategic management process. As domestic and foreign competition intensifies, and during those periods when government's influence on business operations expands, an understanding of strategic management becomes even more essential.

Employees, supervisors, and middle managers must be familiar with strategic management. An appreciation of their organization's strategy helps them relate their work assignments more closely to the direction of the organization, thereby enhancing their job performance and opportunity for promotion and making their organization more effective.

■ Evolving Study of Strategic Management

During the 1950s the Ford Foundation and the Carnegie Corporation funded an analysis of business school curricula and teaching. From this research came the Gordon-Howell report, which concluded that formal business education at universities should be broadened and should conclude with a capstone course that would integrate students' knowledge from such courses as accounting, finance, marketing, management, and economics.[4] Most business schools accepted the conclusions of this report and developed a capstone course that became known as "Business Policy."

The initial thrust of the business policy course was to integrate the functional areas within an enterprise so that it could attain a consistent direction. The direction would be one that capitalized upon its strengths while deemphasizing its weaknesses, relative to the opportunities and threats presented by the organization's external environment.

Over time, the parameters of this capstone course expanded to include more formal analyses of the organization's macroenvironment, industry environment, mission and goals, strategy formulation, strategy implementation, and strategic control. This expanded conception of the field began to be referred to as *strategic management*, as opposed to the more narrow term *business policy*.[5]

In strategic management, it can be argued that the ideal executive of the future will be a leader, not a mere administrator.[6] This ideal executive will be a master servant for the organization's various constituencies. He or she will be a visionary, a team player, and a coach who is global in perspective and capable of capitalizing on diversity.

INFLUENCE ON STRATEGIC MANAGEMENT

As a field of study, strategic management is eclectic, drawing upon a variety of theoretical frameworks. This section examines some of the diverse roots that have influenced our approach to strategic management.

■ Evolution and Revolution Theories

Charles Darwin, the naturalist, proposed a theory of evolutionary change of biological species.[7] In its most basic form, Darwin's theory suggested that environmental change forces each species into incremental, but continuous, mutation or transformation. Through such a change, a living entity can adapt to its environment and survive. A species that cannot conform to its environmental requirements is doomed, eventually becoming extinct.

This perspective of evolutionary change has influenced many management thinkers.[8] As a result, they believe that organizations are influenced by the environment; that environmental change is gradual, requiring concomitant organizational change; and that effective organizations are those that conform most closely to environmental requirements. Firms that cannot or do not adapt to gradual external change eventually find themselves outpaced by their competitors and forced out of business.

A different view of environmental change was proposed by certain natural historians and by the economist Joseph Schumpeter.[9] According to this view, environmental change is not gradual but occurs in revolutionary and abrupt forms. Natural historians in this school of thought believe that species can exist in unaltered form for a lengthy period of time. Then, as a result of sudden, revolutionary environmental change, old species might be destroyed and novel species created. The resultant species then exist for many decades or centuries until the environment again changes abruptly, prompting the creation of still newer species.

Likewise in the field of social science, Schumpeter proposed that an economic environment is characterized by a relatively long period of stability, punctuated by brief periods of discontinuous and revolutionary change. These revolutions are generated by the advent of new entrepreneurial enterprises with novel technologies. The new industries created by these entrepreneurial ventures destroy existing firms and industries by making them obsolete.

Some views of revolutionary change are more moderate, proposing that at least some of the existing firms would be able to adapt to the abrupt environmental change.[10] These adaptive organizations allow the innovative firms to absorb the costs and risks of creating new products and services and then imitate those successful innovations.[11] Even Schumpeter, in 1950, changed from his earlier (1934) position by arguing that some existing firms could survive revolutionary change.[12] Survival, he believed, could come reactively through imitating the revolutionary products or services of newer enterprises or proactively by originating new products or services.

■ Industrial Organization Theory

Industrial organization, a branch of microeconomics, emphasizes the influence of industry environment upon the firm. Implicit in industrial organization theory is the premise of evolutionary change. A firm must adapt to its particular industry's forces to survive and prosper (these forces are discussed in detail in the following chapter), and thus its financial performance is determined by that industry in which it competes. Industries with favorable structures, or forces, offer the opportunity for high returns, whereas the opposite is true for firms operating in industries with less favorable forces.[13]

Industrial organization theory is deterministic because it assumes that an organization's survival depends upon its ability to adapt to industry forces. A firm's strategies, resources, and competencies are reflections of the industry environment.[14] Because the focus of this field is on industry forces, the organizations within an industry are viewed as possessing similar strategies, resources, and competencies. Hence, competing firms in an industry operate in relatively homogeneous ways. If one firm should develop a superior strategy or operating competency, its uniqueness would be short-lived. Less successful firms could imitate the higher-performing firm by purchasing the resources, competencies, or management talent that have made the leading firm so profitable.[15] Recent developments in industrial organization theory have given increased prominence to firm strategy, which not only might affect the strategy of rivals but also might modify the structure of the industry.[16]

The areas that we have briefly examined—theories of evolution and revolution and industrial organization theory—enhance our understanding of how primarily environmental forces can affect organizations. The following theories take a somewhat different perspective by looking not only at the environment but also at the competitive status of the firm. These ideas will complement those theories that we have just discussed.

■ Chamberlin's Economic Theories

Economist Edward Chamberlin, representing another branch of microeconomics, presented his ideas within the context of evolutionary environmental change. He proposed that a single firm could clearly distinguish itself from its competitors:

> [A] general class of product is differentiated if any significant basis exists for distinguishing the goods (or services) of one seller from those of another. Where such differentiation exists, even though it might be slight, buyers will be paired with sellers, not by chance . . . but according to their preferences.[17]

Differentiation can exist for quite some time because of such legal protection as trademarks or patents or because a firm's unique strategies, competencies, and resources cannot be easily duplicated by its competitors.

The premise that buyers will be paired with sellers, not by chance but according to their preferences, emphasizes the need for the firm to structure a compatible fit between its competitive status (its strengths and weaknesses relative to those of its competitors) and the opportunities and threats within its environment. This emphasis on the fit between a firm and its environment is reflected in recent contingency theories.

■ Contingency Theory

Contingency theory also exists within the context of evolutionary environmental change. The basic premise of contingency theory is that higher financial returns are associated with those firms that most closely develop a beneficial fit with their environment. Unlike the earlier theories on evolutionary and revolutionary change and industrial organization, which were framed at a high level of abstraction, contingency theory can be used to view environment-organization interaction at any level of analysis—industry, strategic group (discussed in chapter 6), or individual firm.[18] And, whereas those earlier theories were deterministic, contingency theorists view organizational performance as the joint outcome of environmental forces and the firm's strategic actions. Firms can become proactive by choosing to operate in environments in which the opportunities and threats match the firms' strengths and weaknesses.[19] Should the industry environment change in a way that is unfavorable to the firm, the firm could perhaps leave that industry and reallocate its resources and competencies to other, more favorable industries.

So both Chamberlin and contingency theorists view organizations as heterogeneous firms that can choose their own operating environments. Organizational performance is determined by the fit between the environment's opportunities and threats and the firm's strengths and weaknesses.

■ Resource-Based Theory

Resource-based theory accords even more weight to the firm's proactive choices. Although environmental opportunities and threats are important considerations, a firm's unique resources comprise the key variables that allow it to develop and sustain a competitive strategic advantage. "Resources" include all of a firm's tangible and intangible assets (such as capital, equipment, employees, knowledge, and information).[20] As can be inferred, resource-based theory focuses primarily on individual firms rather than on the competitive environment.

If a firm is to use its resources for sustained competitive advantage, those resources must be valuable, rare, and subject to imperfect imitation, and they must have no strategically relevant substitutes.[21] Valuable resources are those that contribute significantly to the firm's effectiveness and efficiency. Rare resources are possessed by few competitors. Imperfectly imitable resources cannot be fully duplicated by rivals. And resources that have no strategically relevant substitutes enable the firm to operate in a matchless competitive fashion.

Resource-based theory can be framed in the context of either evolutionary or revolutionary change.[22] A firm that possesses unique advantages within an evolutionary environment can continue to compete effectively by making incremental improvements to its resource base. Alternatively, resources that give a firm a competitive advantage within a revolutionary environment do not become irrelevant in newly created settings.

The ideas that we have just examined have important philosophical influences on the field of strategic management. As will become evident, these theories form the basic conceptual underpinnings of the remainder of this textbook.

STRATEGIC DECISIONS

■ Who Makes the Decisions?

The CEO is the individual ultimately responsible for the organization's strategic management. But except in the smallest companies, the CEO relies on a host of other individuals, including members of the board of directors, vice presidents, and various line and staff managers. Precisely who these individuals are depends upon the type of organization. For instance, businesses with centralized decision-making processes generally have fewer managers involved in strategic decisions than do companies that are decentralized. Businesses that are organized around functions (production, marketing, finance, personnel) generally involve the vice presidents of the functional departments in strategic decisions. Firms with product divisional structures (e.g., the home appliance division, the lawn mower division, the hand tool division) usually include the product division managers along with the CEO. Very large organizations often employ corporate-level strategic-planning staffs to assist the CEO and other top managers in making strategic management decisions.

Inputs to strategic decisions can be generated in a number of ways. For example, an employee in a company's research and development department may attend a conference where a new product or production process idea that seems relevant to the company may be discussed. Upon returning from the conference, the employee may relate the idea to his supervisor, who, in turn, may pass it along to her boss. Eventually, the idea may be discussed with the organization's marketing and production managers. As it moves from one area to another, the idea becomes increasingly clear and specific. Ultimately, it may be presented to top management in a formal report. The CEO will eventually decide to adopt or to reject the idea. But can we actually say that this strategic decision was made solely by the CEO? In a sense, the answer is yes because it is the CEO's responsibility to decide which alternative the company will adopt. But from a broader perspective, the answer is no because most strategic decisions result from the streams of inputs, decisions, and actions of many people. Top management is ultimately responsible for the final decision, but its decision is the culmination of the ideas, creativity, information, and analyses of others.

■ Characteristics of Strategic Decisions

In addition to involving more than one area of an organization, strategic decisions usually require obtaining and allocating sizable resources (human, organizational, and physical). Further, strategic decisions involve a lengthy time period, anywhere from several years to more than a decade. Consequently, strategic decisions are future-oriented, with long-term ramifications. In other words, strategic decisions require commitment.[23]

S T R A T E G I C   I N S I G H T

Strategic Decisions

Strategic decisions, by their very nature, are characterized by considerable risk and uncertainty. Dynamic and largely unpredictable environmental changes can quickly transform even the most well-conceived plans into ineffectual strategies. Most strategic decision makers clearly recognize this danger and learn to live with it. Some examples:

• Designing and producing a large commercial aircraft costs as much as $5 billion before any sales revenue is realized. Boeing has taken this enormous risk with its new 777 airliner. The 777 is designed to transport 328 passengers and has a range of 5,000 miles. The design phase began in 1986 when Boeing planners probed the ideas of numerous pilots, passengers, and mechanics about a new type of airliner. As Dean Thornton, head of Boeing's Commercial Airplane Group, puts it: "The 777 causes me to sit bolt upright in bed periodically. It's a . . . gamble. There's a big risk in doing things totally differently."

• American Airlines, the largest airline in the Western Hemisphere, faces—like all major airlines—a number of challenges: steadily rising costs, unstable national economies, uncertain volumes of domestic traffic, and protectionist threats to international traffic. In the face of these threats, CEO Robert Crandall suggests that: "you have to accept the notion at the senior levels of any big company, you rarely know what the outcome of any decision is going to be. . . . Most people at big corporations are rarely certain of what they ought to do. . . . If it were clear what should be done, these jobs wouldn't be nearly so hard."

• Many companies develop "basic beliefs" or "key principles" to guide strategic decision makers through turbulent times. For years, IBM relied on three basic beliefs: the pursuit of excellence, provision of the best customer service, and respect for the individual. However, when outsider Louis V. Gerstner Jr. became IBM CEO, he established new principles for Big Blue, ones emphasizing the marketplace, technology, and entrepreneurial vision. Several top managers noted that modifying the basic philosophy intended to steer decision makers through uncertainty was needed if the company were to see the fruits of its labor. Gerstner put it bluntly: "When it comes to a results-oriented culture, we're not there yet, not by a long shot. . . . There are still a couple of four-minute miles that have to be run."

SOURCES: E. A. Robinson, "America's Most Admired Companies," *Fortune*, 3 March 1997, p. F2; W. M. Carley, "GE and Pratt Agree to Build Engine for Boeing Jumbo Jet," *Wall Street Journal Interactive Edition*, 9 May 1996; J. Cole and C. S. Smith, "Boeing Loses Contest to Become China's Partner in Building Plane," *Wall Street Journal Interactive Edition*, 2 May 1996; B. Ziegler, "IBM Is Growing Again; 'Fires Are Out,' Chief Says," *Wall Street Journal Interactive Edition*, 1 May 1996; L. Hayes, "Gerstner Is Struggling as He Tries to Change Ingrained IBM Culture," *Wall Street Journal*, 13 May 1994, pp. A1, A8 (quotation from p. A1); J. Main, "Betting on the 21st Century Jet," *Fortune*, 20 April 1992, pp. 102–117 (quotation from p. 102); D. Moreau, "From Big Bust to Big Blue: IBM and Its Vigorous Rebirth," *Kiplinger's Personal Finance Magazine*, July 1995, pp. 34–35; J. Sager, "We Won't Stop until We Find Our Way Back," 1 May 1995, pp. 116–118 (quotation from p. 116).

STRATEGIC INSIGHT

Strategy in the Automobile Industry: European and Japanese Inroads

Contrary to popular belief, the world's first workable cars were not manufactured in the United States but in France and Germany. In fact, automakers in these two countries dominated car manufacturing until Henry Ford began producing cars through assembly line techniques. By 1920, Ford alone produced almost half of the cars in the world. The U.S. leadership in car production continued for the next several decades.

By the 1950s, however, U.S. carmakers were becoming complacent. They routinely produced large, heavy cars with powerful engines. Following their policy of "planned obsolescence," U.S. manufacturers gave these cars annual cosmetic changes, designed to make it clear which consumers were driving the latest models. While U.S. car companies were concentrating on styling and sales, European producers were developing an impressive array of technological improvements, including disc brakes, rack-and-pinion steering, front-wheel drive, unitized bodies, and fuel injection systems. By 1970 European automobile exports were 25 times those of the United States.

When the first oil price shock hit the United States in 1974, American carmakers were virtually unprepared. American consumers began to turn to more fuel-efficient European models and, increasingly, to Japan's small economical vehicles. Detroit's carmakers grudgingly began to manufacture smaller cars. But their attitude was best summed up by the comment of Henry Ford II: "Minicars mean miniprofits."

By the late 1970s American consumers were turning to Japanese cars in record numbers. Not only were the cars more economical, but most buyers felt that they were of higher quality than American-made cars. Frightened, U.S. automakers sought government protection. At the behest of the U.S. government, the Japanese "voluntarily" agreed to import restrictions in the early 1980s.

Ironically, however, these restrictions provided Japanese automakers with the impetus to construct plants in the United States to avoid restrictions. Although they originally only assembled cars in America, today Honda, Toyota, and Nissan have established research and development, engineering, and design centers in the United States. In fact, by 1990 Honda was producing cars that were totally planned and built in America—mostly by Americans. More than a million Japanese cars were produced in the United States by 1990, compared with about 1,000 eight years earlier. Honda's Accord even began to vie with Ford's Taurus for the title of best-selling car in the United States.

In the early 1990s the U.S. auto industry had declined to its lowest point, posting record losses. However, cost-cutting programs, quality improvements, attractive new models, and a brighter economy resulted in a resurgence of profits by late 1992. But some analysts believe that overhaul of the Big Three is still only half completed. When the strong yen pushed up Japanese car prices in the mid-1990s, the Big Three responded by raising prices of their own cars instead of gaining market share. As a result, Japanese manufacturers have made significant inroads into the once U.S.-dominated light truck segment.

The Big Three—particularly GM—have begun to experience success marketing their vehicles in Japan. However, the overall success of the Big Three may also be tied to the lucrative European market, where trade barriers are coming down and Ford and GM own over one-third of the market. However, most analysts believe that quality—as perceived by the consumer—will ultimately determine the industry's winners and losers.

Strategy in the Automobile Industry: European and Japanese Inroads

SOURCES: E. A. Robinson, "America's Most Admired Companies," *Fortune*, 3 March 1997, p. F2; "Japan Car Imports Rise 24% on Gains in Overseas Plants," *AP-Dow Jones News Service*, 8 May 1996; M. M. Boitano, "Japan Current Account Fall Seen Hurting GDP," *Dow Jones News Service*, 13 May 1996; H. Sender, "On the Chin: No One Rules Endaka More Than Japan's Carmakers," *Far Eastern Economic Review*, 8 June 1995, pp. 40–41; E. Updike, "Japan's Auto Shock," *Business Week*, 29 May 1995, pp. 44–47; R. L. Simison, D. Lavin, and J. Mitchell, "With Auto Prices Up, Big Three Get a Major Opportunity," *Wall Street Journal*, 4 May 1994, pp. A1, A16; J. Mitchell and N. Templin, "Ford's Taurus Passes Honda's Accord As Best-selling Car in a Lackluster Year," *Wall Street Journal*, 7 January 1993; P. Ingrassia and T. Appeal, "Worried by Japanese, Thriving GM Europe Vows to Get Leaner," *Wall Street Journal*, 27 July 1992; K. Kerwin, J. B. Treece, T. Peterson, L. Armstrong, and K. L. Miller, "Detroit's Big Change," *Business Week*, 29 June 1992; D. Cordtz, "The First Hundred Years: How the U. S. Auto Companies Blew Their Stranglehold on the Industry," *Financial World*, 22 August 1989, pp. 54–56.

STRATEGIC MANAGEMENT: A CONTINUOUS PROCESS

Once a planned strategy is implemented, it often requires modification as environmental or organizational conditions change. These changes are often difficult or even impossible to forecast. In fact, it is a rare situation indeed in which top management is able to develop a long-range strategic plan and implement it over several years without any need for modification.

Hence, an **intended strategy** (what management originally planned) may be realized in its original form, in a modified form, or even in an entirely different form. Occasionally, of course, the strategy that management intends is actually realized, but usually, the intended strategy and the **realized strategy** (what management actually implements) differ.[24] The reason is that unforeseen environmental or organizational events occur that necessitate changes in the intended strategy. The full range of possibilities is illustrated in Table 1.1.

Table 1.1 **Intended Strategy, Realized Strategy, and Results: Range of Possibilities**

1. What is intended as a strategy is realized with desirable results.
2. What is intended as a strategy is realized, but with less than desirable results.
3. What is intended as a strategy is realized in some modified version because of an unanticipated environmental or internal requirement or change. The results are desirable.
4. What is intended as a strategy is realized in some modified version because of an unanticipated environmental or internal requirement or change. The results are less than desirable.
5. What is intended as a strategy is not realized. Instead, an unanticipated environmental or internal change requires an entirely different strategy. The different strategy is realized with desirable results.
6. What is intended as a strategy is not realized. Instead, an unanticipated environmental or internal change requires an entirely different strategy. The different strategy is realized with less than desirable results.

STRATEGIC MANAGEMENT AND WEALTH CREATION

The ultimate purpose of strategic management is to create wealth for the owners (shareholders) of the firm through the satisfaction of the needs and expectations of other stakeholders (e.g., customers, suppliers, employees, discussed in chapter 3). One measure of wealth creation is Tobin's Q. Tobin's Q measures the market's assessment of a firm's value normalized by the replacement cost of its assets.[25]

When Tobin's Q is greater (less) than one, it reflects the market's positive (negative) perception that the combined value of a firm's tangibles and intangibles is greater (less) than the replacement cost of its existing assets (i.e., the cost the firm has to incur to acquire the assets that have the same productive capacity as existing assets).[26]

Currently, many leading firms measure wealth creation through what is referred to as market value added (MVA). This measure of wealth creation has been developed by the New York consulting firm Stern Stewart.[27] The concept is intuitively appealing—the market value of the firm (market value of its outstanding common stock, preferred stock, and long-term debt) less the book value of the capital that has been invested in the firm (such factors as the amount invested by stockholders, what has been lent by banks, and retained earnings). If the firm's market value is greater (less) than the book value of the capital invested in it, then the firm has a positive (negative) MVA, which means that wealth is expected to be created (destroyed) by strategic managers. We believe that a better way to measure MVA is to divide the market value of the firm (market value of its outstanding securities) by the book value of what has been invested in it. This would control for scale differences when one firm's performance is evaluated relative to its smaller or larger rivals.

Many leading firms, such as Quaker Oats, Coca-Cola, and AT&T, use some modified version of MVA to measure their performance.[28] While such firms as Wal-Mart, Intel, Microsoft, Coca-Cola, and Rubbermaid have been wealth creators, others, notably Kmart, TWA, and Morrison Knudsen, have been wealth destroyers in recent years.

Alternatively, a simple measure of wealth creation, and one that we recommend, is the market-to-book ratio. This represents the firm's current stock price divided by its book value per share. If investors view the prospects of the firm positively (negatively), then this ratio should be greater (less) than one.

The reason we argue that the purpose of strategic management is to create wealth for shareholders through the satisfaction of the needs of the various stakeholders is that the support of all stakeholders is needed to create wealth. To maximize shareholder wealth at the expense of other stakeholder groups is myopic. The financial gains of stockholders at the expense of the monetary needs of personnel, for instance, will only alienate the employees, eventually harming the company's financial prospects. Although the maximization of wealth for stockholders has been traditionally proposed as a normative goal in the financial literature, select financial scholars more recently have discussed the importance of being stakeholder-driven.[29]

Professor G. Donaldson of Harvard, for instance, has argued that General Mills has been correct to take an extensive time to restructure (rather than to do so abruptly) in order to be stakeholder-driven. The benefits of taking a longer time to restructure include lowering the number of personnel through a freeze on hiring and accelerated voluntary retirement rather than through abruptly firing people and demoralizing the entire organization; changing suppliers and channels of distribution gradually with longer time notices, thereby avoiding damage to the company's reputation; and selling assets gradually rather than under time pressure, which puts the seller in an unfavorable bargaining position. Professor Donaldson concludes that General Mills has also created more wealth for the shareholders by being stakeholder-driven.

Directors of McKinsey and Company, a leading consulting firm, also argue that firms must be stakeholder driven in order to create wealth for their stockholders.[30] Moreover, many corporations have mission statements that explicitly state their obligations to employees, suppliers, customers, and the community as well as to stockholders. Finally, there is empirical evidence that being stakeholder-driven contributes to competitiveness and an increase in stock price valuation.[31] For instance, firms with quality affirmative action programs are supportive of their human resources and, in turn, may gain through their human resources contributing to lower costs and higher differentiation. Such firms tend to have more committed and productive human resources who have lower absenteeism and turnover—and thereby a reduced cost structure. These corporations also tend to have better problem-solving capabilities and are more creative. Consequently, they are better able to enhance their differentiation. Lower costs and higher differentiation positively impact stock prices.

TEXTBOOK OVERVIEW

This presentation of the strategic management process begins with an analysis of the external environment in which a firm operates. All firms are concerned with two levels of the external environment. The broader of the two is the macroenvironment, which is comprised of political-legal, economic, technological, and social forces that affect all organizations. But each organization also has a more specific external environment(s), known as an industry environment(s), in which it operates. The industry defines the firm's set of customers, suppliers, competitors and so on. The first step in strategic management is analysis of these two levels of the external environment. Chapter 2 provides a framework for understanding and analyzing the macroenvironment and industry environment.

Because strategic management consists of structuring a compatible fit between the organization and its external environment, the reason for the existence of the firm (i.e., its mission) must be defined within its environmental forces as well as in the context of firm resources (strengths and weaknesses). Once the firm's identity is clearly understood, top management must formulate goals to give the organization direction. Establishing the organization's mission and goals through S. W. O. T. (strengths, weaknesses, opportunities, threats) analysis is the subject of chapter 3, which focuses on the internal environment of the firm.

After its mission and goals are established, the organization's strategy must be addressed. Strategy formulation occurs at three organizational levels: corporate, business unit, and functional. Chapters 4 and 5 focus on corporate-level strategy formulation. At this level, the essential question is, In what businesses or industries should we be operating? Chapter 4 presents corporate restructuring and the strategic alternatives that are available to top management. Chapter 5 introduces several analytical frameworks that may be used by corporations that operate multiple businesses.

At the business unit level, the question that must be answered is, How should we compete in each of the businesses or industries in which we have chosen to operate? (The difference between corporate-level and business unit strategies is illustrated via two questions in Figure 1.2.) Chapter 6 identifies the alternative generic business unit strategies that are available to management and explains under what circumstances each is appropriate.

Chapter 7 analyzes the formulation of functional strategies (strategies in production, marketing, research and development, finance, etc.). It emphasizes the interdependence of an organization's functional strategies and their relationship to the company's business unit strategies.

After the examination of strategy formulation at these three levels, the discussion turns to how these strategies can be implemented. The organizational structure adopted by a company plays a key role in strategy implementation. Chapter 8 identifies the structures available to management and discusses the circumstances under which each is likely to lead to effective implementation of the organization's strategies.

Other essential aspects of strategy implementation are presented in chapter 9. How the CEO and the top management team secure the cooperation of the organization's members by exercising leadership and informal power is discussed in some detail. Then, the key role played by organizational culture in implementing strategy is analyzed.

As strategies are implemented, the process of strategic control begins. Strategic control consists of determining the extent to which the organiza-

Figure 1.2   **Corporate- and Business Unit-Level Strategic Questions**

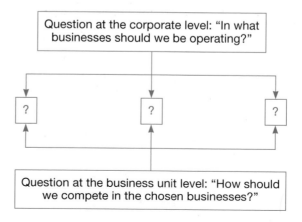

tion's goals are being attained. This process often requires management to modify its strategies or implementation in some fashion so that the company's ability to reach its goals will be improved. Strategic control is the subject of chapter 10.

Strategic management is discussed in the context of the world marketplace in chapter 11. Here, the contents of chapters 2 through 10 are revisited through a distinctly international perspective.

The process of strategic management is applied to not-for-profit organizations in chapter 12. Although the basic principles of strategic management apply equally to profit and not-for-profit organizations, there are some differences that require examination. A diagrammatic overview of chapters 2 through 12 is shown in Figure 1.3.

Figure 1.3   **Overview of the Book**

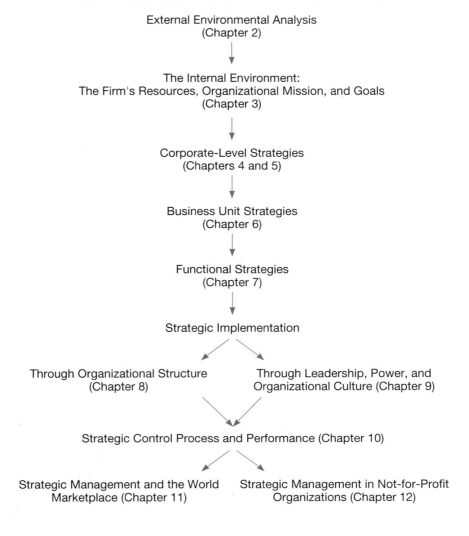

External Environmental Analysis
(Chapter 2)

The Internal Environment:
The Firm's Resources, Organizational Mission, and Goals
(Chapter 3)

Corporate-Level Strategies
(Chapters 4 and 5)

Business Unit Strategies
(Chapter 6)

Functional Strategies
(Chapter 7)

Strategic Implementation

Through Organizational Structure
(Chapter 8)

Through Leadership, Power, and
Organizational Culture (Chapter 9)

Strategic Control Process and Performance (Chapter 10)

Strategic Management and the World
Marketplace (Chapter 11)

Strategic Management in Not-for-Profit
Organizations (Chapter 12)

Finally, the second section of the text begins by presenting an overview of strategic management case analysis. The methodology discussed will help in analyzing the cases contained in the latter part of the text.

Cases, which present the strategies and operations of real companies, provide the opportunity to apply the knowledge gleaned from chapters 1 through 12 to analyses of real situations. Case analysis encourages active, involved learning rather than passive recall of the book's contents.

Some of the cases are narrow, primarily involving single issues. These cases provide opportunities to apply knowledge to a specific issue, problem, or situation. Most, however, are broad, encompassing many different aspects of an organization and its environment. The advantages of such cases are several. First, they encourage the application and integration of what has been learned in this text with knowledge gained from other courses and even from one's work experience. Second, they provide a vehicle for analyzing a total organization versus one narrow aspect or functional area of that company. Third, they promote the awareness that varied aspects of the organization and its environment, and their interrelationships, must be examined to formulate and implement strategies effectively.

SUMMARY

Strategic management refers to the process that begins with determining the mission and goals of an organization within the context of its external environment and its internal strengths and weaknesses. Appropriate strategies are then formulated and implemented. Finally, strategic control is exerted to ensure that the organization's strategies are successful in attaining its goals.

Strategic management, as a field of study, has been influenced by such diverse disciplines as biology (in theories of evolution and revolution) and economics (particularly the views of Schumpeter and Chamberlin and the perspective of industrial organization theory). More recently, the views of contingency theory (that high financial returns are associated with those firms that most closely develop a beneficial fit with their environment) and resource-based theory (that a firm's unique resources are the key variables that allow it to develop and sustain a competitive strategic advantage) have provided useful frameworks for analyzing strategic management.

Determining organizational strategy is the direct responsibility of the CEO, but he or she relies on a host of other individuals, including the board of directors, vice presidents, and various line and staff managers. In its final form, a strategic decision is molded from the streams of inputs, decisions, and actions of many people.

Strategic management is a continuous process. Once a strategy is implemented, it often requires modification as environmental or organizational conditions change. Because these changes are often difficult or even impossible to predict, a strategy may, over time, be modified so that it bears only a slight resemblance to the organization's intended strategy. This realized strategy is the result of unforeseen external or internal events that require changes in the organization's intended strategy. Thus, strategies need to be examined continuously in the light of changing situations. Finally, the reason for strategic management is to create wealth for the owners (shareholders) through the satisfaction of the needs and expectations of other stakeholders.

TAKE IT TO THE NET

We invite you to visit the Wright page on the Prentice Hall Web site at:

http://www.prenhall.com/wright

for this chapter's World Wide Web exercise.

KEY CONCEPTS

Intended strategy   The original strategy that management plans and intends to implement.

Realized strategy   The actual and eventual strategy that management implements. The realized strategy often differs from the intended strategy because unforeseen environmental or organizational events occur that necessitate modifications in the intended strategy.

Strategic management   The continuous process of determining the mission and goals of an organization within the context of its external environment and its internal strengths and weaknesses, formulating appropriate strategies, implementing those strategies, and exerting strategic control to ensure that the organization's strategies are successful in attaining its goals.

Strategy   Top management's plans to attain outcomes consistent with the organization's mission and goals.

DISCUSSION QUESTIONS

1. In what sense does the CEO alone make the company's strategic decisions? In what sense does the CEO *not* make the company's strategic decisions alone?

2. Explain the difference between an intended strategy and a realized strategy. Relate an example of a company whose ultimate realized strategy differed from its original intended strategy.

3. How can an understanding of strategic management be beneficial to your career?

NOTES

1. A. E. Singer, "Strategy as Moral Philosophy," *Strategic Management Journal* 15 (1994): 191–213.

2. See J. B. Barney, "Types of Competition and the Theory of Strategy: Toward an Integrative Framework," *Academy of Management Review* 11 (1986): 791–800; J. Child, "Organizational Structure, Environment, and Performance: The Role of Strategic Choice," *Sociology* 6 (1972): 1–22; J. A. Schumpeter, *The Theory of Economic Development* (New York: Oxford University Press, 1934).

3. J. G. Longenecker and C. D. Pringle, "The Illusion of Contingency Theory as a General Theory," *Academy of Management Review* 3 (1978): 682.

4. R. A. Gordon and J. E. Howell, *Higher Education for Business* (New York: Columbia University Press, 1959).

5. M. Leontiades, "The Confusing Words of Business Policy," *Academy of Management Review* 7 (1982): 46.

6. B. O'Reilly, "Reengineering the MBA," *Fortune*, 24 January 1994, pp. 37–47.

7. S. J. Gould, *Ever Since Darwin* (New York: Norton, 1977).

8. D. A. Gioia and E. Pitre, "Multiparadigm Perspectives on Theory Building," *Academy of Management Review* 15 (1990): 584–602.

9. N. Eldredge and S. J. Gould, "Punctuated Equilibria: An Alternative to Phyletic Gradualism," in T. J. M. Schopf, ed., *Models in Paleobiology* (San Francisco: Freeman, Cooper, 1972), pp. 82–115; Schumpeter, *The Theory of Economic Development*.

10. M. L. Tushman, W. H. Newman, and E. Romanelli, "Convergence and Upheaval: Managing the Unsteady Pace of Organizational Evolution," *California Management Review* 29, no. 1 (1986): 29–44; J. D. Utterback and W. J. Abernathy, "A Dynamic Model of Product and Process Innovation," *Omega* 3 (1975): 639–656.

11. Barney, "Types of Competition and the Theory of Strategy"; R. R. Nelson and S. G. Winter, *An Evolutionary Theory of Economic Change* (Cambridge, Mass.: Harvard University Press, 1982); O. Nodoushani, "The End of the Entrepreneurial Age," *Human Systems Management* 10 (1991): 19–31.

12. J. A. Schumpeter, *Capitalism, Socialism, and Democracy* (New York: Harper & Row, 1950).

13. M. E. Porter, "The Contributions of Industrial Organization to Strategic Management," *Academy of Management Review* 6 (1981): 609–620.

14. J. S. Bain, *Industrial Organization* (New York: Wiley, 1968); F. M. Scherer and D. Ross, *Industrial Market Structure and Economic Performance* (Boston: Houghton-Mifflin, 1990).

15. A. Lado, N. Boyd, and P. Wright, "A Competency-Based Model of Sustainable Competitive Advantage: Toward a Conceptual Integration," *Journal of Management* 18 (1992): 77–91; J. B. Barney, "Strategic Factor Markets: Expectations, Luck, and Business Strategy," *Management Science* 42 (1986): 1231–1241; J. B. Barney, "Firm Resources and Sustained Competitive Advantage," *Journal of Management* 17 (1991): 99–120.

16. A. Seth and H. Thomas, "Theories of the Firm: Implications for Strategy Research," *Journal of Management Studies* 31 (1994): 165–191.

17. E. H. Chamberlin, *The Theory of Monopolistic Competition* (Cambridge, Mass.: Harvard University Press, 1956), p. 231.

18. R. S. Dooley, D. M. Fowler, and A. Miller, "The Benefits of Strategic Homogeneity and Strategic Heterogeneity: Theoretical and Empirical Evidence Resolving Past Differences," *Strategic Management Journal* 17 (1996): 293–305.

19. L. G. Hrebiniak and W. F. Joyce, "Organizational Adaptation: Strategic Choice and Environmental Determinism," *Administrative Science Quarterly* 21 (1985): 41–65.

20. J. B. Barney, "Looking Inside for Competitive Advantage," *Academy of Management Executive* 19 (1995): 49–61.

21. Ibid.

22. R. Rumelt, "Towards a Strategic Theory of the Firm," in R. Lamb, ed., *Competitive Strategic Management* (Englewood Cliffs, N. J.: Prentice Hall, 1984), pp. 556–570; R. Rumelt and R. Wensley, "In Search of the Market Share Effect," in K. Chung, ed., *Academy of Management Proceedings* (1981): 2–6; S. Winter, "Schumpeterian Competition in Alternative Technological Regimes," *Journal of Economic Behavior and Organization* 5 (1984): 287–320.

23. P. Ghemawat, *Commitment: The Dynamic of Strategy* (New York: The Free Press, 1991).

24. H. Mintzberg, "Opening Up the Definition of Strategy," in J. B. Quinn, H. Mintzberg, and R. M. James, eds., *The Strategy Process* (Englewood Cliffs, N. J.: Prentice Hall, 1988), pp. 14–15.

25. See B. H. Hall, *The Manufacturing Sector Master File Documentation: 1959 1967*, Mimeo (University of California at Berkeley, 1990) for computational details.

26. B. C. Reimann, *Managing for Value* (Cambridge, Mass.: Basil Blackwell, 1989).

27. L. Walbert, "America's Best Wealth Creators," *Fortune*, 27 December 1993, pp. 64, 76.

28. B. Cornell and A. Shapiro, "Corporate Stakeholders and Corporate Finance," *Financial Management* 16 (1987): 5–14; G. Donaldson, "Voluntary Restructuring: The Case of General Mills," *Journal of Financial Economics* 27 (1990): 117–141.

29. Donaldson (1990).

30. K. P. Coyne and R. W. Ferguson, "Real Wealth," *The McKinsey Quarterly* 4 (1991): 69–80.

31. P. Wright, S. P. Ferris, J. S. Hiller, and M. Kroll, "Competitiveness through the Management of Diversity: The Effect on Stock Price Valuation," *Academy of Management Journal* 38 (1995): 272–287.

STRATEGIC MANAGEMENT MODEL

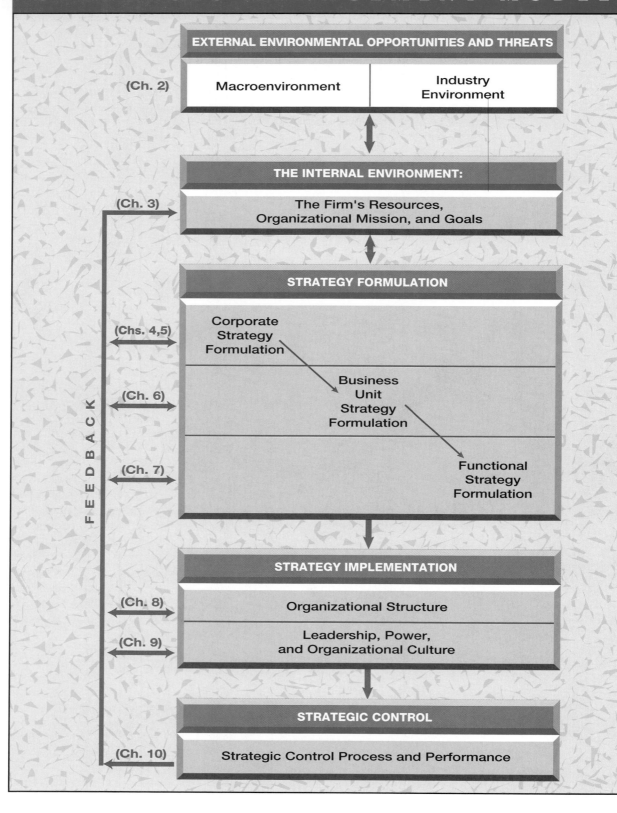

EXTERNAL ENVIRONMENTAL OPPORTUNITIES AND THREATS

(Ch. 2)

Macroenvironment	Industry Environment

THE INTERNAL ENVIRONMENT:

(Ch. 3)

The Firm's Resources, Organizational Mission, and Goals

STRATEGY FORMULATION

(Chs. 4,5) Corporate Strategy Formulation

(Ch. 6) Business Unit Strategy Formulation

(Ch. 7) Functional Strategy Formulation

STRATEGY IMPLEMENTATION

(Ch. 8) Organizational Structure

(Ch. 9) Leadership, Power, and Organizational Culture

STRATEGIC CONTROL

(Ch. 10) Strategic Control Process and Performance

FEEDBACK

2 External Environmental Opportunities and Threats

Strategic management involves three levels of analysis: the organization's macroenvironment, the industry in which the organization operates, and the organization itself. These levels are portrayed in Figure 2.1 on page 24. This chapter focuses upon the first two levels—the macroenvironment and industry. Then, chapter 3 begins our analysis of the firm.

Every organization exists within a complex network of environmental forces. All firms are affected by political-legal, economic, technological, and social systems and trends. Together, these elements comprise the **macroenvironment** of business firms. Because these forces are so dynamic, their constant change presents myriad opportunities and threats or constraints to strategic managers.

Each business also operates within a more specific environment termed an **industry:** a group of companies that produce competing products or services. The structure of an industry influences the intensity of competition among the firms in the industry by placing certain restrictions upon their operations and by providing various opportunities for well-managed firms to seize the advantage over their competitors. As we shall see in this chapter, successful management depends upon forging a link between business and its external environment through the activities of environmental analysis.

ANALYSIS OF THE MACROENVIRONMENT

All organizations are affected by four macroenvironmental forces: political-legal, economic, technological, and social. Although very large organizations (or several firms in association with one another) will occasionally attempt to

23

Figure 2.1   **Three Levels of Analysis**

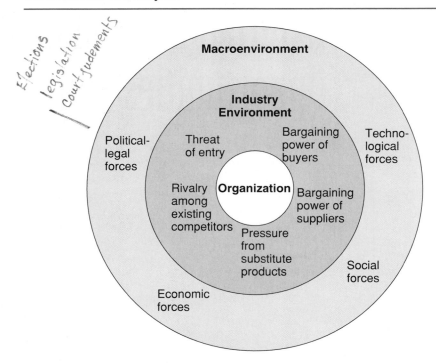

Handwritten annotations: Elections, legislation, Court Judgements

Handwritten annotation (left margin): Military Cars

influence legislation or, through research and development, will pioneer technological or social changes, these macroenvironmental forces are generally not under the direct control of business organizations. Hence, the purpose of strategic management is to enable the firm to operate effectively within environmental threats or constraints and to capitalize on the opportunities provided by the environment. To accomplish this purpose, strategic managers must identify and analyze these national and global macroenvironmental forces, which are described in the following sections.

▪ Political-Legal Forces

Political-legal forces include the outcomes of elections, legislation, and court judgments, as well as the decisions rendered by various commissions and agencies at every level of government. As an example of the impact of these forces, consider the automobile industry. The U.S. government's insistence on legislating gradually increasing fuel economy standards for cars has affected the size and design of cars, their engine size, and their horsepower. Although American automakers have viewed these regulations as a constraint upon the types of models that they can make and sell, Japanese car manufacturers perceived it as an opportunity to make inroads into the prosperous American market.

On the other hand, the U.S. government's imposition of import fees on automobiles and its success in convincing Japanese manufacturers to restrict "voluntarily" their exports to the United States have provided opportunities for American firms to increase their car sales. Unfortunately, the U.S. car producers have not taken advantage of all of these opportunities to increase their market share. But some Japanese carmakers successfully adapted to these constraints by building manufacturing plants in the United States.

As another example, consider the U.S. defense industry. Both the Bush and Clinton administrations and the Congress recommended huge cuts in defense spending through 1998. These reductions resulted in massive layoffs and restructurings among some of the nation's largest corporations. Affected, to some extent, were such prominent firms as General Dynamics, Northrup, LTV, Martin Marietta, McDonnell Douglas, and Lockheed. But an even greater impact was felt by the thousands of small suppliers and subcontractors whose businesses depended almost entirely on defense contracts. We can see, then, that the U.S. political-legal system can have a major impact on business

On a more global scale, the 1985 decision by the Commission of the European Community to form a single European market for the twelve-nation European community presents both opportunities and threats to U.S.-based firms. One of the major opportunities is the attractive nature of this large, affluent market, which some U.S. firms may have avoided up until now because they considered the market too fragmented and its trade regulations overly complicated. However, a possible threat is that a consolidated market may allow European firms to build a solid base upon which they can develop into much stronger world competitors.

A nation's political-legal system greatly influences its business operations and the standard of living of its citizens. Historically, higher standards of living have been associated with nations whose economic systems are pro-business. In the United States, capitalism has contributed significantly over the past two centuries to America's unparalleled economic growth. But even free enterprise has its weaknesses. By the beginning of the twentieth century, such undesirable social consequences as unsafe working conditions, child labor, low wages, monopolistic competition, deceptive advertising, and unsafe products made it clear that some degree of governmental regulation was necessary. Examples of some of the more significant regulations are shown in Table 2.1 on page 26.

Not all of the legislative and judicial movement in American society, however, has been in the direction of greater regulation of business. In the late 1970s and the 1980s, a major shift in national policy occurred, which reversed this trend in several industries. This "deregulation" movement eliminated a number of legal constraints in such industries as airlines, trucking, and banking.

However, while some industries were being deregulated, overall regulation was increasing. The federal government employs approximately 125,000 regulators to oversee this process. The U.S. Chamber of Commerce predicted a 25 percent increase in business regulatory costs during the 1990s, bringing the total cost of regulation to $600 billion annually.[1]

Deregulation presented both new opportunities and new threats to organizations in the affected industries. Airline deregulation, for instance, offered opportunities to entrepreneurs to start companies such as Southwest Airlines. For some established firms, though, like Eastern and Pan Am, the reduction of regulation posed a threat by creating intense cost and price competition, resulting in their eventual demise. In banking, deregulation presented vast opportunities for expansion in services and geographic scope. Banks began offering brokerage services, for example, and mergers across state lines became common. On the other hand, deregulation intensified competition for banks because non-banking firms, such as money market funds and brokerage houses, began competing directly with banks for consumers' savings.

Table 2.1   **Examples of Government Regulation of Business**

Legislation	Purpose
Sherman Antitrust Act (1890)	Prohibits monopoly or conspiracy in restraint of trade
Pure Food and Drug Act (1906)	Outlaws production of unsanitary foods and drugs
Clayton Act (1914)	Forbids tying contracts, which tie the sale of some products to the sale of others
Federal Trade Commission Act (1914)	Stops unfair methods of competition, such as deceptive advertising, selling practices, and pricing
Fair Labor Standards Act (1938)	Sets minimum-wage rates, regulations for overtime pay, and child labor laws
Wheeler-Lea Amendment (1938)	Outlaws deceptive packaging and advertising
Antimerger Act (1950)	Makes the buying of competitors illegal when it lessens competition
Equal Pay (1963)	Prohibits discrimination in wages on the basis of sex when males and females are performing jobs requiring equal skill, effort, and responsibility under similar working conditions
Occupational Safety and Health Act (1970)	Requires employers to provide a working environment free from hazards to health
Consumer Product Safety Act (1972)	Sets standards on selected products, requires warning labels, and orders product recalls
Equal Employment Opportunity Act (1972)	Forbids discrimination in all areas of employer-employee relations
Magnuson-Moss Act (1975)	Requires accuracy in product warranties
Americans with Disabilities Act (1992)	Protects the physically and mentally disabled from job discrimination
Family and Medical Leave Act (1993)	Offers workers up to twelve weeks of unpaid leave after childbirth or adoption, or to care for a seriously ill child, spouse, or parent

■ Economic Forces

Like political-legal systems, economic forces also have a significant impact on business operations. As prime examples, we will consider the impact of growth or decline in gross domestic product and increases or decreases in interest rates, inflation, and the value of the dollar. These changes present both opportunities and threats to strategic managers.

Gross Domestic Product

Gross domestic product (GDP) refers to the value of a nation's annual total production of goods and services and serves as a major indicator of economic growth. Moderate, consistent growth in GDP generally produces a healthy

[handwritten in margin: GBP- refer to nations growth]

economy in which businesses find increasing demand for their outputs because of rising consumer expenditures. Opportunities abound for both established and new businesses during such prosperous times.

On the other hand, a decline in GDP normally reflects reduced consumer expenditures and lower demand for business outputs. When GDP declines for two consecutive quarters, the national economy is considered to be in a recession. During such times, competitive pressures on businesses increase dramatically; profitability suffers and business failure rates increase. However, even recessions provide opportunities for some firms. Movie theaters are normally strong performers during hard economic times, providing escape from financial worries for their patrons. Likewise, trade school enrollments often increase as unskilled laborers attempt to learn trades to improve their job marketability.

Interest Rates

Short- and long-term interest rates significantly affect the demand for products and services. Low short-term interest rates, for instance, are particularly beneficial for retailers such as Sears and Kmart because such rates encourage consumer spending. For other businesses, such as construction companies and automobile manufacturers, low longer-term rates are especially beneficial because they result in increased spending by consumers for durable goods.

Interest rate levels greatly affect strategic decisions. High rates, for instance, normally dampen business plans to raise funds to expand or to replace aging facilities. Lower rates, by contrast, are more conducive to capital expenditures and to mergers and acquisitions. But some businesses may buck these trends. For example, firms that own apartment buildings usually benefit when long-term interest rates rise, because potential homebuyers find that they cannot qualify for mortgage loans and are forced to rent until rates decline significantly.

Inflation Rates

High inflation rates generally result in constraints on business organizations. High rates boost various costs of doing business, such as the purchase of raw materials and parts and the wages and salaries of employees. Consistent increases in inflation rates will constrict the expansion plans of businesses and cause the government to take action that slows the growth of the economy. The combination of government and business restraints can create an economic recession.

Of course, inflation can present opportunities for some firms. For instance, oil companies may benefit during inflationary times if the prices of oil and gas rise faster than the costs of exploration, refining, and transporting. Likewise, companies that mine or sell precious metals benefit because such metals serve as inflation hedges for consumers.

Value of the Dollar

As we have seen, the value of the dollar relative to other major world currencies can be affected by international agreements and the coordinated economic policies of governments. Currency exchange rates, however, can also be affected by international economic conditions. When economic conditions boost the value of the dollar, U.S. firms find themselves at a competitive disadvantage internationally. Foreign customers are less inclined to buy American-made goods because they are too expensive relative to goods produced in their own home markets. Likewise, U.S. consumers find that their strong dollars can be stretched by buying foreign-made products, which are less expensive than goods produced domestically.

For example, in the early 1990s, Caterpillar was in the midst of a major cost-cutting program designed to maintain its position as the world leader in heavy machinery. Yet even as it reduced its cost structure, its efforts were being undermined by the rise in the value of the dollar vis-à-vis the Japanese yen. The resultant difference in exchange rates gave Caterpillar's chief Japanese competitor, Komatsu, such a substantial price advantage in the U.S. market that it completely negated Caterpillar's extensive cost-cutting program. Komatsu even merged its U.S.-based manufacturing and engineering facilities with Dresser Industries, headquartered in Dallas, as a hedge against future currency fluctuations.[2] Subsequently, when the dollar weakened relative to the Japanese yen, Caterpillar benefited.

The dollar's value affects the strategic decisions of managers. When it is strong, American manufacturers tend to locate more of their plants abroad, make purchases from foreign sources, and enter into strategic alliances with firms in other countries. However, when the dollar is relatively weak, less financial incentive exists for American companies to purchase from foreign sources or to build new plants overseas.

■ Technological Forces

Technological forces include scientific improvements and innovations that provide opportunities or threats for businesses. The rate of technological change varies considerably from one industry to another. In electronics, for example, change is rapid and constant, but in furniture manufacturing, change is slower and more gradual.

Changes in technology can affect a firm's operations as well as its products and services. Recent technological advances in computers, robotics, lasers, satellite networks, fiber optics, and other related areas have provided significant opportunities for operational improvements. Manufacturers, banks, and retailers, for example, have used advances in computer technology to perform their traditional tasks at lower costs and higher levels of customer satisfaction.

From another perspective, however, technological change can decimate existing businesses and even entire industries, since it shifts demand from one product to another. Examples of such change include the shifts from vacuum tubes to transistors, from steam locomotives to diesel and electric engines, from fountain pens to ballpoints, from propeller airplanes to jets, and from typewriters to computer-based word processors. Interestingly enough, these new technologies are often invented outside of the traditional industries that they eventually affect.

■ Social Forces

Social forces include traditions, values, societal trends, and a society's expectations of business. Traditions, for instance, define societal practices that have lasted for decades or even centuries. For example, the celebration of Christmas

Christmas spending

US values / entrepreneurship

Health & fitness

↓ hard liquor

Baby Boomers

Stakeholders

in many countries in the Western Hemisphere provides significant financial opportunities for card companies, toy retailers, turkey processors, tree growers, mail-order catalog firms, and other related businesses.

Values refer to concepts that a society holds in high esteem. In the United States, for example, major values include individual freedom and equality of opportunity. In a business sense, these values translate into an emphasis on entrepreneurship and the belief that one's success is limited only by one's ambition, energy, and ability. These values, over the past century, have attracted millions of immigrants to the United States in search of economic and political freedom. We can expect, therefore, to find a more vibrant and dynamic business environment in the United States than in countries that place less value on the freedom of the individual and equality of opportunity.

Societal trends present various opportunities and threats or constraints to businesses. For example, the health-and-fitness trend that began several years ago has led to financial success for such companies as Nike (sport shoes) and Nautilus (exercise equipment) and the makers of diet soft drinks, light beer, and bottled water. This trend, however, has financially harmed businesses in other industries such as cattle raising, meat and dairy processing, tobacco, and liquor.

For example, over the past ten years, the consumption of hard liquor by the 18-to-34-year-old segment of the U.S. population fell significantly. This trend is of considerable concern to distillers because that age group comprises 40 percent of the U.S. population. The reasons include not only the health-and-fitness trend but also a growing nationwide revulsion toward drunk driving, the increased legal liability of hosts who serve alcohol to their guests, and a general increase in "sin taxes" (taxes on alcohol and tobacco products) at the federal and state levels. As a result, many alcohol makers are diversifying into nonalcoholic drinks.[3]

Societal trends also include demographic changes. Fast-food chains, for instance, are currently wrestling with a pressing problem. Teenagers, who comprise 85 percent of the fast-food work force, declined in number by 5 million in total between 1981 and 1995, while the number of preteen children (primary customers for fast food) increased by 4 million. The result is more customers for fast-food restaurants with fewer people to serve them. These pressures are resulting in increased hiring of the elderly, attempts to reduce turnover among teenage employees, and improvements in productivity.[4]

Demographic trends can dramatically affect business opportunities. The baby boom, which lasted from 1945 through the mid-1960s, initially provided opportunities for such businesses as clothing and baby apparel manufacturers, private schools, record companies, candy and snack makers, and so on. Later, as the baby boomers entered the job market, businesses were blessed with a tremendous pool of job applicants. As they continue to age, the baby boomers will shop at home more and will spend vast sums of money for health care needs, leisure activities, and vacation alternatives.[5] Further, this population segment may not be as brand loyal as older Americans.[6]

Finally, a society's expectations of business present other opportunities and constraints. These expectations emanate from diverse groups referred to as **stakeholders.** These groups affect and, in turn, are affected by the activities of companies. Stakeholders include a firm's owners (stockholders), members of the board of directors, managers and operating employees, suppliers, customers, creditors, distributors, and other interest groups.

At the broadest level, stakeholders include the general public. Increasingly, in recent decades, the general public has expected socially responsible behavior from business firms. Although social responsibility will be discussed in chapter 3, consider just one element of social responsibility—pollution. The public's concern about pollution has resulted in various forms of legislation that have constrained the operations of firms in such industries as automobiles, energy, and mining. On the other hand, this legislation has provided an opportunity for firms such as Waste Management to sell its services in reducing pollution.

In a more limited sense, stakeholder groups may hold conflicting expectations of business performance. For example, stockholders and unionized employees may have financial goals that clash. Chapter 3 will elaborate further on this topic.

■ Environmental Scanning

The preceding sections were able to examine only a few of the important macroenvironmental forces that affect organizations. Examples of other significant forces are identified in Table 2.2.

How do managers recognize the various opportunities or threats that arise from changes in the political-legal, economic, technological, and social arenas?

S T R A T E G I C   I N S I G H T

Capitalizing on Technological and Social Forces at Knight-Ridder

Environmental analysis helps a company take advantage of the changing technological and social forces. One such example is Miami-based Knight-Ridder, a firm that has achieved annual sales of $2.3 billion in the information industry.

Founded in 1903, Knight-Ridder was originally a newspaper company. Its first major newspapers were the *Miami Herald* and the *Akron Beacon Journal*. Since that time, it has purchased numerous newspapers and today owns such well-known publications as the *Detroit Free Press*, the *Philadelphia Inquirer*, and the *San Jose Mercury News*. Its newspaper business, which includes a news syndication service, a newsprint mill, and newspaper printing plants in twenty-nine cities, provides 86 percent of its sales revenue.

Increasingly, however, Knight-Ridder is taking advantage of technological innovations to expand its information network. The company owns an on-line newswire service for financial markets, a cable/pay television channel, and an electronic information retrieval service. Its various information services reach more than 100 million people in 129 countries.

The company has also been cognizant of changing social forces. According to its CEO, James Batten, the firm successfully capitalized upon an opportunity provided by demographic changes in Miami several years ago. Observing that the Miami area was becoming home to more than 250,000 residents of Cuban origin, management believed that the time was right to introduce a Spanish-language daily newspaper. The paper, *El Nuevo Herald*, became an instant success and is now the largest of its kind in the United States.

Knight-Ridder may go even further in taking advantage of the opportunities presented by demographics. Management is currently studying the feasibility of tailoring newspapers to specific groups of readers, such as the elderly, households with children, and so on.

Table 2.2

Examples of Additional Macroenvironmental Forces

Political-Legal Forces	Social Forces	Economic Forces	Technological Forces
Tax laws	Attitudes toward product innovations, lifestyles, careers, and consumer activism	Money supply	Expenditures on research and development (government and industry)
International trade regulations	Concern with quality of life	Monetary policy	Focus of research and development expenditures
Consumer lending regulations	Life expectancies	Unemployment rate	Rate of new-product introductions
Environmental protection laws	Expectations from the workplace	Energy costs	Automation
Enforcement of antitrust regulations	Shifts in the presence of women in the work force	Disposable personal income	Robotics
Laws on hiring, firing, promotion, and pay	Birth rates	Stage of economic cycle	
Wage/price controls	Population shifts		

They engage in environmental scanning—the gathering and analysis of information about relevant environmental trends.

Responses to a survey of Fortune 500 firms that were asked to identify the major payoffs of their environmental-scanning activities included an increased general awareness of environmental changes, better strategic planning and decision making, greater effectiveness in governmental matters, and sound diversification and resource allocation decisions. However, the respondents also indicated that the results of their environmental analysis were often too general or uncertain for specific interpretation.[7]

There is also some evidence that top managers may use "selective perception" in scanning the environment; that is, their scanning activities may be influenced by their organization's strategy. One study concluded that the heads of financial institutions that use a "low-cost" strategy (one that focuses upon being the low-cost provider of products or services) emphasize monitoring activities of competitors and regulators. By contrast, scanning activities in financial institutions that use a "differentiation" strategy (one that emphasizes superior products or services) are likely to focus upon opportunities for growth and ways of satisfying customer needs.[8]

Although macroenvironmental forces influence the operations of all firms in a general fashion, a more specific set of forces within an industry directly and powerfully affects the strategic-planning activities of the firms within that industry. Figure 2.2 on page 32 presents a diagrammatic representation of the impact of macroenvironmental and industry forces. These industry forces are discussed in the following section.

Figure 2 .2   **Macroenvironmental and Industry Forces That Present Opportunities and Threats to Firms**

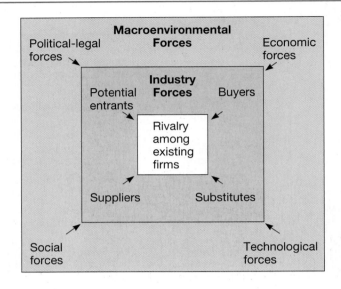

ANALYSIS OF THE INDUSTRY

Professor Michael E. Porter of Harvard University is a leading authority on industry analysis; the following overview of industry forces is based on his work.[9] Porter contends that an industry's profit potential (the long-run return on invested capital) depends on five basic competitive forces within the industry:

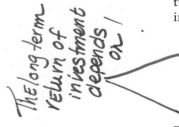

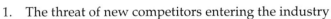

1. The threat of new competitors entering the industry
2. The intensity of rivalry among existing competitors
3. The threat of substitute products or services
4. The bargaining power of buyers
5. The bargaining power of suppliers

These forces can be quite intense in industries such as tires or steel, where returns are generally low, but may be relatively mild in such industries as cosmetics and toiletries, where returns are often high.

The key to competing effectively is for the company to find a position in the industry from which it can influence these five forces to its advantage or can effectively defend itself against them. Such a strategy requires an understanding of these competitive forces, which are described in the following sections.

■ Threat of Entry

As new competitors enter an industry, its productive capacity expands.[10] Unless the market is growing rapidly, a new entry intensifies the fight for market share, thereby bidding prices down and lowering industry profitability. The

Unless the market is expanding new entry intensifies the fight for competition.

likelihood that new firms will enter an industry rests on two factors: barriers to entry and the expected retaliation from existing competitors. Each factor is discussed in the sections that follow.

Barriers to Entry

High barriers and/or expectations of sharp retaliation reduce the threat of entry. There are seven major **barriers to entry,** that is, obstacles to entering an industry. Each barrier is described next.

Economies of Scale.   **Economies of scale** refer to the decline in unit costs of a product or service (or an operation, or a function that goes into producing a product or service) that occurs as the absolute volume of production per period of time increases. Substantial economies of scale deter new entrants by forcing

---

S T R A T E G I C   I N S I G H T

Enormous Barriers to Entry in the Airline Industry

One of the major purposes of deregulating the airline industry in 1978 was to encourage new start-up ventures, thereby increasing the amount of competition in the industry. For a while, deregulation worked; new companies such as Southwest Airlines, Midway Airlines, and People Express helped to lower ticket prices significantly.

But over time, the major airlines have succeeded in erecting enormous barriers to entry. Consider the following obstacles:

- Major carriers hold 20- to 40-year leases on almost all of the passenger-loading gates at big airports.
- They have 95 percent of the landing rights (i.e., permission to take off and land in certain time slots) at four key airports.
- They own the computer reservation systems, pay travel agents (who book 85 percent of all tickets) extra commissions for bringing business to them, and charge small carriers hefty fees for tickets sold through those systems.
- They operate frequent-flier programs that are far too costly for a new airline to offer and that encourage passengers to avoid switching airlines.
- Their computer-pricing systems enable them to selectively offer low fares on certain seats and to cer-

tain destinations, thereby wiping out a start-up airline's pricing edge.
- Most have a large number of U.S. hub airports, a feeder system to those hubs, and international routes that tie into the hubs. Such systems take decades and hundreds of millions of dollars to acquire.
- The dominant major carriers are willing to match or beat the ticket prices of smaller, niche airlines. Most have proved themselves capable of absorbing losses until weaker competitors are driven out of business.

As a result of these obstacles, even two decades after deregulation, the airline industry's best routes and markets are concentrated in the hands of a few carriers. Many analysts predict that newly formed carriers will likely be limited to less desirable routes or small geographical coverage. However, there are signs that many of the barriers to entry are beginning to erode. Surpluses of nonunionized pilots, airplanes, and investors have led to the launching of about a dozen new airlines each year. Although many fail in their first year or two of operation, others like Reno Air have been successful and are filling viable niches in the industry.

SOURCES: S. McCartney, "Conditions Are Ideal for Starting an Airline, and Many are Doing It," *Wall Street Journal*, 1 April, 1996, pp. A1, A7; L.A. *Times* Wire Services, "Boeing 1st-Quarter Profit Off 34%," 30 April 1996; A. L. Velocci Jr., "USAir Defends Aggressive Pricing," *Aviation Week & Space Technology*, 21 August 1995, p. 28; T. K. Smith, "Why Air Travel Doesn't Work," *Fortune*, 3 April 1995, pp. 42–49; D. Greising, P. Dwyer, and W. Zellner, "A Destination But No Flight Plan," *Business Week*, 16 May 1994, pp. 74–75; J. A. Byrne, "The Pain of Downsizing," *Business Week*, 9 May 1994, pp. 60–68; M. J. McCarthy, "Airlines Squeeze Play," *Wall Street Journal*, 18 April 1994, pp. B1, B8; W. Zellner, A. Rothman, and E. Schine, "The Airline Mess," *Business Week*, 6 July 1992, pp. 50–55.

Barrier to Entry

Brand Differentiation
Establish Firms

Distribution

them either to come in at a large scale, thereby risking a strong reaction from existing firms, or to come in at a small scale, with its accompanying cost disadvantages. For example, Xerox and General Electric failed in their attempts to enter the mainframe computer industry some years back, probably because of scale economies in production, research, marketing, and service.

Product Differentiation.   Established firms may enjoy strong brand identification and customer loyalties that are based on actual or perceived product differences, customer service, or advertising. New entrants must spend a great deal of money and time to overcome this barrier. Product differentiation is particularly important in baby care products, over-the-counter drugs, cosmetics, and public accounting. Large brewers, such as Anheuser-Busch, have gone even further by coupling their product differentiation with economies of scale in production, marketing, and distribution.

Capital Requirements.   The need to invest large financial resources to compete creates a third type of entry barrier. Large amounts of capital may be necessary for production facility construction, research and development, advertising, customer credit, and inventories. Some years ago, Xerox cleverly created a capital barrier by renting its copiers rather than only selling them. This move increased the capital needs for new entrants.

Switching Costs.   Switching costs refer to the one-time costs that buyers of the industry's outputs incur if they switch from one company's products to another's. Changing from an established supplier to a new supplier may require the buyer to retrain employees, purchase new ancillary equipment, and/or hire technical help. Most customers are reluctant to switch unless the new supplier offers a major improvement in cost or performance. For example, nurses in hospitals may resist buying from a new supplier of intravenous (IV) solutions and kits, since the procedures for attaching solutions to patients and the hardware for hanging the IV bottles differ from one supplier to another.

Access to Distribution Channels.   To enter the distribution channels already being used by established firms, a new firm must often entice distributors through price breaks, cooperative advertising allowances, or sales promotions. Each of these actions, of course, reduces profits. Existing competitors often have distribution channel ties based on longstanding, or even exclusive relationships, meaning that the new entrant must create a new channel of distribution. Timex was forced to do exactly that decades ago to circumvent the channels dominated by the Swiss watchmakers.

Cost Disadvantages Independent of Scale.   Established firms may possess cost advantages that cannot be replicated by new entrants regardless of their size or economies of scale. These advantages include proprietary product technology (e.g., Polaroid's monopoly on instant photography), favorable access to raw materials (e.g., Texas Gulf Sulphur's control of large salt dome sulphur deposits), favorable locations (e.g., McDonald's locations at interstate highway exits), and the learning or experience curve (the tendency for unit costs to decline as a firm gains experience producing a product or service; an example is Federal Express's efficient operations or Toyota's production process).

Tariffs or Taxes

Government Policy. Governments can control entry to certain industries with licensing requirements or other regulations. For instance, entry into the taxicab business in most large cities is controlled by licensing, and entry into the liquor retail business is heavily regulated by states. Even pollution control requirements can serve as an entry barrier because of the need for a certain level of technological sophistication.

Expected Retaliation

Entry may well be deterred if the potential entering firm expects existing competitors to respond forcefully. These expectations are reasonable if the industry has a history of vigorous retaliation to new entrants or if the industry is growing slowly. Retaliation may also be expected if the established firms are committed to the industry and have specialized fixed assets that are not transferable to other industries, or if the firms have sufficient cash and productive capacity to meet customer needs in the future.[11]

■ Intensity of Rivalry Among Existing Competitors

Competition intensifies when one—or more—of the firms in an industry sees the opportunity to improve its position or feels competitive pressure from others. It manifests itself in the form of price cutting, advertising battles, new-product introductions or modifications, and increased customer service or warranties.[12] The intensity of competition depends on a number of interacting factors, as discussed in the following sections.

Numerous or Equally Balanced Competitors

The number of companies in the industry or how equally balanced they are in terms of size and power may determine intensity of rivalry. Industries with few firms tend to be less competitive, but those that contain a few firms that are roughly equivalent in size and power may be more competitive because each firm will fight for dominance. Competition is also likely to be intense in industries with large numbers of firms, since some of those companies believe that they can make competitive moves without being noticed.[13]

Slow Industry Growth

Firms in industries that grow slowly are more likely to be highly competitive than companies in fast-growing industries. In slow-growth industries, one firm's increase in market share must come at the expense of other firms' shares.

High Fixed or Storage Costs

Companies with high fixed costs are under pressure to operate at near-capacity levels to spread their overhead expenses over more units of production. This pressure often leads to price cutting, thereby intensifying competition. The U.S. airline industry has experienced this problem periodically. The same is true of firms that have high storage costs. For that reason, profits tend to be low in industries such as lobster fishing and hazardous-chemical manufacturing.

Lack of Differentiation or Switching Costs

When products are differentiated, competition is less intense because buyers have preferences and loyalties to particular sellers. Switching costs have the same effect. But when products or services are less differentiated, purchase decisions are based on price and service considerations, resulting in greater competition.

Capacity Augmented in Large Increments

If economies of scale dictate that productive capacity must be added only in large increments, then capacity additions will lead to temporary overcapacity

---

STRATEGIC INSIGHT

Two Equally Balanced Competitors: PepsiCo and Coca-Cola

Consolidated industries that contain only a few companies can be highly competitive. One of the best examples is the soft-drink industry, where Coca-Cola and PepsiCo have been fighting for dominance for many years. Although most consumers probably consider these two fierce competitors to be similar types of firms, they were actually quite different.

A distinction was that most of Coca-Cola's sales came from the soft-drink market, but PepsiCo was more diversified. Over the past twenty years, Coca-Cola has made several attempts at diversification (e.g., motion pictures, coffee, tea, and wine), but none was particularly successful. PepsiCo, on the other hand, consisted of three major product divisions: soft drinks, snack foods (e.g., Frito-Lay), and fast-food restaurants (Pizza Hut, KFC, and Taco Bell). Although in the 1970s and 1980s diversification seemed like a good idea for PepsiCo, by the latter 1990s it was evident that fast food was not going to continue to generate much profits. PepsiCo's restaurants, known for their creativity, began to stall. This was partially due to a proliferation of fast-food stores which had

opened for business in the 1990s. Note that opening fast-food restaurants requires relatively low investments. By 1997 PepsiCo made the decision to spin off its three fast-food restaurant chains. Thus, similar to Coca-Cola, PepsiCo found that diversification was not advantageous.

Currently, the battle arena for the two firms is the soft-drink market. Most of their competition has taken the form of advertising, attempting to maximize shelf space in retail outlets, waging price wars, and introducing new products. PepsiCo and Coca-Cola will likely continue to wage new battles. For instance, U.S. demand for cola drinks has recently declined in favor of such New Age drinks as flavored seltzers, juice drinks, and iced teas. Although Snapple was an early dominating force in this segment, PepsiCo and Coca-Cola countered with naturally brewed versions of their respective Lipton and Nestea brands. Both giants control massive geographical distribution channels and soft-drink machines. Hence, the intensity of rivalry between the two leading soft-drink producers is likely to continue.

SOURCES: "Pepsi Readies Promotion Giving Beepers to Teens," *Wall Street Journal Interactive Edition*, 13 May 1996; M. Wallin and D. Lytle, "PepsiCo Moves to Shore Up S. American Bottler," *Dow Jones News Service*, 9 May 1996; "Hardee's Food Systems Renews Contract With Coca-Cola," *Dow Jones News Service*, 8 May 1996; R. Frank, "Pepsi to Take Control of Latin American Bottler," *Wall Street Journal Interactive Edition*, 10 May 1996; P. Sellers, "PepsiCo's New Generation," *Fortune*, 1 April 1996, pp. 110–118; "The Fortune 500 Largest U.S. Industrial Corporations," *Fortune*, 16 April 1996; G. Collins, "Juice Wars: The Squeeze Is On; Snapple Looks Back to See Coke and Pepsi Gaining", *New York Times*, 15 July 1995, p. 17; N. Deagun, "Pepsi Has Had Its Fill of Pizza, Tacos, Chicken," *Wall Street Journal*, 24 January 1997; G. W. Prince and E. Sfiligoj, "New Age Flourishes," *Beverage Industry Supplement*, March 1994, pp. 21–23; L. Zinn, "Does Pepsi Have Too Many Products?" *Business Week*, 14 February 1994, pp. 64–66; M. J. McCarthy, "Soft-Drink Firms Search for Answers as Volumes Drop," *Wall Street Journal*, 27 July 1992.

in the industry and resultant price cutting. This problem characterizes the manufacture of chlorine, vinyl chloride, and ammonium fertilizer.

Diverse Competitors

Companies that are diverse in their origins, cultures, and strategies will often have differing goals and differing ways of competing. These differences mean that competitors will have a difficult time agreeing on a set of "rules for the game." Industries with foreign competitors and industries with entrepreneurial owner-operators may, therefore, be particularly competitive.

High Strategic Stakes

Rivalry will be quite volatile if firms have high stakes in achieving success in a particular industry. For instance, Sony or Toyota may have perceived a strong need to establish a solid position in the U.S. market to enhance its global prestige or technological credibility. These desires can even involve the willingness to sacrifice profitability.

High Exit Barriers

Exit barriers can be economic, strategic, or emotional factors that keep companies from leaving an industry even though they are earning a low—or possibly negative—return on their investment. Examples of exit barriers are fixed assets that have no alternative uses, labor agreements, strategic interrelationships between that business unit and other business units within the same company, management's unwillingness to leave an industry because of pride, and governmental pressure to continue operations to avoid adverse economic effects in a geographic region.

■ Pressure From Substitute Products

Firms in one industry may be competing with firms in other industries that produce **substitute products,** which are alternative products that satisfy similar consumer needs but differ in specific characteristics. Substitutes place a ceiling on the prices that firms can charge. For instance, the products of fiberglass insulation were unable to raise their prices despite unprecedented demand during a severe winter because of the availability of insulation substitutes such as cellulose, rock wool, and Styrofoam. And movie theaters are coming under increasing competition from pay-per-view cable channels, which show first-run movies at less than half the theater ticket price. In contrast, firms that produce products that have no substitutes are likely to be highly profitable.

■ Bargaining Power of Buyers

The buyers of an industry's outputs can lower that industry's profitability by bargaining for higher quality or more services and playing one firm against another. Buyers are powerful under the following circumstances:

- Buyers are concentrated or purchase large volumes relative to total industry sales. If a few buyers purchase a substantial proportion of an industry's sales, then they will wield considerable power over prices.

- The products that the buyers purchase represent a significant percentage of the buyers' costs. If the products account for a large portion of the buyers' costs, then price is an important issue for the buyers. Hence, they will shop for a favorable price and will purchase selectively.
- The products that the buyers purchase are standard or undifferentiated. In such cases, buyers are prone to play one seller against another.
- The buyers face few switching costs. Switching costs, of course, lock buyers to particular sellers.
- The buyers earn low profits. Low profits create pressure for the buyers to reduce their purchasing costs.
- Buyers can engage in backward integration (they become their own suppliers). General Motors and Ford, for example, use the threat of self-manufacture as a powerful bargaining lever.
- The industry's product is relatively unimportant to the quality of the buyers' products or services. When the quality of the buyers' products is greatly affected by what they purchase from the industry, the buyers are less likely to have significant power over the suppliers.
- Buyers have full information. The more information buyers have regarding demand, actual market prices, and supplier costs, the greater their bargaining power.

■ Bargaining Power of Suppliers

Suppliers can squeeze the profitability out of an industry that is unable to recover cost increases in its own prices. The conditions that make suppliers powerful basically mirror those that make buyers powerful. Hence, suppliers are powerful under the following circumstances:

- The supplying industry is dominated by a few companies and is more concentrated than the industry to which it sells. Selling to fragmented buyers means that concentrated suppliers will be able to exert considerable control over prices, quality, and selling terms.
- There are no substitute products. If buyers have no alternative sources of supply, then they are weak in relation to the suppliers that exist.
- The buying industry is not an important customer of the suppliers. If a particular industry does not represent a significant percentage of the suppliers' sales, then the suppliers have considerable power. If the industry is an important customer, however, suppliers' fortunes will be closely tied to that industry, and they will find that reasonable pricing and assistance in such areas as research and development are in their best interests.
- The suppliers' product is an important input of the buyers' business. If the product is a key element in the buyers' manufacturing process or product quality, the suppliers possess significant power.
- The suppliers' products are differentiated or they have built-in switching costs. Product differentiation or switching costs reduce the buyers' ability to play one supplier against another.
- The suppliers pose a credible threat of forward integration (they can become their own customers). If suppliers have the ability and resources to operate their own manufacturing facilities, distribution channels, or retail outlets, they will possess considerable power over buyers.

We can see, then, that—at one extreme—a company could operate quite profitably in an industry with high entry barriers, low intensity of competition among member firms, no substitute products, weak buyers, and weak suppliers. On the other hand, a company doing business in an industry with low entry barriers, intense competition, many substitute products, and strong buyers and/or suppliers would be hard-pressed to generate an adequate profit. The key, of course, is for management to scan and understand the industry in which it operates and to position its company as favorably as possible within that industry. In fact, the next few chapters are devoted to an examination of this key issue in strategic management.

STRATEGIC INSIGHT

Supplier Power: The Case of NutraSweet

In 1901, John Francisco Queeny was unable to persuade the wholesale pharmaceutical company for which he worked to produce saccharin, the low-calorie sweetener, rather than to continue to import it from Germany. He took $5,000 and started his own company in St. Louis, calling it Monsanto Chemical Works after his wife's family name.

Some eighty-four years later, Monsanto returned to its roots by acquiring G. D. Searle, the pharmaceutical company known for its extremely successful low-calorie sweetener, NutraSweet. Now a separate business unit of Monsanto, NutraSweet manufactures aspartame for beverages, dessert products, and table-top sweeteners (under the brand name Equal). Its sales represented 10 percent of Monsanto's annual revenues of $9 billion, and, in 1992, it controlled 75 percent of the U.S. sweetener market. Furthermore, aspartame's operating margins were an impressive 20 percent.

The secret to this success was NutraSweet's patent protection on aspartame. In fact, for two decades, NutraSweet was the world's only supplier of this artificial sweetener. Its monopoly sometimes resulted in a reputation for high-handedness among its customers. For instance, NutraSweet insisted that its logo be displayed in a certain way on all products that contained aspartame. Its power was further demonstrated through its high prices.

But the days of unilateral power are over. NutraSweet's patent expired in 1992, opening the market for aspartame to numerous competitors. To adapt to its declining clout with customers, top management lowered prices by one-third and pledged its $20 million advertising budget to support customer products that contained NutraSweet.

Shortly before the patent expired, Coca-Cola and PepsiCo, NutraSweet's two largest customers, again signed contracts to buy aspartame from NutraSweet, although Coke also signed a similar contract with Holland Sweetener of The Netherlands. Industry observers suggested that neither of the soft-drink giants wanted to take the risk of replacing an ingredient that already had such high consumer acceptance.

Monsanto's Searle unit is continuing to fund efforts aimed at creating an even better sweetener. The company is committed to developing Sweetener 2000, an artificial sweetener that is hundreds of times sweeter than sugar and yet contains no calories.

SOURCES: M. Wilke, "Sweetener Battle Could Fizz Up," *Advertising Age,* 1 May 1995, p. 39; "America's Most Valuable Companies," *Business Week,* 28 March 1994, pp. 72–127; "Monsanto Posts Sales and Net Gains," *Chemical Marketing Reporter,* 26 July 1993, p. 5; L. Therrien, P. Oster, and C. Hawkins, "How Sweet It Isn't at NutraSweet," *Business Week,* 14 December 1992, p. 42; M. J. McCarthy, "Pepsi, Coke Say They're Loyal to NutraSweet," *Wall Street Journal,* 22 April 1992.

ASSEMBLAGE OF PLAYERS

In the previous section, five industry forces that can have an impact on a firm's profitability were identified. A study of these forces promotes an understanding of firm performance within industries. However, four assumptions are implicit in the preceding section:

- Firms tend to compete in industries with distinct parameters.
- In an industry, the boundaries and identities of each of the five forces are relatively clear-cut.
- The gain of one industry force may result in a loss to another (e.g., one firm gains at the expense of its rivals; a buying organization benefits at a cost to its suppliers).
- Each force may develop independently of other forces (e.g., existing firms develop independently of the buyers they serve).

Although examining the five forces simplifies one's understanding of the performance of firms in an industry, the preceding assumptions are largely violated in many of today's highly complex industries. The pressure for enhanced efficiency and innovation during the last two decades has increased to such an extent that analyzing any one industry does not fully reveal what determines a firm's performance. We can at times benefit by departing from the assumptions of the five-force model and instead examine firm performance in the context of an assemblage of players, which are not confined to a single industry.

The economic prospects for any one firm may in some circumstances be better understood in terms of its interactions with an assemblage of competitive and cooperative firms, called players. For instance, rather than viewing Coca-Cola and PepsiCo as competitors only in the soft-drink industry, we can examine their competition and cooperation with other firms across several industries (Our examination relates to PepsiCo prior to the spin-off of its fast food restaurants). This does not mean that the soft-drink industry classification is irrelevant, but that firm performance may be better understood if factors not solely confined to a specific industry are examined.

■ Exchanges with Cooperative Players

Exchanges with cooperative players refer to the mutually beneficial relationships that develop among firms across different industries, although such exchanges are not always obvious. For instance, a carbon dioxide supplier, a chicken processor, and a soft-drink company might engage in mutually supportive, cooperative exchanges. Liquid Carbonic, Airco, or Air Liquide might supply carbon dioxide to PepsiCo for carbonation. These firms might also provide carbon dioxide to chicken processors such as Tyson Foods for freezing the birds. Moreover, Tyson might supply PepsiCo's KFC and Taco Bell units with frozen chicken.

Exchanges among these firms could be mutually advantageous. Higher demand for frozen chicken by PepsiCo's KFC and Taco Bell businesses might benefit Tyson by enabling the chicken processor to enhance its scale economies. This might make it feasible for Tyson to pass along a portion of its cost savings to KFC and Taco Bell. Moreover, higher demand for carbon dioxide by PepsiCo and Tyson might allow the producers of carbon dioxide to reduce their operating costs, making it possible for Airco, Liquid Carbonic, or Air Liquide to transfer a percentage of the cost savings back to PepsiCo and Tyson.

■ Exchanges with Competitive Players

Examining interactions among competitors can also be instructive. Competition among PepsiCo, McDonald's, Burger King, Wendy's and Disney exists in various markets. PepsiCo has been prevented from selling its soft drinks to the latter businesses because PepsiCo's restaurants—Pizza Hut, Taco Bell, and KFC—are rivals of McDonald's, Burger King, Wendy's, and Disney-owned establishments. PepsiCo is also excluded from co-branding and merchandising ventures with Disney, whereas Coca-Cola is Disney's partner in such ventures. Alternatively, Coca-Cola cannot bid for the soft-drink needs of Pizza Hut, Taco Bell, and KFC.

Some firms beneficially anchor one competitor to another. For instance, a carbon dioxide supplier such as Airco, Liquid Carbonic, or Air Liquide could serve as an anchor by supplying both PepsiCo and Coca-Cola. Alternatively, Tyson Foods could supply chicken to PepsiCo's units as well as to units of its competitors. In this way competitors may indirectly engender mutual benefits through anchor firms. The heavy demands of Coca-Cola and PepsiCo for carbonation may enable a producer of carbon dioxide to reduce costs and ultimately share a portion of the cost savings with the two firms. Similarly, Tyson, as an anchor firm may simultaneously lower the cost of chicken for PepsiCo's restaurants and for the restaurants owned by McDonald's, Burger King, and Wendy's, because the combined demand of these restaurants provides greater economies of scale for Tyson.

■ Existence of Cooperation and Competition

Whereas exchanges among mutually supportive firms are cooperative as they interact to create value, the relationship turns competitive over the division of spoils. Thus, both cooperative and competitive behavior may exist among mutually supportive firms, although they will be more interested in cooperation than in competition. In some situations, adversaries may collaborate for mutual gain, such as in setting technical standards or by sharing research, as the U.S. automakers have done in developing battery technology for electric vehicles.

■ Changing Nature of Exchanges and Roles

The nature of exchanges and the roles of competitors or collaborators may change over time. For instance, cooperative exchanges once existed between PepsiCo and Burger King. Before PepsiCo diversified into three restaurant chains, Burger King sold Pepsi products through its outlets. However, after PepsiCo became one of Burger King's prime competitors, the nature of their exchange shifted from cooperation to competition; their roles changed from being mutually supportive to being adversarial (The nature of their exchanges may again change due to the spin-off).

Moreover, the interactive roles some firms play may not be clear-cut. For example, Novell has performed well by consistently converting rivals into partners or customers through the development and use of its NetWare software.

Alternatively, on any given day AT&T finds Motorola to be simultaneously a competitor, partner, supplier, and customer.[14] In this context, only firms capable of cooperating and competing simultaneously will be top performers.[15]

■ The Process of Mutual Development

The conceptualization of an assemblage of players may help shed light on the process of mutual development through cooperative and competitive firm behavior.[16] In many respects, behavior among firms is analogous to activity in the animal kingdom. For instance, lions, hyenas, and zebras develop together in the wild. The lion culls the weak and slow zebras, thus strengthening the herd of zebras over time. But to prevail over a stronger and faster herd, the lion must also become more adept. Similarly, the hyena, which competes for the zebra, must become stronger and faster in order to feast on the zebra.

Interactions in the animal kingdom, however, also entail both competitive and cooperative behaviors. Although male zebras compete with each other for mates, their herd behavior to evade predators protects their potential mates as well as their male rivals. Also, although lions (or hyenas) may cooperate in hunting the zebra, they inevitably compete over the kill. Additionally, hyenas may chase the zebra herd toward the lions (or lions toward hyenas), demonstrating an unintentional but effective cooperation between the lion and the hyena.

Competitive or cooperative behavior is instinctive in the animal kingdom, but firms tend to cooperate or compete intentionally. Mutual development among organizations may be based on their competitive or cooperative behavior. Enterprises confronted with strong rivalry may develop into more efficient and innovative units. Alternatively, without viable rivals, firms may lack the incentive to advance, causing them to become less efficient and productive. Such was the case in the 1960s and 1970s when U.S. automakers lacked strong international rivals and became complacent.

Mutual development can occur not only through rivalries, but also through interactions such as between suppliers and buyers. For example, IKEA provides research assistance to its suppliers and leases equipment to them, allowing the supplier firms to keep pace with technological developments. The assistance IKEA provides to its suppliers not only strengthens the suppliers but benefits IKEA by allowing it to produce outputs with reliable components that facilitate operational efficiencies. As firms develop efficiencies and innovations, competitive pressure is even exerted on firms that produce substitute products or services. For instance, the enhanced efficiency of airlines, resulting in lower prices, has exerted pressure on bus and railroad companies to emphasize efficiencies.

FORECASTING THE ENVIRONMENT

Macroenvironmental and industry scanning and analyses are only marginally useful if all they do is reveal current conditions. To be truly meaningful, such analyses must forecast future trends and changes. Although no form of forecasting is foolproof, several techniques can be helpful: time series analysis, judgmental forecasting, multiple scenarios, and the Delphi technique. Each method is described in the following sections.

■ Time Series Analysis

Time series analysis attempts to examine the effects of selected trends (such as population growth, technological innovations, changes in disposable personal income, or changes in number of suppliers) on such variables as a firm's costs, sales, profitability, and market share over a number of years. This methodology also enables management to relate such factors as seasonal fluctuations, weather conditions, and holidays to the firm's performance. Likewise, time series analysis can reveal the effect of economic cycles on the organization's sales and profits. The purpose is to make a prediction about these variables.

Because time series analysis projects historical trends into the future, its validity depends upon the similarity between past trends and future conditions. Any significant departure from historical trends will weaken the forecast dramatically. Unfortunately, departures from historical trends seem to be occurring with increasing frequency.

A second potential weakness in time series analysis is that it provides quantitative answers. Managers must take care that they do not place too much confidence in these results. The use of numbers and equations often gives a misleading appearance of scientific accuracy.

■ Judgmental Forecasting

When the relationships between variables are less clear than they are in time series analysis or when they cannot be adequately quantified, judgmental forecasting may be used. In **judgmental forecasting,** an organization may use its own employees, customers, suppliers, or trade association as sources of qualitative information about future trends. For instance, sales representatives may be asked to forecast sales growth in various product categories from their knowledge of customers' expansion plans. Survey instruments may be mailed to customers, suppliers, or trade associations to obtain their judgments on specific trends.

For example, Allied Corporate Investments, a Los Angeles broker for buyers and sellers of businesses, originally specialized in relatively low-priced small businesses. In 1984, however, it conducted a judgmental forecast, asking its research staff, sales force, and outsiders (such as banks, customers, and the chamber of commerce) to forecast what business opportunities might be available in the future. The consensus of the forecast was that the Los Angeles economy would expand and the value of businesses would be substantially bid up. In response, Allied opened several more offices, contacted commercial sections of foreign embassies to inform them of business opportunities, and brokered more expensive businesses. As a result of its judgmental forecast, its volume of business increased by ten times. Judgmental forecasting should be done periodically to ensure that recent events are taken into account. Unfortunately, Allied did not update its forecast. The recession of the early 1990s, the bankruptcy of Orange County in 1994, and natural disasters severely impacted its operations, leading to a reduced business base and layoffs.

■ Multiple Scenarios

The increasing unpredictability of environmental changes makes it incredibly difficult to formulate dependable assumptions upon which forecasts can be based. One means of circumventing this troublesome state is to develop multiple scenarios about the future. In **multiple scenarios,** the manager formulates several alternative descriptions of future events and trends.[17]

One scenario, for example, may specify the economic conditions thought most likely to occur at some future point. Alternative scenarios may use a more optimistic assumption and a more pessimistic assumption. The same process can just as easily be used to express differing assumptions about technology, political elections, environmental regulation, oil prices, strikes, and other events.

For example, Royal Dutch/Shell Group, the world's second largest corporation, with annual sales exceeding $103 billion, currently uses two scenarios to formulate strategy. One assumes that European economic unification is successful, Japan and the United States avoid a trade war, and stable economic growth occurs throughout most of the world. In such a case, the physical environment will receive increasing attention, meaning governments will formulate additional emission restrictions and natural gas will take precedence over oil as a source of energy. The second scenario assumes international trade wars and widespread recession. Under such conditions, environmental regulations will be de-emphasized and oil consumption will increase dramatically. The point is not to predict which outcome will occur but to encourage managers to analyze a variety of "what if" possibilities.[18]

In formulating scenarios, strategic managers must identify the key forces in the macroenvironment and industry, assess their likely interrelationships, and estimate their influence upon future events. Contingency plans can then be prepared to cover the various conditions specified in the multiple scenarios. These plans may be general statements of action to be taken, without completely specifying the intended operational details. Contingency plans usually specify trigger points—events that call for implementing particular aspects of a plan.[19]

■ Delphi Technique

In certain cases, the **Delphi technique** may be used to forecast the future.[20] If the trend to be forecasted lies within a particular field of study, then experts in that field can be identified and questioned about the probability of the trend's occurring. For instance, if a home building firm would like to know when it will become feasible to build entire housing developments with solar energy as the sole source of electricity, heating, and cooling, the firm would compile a list of experts in the field of solar energy. Each expert would then be mailed a questionnaire asking for his or her judgments as to when knowledge of solar energy will be sufficiently advanced to rely solely on it for home energy needs. The respondents will fill out the questionnaires, without communicating with one another, and return them to the home building company.

The company will compile a summary of the results and send it to each respondent along with a second questionnaire. After reviewing the summary and observing the other experts' judgments, each respondent will fill out and mail in the second questionnaire. Some respondents may alter their judgments on this questionnaire after reviewing the judgments of the other members. This process of responding–receiving–feedback–responding continues until consensus is reached. The home builder will then rely, at least partially, on this consensus in formulating the firm's plans for the future.

In the previous paragraphs, several forecasting techniques were presented. Examples of others are shown in Table 2.3.

Table 2.3	**Other Forecasting Techniques**		
Technique	*Description*	*Weakness*	
Econometric forecast	Simultaneous multiple regression systems	Assumes past relationships will continue into the future	
Sales force forecast (judgmental)	Aggregate sales force estimate	Potential bias in opinions	
Managerial forecast (judgmental)	Aggregation of estimates made by research and development, production, finance, and marketing managers	Potential bias in opinions	
Consumer survey (judgmental)	Aggregate preferences of consumers	Potential bias in opinions	
Brainstorming (judgmental)	Idea generation in supportive group interaction	Potential bias in opinions	

SUMMARY

Each organization exists within a complex network of environmental forces comprised of (1) the national and global macroenvironment and (2) the industry in which the organization competes. Because these forces are dynamic, their constant change presents numerous opportunities and threats to strategic managers.

Four macroenvironmental forces affect an organization. Political-legal forces, in the broadest sense, include a government's basic stance toward business operations and, more narrowly, the outcomes of elections, legislation, and court judgments, as well as the decisions of various commissions and agencies at all levels of government. Economic forces comprise elements such as the impact of growth or decline in GDP and increases or decreases in interest rates, inflation, and the value of the dollar. Technological forces include scientific improvements and innovations that affect a firm's operations and/or its products and services. Social forces include traditions, values, societal trends, and a society's expectations of business. To identify and understand changes and trends in these forces, managers engage in environmental scanning.

A more specific set of forces within a firm's industry directly and powerfully affects management's strategic planning. Professor Porter has identified five basic competitive industry forces: the threat of new entrants in the industry, the intensity of rivalry among existing competitors in the industry, the pressure from producers of substitute products or services, the bargaining power of buyers of the industry's outputs, and the bargaining power of suppliers to the industry's companies. The goal of a competitive strategy for a firm is to find a position in the industry from which it can best defend itself against these competitive forces or can influence them to its advantage.

An alternative way we can examine firm performance is in the context of an assemblage of competitive as well as cooperative players. Exchanges among cooperative firms refer to the mutually supportive interactions of an assemblage of firms across different industries. Exchanges with competitive players consist of interactions of adversarial firms in various industries. Both cooperative and competitive firm behavior may prevail among supportive or adversarial players. The nature of exchanges and the roles of players, however, may change over time. Also, the roles played by some firms as they interact with each other may not always be clear-cut. Moreover, mutual development may occur among cooperative or competitive organizations.

Strategic planners must not only understand the current state of the macroenvironment and their industry but must also be able to forecast the future states. Although forecasting is an inexact science, four techniques can be particularly helpful: time series analysis, judgmental forecasting, multiple scenarios, and the Delphi technique.

TAKE IT TO THE NET

We invite you to visit the Wright page on the Prentice Hall Web site at:

http://www.prenhall.com/wright

for this chapter's World Wide Web exercise.

KEY CONCEPTS

Barriers to entry Obstacles to entering an industry. The major barriers to entry are economies of scale, product differentiation, capital requirements, switching costs, access to distribution channels, cost disadvantages independent of scale, and government policy.

Delphi technique A forecasting procedure in which experts in the appropriate field of study are independently questioned about the probability of some event's occurrence. The responses of all the experts are compiled, and a summary is sent to each expert, who, on the basis of this new information, responds again. Those responses are then compiled and a summary is again sent to each expert, with the cycle continuing until consensus is reached regarding the particular forecasted event.

Economies of scale The decline in unit costs of a product, an operation, or a function that goes into producing a product, which occurs as the absolute volume of production per period of time increases.

Environmental scanning The gathering and analysis of information about relevant environmental trends.

Exit barriers Obstacles to leaving an industry. Exit barriers can be economic, strategic, or emotional.

Industry A group of companies that produces products or services that are in competition.

Judgmental forecasting A forecasting procedure in which employees, customers, suppliers, and/or trade associations serve as sources of qualitative information regarding future trends.

Macroenvironment   The general environment that affects all business firms. Its principal components are political-legal, economic, technological, and social systems and trends.

Multiple scenarios   A forecasting procedure in which management formulates several plausible hypothetical descriptions of sequences of future events and trends.

Stakeholder   An individual or group who is affected by—or can influence—an organization's operations.

Substitute products   Alternative products that may satisfy similar consumer needs and wants but that differ somewhat in specific characteristics.

Switching costs   One-time costs that buyers of an industry's outputs incur if they switch from one company's products to another's.

Time series analysis   An empirical forecasting procedure in which certain historical trends are used to predict such variables as a firm's sales or market share.

DISCUSSION QUESTIONS

1. Give an example, other than those in the text, of how political-legal forces have presented an opportunity or a threat to a particular industry or business organization.

2. Explain how changes in the value of the dollar affect the domestic and international sales of U.S.-based companies.

3. Give an example, other than those in the text, of how technological forces have presented an opportunity or a threat to a particular industry or business organization.

4. Select a specific business organization and identify the stakeholders of that particular firm.

5. Using your university as an example, explain how political-legal, economic, technological, and social forces have affected its operations over the past decade.

6. Identify an industry that has low barriers to entry and one that has high barriers. Explain how these differences in barriers to entry affect the intensity and form of competition in those two industries.

7. Give some specific examples of exit barriers. How do they affect competition in those industries?

8. Aside from the examples given in the text, identify some products whose sales have been adversely affected by substitute products.

9. Identify an industry in which the suppliers have strong bargaining power and another industry in which the buyers have most of the bargaining power.

10. What are the strengths and weaknesses of time series analysis as a forecasting technique?

STRATEGIC MANAGEMENT EXERCISES

1. Select a specific company with which you are somewhat familiar. From your recollection of current events (events you may have read about in newspapers or magazines or have heard about on television or radio), identify some of the important macroenvironmental opportunities and threats for this company.

2. From your recollection of current events (events you may have read about in newspapers or magazines or have heard about on television or radio), identify and analyze the industry forces for an automobile company of your choice.

3. Select a major company for which there is considerable information available in your university library. Conduct a macroenvironmental analysis for that company. Your analysis should contain four sections: political-legal forces, economic forces, technological forces, and social forces. (See Appendix 2A for help in locating sources of macroenvironmental information.) Worksheet 1 may help to structure your analysis.

   You need not limit yourself to the terms listed under "Important Information." In some cases, other items that you discover in your research will be of equal or greater importance.

   Once you have identified the important components of each macroenvironmental force, you should determine whether each presents an opportunity or a threat to your company. You might assign a "+" to opportunities and a "−" to threats, or you might list each item under the subheadings "Opportunities" and "Threats." (You can refer to the beginning of the case section, "Strategic Management Case Analysis," for further details.)

4. Conduct an industry analysis for the company that you selected in Exercise 3. Your analysis should contain information in five areas: threat of entry, intensity of rivalry among existing competitors, pressure from substitute products, bargaining power of buyers, and bargaining power of suppliers. (See Appendix 2A for help in locating sources of industry information.) Worksheet 2 should help you to organize your work.

5. Assume that you have been asked to develop an environmental forecast for the bookstore at your university, using the judgmental forecasting technique. Attempt to forecast the environment of the bookstore by writing a summary report based on questions that you ask several employees and customers of the bookstore. Inasmuch as you may not have access to suppliers or trade associations, include your own judgment of what opportunities and threats the environment holds for the bookstore.

Worksheet 1   **Macroenvironmental Analysis**

Macroenvironmental Force	*Important Information*
Political-legal	Outcomes of elections, legislation, court judgments, and decisions rendered by various federal, state, and local agencies
Economic	GDP, short- and long-term interest rates, inflation, and value of the dollar
Technological	Scientific improvements, inventions, and the rate of technological change in the industry
Social	Traditions, values, societal trends, consumer psychology, and the public's expectations of business

Worksheet 2   **Industry Analysis**

Industry Sector	*Important Information*
Threat of entry	Extent to which the following factors prevent new companies from entering the industry: economies of scale, product differentiation, capital requirements, switching costs, access to distribution channels, cost disadvantages independent of scale, government policy, and expected retaliation
Intensity of rivalry among existing competitors	Number and relative balance of competitors, rate of industry growth, extent of fixed or storage costs, degree of product differentiation and switching costs, size of capacity augmentation, diversity of competitors, extent of strategic stakes, and height of exit barriers
Pressure from substitute products	Identification of substitute products, and analysis of the relative price and quality of those products
Bargaining power of buyers	Concentration of buyers, their purchase volume relative to industry sales and to the buyers' costs, product differentiation, buyers' switching costs, buyers' profits, possibility of buyers integrating backward, importance of the product to the quality of the buyers' products, and amount of information possessed by the buyers
Bargaining power of suppliers	Number and concentration of suppliers, availability of substitute products, importance of the buying industry to the suppliers, importance of the suppliers' product to the buyer's business, differentiation and switching costs associated with the suppliers' product, and possibility of suppliers integrating forward

NOTES

1. J. Sadler, "Small Businesses Complain that Jungle of Regulations Jeopardize Their Futures," *Wall Street Journal*, 11 June 1992; R. W. Duesenberg, "Economic Liberties and the Law," *Imprimis* 23 (April 1994): 1–4.

2. K. Kelly, "A Dream Marriage Turns Nightmarish," *Business Week*, 29 April 1991, pp. 94–95; R. L. Rose, "Caterpillar Sees Gains in Efficiency Imperiled by Strength of Dollar," *Wall Street Journal*, 6 April 1990.

3. T. Y. Wiltz, "It's Enough to Drive the Distillers to Drink," *Business Week*, 25 June 1990, pp. 98–99; M. Charlier, "Youthful Sobriety Tests Liquor Firms," *Wall Street Journal*, 14 June 1990.

4. A. Miller, "Burgers: The Heat Is On," *Newsweek*, 16 June 1986, p. 53.

5. K. J. Marchetti, "Customer Information Should Drive Retail Direct Mail," *Marketing News*, 28 February 1994, p. 7.

6. S. Ratan, "Why Busters Hate Boomers," *Fortune*, 4 October 1993, pp. 56–69; B. W. Morgan, "It's the Myth of the '90s: The Value Customer," *Brandweek*, 28 February 1994, p. 17.

7. J. Diffenbach, "Corporate Environmental Analysis in Large U.S. Corporations," *Long Range Planning* 16, no. 3 (June 1983):109, 112–113.

8. D. F. Jennings and J. R. Lumpkin, "Insights Between Environmental Scanning Activities and Porter's Generic Strategies: An Empirical Analysis," *Journal of Management* 18 (1992): 791–803.

9. M. E. Porter, *Competitive Strategy* (New York: Free Press, 1980), pp. 3–4, 7–14, 17–21, 23–28. Reprinted with permission of The Free Press, a division of Macmillan, Inc., from *Competitive Strategy for Analyzing Industries and Competitors*, by Michael E. Porter. Copyright © 1980 by The Free Press.

10. See A. Taylor III, "Korea Revs Up for Jeep Country," *Fortune*, 10 January 1994, p. 20.

11. M. J. Chen and D. Miller, "Competitive Attack, Retaliation, and Performance: An Expectancy-Valence Framework," *Strategic Management Journal* 15 (1994): 85–102.

12. J. R. Graham, "Bulletproof Your Business Against Competitor Attacks," *Marketing News*, 14 March 1994, pp. 4–5; J. Hayes, "Casual Dining Contenders Storm 'Junior' Markets," *Nation's Restaurant News*, 14 March 1994, pp. 47–52.

13. See A. Taylor III, "Will Success Spoil Chrysler?" *Fortune*, 10 January 1994, pp. 88–92.

14. G. Hamel and C. K. Prahalad, *Competing for the Future* (Cambridge: Harvard Business School Press, 1994).

15. See A. A. Lado, N. G. Boyd, and S. C. Hanlon, "Competition, Cooperation and the Search for Economic Rents: A Syncretic Model," *Academy of Management Review*, 22 (1997): 110–141.

16. See J. F. Moore, "Predators and Prey: A New Ecology of Competition," *Harvard Business Review*, 71 (1993): 75–86.

17. L. Fahey and V. K. Narayanan, *Macroenvironmental Analysis for Strategic Management* (St. Paul, Minn.: West, 1986), p. 215.

18. C. Knowlton, "Shell Gets Rich by Beating Risk," *Fortune*, 26 August 1991, p. 82.

19. C. D. Pringle, D. F. Jennings, and J. G. Longenecker, *Managing Organizations: Functions and Behaviors* (Columbus, Ohio: Merrill, 1988), p. 114.

20. N. C. Dalkey, *The Delphi Method: An Experimental Study of Group Opinion* (Santa Monica, Calif.: Rand Corporation, 1969).

Appendix 2A: Sources of Environmental and Industry Information

Much valuable information on environmental and industry conditions and trends is available from published or other secondary sources. Managers should consult these sources prior to gathering expensive primary data.

Local libraries, for instance, contain introductory information on the political-legal, economic, technological, and social components of the macroenvironment in almanacs and encyclopedias. University libraries provide government publications that are rich with political-legal and economic data. Additional information can be obtained from business literature indexes, business periodicals, and reference services. Regularly published periodicals and newspapers such as *Business Week*, the *Wall Street Journal*, and *Fortune* provide excellent, timely macroenvironmental and industry information. More specific sources of information that may be found in many libraries are listed in Table 2A.1 on page 52.

Other highly specific information may be obtained from the annual reports of companies, reports of major brokerage firms (such as Merrill Lynch), and trade publications (examples include *American Paints and Coatings Journal, Modern Brewery Age, Quick Frozen Foods*, and *Retail Grocer*).

Information on the macroenvironment and industries may also be assimilated from radio business news, television shows (such as "Wall Street Week" and "Money Line"), and suppliers, customers, and employees within the industry. And a visit to a branch office of the U.S. Commerce Department can be helpful. The Commerce Department has an extensive bibliography of its own publications, which is available at the branch offices.

Managers can use these sources of information along with assistance from consultants to forecast changes so that the firm can modify its strategy appropriately. Professional consulting firms are available in all major cities and many midsize locales. University professors in all areas of business administration and other disciplines such as sociology, psychology, engineering, and the sciences can also provide expert counseling in relevant areas.

Table 2A.1	Major Sources of Information on the Business Environment	
Name of Index	**Breadth of Information**	**Description**
Business Periodicals Index	Political-legal Economic Technological Social Industry	Identifies periodicals in all aspects of business and industry. Its "Book Review" covers publications on a variety of topics.
Funk & Scott Index of Corporations and Industries	Industry Economic Suppliers Competitors	Identifies periodicals and brokerage reports on all SIC (Standard Industrial Classification) Industries. Its yellow pages provide weekly updates, its green pages provide lists of articles and dates, and its white pages list information on articles about specific companies.
New York Times Index	Political-legal Economic Technological Social Industry	Provides an index of articles published in the New York Times.
Public Affairs Information Service Bulletin	Social Economic Political-legal	Provides a subject listing on national and international journals, books, pamphlets, government publications, and reports of private and public agencies.
Reader's Guide to Periodical Literature	Political-legal Economic Technological Social Industry	Provides an author and subject index on periodicals and books.
Social Science Index	Political-legal Economic Social	Provides an author and subject index on periodicals and books.
Wall Street Journal/ Barron's Index	Political-legal Economic Technological Social Industry	Provides an index of articles published in the Wall Street Journal and Barron's. Also includes a list of book reviews.
U.S. Industrial Outlook	Political-legal Economic Technological Social Industry	Gives the U.S. Department of Commerce's annual forecasts for over 350 industries.
Predicasts Forecasts	Political-legal Economic Technological Social Industry	Provides forecasts (as a quarterly service) of products, markets, and industry and economic aggregates for the United States and North America. Forecasts are grouped by SIC numbers and many go into the twenty-first century.

Table 2A.1   **Major Sources of Information on the Business Environment (cont'd.)**

Name of Index	Breadth of Information	Description
Standard and Poor's Industry Surveys	Political-legal Economic Technological Social Industry	Profiles and analyzes thirty-three basic industry groups. Trends and projections are detailed. Also contains analyses of each industry's leading performers.
Corporate & Industry Research Reports	Political-legal Economic Technological Social Industry	Provides analyses and forecasts of 8,000 U.S. companies and 600 industries from analytical research reports of 68 securities and institutional investment firms.

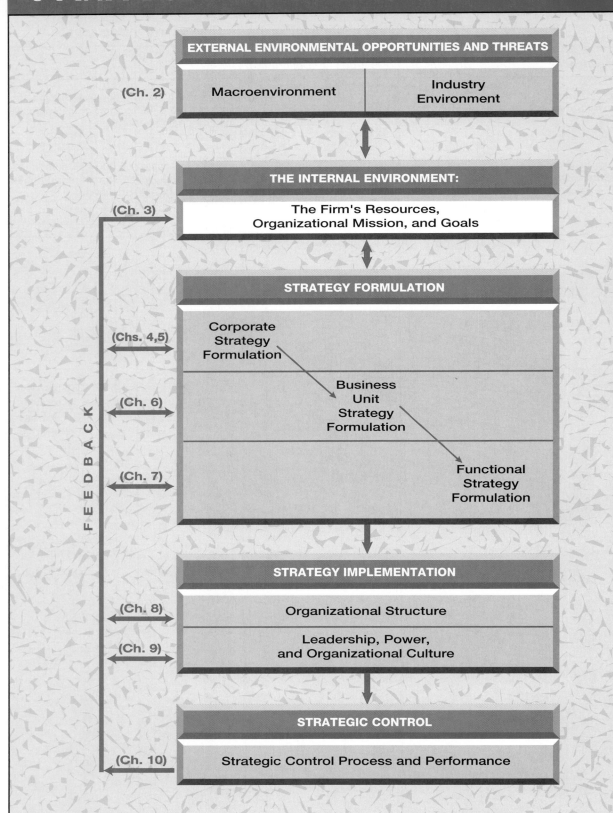

STRATEGIC MANAGEMENT MODEL

EXTERNAL ENVIRONMENTAL OPPORTUNITIES AND THREATS

(Ch. 2)

Macroenvironment	Industry Environment

THE INTERNAL ENVIRONMENT:

(Ch. 3)

The Firm's Resources, Organizational Mission, and Goals

STRATEGY FORMULATION

(Chs. 4,5)

Corporate Strategy Formulation

(Ch. 6)

Business Unit Strategy Formulation

(Ch. 7)

Functional Strategy Formulation

STRATEGY IMPLEMENTATION

(Ch. 8)

Organizational Structure

(Ch. 9)

Leadership, Power, and Organizational Culture

STRATEGIC CONTROL

(Ch. 10)

Strategic Control Process and Performance

FEEDBACK

3 The Internal Environment: The Firm's Resources, Organizational Mission, and Goals

A s we saw in the preceding chapter, an assessment of the opportunities and threats in the organization's external environment is essential in formulating strategy. In this chapter, we turn from the external environment to take an inward look at the firm. This step in the strategy process—establishing the organization's mission and goals—requires management to determine the direction in which the organization is to move within its external environment.

Organizational direction is difficult to determine unless management and the board of directors, with input from diverse stakeholders, have clearly delineated the firm's purpose. The purpose of a firm is delineated in order to strategically create wealth for the shareholders through the satisfaction of the needs and expectations of various stakeholders. According to H. B. Fuller's top manager, Tony Anderson, a firm "exists to make money for its shareholders, but if you have happy customers and employees . . . , the payoff to stockholders will work itself out."[1] A firm's purpose may be conceptualized in the context of **S.W.O.T. analysis** (the strengths and weaknesses of the firm relative to its competitors as well as the opportunities and threats in the external environment). Hence, this chapter begins with a discussion of S. W.O. T. analysis and more specifically the firm's resources, which comprise its strengths and weaknesses, before we examine the organization's mission, its reason for existing. Goals and objectives, as well as other related topics, are subsequently examined.

S.W.O.T. ANALYSIS

Underlying the organization's mission is an analysis of its internal strengths and weaknesses and the opportunities and threats that are posed in the external environment. The framework presented in Table 3.1 identifies many of the variables that management should analyze. The point of the analysis is to enable the firm to position itself to take advantage of particular opportunities in the environment and to avoid or minimize environmental threats. In doing so, the organization attempts to emphasize its strengths and moderate the impact of its weaknesses. The analysis is also useful for uncovering strengths that have not yet been fully utilized and in identifying weaknesses that can be corrected. Matching information about the environment with a knowledge of the organization's capabilities enables management to formulate realistic strategies for attaining its goals.

A firm's resources constitute its strengths and weaknesses.[2] They include **human resources** (the experience, capabilities, knowledge, skills, and judg-

Table 3.1

Framework for S.W.O.T. Analysis

Sources of Possible External Environmental Opportunities and Threats

Economic forces	Political-legal forces	Social forces	Technological forces
Industry forces			

Possible Organizational Strengths and Weaknesses

Access to raw materials	Distribution	Management	Purchasing
Advertising	Economies of scale	Manufacturing and operations	Quality control
Board of directors	Environmental scanning	Market share	Research and development
Brand names	Financial resources	Organizational structure	Selling
Channel management	Forecasting	Physical facilities/ equipment	Strategic control
Company reputation	Government lobbying	Product/service differentiation	Strategy formulation
Computer information system	Human resources	Product/service quality	Strategy implementation
Control systems	Labor relations	Promotion	Technology
Costs	Leadership		
Customer loyalty	Location	Public relations	Inventory management
Decision making			

ment of all the firm's employees), **organizational resources** (the firm's systems and processes, including its strategies, structure, culture, purchasing/materials management, production/operations, financial base, research and development, marketing, information systems, and control systems), and **physical resources** (plant and equipment, geographic locations, access to raw materials, distribution network, and technology). In an optimal setting, all three types of resources work together to give a firm a **sustained competitive advantage,** as illustrated in Figure 3.1. Sustained competitive advantage refers to valuable strategies that cannot be fully duplicated by the firm's competitors and that result in high financial returns over a lengthy period of time.

Just as chapter 2 explored the external environmental opportunities and threats, the following paragraphs will briefly examine each of the three types of resources that comprise a firm's internal strengths and/or weaknesses.

▪ Human Resources

Because even the most superb organizational and physical resources are useless without a talented work force of managers and employees, we place most of our emphasis on a firm's human resources. These resources can be examined at three levels—the board of directors; top management; and middle management, supervisors, and employees.

Board of Directors

At the top of the human resource hierarchy sits the board of directors. Because board members are becoming increasingly involved in corporate affairs, they can materially influence the firm's effectiveness. In examining their strengths and weaknesses, the following questions may be asked.

- What contributions do the board members bring to the firm? Strong board members possess considerable experience, knowledge, and judgment, as well as valuable outside political connections.
- Are the members internal or external, and how widely do they represent the firm's stakeholders? Although it is common for several top managers to be board members, a disproportionate representation of them diminishes

Figure 3.1   **Route to Sustained Competitive Advantage**

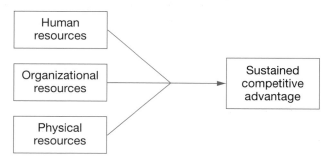

the identity of the board as a group apart from top management. Ideally, board members should represent diverse stakeholders, including minorities, creditors, customers, and the local community. A diverse board membership can contribute to the health of the firm.

- Do the members own significant shares of the firm's securities? Significant stock ownership may increase the board's responsiveness to stockholders, while significant bond holdings may enhance its concern with the firm's creditworthiness.

- How long have the members served on the board? Long-term stability enables board members to gain knowledge about the firm, but some turnover is beneficial because new members often can bring a fresh perspective to strategic issues. More is stated on boards of directors subsequently.

Top Management

The organization's top executives must establish and communicate a vision for the firm that encompasses the needs and desires of the firm's various stakeholders. Strategic leadership will be discussed further in chapter 9. Ideally, then, top managers should assume the role of "selfless stewards" concerned primarily with attaining stakeholders' goals.[3] Several questions might be asked in assessing the strengths and weaknesses of any firm's top management.

- Who are the key top managers, and what are their strengths and weaknesses in job experience, managerial style, decision-making capability, team building, and understanding of the business? There are advantages, for instance, in having executives who have an intimate knowledge of the firm and its industry. On the other hand, managers from diverse backgrounds may generate innovative strategic ideas. And, of course, an organization's management needs may change as the firm grows and matures. For instance, start-up firms are often headed by entrepreneurs who are innovative but may be weak in administrative abilities. More mature firms need strong administration but must continue to be innovative.

- How long have the key top managers been with the firm? Lengthy tenure can mean consistent and stable strategy development and implementation, yet low turnover may breed conformity, complacency, and a failure to explore new opportunities.

- What are top management's strategic strengths and weaknesses? Some executives may excel in innovative strategy formulation, for instance, but may be weak in implementing strategy. Some may spend considerable time interacting with external constituents, whereas others concentrate on internal stakeholders and operations.

Middle Management, Supervisors, and Employees

A firm can have brilliant top managers and board members but if its work force is less than top-notch, even the most ingenious strategies cannot be implemented effectively. Each firm's human resources are unique. That uniqueness stems not only from the fact that every organization employs a different set of human beings, but also from the specific synergies that result from combining each firm's human resources with its particular organizational and physical resources. In this context, a firm's personnel and their knowledge, abilities, commitment, and performance tend to reflect the firm's human resource programs. These factors can be explored by asking several key questions about those programs to ascertain the strengths and weaknesses of the organization's managers and employees.

- Does the organization have a comprehensive human resource planning program? Developing such a program requires that the firm estimate its personnel needs, including types of positions and requisite qualifications, for the next several years based on its strategic plan. Many organizations do little planning in this area, and such short-term thinking rarely results in effective operations.

- How much emphasis does the organization place on training and development programs? Firms that ignore personnel training and development are virtually doomed to stagnation.

- What is the organization's personnel turnover rate compared to the rest of the industry? High turnover rates, compared to those of competitors, generally reflect personnel problems, such as poor management–employee relations, low compensation or benefits, weak personnel policies, or low job satisfaction due to other causes.

- How much emphasis does the firm place on performance appraisal? Effective programs provide accurate feedback to managers and employees, link rewards to actual performance, show managers and employees how to improve performance, and comply with all equal employment opportunity programs.

- How well does the organization manage a work force that increasingly reflects society's changing demographics? Many firms have begun to evaluate and adjust practices that were designed for yesterday's more homogeneous work force. Those firms that lead the way in promoting diversity have a decided advantage in attracting and retaining a highly qualified work force. Human resources are further discussed in chapter 7.

■ Organizational Resources

The assessment of organizational resources basically hinges on the question of whether the resources are properly aligned with the firm's strategies and whether they are sufficient for the strategies' implementation. Although the issues are too numerous to cover completely here, some of the key questions are discussed.

- Are the corporate, business unit, and functional strategies consistent with the organization's mission and goals? The mission, goals, and strategies must be compatible and reflect a clear sense of identity and purpose.

- Are the organization's corporate, business unit, and functional strategies, discussed in chapters 4, 5, 6, and 7 respectively, consistent with one another? These three levels of strategy must be closely intertwined and highly consistent. Hence, managers at the corporate, business unit, and functional level should be represented at each level of strategic planning. Recall that corporate strategies should influence business unit strategies, which, in turn, should influence functional strategies. But, at the same time, functional strategies affect business unit strategies, which then affect corporate strategies.

- Is the organization's formal structure appropriate for implementing its strategy? The content of chapter 8 is entirely devoted to this topic.

- Are the organization's decision-making processes effective in implementing its strategies? Issues of centralization versus decentralization are covered in chapter 5 and chapter 9. Chapter 9 also includes an analysis of leadership team processes.
- Is the organization's culture consistent with its strategy? A part of chapter 9 focuses on the role of culture in strategy formulation and implementation.
- How effective are the organization's strategic control processes? Chapter 10 examines this crucial issue.

■ Physical Resources

Although the types of physical resources possessed by firms differ considerably from one organization to another (consider, e.g., the different physical plants required by an automobile maker versus a management consulting firm), some general questions assessing the strengths and weaknesses of physical resources might take the following form.

- Does the organization possess up-to-date technology? Whereas cutting-edge technology is no guarantee of success, competitors who have superior technology and know how to use it have a decided advantage in the marketplace.
- Does the organization possess adequate capacity? Although a continual backlog of orders indicates market acceptance of a firm's product, it may conceal the lost business and declining customer goodwill that accompany insufficient capacity. We emphasize that numerous firms have restructured their operations in recent years, eliminating excess capacity.
- Is the organization's distribution network an efficient means of reaching customers? Note that distribution networks do not apply only to firms that manufacture products. American Airlines' domination of passenger gates at Dallas–Fort Worth Airport and United's similar control at O'Hare Field give both of these service companies a competitive advantage.
- Does the firm have reliable and cost-effective sources of supply? Suppliers who are unreliable, do not have effective quality control programs, or cannot control their costs well put the buying firm at a decided competitive disadvantage.
- Is the organization (and its branches) in an optimum geographic location? Appropriate location may depend on cost factors (land, building, and labor); the availability of skilled labor, natural resources, and sources of supply; customer convenience; and shipping costs.

What should be emphasized, according to resource-based theory, is the unique combination of human, organizational, and physical resources possessed by a firm. As the firm acquires additional resources, unique synergies occur between its new and existing resources. Because each firm already possesses a distinct combination of human, organizational, and physical resources, the particular types of synergies that occur will differ from one firm to another. For example, if the quality of a new resource in the external environment is represented by Z, once that resource is acquired by organization A the quality of the resource is transformed to ZA. If this resource were instead purchased by organization B, then Z's resultant quality would be transformed to ZB. ZB, of course, represents a qualitatively different value than ZA.

people -service -profit

■ The Organization's Mission

Having examined the firm's external environment in the previous chapter and its potential resource strengths and weaknesses in the preceding paragraphs, we now examine the organization's mission. Organizations are founded for a purpose. Although this purpose may change over time, it is essential that stakeholders understand the reason for the organization's existence, that is, the organization's **mission**. Often, the organization's mission is defined in a formal, written **mission statement**—a broadly defined but enduring statement of purpose that identifies the scope of an organization's operations and its offerings to the various stakeholders.[4]

As suggested before, a firm's mission should evolve in the context of S.W.O.T. analysis.[5] In the following section, we examine the organization's mission at both the corporate and business unit levels. Changes in the organization's mission over time are then discussed, followed by an overview of the relationship between the organization's mission and its strategy. Goals and objectives, as well as other related topics, are subsequently probed.

Mission and Organizational Level

The mission of an organization, at the corporate level, is stated in fairly broad terms. For instance, the management of General Motors (GM) has stated the firm's overall mission as follows:

> The fundamental purpose of General Motors is to provide products and services of such quality that our customers will receive superior value, our employees and business partners will share in our success, and our stockholders will receive a sustained, superior return on their investment.[6]

pure compentition

Buyer has the advantage

Certainly, a large number of activities can be covered by such a broad statement. Such disparate GM undertakings as manufacturing vehicles, producing electronics and defense products, and providing technology can all be included in this mission statement. However, in each of these cases, the statement indicates that GM intends to furnish superior value to customers, to have employees and business partners share in the firm's success, and to provide a sustained, superior return to stockholders on their investment. So even though very broad, this corporate-level statement does provide direction to the company.

At the business unit level, the mission becomes narrower in scope and more clearly defined. For example, the mission of the Chevrolet business unit would include manufacturing safe and reliable economy cars, sport cars, sedans, and trucks. The Hughes Aircraft subsidiary's mission would be to produce electronic components and systems for defense and industrial customers.

The mission of some business units even specifies in which country the products will be manufactured and strategically links the business unit to the corporate level in some manner—such as through the transfer of knowledge and technology. For example, GM's Saturn business unit has the following mission statement:

> The mission of Saturn is to market vehicles developed and manufactured in the United States that are world leaders in quality and customer satisfaction through the integration of people, technology and business systems and to transfer knowledge, technology and experience throughout General Motors.[7]

Mission and Change

Corporate and strategic business-level missions will generally change over time. In many cases, the change will be slow and gradual, but in some instances, the change may take place very rapidly. As an example of a firm whose mission changed gradually, consider Primerica. At one time, Primerica was known as American Can Company and was engaged in the container manufacturing and packaging businesses. Over the years, the company diversified into financial services and specialty retailing. When it finally sold its can and packaging operations, its name no longer fit its businesses, and it was renamed Primerica. Obviously, its mission had also gradually changed from manufacturing to services. Now its mission is to provide life insurance to individual consumers, originate home mortgages, provide mutual and pension fund management and brokerage services, and offer retail services for recorded music and audio and video products.

UAL, Inc. (United Airlines), serves as a classic example of a firm whose mission changed quickly. In 1987, UAL's chief executive officer, Richard Ferris, decided to broaden the company's mission. Rather than only provide air travel, UAL would become an integrated travel service company with operations encompassing the total service requirements of travelers. The firm would expand into rental cars (to provide customers transportation to and from airports) and hotels (where customers could stay while on trips). To reflect this broadened mission, the firm's name was changed from United Airlines to Allegis. The new mission was quite controversial, and various groups that had vested interests in the company believed that those interests would be better served by the firm's original mission—passenger and cargo air transportation. Within four months, Ferris was fired and the company's name and mission reverted to their previous forms.

Boston Consulting Group's Jeanie Duck has argued that change is very personal. For change to occur in any firm, each person and group must adopt a different attitude and perform an aspect of his or her job differently. This argument may be extended to change and stakeholder groups. If a mission of a firm is to change, stakeholder groups must be positively predisposed toward the change. Otherwise, the change will not occur successfully or will be short-lived, as was the case with United Airlines.[8]

Mission and Strategy

An organization with a keen sense of its own identity is far more likely to be successful than one that has no clear understanding of its reason for existence. For example, Armco diversified widely more than a decade ago in an attempt to shelter itself from fluctuations in the steel industry. But it found itself in alien territory when it moved into financial services and insurance. After acquiring an insurance holding company, Armco's managers discovered that they "had very few people in [their] management group who could ask the right questions and trouble shoot in that part of [their] operations."[9] They determined to limit future diversification to markets with which they were familiar. Sears, another example of a firm with a blurred mission, is discussed in the Strategic Insight box.

By contrast, Wal-Mart transformed the discount retailing industry by identifying itself as a general merchandiser, committed to low-cost operations with

STRATEGIC INSIGHT

A Blurred Mission at Sears

Prior to 1975, Sears, Roebuck was the dominant national force in U. S. retailing. As a full-line general merchandiser with 850 stores, Sears was a regular shopping stop for most of America's families. That dominance ended abruptly, however, as the retail industry experienced rapid and dramatic changes. Sears' private-label business was eroded by the growing popularity of specialty retailers, such as Circuit City and The Limited, and its cost structure was successfully challenged by such low-overhead discounters as Wal-mart and Best Buy.

Initially, Sears reacted by attempting to emphasize fashion with such labels as Cheryl Tiegs sportswear. But high-fashion models did not mesh well with Sears' middle-America image. In fact, Sears allowed the key post of women's fashion director to remain vacant from 1980 until 1989. Turning next to diversification, Sears tried to convert its dowdy image into a "financial supermarket" by purchasing Dean Witter Financial Services and Coldwell Banker Real Estate. But in-store kiosks never caught on with customers, and the expected synergy between these two subsidiaries and Sears' Allstate Insurance Business unit and its Discover Card failed to materialize. Eventually, Sears decided to spin off its Dean Witter Financial Services Group and its Coldwell Banker real estate holdings to permit the firm to sharpen its focus on its core retailing business.

Next, management modified the store's image to one that sold nationally branded merchandise along with private-label brands at "everyday low prices." The idea was to create individual "superstores" within each of the Sears outlets to compete more effectively with powerful niche competitors. Sears' original intent, which was widely publicized, was to depart from its traditional practice of holding weekly sales in order to save on advertising expenses and inventory handling while offering stable, everyday low prices. But the "everyday low prices" turned out to be, in some cases, higher than Sears' old sale prices, advertising expenses climbed rather than declined, and Sears continued to run special sales. By this time, customers were totally confused. Sears' response was to announce that, once again, it was going to emphasize women's fashions and would advertise them in such magazines as *Vogue* and *Mademoiselle*. But, in 1992 alone, Sears lost $3.9 billion, its worst performance ever.

In 1993, Sears terminated its big catalog operations, began spinning off some of its businesses unrelated to general merchandising, overhauled its clothing lines, eliminated more than 93,000 jobs, and closed 113 stores. In 1995, Sears reentered the catalog business. This time, instead of a big book Sears catalog, it set up joint ventures to provide smaller catalogs. Sears provides its name and its 24 million credit card customers database. Its partners select the merchandise, mail catalogs, and fill orders. By 1998, Sears had begun to benefit from its strategic shift to moderately priced apparel and home furnishings. If Sears can maintain a clear mission and present a consistent image during the late 1990s, the retail giant may sustain profits once again. As CEO Arthur Martinez put it, "We've established our platforms for future growth. They're in home stores, home services, credit, and automotive. Sears will stay close to things we're known for and things we're good at."

SOURCES: E. A. Robinson, "America's Most Admired Companies," *Fortune*, 3 March, 1997, p. F3; A. Ward, "Sears 'On Course' Despite Hard Retail Conditions, CEO Says," *Wall Street Journal Interactive Edition*, 9 May 1996 (source of quotation); K. Fitzgerald, "Sears, Ward's Take Different Paths," *Advertising Age*, 31 July 1995, p. 27; S. Chandler, "Sears' Turnaround is For Real—For Now," *Business Week*, 15 August 1994, pp. 102-104; D. Longo, "Kmart Can Learn Some Lessons From Sears," *Discount Store News*, 21 February 1994, p. 9; J. Kirk, "Sears' 'Many-Sided' Look," *Adweek*, 14 February 1994, p. 3; A. Markowitz, "Sears Takes Steps to Strengthen and Revitalize," *Discount Store News*, 7 February 1994, pp. 2, 91; J. A. Parnell, "Strategic Change Versus Flexibility: Does Strategic Change Really Enhance Performance?" *American Business Review*, Vol. 12(2) (1994): 22–30; "Sears Loses $3.93 Billion in '92, *Harrisonburg (VA) Daily News-Record*, 10 February 1993.

"everyday low prices." Through concentrating its efforts on discount retailing, Wal-Mart Stores developed its innovative logistics system, known as *cross-docking*. Products are continuously delivered to its warehouses, where they are normally repacked and transferred to stores within two days, maximizing inventory turnover. The products purchased by Wal-Mart cross from an incoming loading dock to an outgoing dock, enabling this firm to have the lowest cost operation in the discount retailing industry. Wal-Mart's low-cost strength has matched well an external opportunity—customers' demand for low-priced general merchandise.[10]

Hence, effective management requires not only an understanding of the environment, but also a focus on the organization's mission (in the context of its strengths and weaknesses). A clear sense of purpose is necessary in establishing goals, because it is difficult to know where one is going if one does not first know who one is. Firms with a clear sense of their mission are able to determine which activities fit into their strategic direction and which ones do not.

Management consultant C. K. Prahalad emphasizes that organizations should spend more time understanding what proficiencies they possess. For instance, Sony has used its skills in miniaturizing audio, video, and electronics products as its particular strategic competence. Likewise, AT&T's diversification into the credit card field was an application of its strategic competence in transaction processing, based on its extensive billing experience in the telephone industry.[11] Figure 3.2 summarizes the discussion up to this point.

Figure 3.2   **The Role of the Organization's Mission**

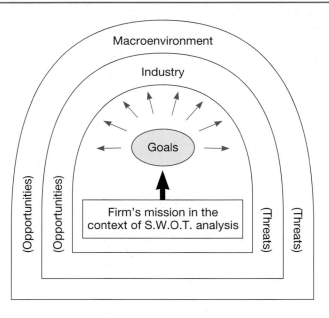

THE ORGANIZATION'S GOALS AND OBJECTIVES

This section focuses on organizational goals and objectives. On the surface, it appears that establishing organizational goals is a fairly straightforward process. As will become evident, however, this process is actually quite complex. Various stakeholder groups have different goals for the firm. The organizational goals that eventually emerge must balance the pressures from the different stakeholder groups so that the continuing participation of each is assured.

■ Goals and Objectives Defined

Whereas the mission is the reason for the existence of the firm, the organization's **goals** represent the desired general ends toward which efforts are directed. **Objectives** are specific, and often quantified, versions of goals. For example, management may establish a goal "to expand the size of the firm through internal growth." From this goal, a number of specific objectives may be derived, such as "to increase sales by 10 percent each year for the next eight years." As another example, management's goal may be "to become the innovative leader in the industry." On the basis of this goal, one of the specific objectives may be "to have 25 percent of sales each year come from new products developed during the preceding three years."

As you can see, objectives are verifiable and specific. That is, with the objectives in the preceding paragraph, management will be able to answer the question: "Has this objective been attained?" Without verifiability and specificity, objectives will not provide a clear direction for managerial decision making, nor will they permit an assessment of organizational performance.

■ Goals and Stakeholders

Various stakeholders will have different goals for the firm. Each stakeholder group—owners (stockholders), members of the board of directors, managers, employees, suppliers, creditors, distributors, and customers—views the firm from a different perspective. To illustrate this point, Table 3.2 on page 66 delineates the goals of selected stakeholders for Kellogg Company.

Rationality suggests that stakeholders establish goals from the perspective of their own interests. Because of the diversity of these interests, top management faces the difficult task of attempting to reconcile and satisfy each of the stakeholder groups while pursuing its own set of goals. Because the interests of various stakeholder groups are quite different, a close examination of some of their interests can be enlightening.

■ Influence on Goals

Who has the most influence on a firm's goals and who determines what the organization does? The traditional view is one of a shareholder-driven corporation. From this perspective, both top management and the board of directors are primarily accountable to the owners (the shareholders) of the corporation. Top management is responsible for enhancing the financial value of the firm, and the board of directors is charged with overseeing top management's decisions to ensure that those decisions enhance firm value.

Table 3.2

General Goals of Kellogg's Stakeholders

Stakeholders	Goals
Customers	Customers would likely want Kellogg's goals to include providing healthy, quality foods at reasonable prices.
General public	The general public would likely want Kellogg's goals to include providing goods and services with minimum costs (i.e., pollution), increasing employment opportunities, and contributing to charitable causes.
Suppliers	Suppliers would likely want Kellogg's goals to include remaining with them for the long term and purchasing from them at prices that allow the suppliers reasonable profit margins.
Employees	Employees would likely want Kellogg's goals to include providing good working conditions, equitable compensation, and promotion opportunities.
Creditors	Creditors would likely want Kellogg's goals to include maintaining a healthy financial posture and a policy of on-time payment of interest and principal.
Distributors	Wholesalers and retailers would likely want Kellogg's goals to include remaining with them for the long term and selling to them at prices that allow for reasonable profit margins.
Stockholders	Stockholders would likely want Kellogg's goals to be the enhancement of returns on their equity.
Board of directors	Directors would likely want Kellogg's goals to be to keep them as directors and to satisfy the demands of the other stakeholders so that the directors would not be liable to lawsuits.
Managers	Managers would likely want to benefit personally from Kellogg. Other management goals are to expand Kellogg's market share in the cereal business, to make compatible growth-oriented acquisitions, to boost capacity, to improve productivity, and to launch new cereals worldwide.

An argument exists, however, that if owners are to experience enhanced financial returns, the corporation must be customer-driven. Consumer advocate Ralph Nader, for instance, has argued for more than thirty years that large corporations must be more responsive to customers' needs.[12] In addition, the marketing strategy literature emphasizes the necessity for firms to maintain strategic adaptability based on changes in customer desires.[13]

A broader viewpoint recognizes that, because corporations are complex and depend upon environmental resources, they cannot maximize any single stakeholder group's interests. Rather, corporation must be broadly stakeholder-driven, attempting to balance the desires of all stakeholders.[14] Maximizing any one stakeholder group's interests at the expense of other groups can seriously jeopardize the corporation's effectiveness. A firm cannot emphasize the financial interests of shareholders over the monetary needs of employees, for example, without alienating the employees and eventually harming the firm's financial returns. Likewise, raising prices to please stockholders will cause customers to take their business elsewhere.

Because various stakeholders' desires may conflict, management must re-solve these opposing demands.[15] Fortunately, however, some stakeholders may have more than a unidimensional self-interest. For instance, although some stockholders may desire high financial returns, they may be unwilling to invest in corporations that produce tobacco products, even though higher re-turns may be associated with such investment opportunities. Moreover, some consumers may be willing to pay higher prices for products that do not harm the environment.

Ideally, top managers recognize that the corporation must be managed to balance the pluralistic demands of various stakeholder groups. Obviously, this requirement poses a considerable challenge. A careful reading of the goals in Table 3.2 illustrates this point. In the following paragraphs, select stakeholder groups are discussed in the context of their paramount goals.

■ Goals of Top Management

Ideally, the goals of top management should be attempts to enhance the return to stockholders on their investment while simultaneously satisfying the inter-ests of other stakeholders. However, the motivation of top management to en-hance profits has been questioned for many years. In fact, for as long as absen-tee owners (stockholders) have been hiring professional managers to operate their companies, questions have been raised concerning the extent to which these managers actually attempt to increase the wealth of the absentee owners. On the one hand, it has been argued that management primarily serves its own interests. On the other hand, some have proposed that management shares the same interests as the stockholders.

Management Serves Its Own Interests

The argument of researchers adhering to this viewpoint is that hired top man-agers tend to pursue strategies that ultimately increase their own rewards.[16] In particular, top executives are likely to increase the size of their firms since larger rewards usually accompany larger organizational size and its greater re-sponsibilities.

Perhaps the major work in this area can be traced to Herbert A. Simon,[17] who won the 1978 Nobel Prize in economics for his research on managerial decision-making behavior. Building on Roberts's study of executive compensa-tion, Simon suggests that a reward differential exists at each managerial level in an organizational hierarchy.[18] That is, first-level supervisors receive the lowest managerial salaries, but salaries increase with each succeeding level in the or-ganization up through the chief executive officer's (CEO's) salary. The larger the organization and the greater the number of levels in its hierarchy, the greater the rewards will be for top-level executives. Hence, top managers have a powerful incentive to increase the size of their firms. Other researchers have empirically demonstrated that larger firm size is positively associated with greater rewards.[19] One study concluded that "the size/pay relation is causal and . . . CEOs can increase their pay by increasing firm size, even when the in-crease in size reduces the firm's market value."[20]

Top managers may also be selfishly motivated to increase the size of their firms through diversification, by acquiring companies in other industries. Diversification not only increases a firm's size but may also reduce the top managers' job risks, for when an organization falters, its top managers often lose their jobs. Diversification should spread this risk and help upper-level managers preserve their positions. Although diversification can benefit top management, it may not similarly advance stockholders' interest. They can more effectively reduce their financial risks by diversifying their personal financial portfolios.[21]

This interest in organizational growth does not necessarily mean that top management is unconcerned with the firm's profitability or market value, but it does suggest to researchers that top managers are likely to emphasize business performance only to the extent that it discourages shareholder revolts and hostile takeovers. Simon suggests, for instance, that the difference between what a firm's profits can be and what its profits actually are represents "organizational slack," which will only be reduced if outside pressure is applied.[22]

Management Shares the Same Interests as Stockholders

A second viewpoint contradicts the preceding view by proposing that the interests of top management are the same as those of the stockholders. Indeed, some studies do reveal positive associations between business performance and managerial rewards. One study, for example, found that profits, not the size of firms, can determine top management rewards.[23] Also, there can be a significant relationship between common stock earnings and the rewards of top executives.[24]

In a widely cited theoretical work, Eugene F. Fama argues that the self-interest of top managers requires that they behave in ways that benefit the stockholders.[25] His argument is based on the premise that the market for managerial talent provides an effective disciplining force. If top managers do not promote the interests of stockholders, this information will result in a lowering of their value in the managerial labor market. This lowered value will adversely affect the managers' alternative employment opportunities.[26] Managerial performance may also be indirectly evaluated by the stock market, because it implicitly judges top management's performance by bidding the firm's stock price either up or down.[27]

From a different perspective, John Child proposes that stock option plans and high salaries bring the interests of top management and stockholders closer together.[28] According to his reasoning, top executives wish to protect their salaries and option plans and can do so only by striving for higher business performance.

This concept of congruent interests has gained support from other scholars, but for different reasons.[29] They suggest that managerial jobs contain "structural imperatives" that force managers to attempt to enhance profits.

> Before the rise of the large stock corporation, individuals who filled the roles of entrepreneur were probably motivated to realize profits. If they did not act as if they were so motivated, however, the failure of their firms would eventually remove them from their positions. . . . The behavior exhibited by entrepreneurs was a structural requirement of the position of entrepreneur itself rather than merely a function of the motivation of individuals who became entrepreneurs.[30]

Similarly, managers would be removed from their positions if they failed to increase profits. Therefore, these scholars reason that top managers will be

S T R A T E G I C   I N S I G H T

CEO Compensation

Excessive CEO compensation has been roundly criticized in recent years. Although no firm standards exist for defining what is "excessive," a number of CEOs have come under fire for their annual compensation. For example, over the past several years, angry shareholders have noted that Champion Paper's annual return has been less than the average annual return on risk-free U. S. treasury notes. Yet Champion's CEO, Andrew Sigler, receives more than $1 million in annual compensation and has been awarded a bonus for more than twenty consecutive years.

Consider also that AT&T Chairman and CEO Robert Allen earned about $11 million in 1995 but drew heavy criticism when he announced 40,000 layoffs as part of the firm's restructuring plan. Since Allen's appointment, AT&T shares have appreciated at the same rate as the S&P 500.

The stock prices of H. J. Heinz, Masco, and Torchmark all fell behind the S&P 500 annual average return over the past five years, yet their CEOs earned $120 million, $38 million, and $37 million, respectively, over the period. And even defenders of high salaries called it excessive when Gibson Greetings fired its CEO, Benjamin Sottile, in early 1996, but agreed to pay his salary and benefits through 1998.

According to several recent surveys, most managers believe CEOs earn too much. During the 1980s, CEO compensation rose by 212 percent, compared to 54 percent for factory workers, 73 percent for engineers, and 95 percent for teachers. After a brief decline in the early 1990s, CEO salaries have begun to climb once again. In 1997, chief executives of American firms with more than $2.5 billion in annual revenues averaged $950,000 in salary alone. Their counterparts in Germany, Great Britain, and Japan earned $775,000, $580,000, and $450,000, respectively.

While cash compensation has risen considerably, CEOs also typically receive stock options and bonuses, revenues from profitsharing plans, retirement benefits, interest-free loans, and the like. As a result, CEOs in America's largest publicly held corporations average more than $4 million in earnings annually.

Numerous studies have demonstrated that CEO salary is more closely tied to company size than to performance. Part of the reason for the historically low correlation between CEO pay and performance is the way in which the typical CEO's compensation is set. Determining that compensation is the responsibility of the compensation committee of the board of directors. The board is usually appointed by the CEO and guided by a compensation consultant appointed by the CEO. Often, the CEO does not even leave the room when his or her compensation is discussed.

Recently, however, firms have begun to tie compensation more closely to corporate performance. DSC Communications Chairman James Donald earned more than $25 million in 1994, but the majority of that came from stock gains. Between 1992 and 1994, Green Tree Financial's CEO, Lawrence Coss, took home more than $55 million, most of which was attributed to a twelvefold increase in the company's stock price. While GE's John Welch was the highest paid CEO in 1995, netting more than $22 million, including benefits and stock options, his earnings were accompanied by strong performance throughout the company. Most firms appear willing to continue to pay large sums to chief executives, provided the corporation performs equally well.

SOURCES: G. Burns, "Fat Wallets," *Business Week*, 3 March 1997, p. 6; C. Duff, "Top Executives Ponder High Pay, Decide They're Worth Every Cent," *Wall Street Journal Interactive Edition*, 13 May 1996; W. Bounds, "Ousted Chairman of Gibson to Get Pay Until April 1998," *Wall Street Journal Interactive Edition*, 29 April 1996; "Is Chairman Allen of AT&T Overpaid?" *Wall Street Journal*, 29 February 1996, p. B1; C. Farrell, "Why Some Compensation Is Clean Outta Sight," *Business Week*, 4 September 1995, p. 60; J. Flynn, "Continental Divide over Executive Pay," *Business Week*, 3 July 1995, pp. 40–41; "Random Numbers: Executive Pay," *Economist*, 3 June 1995; E. S. Hardy, "America's Highest Paid Bosses," *Forbes*, 22 May 1995, pp. 180–182; P. G. Wilhelm, "Application of Distributive Justice Theory to the CEO Pay Problem: Recommendations for Reform," *Journal of Business Ethics*, 12(1993): 469–482; J. A. Byrne, L. Bongiorno, and R. Grover, "That Eye-Popping Executive Pay," *Business Week*, 25 April 1994, pp. 52–58.

motivated to enhance profitability, and "even if they are not so motivated, they must act as if they are if they wish to remain in their positions of authority."[31]

As we can see from the preceding discussion, the issue of whether top managers will attempt to enhance their firms' returns or whether they will pursue a more narrow goal of self-enrichment has not been satisfactorily resolved. Compelling evidence and logic exist on both sides of the controversy. Also unresolved is how motivated top managers are to satisfy the interests of stakeholders beyond the owners of the firm. We turn now to another controversial area—the goals of the board of directors.

■ Goals of Boards of Directors

Legally, boards of directors are responsible for such aspects of corporate leadership as selecting (and replacing) the chief executive officer, setting his or her rewards, advising top management, and monitoring managerial and company performance in order to promote the interests of shareholders. There is evidence, however, that board members have, in many cases, failed to fulfill their legal roles.[32] A common explanation for this failure is that boards have long

---

STRATEGIC INSIGHT

The Growing Responsiveness of Boards

For years, corporate boards have been referenced as "rubber stamps" for top managers. However, the directors of many prominent corporations have become increasingly responsible to stockholder interests in recent years. Leading the charge has been the increased influence of institutional shareholders, which now control the majority of shares of publicly traded companies. These large investment companies hold substantial numbers of shares in various firms and have the savvy and clout necessary to pressure board members for change.

But many analysts and executives believe that there is still a long way to go. According to David Leighton, former chairman of the board at Nabisco Brands, Ltd., companies need to seek out more independent and better qualified board members. Further, companies make fewer mistakes and earn greater profits when they are governed by active boards. Too often, Leighton claims, the critical issues of strategy and firm growth are not aggressively considered by boards.

In some instances, boards of directors, pressured by institutional investors, have forced the turnover of top managers. For example, GM experienced poor performance during the 1980s and the early 1990s. Between 1981 and 1992, GM's market share declined from 44 to 33 percent. Its 1991 and 1992 losses were record-setting. In 1992, the California Public Employees Retirement System, a significant shareholder, pressured the eleven outside board members (a majority of the fifteen-member board) to reassert strategic control over the firm. As a result, a complete overhaul of senior executives was forced at GM, the first since 1920. GM generated profits in subsequent years.

This incident illustrates that the system of corporate governance many not need overhauling. Rather, the system simply needs to be made to work as intended.

SOURCES: C. Torres, "Firms' Restructuring Often Hurt Foreign Buyers," *Wall Street Journal Interactive Edition*, 13 May 1996; M. L. Weidenbaum, "The Evolving Corporate Board," *Society*, March–April 1995, pp. 9–16; J. W. Lorsch, "Empowering the Board," *Harvard Business Review*, (1995) 73(1): 107–117; *General Motors 1995 Annual Report* (Detroit: General Motors Corporation); R. Litchfield, "Conversation: Board Games," *Canadian Business*, October 1993, pp. 53–55; P. G. Stern, "The Power and the Process," *Directors and Boards*, Spring 1993, pp. 6–9.

been considered "creatures of the CEO."[33] Often, board members are nominated by the CEO, who, in turn, expects the directors to support his or her strategic decisions. For their support, the directors receive generous compensation. One British member of several corporate boards once described board membership as follows:

> No effort of any kind is called for. You go to a meeting once a month in a car supplied by the company. You look both grave and sage, and on two occasions say "I agree," say "I don't think so" once, and if all goes well, you get 500 [pounds] a year. If you have five of them, it is total heaven, like having a permanent hot bath.[34]

Directors sometimes behave in this fashion, not only because they wish to show their loyalty to the CEO, who appoints and compensates them (average annual compensation is more than $50,000 for serving on the board of a major corporation), but also because they often make decisions based primarily on information provided by the CEO.[35] As one CEO put it: "[My board members] often have to have blind faith in management. It would take them a month to really understand some of the decisions they make."[36]

In theory, the primary goal of the board is to safeguard the interests of the stockholders. Technically speaking, board members are elected by the stockholders. In reality, however, stockholders are limited to casting a yes or no vote for each individual nominated to the board by top management. Each nominee's credentials are briefly stated in management's mailed "notice of annual meeting of shareholders," and few stockholders will have much knowledge regarding the nominees beyond these basic facts. Hence, most stockholders will simply follow the recommendations of top management.

Therefore, it is not surprising to find that board members are often beholden to top management for their positions. In such cases, the directors' basic loyalties lie with the CEO rather than with the stockholders. Frequently, this loyalty takes the form of approval of lavish compensation packages for top management. In some cases, these packages may even conceal the actual amounts that top managers receive. For example, stockholders did not know that F. Ross Johnson was granted 40,000 shares of stock before RJR Nabisco was acquired by Kohlberg Kravis Roberts. One account described it as follows:

> Johnson received around $20 million, most of which the shareholders didn't know he had coming until the takeover. . . . Shareholders may not always have a legal right to override the decisions of their own board of directors. But they surely have a right to know what their boards have decided.[37]

Ignoring the stockholders' interests has begun to diminish in recent years, however. The turning point was the 1985 decision by the Delaware Supreme Court that Trans Union Corporation's directors had accepted a takeover bid too quickly. They were accused of failing to read the sales contract before approving it, not soliciting an independent, outside opinion on the fairness of the sales price, and approving the sale of the company in a hasty, two-hour meeting dominated by the CEO. They were held personally liable for the difference between the offer they accepted and the price the company might have received in an open sale. The directors had to pay $13.5 million of the $23.5 million settlement—the excess over their liability insurance coverage.[38]

The pressure on directors to acknowledge stockholder wishes continues to increase. For instance, stockholder suits against directors rose by almost 70 percent over the past fifteen years.[39] But the major source of pressure in recent years has come from institutional investors. These stockholders—chiefly pension funds, mutual funds, and insurance companies—own $1 trillion of stock in U. S. corporations. By virtue of the size of their investments, they wield considerable power and are becoming more active in using it. For example, the California Public Employees' Retirement System and the Pennsylvania Public School Employees' Retirement System recently launched a proxy battle that led Honeywell's management to restructure the company. Considering that institutional investors own large chunks of many major companies (e.g., 82 percent of Lotus Development, 81 percent of Southwest Airlines, and 80 percent of Whirlpool), their potential power is quite impressive.[40]

On the other side, however, it should be emphasized that some board members have played effective stewardship roles. Many directors promote strongly the best interests of the firm's shareholders and various other stakeholder groups as well. Research indicates, for instance, that board members are invaluable sources of environmental information.[41] By conscientiously carrying out their duties, directors can ensure that management does not solely pursue its own interests by focusing management's attention on company performance.[42] Directors do exist who believe that their job is to represent shareholders. For example, the chairman of the board of Compaq Computer states that "the owners of the company should be represented by the directors. That has ceased to happen at lots of companies where management dominates the board."[43] Murray Weidenbaum, an economist who serves on three corporate boards, does not "view the director's role as helping the CEO. The role of the director, the legal obligation, is to represent the shareholders."[44]

▪ Goals of Creditors

Creditors of a corporation include bondholders, banks, and other financial institutions. Their primary goal is to influence the firm to maintain a healthy financial posture in order to safeguard both the principal and interest on their loaned funds. Recent trends toward acquisitions and mergers that involve financial leverage have given creditors increasingly powerful roles in corporate America. In cases in which heavy debt financing exists, an increasing number of business decisions may be transferred to creditors. Such decisions could include choices as crucial as the selection of top management, the identification of acquisition targets, and the determination of which products to produce and where and how to produce them. Furthermore, as mergers and acquisitions continue, fewer competitors will remain in the marketplace, and many of those who do remain will be heavily financed by creditors.

The increased power of creditors can result in market distortions. For example, now-defunct Pan Am Corporation, which operated one of the oldest fleets of airplanes in the airline industry, was on the brink of bankruptcy for years. Yet in 1989, after losing $2.5 billion over the preceding decade, it tried (but failed) to buy Northwest Airlines—a much larger and more profitable competitor. It could only attempt this through the strong support of a group of creditors—such as Bankers Trust, Morgan Guaranty, Citicorp, and Prudential-Bache—that was willing to provide financing of $2.7 billion.

▪ Conflicting Goals

It is evident from the preceding discussion that the goals of top managers, boards of directors, and creditors are not always congruent with the goals of the firm's shareholders or other stakeholder groups. Broadly speaking, of

firm to function as a viable entity

course, the goals of all stakeholders are best served when the firm functions as a viable entity. It is then able to supply goods to customers, contribute to society's standard of living, provide employment, and channel financial and nonfinancial benefits to all stakeholders.

We must realize, however, that a viable firm has the power to benefit each stakeholder group differently. For instance, tough bargaining with suppliers will transfer benefits from suppliers to stockholders, managers, and customers. Shirking responsibility for controlling environmental pollution transfers benefits from society (because the general public bears the costs of pollution) to a number of stakeholders who benefit from the financial savings. Bestowing extremely generous compensation on top management transfers benefits from stockholders, employees, and customers to upper-level managers.

Perhaps the most common suggestion for making the goals of top management and stockholders more congruent is to award shares of stock or stock options to top management. The rationale is that significant stock ownership would align the interests of top management with the interests of shareholders. Select scholars have theoretically argued[45] and empirically found[46] that as managerial ownership rises, the interests of managers and shareholders begin to converge. Other scholars have concluded that interests of top managers and shareholders have become more congruent with managerial ownership only up to a point.[47] When managers are major shareholders, however, they become entrenched and may adopt strategies that are beneficial to themselves but not necessarily to the shareholders.[48] Attempts to align the interests of upper-level management with those of other stakeholder groups have also been negatively imposed through lawsuits—that is, fines imposed on the firm by various public agencies and court decisions.

CORPORATE GOVERNANCE

Although top managers are charged with creating wealth for shareholders through strategies that are meant to satisfy the needs of the various stakeholders, these managers may not always comply with their responsibilities. Consequently, publicly traded firms have **corporate governance** systems. Corporate governance refers to the board of directors, institutional investors (e.g., pension and retirement funds, mutual funds, banks, insurance companies, among other money managers), and blockholders (individuals or families with significant shareholdings) who monitor firm strategies to ensure managerial responsiveness.

Boards of directors and institutional investors should be the most influential in the governance systems. Boards of directors represent the owners of the firm and are legally authorized to monitor firm strategies. They are also responsible for the selection, evaluation, and compensation of top managers. Institutional investors own more than half of all shares of publicly traded firms; therefore, they are influential because of their substantial ownership. Although blockholders are significant shareholders, they are less influential because their ownership ordinarily is less than 20 percent and some of them are passive investors.[49]

Professor Walter Salmon of Harvard has observed that prior to the 1990s, boards of directors normally tolerated mediocre management.[50] Board members were reduced to damage control in response to demands for restructuring and objections of shareholders against unworthy acquisitions through corporate assumption of substantial debt.[51] Moreover, from the 1960s through the middle of the 1970s, senior management comprised the majority of board membership. From the mid-1970s to the 1990s, however, the presence of senior managers on boards of directors has been reduced—from an average of five insiders (senior managers who are board members) and eight outsiders (board members from outside the firm) to an average of three insiders and nine outsiders. This has enabled board members to more effectively oversee managerial decisions.[52]

Because institutional investors are majority owners of publicly traded firms, on the one hand they face increased pressure to influence managerial strategies in order to push for national competitiveness and social causes as well as to promote the enhancement of firm value. On the other hand, institutional investors have been criticized for becoming too involved in influencing managerial strategies. The CEO of Contel, Charles Wohlstetter, for instance, has argued that although institutional investors are increasingly in control of large firms, they have no managerial skills, "no experience in selecting directors, no believable judgment in how much should be spent for research and marketing—in fact, no experience except that which they have accumulated controlling other people's money."[53]

A working group of experts, representing both large publicly traded corporations and leading institutional investors, has made a number of recommendations on how to promote an effective governance system. For the board of directors, the recommendations include that outside directors should be the only ones to evaluate the performance of top managers against established mission and goals; that all outside board members should meet alone at least once annually; and that boards of directors should establish appropriate qualifications for board membership (and shareholders should be informed of these qualifications). For institutional shareholders, the suggestions include that institutions (and other shareholders) should act as owners and not just investors; that they should not interfere with day-to-day managerial decisions; that they should evaluate the performance of the board of directors regularly; and that they should recognize that the prosperity of the firm benefits all shareholders.[54]

STAKEHOLDERS AND TAKEOVERS

What happens when top managers of a firm with ineffective board members continue to mismanage the firm? In such cases of mismanagement, institutional investors, blockholders, and other shareholders may sell their shares, depressing the market price of the company's stock. Depressed prices often attract takeover attempts, as is discussed in the following paragraphs.

■ An Overview

Any firm whose stock is publicly traded faces the possibility of a takeover. Depending upon the form in which a takeover occurs, different groups of stakeholders will be affected in various ways.

A **takeover** refers to the purchase of a significant number of shares of a firm by an individual, a group of investors, or another organization. Takeovers may be attempted by outsiders or insiders.

Attempts to take over a company by those outside the organization may be friendly or unfriendly. A friendly takeover is one in which both the buyer and seller desire the transaction. In recent years, General Electric's takeover of RCA, Disney's takeover of Capital Cities/ABC, and Greyhound's takeover of Trailways illustrate friendly takeovers. An unfriendly takeover is one in which the target firm resists the sale. Examples of unfriendly takeovers include Carl Icahn's successful bid for TWA and Sir James Goldsmith's unsuccessful bid for Goodyear.[55]

Unfriendly takeovers are sometimes precipitated by **raiders**—individuals who believe that the way a company is being managed can be significantly improved. Raiders purchase a large number of shares in the target firm either to force a change in top management personnel or to manage the firm themselves.

Other reasons for takeovers by outsiders include acquisitions by investors or creditors for financial purposes or acquisitions by another firm for strategic reasons. For example, Chrysler's takeover of American Motors several years ago provided Chrysler with immediate expansion of product lines, production capacity, and market share.

Transfer of ownership to organizational insiders, such as employees or top managers, may occur gradually through special types of takeovers known as **employee stock ownership plans (ESOPs).** Since the enactment of a tax law in 1974 that encouraged ESOPs, many closely held firms (those with only a few stockholders whose shares are not traded publicly) have been partially turned over to their managers and employees. This process usually begins when the principal owner of the closely held firm retires or when an ESOP plan is developed as a benefit or motivational incentive for the firm's employees. As the employees receive more and more shares of stock over a period of time, the ownership of the firm is gradually turned over to them.

The transfer of ownership to insiders may also occur suddenly through a takeover by the firm's employees or top managers. In one of the most publicized takeover attempts in American business, F. Ross Johnson, the CEO of RJR Nabisco, and his top management group attempted to take the firm private (concentrate its ownership in their hands). However, their bids were topped by the investment firm of Kohlberg Kravis, which paid about $25 billion for the firm.

Sudden takeover attempts often (but not always) rely heavily on borrowed funds to finance the acquisition. Borrowing funds to purchase a firm is referred to as a **leveraged buyout (LBO).** When a takeover is financed in this fashion, the company is burdened with heavy debt, which must be paid back either by funds generated from operations or by the sale of company assets, such as subsidiaries or product divisions.

■ Pros and Cons

Takeovers have been both defended and criticized. Their defense generally consists of pointing out the useful role that takeovers play in replacing ineffective management. For instance, T. Boone Pickens Jr., a renowned corporate raider, has argued:

After decades of sovereign autonomy, the professional managers of many large, publicly held corporations are finding themselves on the firing line. They are being asked to justify lackluster performance and questionable strategies. They are being called on to address the chronic undervaluation of their securities.[56]

Takeovers have been criticized from several perspectives. One argument is that the primary goal of some takeover attempts is for the raider to make short-term profits. Even the bidder who ultimately loses out to a higher bidder usually pockets a considerable profit because of the increase in the stock's price brought about by the bidding. In some cases, management will attempt to take the firm private, usually through an LBO, to prevent the unfriendly takeover. This action will limit the firm's future strategic options because it must make heavy interest payments on its newly acquired debt for many years. These payments make it difficult for the firm to finance research and development activities, to explore new markets, and to promote and advertise its goods and services.

Bondholders, too, suffer from LBOs. As company debt increases following an LBO, the firm's bonds become more risky, since their ultimate redemption is less certain. This increase in risk results in a deterioration of the credit rating of the firm's bonds and a loss of value to the bondholders.

Finally, most takeovers are followed by layoffs of employees and managers. But more than those employees and their families are affected. For example, when Gulf Oil was taken over by Chevron, Gulf's Pittsburgh headquarters was closed. Nearly 6,000 employees either were transferred from Pittsburgh or were fired. This move had a significant negative impact on the many Pittsburgh-area firms that supplied various products and services to Gulf. Additionally, the city suffered because of lower tax revenues, and the price of real estate throughout the city declined.

For these reasons, some states have passed laws that protect their firms from takeovers. For example, when T. Boone Pickens attempted, in 1987, an un-friendly takeover of Boeing, the largest employer in the state of Washington, a bill was passed by state legislators that put a five-year ban on the sale of Boeing's assets to pay off creditors. This act effectively nullified Pickens's bid, because his only way to repay the debt he would incur in buying the company was to sell off some of its assets.

SOCIAL RESPONSIBILITY AND ETHICS

One of an organization's primary goals is its obligation to operate in a socially responsible manner. This section examines corporate social responsibility and the related area of managerial ethics.

■ Corporate Social Responsibility

Our society grants considerable freedom to business organizations. In return, businesses are expected to operate in a manner consistent with society's interests. **Social responsibility** refers to the expectation that business firms should act in the public interest. Certainly, businesses have always been expected to provide employment for individuals and to provide goods and services for customers. But social responsibility implies more than that. Today, society expects business to help preserve the environment, to sell safe products, to treat its employees equitably, to be truthful with its customers, and, in some cases, to go even further by training the hard-core unemployed, contributing to education and the arts, and helping revitalize urban slum areas.

Some observers, ranging from Adam Smith to Milton Friedman, have argued that social responsibility should not be part of management's decision-making process.[57] Friedman has maintained that business functions best when it sticks to its primary mission—profitably producing goods and services within society's legal restrictions. Indeed, its sole responsibility is to attempt to maximize returns. When it goes further than that by tackling social problems, business is spending money that should more properly be returned to its stockholders. The stockholders, who have rightfully earned the money, should be able to spend that money as they see fit, and their spending priorities may differ from those of business.

In reality, however, business is part of society, and its actions have both economic and social ramifications. It would be practically impossible to isolate the business decisions of corporations from their economic and social consequences. For instance, Federal Express's insistence that its South African partners, XPS Services, employ a 50/50 ratio of minority and white managers and Microsoft's development of an internship program for South Africans at its U.S. headquarters advance the social aims of both the South African and the U.S. governments.[58]

In fact, top managers may find a number of areas where their interests, various stakeholders' interests, and society's interests are mutually compatible.[59] For example, a firm that pollutes the atmosphere because it fails to purchase costly antipollution equipment is harming not only society but also, ultimately, its own stakeholders. With a polluted environment, the quality of life of the firm's stockholders, directors, managers, employees, suppliers, customers, and creditors suffers. As another example, if businesses do not contribute to the education of young people, their recruitment efforts will suffer and they will eventually experience a decline in the quality of their work force. This result benefits no group of stakeholders.

Many government regulations over business operations came into being because some firms refused to be socially responsible. Had organizations not damaged the environment, sold unsafe products, discriminated against some employees, and engaged in untruthful advertising, laws in these areas would not have been necessary. The threat of ever more government regulation exists unless companies operate in a manner consistent with society's well-being.

Ideally, then, firms that are socially responsible are those that are able to operate profitably while simultaneously benefiting society. But realistically, it is not always clear exactly what is good for society. For example, society's needs for high employment and the production of desired goods and services must be balanced against the pollution and industrial wastes that are generated by these operations. Despite these difficulties, however, many firms in their annual reports express, at least in general terms, how they are socially responsible. General Motors, for instance, has published an annual *Public Interest Report* for more than twenty years. A recent issue described GM's efforts in such areas as clean air, ozone depletion, global warming, waste management, automotive safety, minority programs, philanthropic activities, higher quality products, and greater operating efficiency.

S T R A T E G I C   I N S I G H T

Social Responsibility at GM

Each year, GM publishes a *Philanthropic Annual Report* and an *Environmental Report* detailing its corporate activities in the area of social responsibility. A few of the more noteworthy activities in which GM is involved are listed here:

- In 1995, GM made charitable contributions in excess of $55 million, including $4.4 million to United Way chapters.
- In 1994, GM provided 842 scholarships, totaling more than $1.8 million, to outstanding business and engineering students.
- GM has entered into a partnership with The Nature Conservancy, an international environmental organization, in which GM will spend $1 million annually to assist in the preservation of land and water systems in North America, Latin America, the Caribbean, and the Asia/Pacific region.
- Under the GM Mobility Program for Persons with Disabilities, GM will reimburse up to $1,000 of the cost of any aftermarket adaptive driving equipment or passenger aids installed in a GM vehicle.

GM works in conjunction with the University of Michigan and local public schools to implement the Global Rivers Environmental Education Network (GREEN) in GM plant cities worldwide. GREEN is designed to teach students to monitor water quality, analyze watershed usage, and identify the socioeconomic determinants of river degradation.

GM contributed more than $600,000 to assist victims of the Midwest floods in the summer of 1993, and (with the United Auto Workers) contributed more than $1.4 million to the American Red Cross and Salvation Army to assist victims of the January 1994 earthquake in Southern California.

All of GM's Mexican operations support local charities to improve education and health care.

SOURCES: G. Collins, "G.M. to Sponsor AIDS Supplement," *New York Times*, 26 April 1995, p. D9; *General Motors Environmental Report 1995* (Detroit: General Motors Corporation); *GM Philanthropic Annual Report 1994* (Detroit: General Motors Corporation); *General Motors Public Interest Report 1994* (Detroit: General Motors Corporation).

▪ Managerial Ethics

Closely related to issues of corporate social responsibility are the ethics of individual managers. **Ethics** refers to standards of conduct and moral judgment—that is, whether managers' decisions and behaviors are right or wrong. (Table 3.3 presents two companies' views of ethical behavior.) What is morally right or wrong, of course, has been argued since the beginning of civilization, and as we might expect, there are few generally accepted global standards of ethical behavior. Even in the same nation, various people may look at ethical issues from different perspectives. Over the past several years, for example, many American corporations have "restructured" to become more competitive. Part of the restructuring process inevitably involves mass layoffs of employees. Is it right to lay off employees so that a company can compete more effectively with foreign firms and—in essence—assure its survival, or is it wrong to put people with family and financial responsibilities and obligations out of work?

Ethical behavior can be viewed in several different ways. First, it may be considered from the perspective of self-interest. Adam Smith proposed that if each individual pursued his or her own economic self-interests, society as a whole would benefit. Milton Friedman, as mentioned earlier, believed that

Table 3.3	Codes of Ethics

A Large Business: Electronic Data Systems (EDS)*

We conduct EDS' business in accordance with both the letter and spirit of the applicable laws of the United States and of those foreign countries in which EDS does business. We will conduct our business in the center of the field of ethical behavior—not along the sidelines, skirting the boundaries. . . . We must be honest in all our relationships and must avoid even the appearance of illegal or unethical conduct. For example, no employee of EDS will give or receive bribes or kickbacks; make improper political contributions; abuse proprietary or trade secret information, whether EDS' or our suppliers', business partners' or customers'; or misuse the company's funds and assets. . . .

The success of EDS rests directly on the quality of our people and our services. The integrity of all our people is an essential part of this quality that we offer to our customers. If our integrity ever became suspect, the future of EDS would be in jeopardy. . . .

When in doubt, measure your conduct against this Golden Rule of Business Ethics: Could you do business in complete trust with someone who acts the way you do? The answer must be YES.

A Small Business: Schilling Enterprises (operates automobile dealerships in Tennessee and Arkansas and a heating/air-conditioning distributorship in Alabama)**

Schilling's Guiding Principles:

- Practice honesty, integrity and fairness in everything we do.
- Assure every customer receives value, quality, and satisfaction.
- Create an environment in which our employees can succeed.
- Return to the community a share of the success we experience.
- Consistently promote these principles through our Christian behavior.

*Excerpted from *EDS Code of Conduct*.

**Excerpt from statements made to the authors by Harry Smith, chairperson of the board, and Rex Jones, president of Schilling Enterprises.

firms that attempt to maximize their returns within the legal regulations of society behave ethically.

Smith and Friedman viewed ethics economically, but Charles Darwin approached the issue from a biological perspective. In this sense, ethics can be explained implicitly in terms of survival of the fittest. Some species survive at the expense of other species. The survivors are those who are either instinctively or deterministically able to structure compatible fits with their environments. Ethical behavior, in a Darwinian sense, then, may encompass survival of one at the expense of the destruction of another. Hence, self-interest is at the heart of the approaches of Darwin, Smith, and Friedman. It is ethical to take care of oneself.

A second way of viewing ethics also involves the concept of self-interest, but in a broader sense. From this perspective, if an individual always promotes his or her interests at the expense of others, eventually the individual will be isolated by others. Selfish children find themselves without playmates, just as selfish managers are unable to fully secure the cooperation of their employees, peers or supervisor. Hence, individuals should be concerned with the welfare of others because it serves their own interests in the long run.

A third common perspective of ethics bases the concepts of right and wrong on religious beliefs. In the United States, the strongest religious tradition is the Judeo-Christian heritage, although other religious viewpoints also prevail. From this perspective, it is "God's will" for individuals to behave in ways that benefit others. Behaving in a correct manner involves treating other people as one would wish to be treated. The concept of selfishness is frowned upon, and individuals are cautioned against ignoring the plight of others who are less fortunate.

Another view of ethics differs from all of the preceding by holding that human beings are inherently concerned with others. This concern is not based on either selfish or religious reasons but is simply a natural condition of humankind. In wars, soldiers help the wounded at the expense of their own lives. In natural disasters, individuals sacrifice their own lives in attempts to save others. Such naturally unselfish behavior is not without precedent, for it also occurs outside the domain of human beings. Certain species of animals, such as elephants, dolphins, and bison, routinely show great concern for the welfare of their family members, even to the point of protecting them with their own lives.

However ethical behavior is viewed, evidence exists that ethical operations may be related to organizational success. For instance, in certain parts of the country, Quaker and Mennonite entrepreneurs are often successful because of their reputations for being conscientious, reliable, trustworthy, and willing to stand behind their firms' products or services. And some institutional investors invest only in stocks that represent firms known for their high social and ethical standards. In brief, behavior that is ethically considerate of other stakeholders and socially responsible makes good business sense.

SUMMARY

Underlying the organization's mission is an analysis of its internal strengths and weaknesses in the context of the external opportunities and threats. A firm's strengths and weaknesses reside in its human, organizational, and physical resources. Ideally, these resources work together to give the firm a sustained competitive advantage.

Organizations are founded for a particular purpose, known as the organization's mission. The mission, at the corporate level, is stated in fairly broad terms but is sufficiently precise to give direction to the organization. At the business unit level, the mission is narrower in scope and more clearly defined. It is essential that an organization carefully understand its mission, because a clear sense of purpose is necessary for an organization to establish appropriate goals.

Goals represent the desired general ends toward which organizational efforts are directed. From the organization's goals, management formulates objectives—specific, verifiable versions of goals. However, various stakeholder groups, because of their own interests, will desire different goals for the firm. Because of the diversity of these interests, top management faces the difficult task of attempting to reconcile and satisfy the interests of each of the stakeholder groups while pursuing its own set of goals.

Controversy exists over the extent to which top management actually attempts to enhance return on the stockholders' investment. One viewpoint argues that top managers pursue strategies, such as increasing the size of their firm, that ultimately increase their own rewards. Another proposes that top management's interests coincide with those of the firm's stockholders for various reasons.

Controversy also exists over the extent to which boards of directors serve as "creatures of the CEO" versus the degree to which they represent the interests of the stockholders. Certainly, recent legal trends have emphasized the boards' stewardship of the stockholders' interests. Publicly traded firms have corporate governance, which monitors firm strategies to ensure managerial responsiveness. Components of corporate governance are the board of directors, institutional investors, and blockholders.

Stakeholder groups are affected by corporate takeovers. Their impact differs, depending upon whether the takeover is friendly or unfriendly and whether it is engineered by outsiders or insiders. Takeovers, from a societal viewpoint, have both defenders and critics.

Of considerable concern in the strategic decision-making process are the concepts of corporate social responsibility and managerial ethics. Social responsibility refers to the extent to which business firms should act in the public interest while conducting their operations. Ethical considerations involve questions of moral judgment in managerial decision making and behavior. Society today demands that companies operate in a socially responsible manner and that managers exhibit high ethical behavior.

TAKE IT TO THE NET

We invite you to visit the Wright page on the Prentice Hall Web site at:

http://www.prenhall.com/wright

for this chapter's World Wide Web exercise.

KEY CONCEPTS

Corporate governance   The board of directors, institutional investors, and blockholders who monitor firm strategies to ensure managerial responsiveness.

Employee stock ownership plan (ESOP)   A formal program, administered by a trust, that transfers ownership of a corporation—through shares of stock—to its employees. The program is usually initiated by the organization's owners for financial, tax, and/or motivational reasons.

Ethics   Standards of conduct and moral judgment.

Goals   Desired general ends toward which efforts are directed.

Human resources   The experience, capabilities, knowledge, skills, and judgment of the firm's employees.

Leveraged buyout (LBO)   A takeover in which the acquiring party borrows funds to purchase the firm. The resulting interest payments and principal are paid back by funds generated from operations and/or the sale of company assets.

Mission   The reason for an organization's existence.

Mission statement   A broadly defined but enduring statement of purpose that identifies the scope of an organization's operations and its offerings to the various stakeholders.

Objective   A specific, verifiable, and often quantified version of a goal.

Organizational resources   The firm's systems and processes, including its strategies, structure, culture, purchasing/materials management, production/operations, financial base, research and development, marketing, information systems, and control systems.

Physical resources   An organization's plant and equipment, geographic locations, access to raw materials, distribution network, and technology.

Raider   An individual who attempts to take over a company because he or she believes that its management can be significantly improved. Raiders purchase a large number of shares in the target firm either to force a change in top management personnel or to manage the firm themselves.

Social responsibility   The expectation that business firms should act in the public interest.

Sustained competitive advantage   A firm's valuable strategies that cannot be fully duplicated by its competitors and that result in high financial returns over a lengthy period of time.

S.W.O.T. analysis   An analysis intended to match the firm's strengths and weaknesses (the *S* and *W* in the name) with the opportunities and threats (the *O* and *T*) posed by the environment.

Takeover   The purchase of a significant number of shares in a firm by an individual, a group of investors, or another organization. Takeovers may be friendly—in which both the buyer and the seller desire the transaction—or unfriendly—in which the target firm resists the sale.

DISCUSSION QUESTIONS

1. Do corporate-level missions and business unit missions usually change over time? Why or why not?

2. Explain the relationship between an organization's mission and its strategy.

3. Explain the difference between a goal and an objective. Give an example of each, different from those given in the text.

4. Why is it essential that objectives be verifiable?

5. Why do various groups that are stakeholders in the same organization have different goals? Should they not all be pulling together in the same direction?

6. How might the goals of top management differ from those of the firm's board of directors? How might they be similar?

7. What might be the impact of a takeover on various stakeholder groups?

8. What are the risks for the acquiring party in a leveraged buyout?

9. Explain the relationship between managerial decisions and social responsibility.

10. Explain the relationship between managerial decisions and ethics.

STRATEGIC MANAGEMENT EXERCISES

1. Select a well-known company about which there is a considerable amount of published information. Using Table 3.1 and the question on human, organizational, and physical resources as your outline, conduct a S.W.O.T. analysis for this firm. (Note that you may be unable to address all of the issues covered in the chapter because of a lack of information, and as you conduct your research, you may be able to identify factors not addressed in the chapter.) Explain your rationale.

2. Select a particular type of business that you may wish to start.
   a. Develop a written mission statement for that business.
   b. Construct a set of goals for the business.
   c. From the set of goals developed in part (b), formulate specific, verifiable objectives.
   d. Devise a statement of social responsibility for the business.

3. Select a company that has a written mission statement. Evaluate its mission statement along each of the following criteria:

a. Is the mission statement all-encompassing yet relatively brief?

b. Does the mission statement delineate, in broad terms, what products or services the firm is to offer?

c. Does the mission statement define the company's geographical operating parameters (whether it will conduct business locally, regionally, nationally, or internationally)?

d. Is the mission statement consistent as it moves from the corporate level to the business unit level?

e. Is the mission statement consistent with the company's actual activities and competitive prospects at the corporate level? (For instance, Chrysler's mission of using its technology to operate both in the automobile industry and in the defense industry failed to match its competitive stance. Facing powerful international competition in the automobile industry required Chrysler to concentrate totally on that industry. As a result, it was forced to sell its nonvehicle businesses.)

f. Is the mission statement consistent with the company's actual activities and competitive prospects at the business unit level? (For instance, GM's mission of providing quality outputs matches the operation of its Electronic Data Systems business unit, but the quality of its vehicle products has been questioned over the years by many industry observers and customers.)

NOTES

1. P. Sellers, "Who Cares About Shareholders?" *Fortune*, 15 June 1992, p. 122.

2. J. Barney, "Firm Resources and Sustained Competitive Advantage," *Journal of Management* 17 (1991): 99–120; A. Lado, N. Boyd, and P. Wright, "A Competency-Based Model of Sustainable Competitive Advantage: Toward a Conceptual Integration," *Journal of Management* 18 (1992): 77–91.

3. R. Jacob, "The Search for the Organization of Tomorrow," *Fortune*, 18 May 1992, p. 93. Also see O. Nodoushani, "The Professional Ideal in Management History," *Human Systems Management* 14 (1995): 335–345.

4. J. A. Pearce II, "The Company Mission as a Strategic Tool," *Sloan Management Review* 23 (Spring 1982): 15.

5. See A. Davidson, "Frank Barlow," *Management Today*, February 1994, pp. 50–54.

6. J. K. Clemens, "A Lesson from 431 B.C." *Fortune*, 13 October 1986, p. 164.

7. G. Fuchsberg, "Visioning Mission Becomes Its Own Mission," *Wall Street Journal*, 7 January 1994, p. B1.

8. J. D. Duck, "Managing Change: The Art of Balancing," *Harvard Business Review* 71 (1993): 109–118. See also P. Strebel, "Why Do Employees Resist Change?" *Harvard Business Review* 74 (1996): 86–92.

9. G. Brooks, "Some Concerns Find That the Push to Diversify Was a Costly Mistake," *Wall Street Journal*, 2 October 1984, p. B1.

10. G. Stalk, P. Evans, and L. E. Shulman, "Competing on Capabilities: The New Rules for Corporate Strategy," *Harvard Business Review* 70 (1992): 57–69.

11. M. Schrage, "Consultant's Maxim for Management: Ignore Markets, Build on Competence," *Washington Post*, 17 May 1991, p. 12.

12. For an example of his early work, see R. Nader, *Unsafe at Any Speed: Design and Dangers of the American Automobile* (New York: Grossman, 1964).

13. D. O. McKee, R. Varadarajan, and W. M. Pride, "Strategic Adaptability and Firm Performance: A Market Contingent Perspective," *Journal of Marketing* 53 (1989): 21–35.

14. H. A. Simon, "On the Concept of Organizational Goal," *Administrative Science Quarterly* 9 (1964): 1–22; J. Pfeffer and G. Salancik, *The External Control of Organizations* (New York: Harper & Row, 1978).

15. R. M. Cyert and J. G. March, *A Behavioral Theory of the Firm* (Englewood Cliffs, N.J.: Prentice Hall, 1963); J. G. March and H. A. Simon, *Organizations* (New York: John Wiley & Sons, 1958).

16. M. Kroll, P. Wright, L. Toombs, and H. Leavell, "Form of Control: A Critical Determinant of Acquisition Performance and CEO Rewards," *Strategic Management Journal* (in press).

17. H. A. Simon, "The Compensation of Executives," *Sociometry* 20 (1957): 32–35.

18. D. R. Roberts, "A General Theory of Executive Compensation Based on Statistically Tested Propositions," *Quarterly Journal of Economics* 20 (1956): 270–294.

19. K. J. Murphy, "Corporate Performance and Managerial Remuneration: An Empirical Analysis," *Journal of Accounting and Economics* 7 (1985): 11–42; Aoki, *Co-Operative Game Theory of the Firm*; A. A. Berle and G. C. Means, *The Modern Corporation and Private Property*, rev. ed. (New York: Harcourt, Brace & World, 1968).

20. G. P. Baker, M. C. Jensen, and K. J. Murphy, "Compensation and Incentives: Practice vs. Theory," *Journal of Finance* 43 (1988): 609.

21. D. J. Teece, "Towards an Economic Theory of the Multiproduct Firm," *Journal of Economic Behavior and Organization* 3 (1982): 39–63.

22. H. A. Simon, *Administrative Behavior* (New York: Macmillan, 1957).

23. M. Kroll, P. Wright, L. Toombs, and H. Leavell, "Form of Control: A Critical Determinant of Acquisition Performance and CEO Rewards," *Strategic Management Journal* 18(1997): 85–96.

24. Ibid.

25. E. F. Fama, "Agency Problems and the Theory of the Firm," *Journal of Political Economy* 88 (1980): 288–307.

26. Y. Amihud, J. Y. Kamin, and J. Romen, "Managerialism, Ownerism, and Risk," *Journal of Banking and Finance* 7 (1983): 189–196.

27. Fama, "Agency Problems and the Theory of the Firm."

28. J. Child, *The Business Enterprise in Modern Industrial Society* (London: Collier-Macmillan, 1969).

29. D. R. James and M. Soref, "Profit Constraints on Managerial Autonomy: Managerial Theory and the Unmaking of the Corporation President," *American Sociological Review* 46 (1981): 1–18.

30. Ibid., p. 3.

31. Ibid.

32. J. Bacon, *Corporate Directorship Practices: Membership and Committees of the Board* (New York: The Conference Board, 1973); J. C. Baker, *Directors and Their Functions* (Cambridge: Harvard University Press, 1945); Berle and Means, *The Modern Corporation and Private Property*; B. K. Boyd, "Board Control and CEO Compensation," *Strategic Management Journal* 15 (1994): 335–344; C. C. Brown and E. E. Smith, *The Director Looks at His Job* (New York: Columbia University Press, 1957); E. J. Epstein, *Who Owns the Corporation? Management vs. Shareholders* (New

York: Priority Press, 1986); J. M. Juran and J. K. Louden, *The Corporate Director* (New York: American Management Association, 1966); H. Koontz, *The Board of Directors and Effective Management* (New York: McGraw-Hill, 1967); J. K. Louden, *The Director: A Professional's Guide to Effective Board Work* (New York: Amacom, 1982); M. L. Mace, *Directors: Myth and Reality* (Cambridge: Harvard University Press, 1971); O. E. Williamson, *The Economics of Discretionary Behavior: Managerial Objectives in a Theory of the Firm* (Englewood Cliffs, N.J.: Prentice Hall, 1964); S. G. Winter, "Economic Natural Selection and the Theory of the Firm," *Yale Economic Essays* 4 (1964): 225–231.

33. A. Patton and J. C. Baker, "Why Won't Directors Rock the Boat?" *Harvard Business Review* 65, no. 6 (1987): 10–18.

34. L. Herzel, R. W. Shepro, and L. Katz, "Next-to-the-Last Word on Endangered Directors," *Harvard Business Review* 65, no. 1 (1987): 38.

35. C. Loh, "The Influence of Outside Directors on the Adoption of Poison Pills," *Quarterly Journal of Business and Economics* 33, no. 1 (1994): 3–11.

36. S. P. Sherman, "Pushing Corporate Boards to Be Better," *Fortune*, 18 July 1988, p. 60.

37. G. S. Crystal and F. T. Vincent Jr., "Take the Mystery Out of CEO Pay," *Fortune*, 24 April 1989, p. 220.

38. M. Galen, "A Seat on the Board Is Getting Hotter," *Business Week*, 3 July 1989, p. 72; Sherman, "Pushing Corporate Boards to Be Better," p. 62.

39. W. E. Green, "Directors' Insurance: How Good a Shield?" *Wall Street Journal*, 14 August 1989.

40. B. D. Fromson, "The Big Owners Roar," *Fortune*, 30 July 1990, pp. 66–78.

41. J. Pfeffer, "Size, Composition, and Function of Hospital Boards of Directors: A Study of Organization-Environment Linkage," *Administrative Science Quarterly* 18 (1973): 349–364; Pfeffer and Salancik, *External Control of Organizations*; and K. G. Provan, "Board Power and Organizational Effectiveness Among Human Service Agencies," *Academy of Management Journal* 23 (1980): 221–236; J. Goldstein, K. Gautum, and W. Boeker, "The Effects of Board Size and Diversity on Strategic Change," *Strategic Management Journal* 15 (1994): 241–250.

42. M. S. Mizruchi, "Who Controls Whom? An Examination of the Relation Between Management and Board of Directors in Large American Corporations," *Academy of Management Review* 8 (1983): 426–435.

43. Sherman, "Pushing Corporate Boards to Be Better," p. 58.

44. Ibid., p. 60.

45. M. C. Jensen and W. H. Meckling, "Theory of the Firm: Managerial Behavior, Agency Cost and Ownership Structure," *Journal of Financial Economics* 3 (1976): 305–360.

46. S. L. Oswald and J. S. Jahera, "The Influence of Ownership on Performance: An Empirical Study," *Strategic Management Journal* 12 (1991): 321–326.

47. J. J. McConnell and H. Servaes, "Additional Evidence on Equity Ownership and Corporate Value," *Journal of Financial Economics* 27 (1990): 595–612; R. A. Morck, A. Shleifer, and R. Vishny, "Managerial Ownership and Market Valuation: An Empirical Analysis," *Journal of Financial Economics* 20 (1988): 293–315.

48. P. Wright, S. P. Ferris, A. Sarin, and V. Awasthi, "Impact of Corporate Insider, Blockholder, and Institutional Equity Ownership on Firm Risk Taking," *Academy of Management Journal* 39 (1996): 441–463.

49. J. J. McConnell and H. Servaes, "Additional Evidence on Equity Ownership and Corporate Value," *Journal of Financial Economics* 27 (1990): 595–612; A. Shleifer and R. Vishny, "Large Shareholders and Corporate Control," *Journal of Political Economy* 94 (1986): 461–488.

50. W. J. Salmon, "Crisis Prevention: How to Gear Up Your Board," *Harvard Business Review* 71 (1993): 68–75.

51. Ibid.

52. *Harvard Business Review*, The Working Group on Corporate Governance, "A New Compact for Owners and Directors," *Harvard Business Review* 69 (1991): 141–143.

53. C. Wohlstetter, "Pension Fund Socialism: Can Bureaucrats Run the Blue Chips?" *Harvard Business Review* 71 (1993): 78.

54. *Harvard Business Review* (1991).

55. T. B. Pickens Jr., "Professions of a Short-Termer," *Harvard Business Review* 64, no. 3 (1986): 75.

56. Ibid.

57. A. Smith, *An Inquiry into the Nature and Causes of the Wealth of Nations* (Chicago: Encyclopedia Britannica, 1952); M. Friedman, "The Social Responsibility of Business Is to Increase Its Profits," *New York Times Magazine*, 13 September 1970, pp. 33, 122–125.

58. B. Bremmer, A. Fine, and J. Weber, "Doing the Right Thing in South Africa?" *Business Week*, 27 April 1992, pp. 60, 64.

59. C. Smith, "The New Corporate Philanthropy," *Harvard Business Review* 72 (May/June 1994), 105–116; For further discussion, see M. B. E. Clarkson, "A Stakeholder Framework for Analyzing and Evaluating Corporate Social Performance," *Academy of Management Review* 20 (1995): 92–117.

STRATEGIC MANAGEMENT MODEL

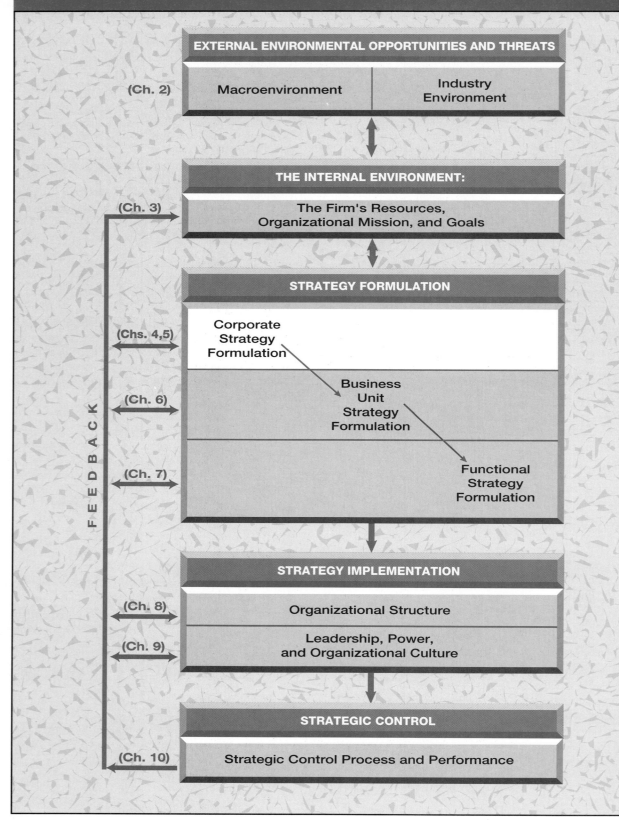

EXTERNAL ENVIRONMENTAL OPPORTUNITIES AND THREATS

(Ch. 2)

| Macroenvironment | Industry Environment |

THE INTERNAL ENVIRONMENT:

(Ch. 3)

The Firm's Resources, Organizational Mission, and Goals

STRATEGY FORMULATION

(Chs. 4,5)

Corporate Strategy Formulation

(Ch. 6)

Business Unit Strategy Formulation

(Ch. 7)

Functional Strategy Formulation

STRATEGY IMPLEMENTATION

(Ch. 8)

Organizational Structure

(Ch. 9)

Leadership, Power, and Organizational Culture

STRATEGIC CONTROL

(Ch. 10)

Strategic Control Process and Performance

FEEDBACK

4 Corporate-Level Strategies

Once the organization's mission, goals, and objectives are delineated, as was discussed in the preceding chapter, top management can formulate the firm's strategy. Strategy exists at three levels: the corporate level, the business unit level, and the functional level. The focus of this chapter and the one following it is **corporate-level strategy**—the strategy top management formulates for the overall corporation. The subsequent two chapters will discuss business unit and functional strategies. Although each of these chapters emphasizes strategy at a separate level, in reality, all three levels are closely intertwined.

At the corporate level, the basic strategic question facing top management is, In what particular businesses or industries should we be operating? The answer to this question depends upon the firm's particular strengths and weaknesses and the opportunities and threats posed by the external environment. This chapter explores strategic alternatives at the corporate level.

Although in this and the next chapter we primarily focus on strategic alternatives and portfolio management at the corporate level, we initially discuss a phenomenon that has been in vogue in the 1980s and the 1990s—corporate restructuring. The study of corporate restructuring goes back several decades although it has received greater emphasis since the 1980s.

CORPORATE RESTRUCTURING

Corporate restructuring may include a broad set of decisions and actions, such as changing the organization of work itself in the firm, reducing the amount of cash under the discretion of senior executives (through the assumption of higher corporate debt or an increase in dividend payments or the declaration of a special one-time dividend or corporate share buybacks), and acquiring or divesting business units. Ideally, the purpose of corporate restructuring is to enhance the wealth of the shareholders by satisfying the needs of various stakeholders.

Firms that manage shareholder value through voluntary restructuring as needed ordinarily do not have to be concerned with hostile takeover bids and externally forced, involuntary restructuring. For instance, General Mills has voluntarily restructured a number of times. The benefits of voluntary restructuring for General Mills have included lowering the number of personnel through a freeze on hiring and accelerated voluntary retirement rather than through abruptly firing people and demoralizing the entire organization; changing suppliers and channels of distribution gradually with longer time notices, so as not to gain a poor corporate reputation; and selling assets gradually rather than under a time pressure that puts the seller in an unfavorable bargaining position. This stakeholder approach to restructuring has also created more wealth for the shareholders of General Mills.[1] Firms that do not manage for value may eventually be forced to restructure by outsiders. Involuntary restructuring normally is costly and creates trauma for the stakeholders. Corporate restructuring has three interrelated dimensions. They are organizational, financial, and portfolio dimensions.[2]

Organizational restructuring refers to fundamentally changing the organization of work itself at the corporate level or radically reconfiguring activities and relationships at the business unit level (discussed in chapter 6). Organizational restructuring was studied by Alfred Chandler more than three decades ago.[3] His conclusion was that as corporate strategy changes, organization of the corporate entity must also change in order to get the work done efficiently. For instance, a functional organization (discussed in chapter 8) may be appropriate if a firm is in a single business. With diversification, however, the functional organization may not serve as an efficient means of organizing the firm's work. Thus, an organizational restructuring may be required.

Organizational restructuring may be undertaken in parts of the corporation or in its entirety. The goal, in either case, is to heighten effectiveness and efficiency. For instance, Paramount Publishing Group at one time had two divisions—Prentice Hall and Allyn & Bacon—which sold a variety of textbooks to universities. Subsequently, Paramount also acquired MacMillan Publishing, with its own variety of books. Rather than having each publisher sell a variety of books, the publishing work was reorganized so that Prentice Hall could concentrate on business texts and Allyn & Bacon on social science, health, education, and the physical sciences. MacMillan was dissolved, and its titles were transferred to Prentice Hall or Allyn & Bacon.

Organizational restructuring may be done proactively, as was the case with Paramount, or in response to changes in the environment. For instance, colleges and universities have had to organizationally restructure because students have progressively become more interested in specialized areas of education rather than in a traditional liberal arts education.[4]

Financial restructuring refers to reducing the amount of cash available to senior executives so that they are not tempted to waste shareholders' wealth on unprofitable projects that may be personally appealing to the managers. Reducing the amount of cash also puts pressure on the executives to emphasize efficiency as financial slack is reduced. Cash at the disposal of executives may be reduced by channeling it to the stockholders through stock buybacks or special dividends. An increase in regular dividends also takes away cash from managerial discretion and gives it to the stockholders.

Financial restructuring is driven by agency theory. The premise of agency theory is that top managers are often compensated and rewarded on the basis of strategies that are self-serving and do not necessarily benefit the shareholders. For instance, managerial rewards may be increased more through growth and diversification than through enhancement of firm value. Some scholars have even argued that managerial rewards may be independent of their incentives.[5] Thus, financial restructuring is instituted in order to reduce agency costs. Emphasis should be made that financial restructuring has become more prominent as the number and size of institutional investors and blockholders have increased. Since the 1980s institutional investors and blockholders have become significant shareholders and, because of this substantial ownership, can force management to financially restructure to enhance firm value.

Portfolio restructuring refers to the acquisition or divestment of business units to enhance corporate value. Portfolio restructuring is comprehensively addressed in the next section through a discussion of strategic alternatives, and in chapter 5 under corporate portfolio frameworks.

STRATEGIC ALTERNATIVES

Most firms begin their existence as single-business companies. Some enterprises continue to thrive while remaining primarily a single industry. Examples of such companies include Federal Express, Wal-Mart, Wrigley, Xerox, Campbell Soup, McDonald's, Anheuser-Busch, and Timex.

By competing in only one industry, a firm benefits from the specialized knowledge that it derives from concentrating on a limited business arena. This knowledge can help firms offer better products or services and become more efficient in their operations. McDonald's, for instance, has been able to develop a steadily improved product line and maintain low per-unit cost of operations over the years by concentrating exclusively on the fast-food business. Wal-Mart has also benefited from operating primarily in the retailing industry. And Anheuser-Busch has limited its scope of operations largely to the brewing industry, from which it derives more than 80 percent of its sales and 90 percent of its profits.

Operating primarily in one industry, however, may increase a firm's vulnerability to business cycles. Also, should industry attractiveness decline, through a permanent decrease in consumer demand for the firm's products or an onslaught of severe competition from existing or new competitors (in the same industry or substitute industries), the firm's performance is likely to suffer.

These disadvantages can be overcome by operating in different industries through diversification. In fact, senior executives often justify diversifying their firms (having corporate presence in more than one industry) by claiming that it reduces uncertainties associated with being tied to only one industry. Note should be made that the majority of U.S. firms today are active in more than one industry.

Firms may diversify into unrelated or related businesses. Unrelated diversification is driven by the desire to capitalize on profit opportunities in any industry. Unrelated diversification often involves the corporation in businesses that typically have no similarities or complementarities (along important strategic dimensions) among them.

Related diversification involves diversifying into other businesses that have similarities or complementarities along important strategic dimensions. More is stated on related and unrelated diversification throughout this chapter. We emphasize, however, that although executives justify diversification by arguing that it reduces uncertainties associated with being involved in one industry, in reality, diversifying wildly into numerous unrelated businesses also presents its own set of uncertainties. The uncertainties of being in one industry may be compared to putting all of one's eggs into a single basket, whereas being in numerous unrelated businesses may result in uncertainties associated with losing touch with the fundamentals of each business and the difficulty of analyzing the numerous disaggregate external opportunities and threats inherent in unrelated industries. In fact, select authors have empirically concluded that an important way for firms to minimize uncertainties is to diversify into similar industries, rather than remain in just one industry, or to diversify into very different industries.[6] Broadly speaking, senior managers have three corporate-level strategies from which to choose. They may elect to pursue a strategy of growth, stability, or retrenchment. The available strategies are listed in Table 4.1.

■ Growth Strategies

Ideally, a firm should select a **growth strategy** that results in an increase in sales or market share only if that growth is expected to result in an increase in firm value. Growth may be attained in a variety of ways. In the following subsections, we describe key growth strategies firms can adopt.

Internal Growth

Internal growth is achieved through increasing a firm's sales, production capacity, and work force. Some companies consciously pursue this route to growth rather than the alternative route of acquiring other firms. Their belief is

---

Table 4.1   **Corporate-Level Strategies**

1. Growth strategies
   a. Internal growth
   b. Horizontal integration
   c. Horizontal related diversification
   d. Horizontal unrelated diversification (conglomerate diversification)
   e. Vertical integration of related businesses
   f. Vertical integration of unrelated businesses
   g. Mergers
   h. Strategic alliances
2. Stability strategy
3. Retrenchment strategies
   a. Turnaround
   b. Divestment
   c. Liquidation

that internal growth better preserves their organizational culture, efficiency, quality, and image. McDonald's, for instance, has never purchased other fast-food restaurant chains. To maintain its high standards for cleanliness, service, and product consistency, it has grown by granting franchises only to people who are willing to be trained in the McDonald's way.

Likewise, American Airlines prefers to grow internally. American was the only U.S.-based airline to expand its services to three continents (Europe, Asia, and South America) at once, and its chairman, Robert L. Crandall, was asked why American did not buy ailing Pan Am or TWA as a quick way to enter these overseas markets. He responded:

> We've always said we don't want to buy another airline. We don't want to acquire another airline's airplanes. We don't want another airline's people. . . .[7]

Internal growth not only includes growth of the same business but also the creation of new businesses, either in a horizontal or vertical direction. **Horizontal internal growth** may involve creating new companies that operate in related or unrelated businesses. Recall that Blockbuster was initially in the video-rental business. Subsequently, it created its music stores, which sell CDs and tapes. This demonstrates Blockbuster's horizontal internal growth. **Vertical internal growth** refers to creating related or unrelated businesses within the firm's vertical channel of distribution and takes the form of supplier-customer relationships. For example, airlines normally purchase their in-flight meals from outside suppliers, such as Dobbs International, that prepare and deliver meals to the air carriers. However, United Airlines has created its own in-flight food service; hence its food service business serves as a supplier to its in-house customer, the airline.

As already emphasized, internal growth helps preserve the organization's culture, efficiency, quality, and image. The chief disadvantages to internal growth, however, are the rising bureaucratic and coordinating costs that generally accompany internal growth. United's in-flight food service, for example, requires its own management team, personnel procedures, and accounting systems. Moreover, its operations need to be coordinated with those of the airline. Therefore, creating new businesses should only be undertaken when their benefits exceed their costs. Note should be made that cost-benefit analysis, in a strategic context, involves important decision components that are difficult to quantify. For instance, a firm may elect to grow internally to maintain its employment level rather than to subcontract its needs to suppliers who may be able to provide their work at marginally lower costs. This may obviate reducing the number of employees (and the costs associated with lower organizational morale).

Horizontal Integration

Some firms expand by acquiring other companies in the same line of business, a process called **horizontal integration.** ConAgra, for instance, has acquired Banquet Foods, Armour Foods, RJR Nabisco Frozen Foods (Morton, Patio, and Chun King), Beatrice (Hunt's, Wesson, Swift, Eckrich, Butterball, and Orville Redenbacher's), and Golden Valley Microwave Foods (Act II).[8] There are several reasons for engaging in horizontal integration. One of the primary reasons is to increase market share. Along with increasing revenues, larger market share provides the company with greater leverage to deal with its suppliers and customers.[9] Greater market share should also lower the firm's costs through scale economies. Increased size enables the firm to promote its products and services more efficiently to a larger audience and may permit greater access to channels of distribution. Finally, horizontal integration can result in increased operational flexibility.

An example of horizontal integration is Chrysler's purchase of American Motors some years ago. The combination of these two firms is a greater competitive threat to other automobile manufacturers than were the two firms owned and operated separately. The combined firm is larger and financially stronger and can appeal to a broader group of customers through its more diverse product line.

Antitrust legislation, of course, restricts some forms of horizontal integration. The Chrysler purchase of American Motors was approved because Chrysler was far smaller and weaker than either General Motors (GM) or Ford and because American Motors was close to being forced out of business. But many horizontal integrations that would substantially lessen competition in an industry—such as a hypothetical one between GM and Ford—are usually prohibited by the U.S. Justice Department.

S T R A T E G I C   I N S I G H T

Horizontal Integration in the Paper Industry:
Union Camp and Georgia-Pacific

The horizontal growth of one major firm in an industry is likely to affect all of its competitors. Consider the U. S. paper industry. For decades, the industry was characterized by nonantagonistic competition. Even when horizontal integrations occurred, they were considered friendly. Because competition was not cutthroat, firms like the $2.75 billion Union Camp Corporation were able to survive even during economic downturns.

Then in 1990, Union Camp's largest competitor, Georgia-Pacific, changed the rules of the game by acquiring Great Northern Nekoosa in a hostile takeover. The purchase gave Georgia-Pacific annual sales of more than $10 billion, placing it thirty-fourth on the 1990 Fortune 500. Overnight, Georgia-Pacific became the world's largest paper products producer. Its new size and efficient fit with Great Northern Nekoosa gave it such economies of scale that Georgia-Pacific became the lowest-cost producer of several major liens of paper products.

Georgia-Pacific's low-cost position, combined with an economic recession, placed significant pressure on Union Camp and other companies in the industry to reduce their costs dramatically. As price pressures and discounting increased, these firms faced the unpleasant prospect of being underbid in the industry's price competition.

Union Camp, however, did enjoy some advantages. Its strong balance sheet enabled it to continue expanding aggressively, primarily through internal growth. Georgia-Pacific, on the other hand, found that its acquisition of Great Northern Nekoosa increased its interest expense substantially, forcing it to reduce capital spending and sell more than $2 billion in assets, as well as close sixty distribution centers in 1996.

SOURCE: "Georgia-Pacific to Close 60 Distribution Centers," *New York Times*, 30 June 1995, p. 3D.

Horizontal Related Diversification

When a corporation acquires a business that is in an industry outside of its present scope of operations (through a payment of cash or stock or some combination of the two) but is related to the corporation's core competencies, the corporation has engaged in **horizontal related diversification.** Relatedness suggests that similar or complementary core competencies may be transferred or shared between the corporation and the acquired business. **Core competencies** are the major resource strengths (human, organizational, physical—present or potential) of organizations. Broadly speaking, core competencies can include, among others, operations excellence, superior technology, cutting edge research and development, and effective marketing. For example, one firm acquiring another with **similar core competencies** in marketing may strengthen both of their overall competitive positions.

Alternatively, two firms may combine **complementary core competencies.** A firm, for instance, that possesses a competency in its product distribution network but limited competence in research and development may acquire a firm that is a leader in research and development but weak in distribution. Each firm would presumably benefit from the acquisition.

Coca-Cola is a good example of shared or transferred competencies. Coca-Cola's expertise in promoting consumer products could be transferred from its soft-drink business to the fruit-juice business (Minute Maid) that it acquired. Also, Coca-Cola's sales force competency may be shared by these two units by a common sales force that simultaneously sells Coca-Cola and Minute Maid products. Examples of two other consumer products companies that have undertaken a number of horizontal related diversifications are shown in Table 4.2.

As is evident, the primary impetus for acquiring horizontal related businesses is to achieve synergy and to strengthen a firm's core competencies.[10] Synergy is attained when the combination of two firms results in higher effectiveness and efficiency than the total yielded by them separately. Three major

---

Table 4.2   **Examples of Corporations That Have Undertaken Horizontal Related Diversifications**

Johnson & Johnson	*Gillette*
Dental products	Razors and blades
Oral contraceptives	Toiletries
Wound care products	Electrical shavers, curlers, toothbrushes, alarm clocks, coffee makers
Prescription drugs	
Hospital products	Stationery products and writing instruments
Over-the-counter drugs	
Diapers	
Feminine hygiene products	
Infant products	

synergistic advantages may be associated with horizontal related acquisitions: horizontal scope economies, horizontal scope innovations, and a combination of the two. Each of these possible advantages is discussed next.

Horizontal scope economies occur when a firm's multiple business units are able to share purchasing, research and development, marketing, or other functional activities at a lower total or per-unit cost than would be available if the business units did not share. For instance, a firm that has several business units, each producing a type of major appliance, could reduce its total or per-unit advertising expenses by spreading those costs over a broad range of appliances. Similarly, a corporation may receive a quantity discount by purchasing common parts or supplies for several of its business units.

Horizontal scope innovations refer to improvements or innovations that can be transferred or shared across the corporation's business units. Consider Daimler-Benz, for example. This producer of Mercedes-Benz vehicles has, over the past decade, acquired business units in defense electronics, aerospace, automation systems, appliances, and financial services. Together, Daimler-Benz's business units share research and development innovations that help each of them offer superior, state-of-the-art products.

Daimler-Benz also illustrates the **combination of horizontal scope economies and scope innovations.** By acquiring those business units, Daimler-Benz not only benefits from technological and product innovations but also lowers its total research and development costs by spreading them among the business units.

Horizontal related diversification is often accompanied by two disadvantages: increased bureaucratic costs and greater costs of coordinating the activities of the multiple business units. As a result, such diversification should be preceded by a careful cost-benefit analysis.

Horizontal Unrelated Diversification (Conglomerate Diversification)

When a corporation acquires a business in an unrelated industry, it has undertaken a **horizontal unrelated diversification** or **conglomerate diversification.** Whereas horizontal related diversification is based on the premise of strategically managing and coordinating related businesses to create synergy and value, conglomerate diversification decisions are made primarily for financial investment reasons. The assumption, in the latter case, is that structuring a portfolio of businesses based on their potential financial benefits will create value.[11] Thus, whereas diversifying into related industries is strategically driven, diversifying into unrelated industries is largely financially driven.[12]

In one sense, conglomerate diversification is simpler than horizontal related diversification because it is based on financial analysis without concern for the potential synergistic effects of combining core competencies. Also, since the acquired business units are unrelated to the firm's existing businesses, the costs of coordination are relatively few. Bureaucratic costs, however, tend to increase with unrelated diversification. Again, firms are well advised to undertake a cost-benefit analysis before acquiring unrelated businesses.[13]

USX provides an example of horizontal unrelated diversification. Formerly known as U.S. Steel, this firm began to diversify out of the declining steel industry and into the more attractive energy industry by acquiring Marathon Oil. The firm hoped to increase its financial returns by entering an industry with greater opportunities.

STRATEGIC INSIGHT

Horizontal Related Diversification at Daimler-Benz

Sometimes acquisitions do not appear to be in related areas, but, upon more careful examination, common attributes become evident. Take, for example, Daimler-Benz. One of the world's largest companies with $62 billion in annual sales, Daimler-Benz conducts manufacturing and marketing operations around the world. Almost two-thirds of its sales stem from transactions outside its home base of Germany.

This corporate giant operates four distinct business units: Mercedes-Benz cars and trucks, Deutsche Aerospace defense and military electronics, AEG nondefense electronics and consumer products, and Debis financial services. At first glance, washing machines, coffee makers, luxury cars, and military electronics seem to share few attributes. But closer inspection reveals that these businesses have a common technological core.

For instance, developments in technology at Deutsche Aerospace are helping engineers at the Mercedes-Benz car and truck division to design vehicles that can detect road hazards and improve the driver's vision. In fact, Daimler-Benz has formed a centralized research and development center charged with creating innovations that can be transferred from one business unit to another. Daimler's chief executive officer insists that every product line, from washing machines to jet fighters, incorporate innovations using microelectronics and new materials. The central research and development facility is responsible for helping transfer these new technologies from one product or service to another.

SOURCES: "Germany Daimler Releases Unit-By-Unit Plan for 1996/1997," *AP-Dow Jones News Service*, 26 April 1996; "Le Shuffle," *Economist*, 8 July 1995, p. 7; "Cap Gemini Sogeti: Genesis or Exodus?" *Economist*, 26 February 1994, p. 67; "Daimler-Benz: A Slow Recovery," *Economist*, 18 December 1993, pp. 60–61; J. Templeman, D. Woodruff, and S. Reed, "Downshift at Daimler," *Business Week*, 16 November 1992, pp. 88–90.

A desire to reduce risk may lead to conglomerate diversification for firms operating in volatile industries that are subject to rapid technological change. However, financial economists argue that, from the perspective of the owners, risk reduction should not drive acquisition strategies. Their point is that individual stockholders can reduce their financial risk more efficiently by diversifying their personal financial portfolios rather than by owning stock in diversified firms.

Some conglomerates are managed quite effectively. TRW, for instance, has generally demonstrated successful financial performance. This firm, which began in Ohio as The Steel Products Company in 1916, now produces such diverse products and services as spacecraft, software and systems engineering support services, electronic systems, original and replacement automotive equipment, consumer and business credit information services, computer maintenance, pumps, valves, and energy services.

Another conglomerate that has performed well throughout the years is Dover Corporation. This firm has more than 70 different businesses, which produce elevators, valves and welding torches, and garbage trucks, among others. According to Dover CEO Thomas Reece, making a conglomerate a winner requires giving near-total autonomy to heads of business units, buying good companies at reasonable prices and retaining their existing managers, keeping headquarters staff and overhead at a minimum, and not being concerned with synergy.[14]

Carlson Companies: From Conglomerate to Horizontal Related Diversification

In the 1960s, Carlson Companies operated in a single business, trading stamps, as the Gold Bond Trading Stamp Company. However, it followed the path of many other enterprises in the 1970s, diversifying into unrelated businesses. By the end of that decade, Carlson Companies had become a conglomerate involved in eleven different business lines. Carlson soon learned the lesson, however, that many other conglomerates did: It is difficult to manage divergent businesses profitably. Consequently, Carlson Companies sold most of its businesses to concentrate in only three related areas—travel, hospitality, and marketing services.

Today, Carlson is one of the nation's largest privately owned firms, with about $10 billion in annual sales and about 70,000 employees. Curtis L. Carlson serves as chairman of the board and CEO.

Management describes the firm as "synergistically diversified." Its individual business units complement, support, and create business for one another. For instance, its travel agents and tour companies book reservations in its hotels, resorts, motels, and inns. One of its hotel chains, Radisson Hotels, hosts conventions and meetings often arranged by one of Carlson's marketing services. Next door to the Radisson

may be a TGI Friday's or a Dalts, two of the restaurant chains owned by Carlson. Even more synergy should flow from Carlson's superluxury cruise ship, SSC Radisson Diamond. Designed to serve the most upscale segment of the market, the huge ship has fully equipped meeting facilities.

To take advantage of the falling trade barriers in Europe, Carlson bought a London-based marketing group. The firm already provides twenty-eight different marketing services to businesses in the United States, Australia, and Japan. It is now expanding those services to France, Germany, Italy, and Spain.

Carlson Companies is extremely aggressive, continuing to expand its operations. The firm has grown at an annual rate of about 20 percent during the past decade. Leading the way is the Radisson Hotel chain, with locations in the United States, Russia, Eastern Europe, Australia, India, Mexico, Switzerland, Spain, Thailand, Canada, and the Caribbean. Carlson plans to add a new hotel every ten days until the year 2000; it is presently adding one every six days. Over the past decade, the number of hotel units has increased more than tenfold, making Radisson one of the top hotel companies in the world.

SOURCES: "Radisson Expands into Asia," *New York Times*, 31 March 1995, p. C5; M. Torchia, "How Twin Cities Employers Are Reshaping Health Care," *Business and Health*, February 1994, pp. 30–35; P. Grant, "Bringing Claims Administration Home," *Business and Health*, September 1993, pp. 54–60; R. Donoho, "Lofty Ambitions," *Successful Meetings*, August 1993, pp. 80–86; S. Pesmen, "Bad Times Good for Carlson," *Business Marketing*, July 1993, p. 48.

Vertical Integration of Related Businesses

Vertical integration refers to merging into a functional whole various stages of activities backward into sources of supply or forward in the direction of final consumers. Vertical integration may be partial or full. Performing all stages of activities ranging from raw materials to final outputs may be referred to as full integration. Performing some of these activities comprises partial integration. Acquiring a company with similar or complementary core competencies in the vertical distribution channel may be referred to as **vertical integration of related businesses.** Here also, relatedness suggests that pertinent organizational competencies or strengths may be transferred or shared.

Vertical integration may be either backward or forward in the distribution channel. Backward vertical integration occurs when the companies acquired supply the firm with products, components, or raw materials. An example of backward vertical integration is DuPont's purchase several years ago of Conoco. Conoco, an oil company, supplies petroleum products that DuPont uses in manufacturing its chemicals. By buying its suppliers, a firm assures itself of a steady source of supply.

A firm engages in forward vertical integration when it acquires companies that purchase its products. The acquired companies are closer to the end user. For example, when a manufacturer of navigation and guidance systems purchases an aircraft manufacturer, it has engaged in forward vertical integration.[15] The navigation and guidance systems are installed in the aircraft before it is sold to the airlines.

Four principal advantages are associated with vertical integration of related businesses. **Vertical chain economies** may result from eliminating production steps, reducing overhead costs, and coordinating distribution activities to attain greater synergy. **Vertical chain/horizontal scope economies** can occur when a corporation's horizontally related business units purchase from one of the corporation's business units that serves as a supplier. If sufficiently large, such purchases can improve the supplier's economies of scale while reducing purchasing costs for the horizontal business units. Take, for example, a corporation with horizontal business units that produce hair dryers, industrial fans, cooling systems for electronic equipment, and electric pencil sharpeners. The electric motor parts for all these products are produced by another of the corporation's business units in its vertical chain. As a result of the large combined internal demand for these motor parts, the supplier business unit benefits from scale economies, which lower its per-unit costs of operations. These lower costs are then passed along to the purchasing business units, which, in turn, can subsequently sell their products at highly competitive prices.

Vertical chain innovations refer to improvements or innovations that may be transferred or shared among the corporation's business units in the distribution channel. For example, firms such as IBM, Ford, and Digital Equipment acquire suppliers that conduct research and development on promising technology.[16] Vertical chain innovations not only can promote the development of technologically superior outputs, but they can also help the firm differentiate its outputs through improved design, faster delivery, or better marketing practices.

A final advantage is a **combination of vertical chain economies and chain innovations.** As an example, consider Admiram Corporation. One of its business units produces electric switches and plugs, for which it purchases plastic fasteners from another of Admiram's business units. Several years ago that same supplier produced steel fasteners for switches and plugs. As a result of extensive communication between the managers of the two business units, the fastener unit developed sturdy plastic fasteners to replace those made of steel. The business unit that produced the switches and plugs then redesigned its products around the new plastic fasteners. The shift from steel to plastic parts and the subsequent redesigned products resulted in substantial cost savings in supplies, production, and assembly. Customers benefited from redesigned products not only because of the improved design but also because of the product's lighter weight, which led to reduced transportation and handling costs.

Although vertically integrated firms with related businesses in the distribution channel may be better positioned to gain on efficiency and innovation potentials internally, their disadvantage is that they are not predisposed to capitalize on such potentials developed in the external environment.[17] The reason is that such firms focus on internal coordination of activities meant to promote efficiencies and innovations. Firms with vertically unrelated business units, discussed next, are not as strictly subject to internal coordination needs. For instance, the activities of brewing beer and producing aluminum cans need not be coordinated for gains in efficiency or innovation. A brewer of beer with its own aluminum can production may seek external ideas to improve its brewing as well as its aluminum can operations. Note that this points out the disadvantage of being in vertically related businesses and, on the other hand, the advantage of being in vertically unrelated businesses.

We should also point out that firms that adhere to vertical integration of related businesses tend to have more complex patterns of integration. Although the uncertainty of suppliers and customers may have been the motivation to structure complex patterns, the complexity may lead to increased risk, especially in more dynamic environments.[18] Thus, outsourcing for suppliers and distributors may be beneficial in more dynamic environments.

Certain other disadvantages are also associated with vertical integration of related businesses. When market demand varies unpredictably over time, it becomes difficult to coordinate vertically integrated activities. Another disadvantage is that a technological innovation in the vertical channel may require all of the vertically linked businesses to modify their operations. Next, a firm that buys all of its needs internally may pay more if less expensive external sources of supply exist. Finally, the longer the chain, the greater will be the costs associated with increased coordination and bureaucracy. Obviously then, potential costs and benefits must be compared before engaging in vertical integration of related businesses.

Vertical Integration of Unrelated Businesses

Whereas vertical integration of related businesses centers on transferring or sharing pertinent complementary or similar core competencies, **vertical integration of unrelated businesses** is undertaken with limited possibilities for transferring or sharing core competencies.[19] The purchase by American Agronomics (a producer of citrus juices) of Precision Plastics (a manufacturer of plastic containers) is an example of vertical integration of unrelated businesses. Some juices, of course, can be marketed in plastic containers, but these containers also have multiple other uses. Also, the combination of a juice producer and a plastics company allows limited possibilities for transferring or sharing core competencies. Thus, there are limited potentials for achieving synergy.

Emphasis should be made that some stages of vertical integration may be related while others may be unrelated, as suggested by a number of scholars.[20] For instance, operational technology, managerial approaches, and organizational formats may be much more similar between wholesaling and retailing but quite different from those for manufacturing and processing. A firm that is vertically connected in two stages—component production and manufacturing—may be vertically related in these stages. If this firm additionally acquires its own wholesaling or retailing, however, then it will have vertically integrated into an unrelated business.

As already suggested, one advantage of vertically unrelated businesses is that they are normally more likely to adopt improvements and innovations of outsiders. This leads to a second advantage. Particularly in dynamic industry environments, they face lower risk of technological obsolescence because they are externally oriented.

Managing vertically unrelated businesses can be associated with two major disadvantages: The more vertical businesses the firm owns, the higher the costs of bureaucracy—and perhaps coordination—are likely to be, and a firm that commits itself to buying all of its needs internally may pay higher costs by failing to seek competitive bids from outside suppliers.

Note that some acquisitions do not fall neatly into either a horizontal or a vertical category. For example, PepsiCo's purchase of KFC, Pizza Hut, and Taco Bell can be viewed as horizontal related diversification. Their common core would be the marketing of fast food and soft drinks within the restaurant industry. But these same purchases can also be viewed as forward vertical integration of related businesses in that PepsiCo supplies soft drinks to KFC, Pizza Hut, and Taco Bell. Recall that relatedness did not pay off for PepsiCo so it spun-off these business units.

As is evident, some of the growth strategies discussed consist of acquiring other companies—either in a horizontal or a vertical direction. Growth may also be pursued through the voluntary merging of two independent companies.

Mergers

Many firms elect to grow through mergers. A **merger** occurs when two or more firms, usually of roughly similar sizes, combine into one through an exchange of stock. Mergers are undertaken to share or transfer resources and gain in competitive power. For example, Sperry and Burroughs merged to form Unisys several years ago in an attempt to compete more effectively in the computer industry.

The overall reason for a merger is to take advantage of the benefits of synergy. When the combination of two firms results in greater effectiveness and efficiency than the total yielded by them separately, then synergy has been attained. Synergy can result from either horizontal mergers, such as that between NCNB and C&S/Sovran (now named NationsBank), or from vertical mergers. The merger of Ocean Drilling and Exploration (an oil exploration and drilling firm) with Murphy Oil (a refiner) illustrates a vertical merger.

Because either type of merger usually results in increased bureaucratic and coordination costs, they should be undertaken only when the projected benefits exceed the merger's estimated costs.

Strategic Alliances

Strategic alliances are partnerships in which two or more firms carry out a specific project or cooperate in a selected area of business. The firms comprising the alliance share the costs, risks, and benefits of exploring and undertaking new business opportunities.[21] Such arrangements include joint ventures, franchise/ license agreements, joint research and development, joint operations, joint long-term supplier agreements, joint marketing agreements, and consortiums. Strategic alliances can be temporary, disbanding after the project is finished, or long term. Ownership of the firms, of course, remains unchanged.

Strategic alliances may be undertaken for a variety of reasons—political, economic, or technological. In certain countries, for instance, a foreign firm may be permitted to operate only if it enters into a strategic alliance with a local partner. In other cases, a particular project may be so large that it would strain a single company's resources. Thus that company may enter into a strategic alliance with another firm to gain the resources to accomplish the job. Other projects may require multidimensional technology that no one firm possesses. Hence, firms with different, but compatible, technologies may join together. Or in other cases, one firm may contribute its technological expertise while another contributes its managerial talent.

There are many examples of strategic alliances. IBM and Apple Computer recently agreed to exchange technology in an attempt to create a new computer operating system that would dominate the industry. The major U.S. automakers—GM, Ford, and Chrysler—are jointly conducting research, with the assistance of $120 million from the U.S. Department of Energy, to develop battery technology for electric cars. And GM, Lockheed, Southern California Edison, and Pacific Gas & Electric have formed a consortium to speed the development of widely used electric vehicles and advanced mass transportation systems.

Strategic alliances have two major advantages. The first, due to the companies' remaining separate and independent, is little increase in bureaucratic and coordination costs. Second, each company can benefit from the alliance without bearing all the costs and risks of exploring new business opportunities on its own. On the other hand, the major disadvantage of forming a strategic alliance is that one partner may take more than it gives. That is, some partners in the alliance possess less knowledge and less advanced technology than other partners and may, in the future, use their newly acquired knowledge and technology to compete directly with their more progressive partners. In addition, the profits from the alliance must be shared.

■ Stability Strategy

Corporate growth strategies may be adopted for a period of time but inevitably the firm may choose to adopt the stability strategy, or perhaps one of the retrenchment strategies discussed in the next section. It needs to be emphasized that when a firm is in different businesses, corporate strategy addresses what businesses to be in, and business unit strategy, discussed in chapter 6, emphasizes how to compete in those businesses. However, when a firm is in a single business, corporate strategy and business unit strategy become synonymous.

The **stability strategy** for a firm (that has operations in more than one industry) is the maintenance of the current array of businesses. There are two reasons for adopting the corporate stability strategy. First, this strategy enables the corporation to focus managerial efforts on the existing businesses with the goal of enhancing their competitive postures. That is, rather than continuing to add new businesses to the corporation and working hard to manage numerous different business units, management can concentrate on improving the productivity and innovation of existing businesses. Second, senior managers may perceive that the cost of adding new businesses may be more than the potential benefits. With the passage of time, however, the corporation may forgo the stability strategy and under favorable circumstances again adopt one of the growth strategies or, under less favorable conditions, one of the retrenchment strategies.

For a single-industry firm the stability strategy is one that maintains approximately the same operations without seeking significant growth in revenues or

International Strategic Alliances

Strategic alliances between firms headquartered in different countries have become increasingly popular in recent years. Consider the following examples:

Nestlé and General Mills

Nestlé, the world's largest food company, headquartered in Switzerland, has joined with U. S.-based General Mills to form Cereal Partners Worldwide (CPW). Using Nestlé's powerful channels of distribution, General Mills is penetrating such markets as Europe, Asia, Africa, and Latin America with its Wheaties and Cheerios brands.

General Motors and Toyota

In 1984, General Motors and Toyota established a joint production venture in California known as the New United Motor Manufacturing, Inc. (NUMMI). Although some GM executives were skeptical, CEO Roger Smith recognized that GM lacked the technology—from research and development through sales—to produce a high-

quality small car. Toyota sought the joint venture because it wanted a production facility in the United States without going it alone. Much of the Saturn philosophy that has contributed to its present success—from long-term relationships with supplies to just-in-time manufacturing—was gleaned from the GM–Toyota alliance.

Northwest and KLM

U.S.-based Northwest Airlines teamed up with Netherlands-based KLM to make Northwest more competitive in the North Atlantic market and to give KLM access to critical U. S. routes. The alliance allowed both carriers to act as a single airline. However, such alliances can bring about strained relationships between the participating firms. KLM has considered dissolving the alliance in part because of a Northwest shareholders-rights plan that caps KLM's stake in Northwest.

SOURCES: C. Goldsmith, "KLM Considers Dissolving Tie with Northwest Airlines," *Wall Street Journal Interactive Edition*, 2 May 1996; "Nestle Lays Off 43 Workers at Fulton, NY Chocolate Plant," *Dow Jones Business News*, 9 May 1996; E. H. Phillips, "Northwest Calls KLM Pact 'Strategic Asset'," *Aviation Week and Space Technology*, 31 October 1994, pp. 56–57; W. Webb, "Partnering with New Media Companies," *Editor and Publisher*, 15 April 1995, pp. 29–30; J. Bleeke and D. Ernst, "Is Your Strategic Alliance Really a Sale?" *Harvard Business Review*, January–February 1995, pp. 97–105; T. Sasaki, "What the Japanese Have Learned from Strategic Alliances," *Long Range Planning*, 26(3) (1994): 41–53; C. Knowlton, "Europe Cooks Up a Cereal Brawl," *Fortune*, 3 June 1991, pp. 175, 179.

in the size of the business. Why might a firm in a single business adopt this strategy? In some cases, it may be forced to do so if it operates in a low-growth or no-growth industry. Second, it may find that the cost of expanding its market share or of entering new-product or new-market areas is higher than the benefits that are projected to come with that growth. Third, a firm that dominates its industry through its superior size and competitive advantage may pursue stability to reduce its chances of being prosecuted for engaging in monopolistic practices. And finally, smaller enterprises that concentrate on specialized products or services may choose stability because of their concern that growth will result in reduced quality and customer service.

As an example of the last reason, consider Peet's Coffee and Tea, a group of eight coffeehouses that employs 170 people in the San Francisco Bay area. These establishments serve only the finest freshly roasted coffee to the accompaniment of piped-in classical music. Although the owner of Peet's, Gerald Baldwin, has received numerous lucrative offers to franchise his business nationwide, he has always refused. His concern is that with growth, quality may suffer. He fears, for instance, that some franchisees might serve coffee that was not freshly roasted in order to cut their costs and to increase their profits.

■ Retrenchment Strategies

Growth strategies and the stability strategy are normally adopted by firms that are in satisfactory competitive positions. But when the performance of a firm's business units is disappointing or, at the extreme, when its survival is at stake, then **retrenchment strategies** may be appropriate. Retrenchment may take one of three forms: turnaround, divestment, or liquidation.

Turnaround

The intent of a **turnaround** is to transform the corporation into a leaner and more effective firm. Turnaround includes such actions as eliminating unprofitable outputs, pruning assets, reducing the size of the work force, cutting costs of distribution, and rethinking the firm's product lines and customer groups.[22]

Take, as an example, what may be the most famous turnaround in American history. Chrysler Corporation, by the late 1970s, was on the verge of bankruptcy. Its newly hired CEO, Lee Iacocca, implemented a dramatic turnaround strategy. Large numbers of blue- and white-collar employees were laid off, the remaining workers agreed to forgo part of their salaries and benefits, and twenty plants were either closed or consolidated. These actions lowered the firm's break-even point from an annual sales level of 2.4 million cars and trucks to about 1.2 million. Iacocca also implemented a divestment strategy (discussed in the following section) by selling Chrysler's marine outboard motor division, its defense business, its air-conditioning division, and all of its automobile manufacturing plants located outside the United States. By 1982, Chrysler began to show a profit, after having lost $3.5 billion in the preceding four years.

Unfortunately, the turnaround failed to last. By 1991, Chrysler was losing over $2 million a day and had been replaced by Honda as the third-largest seller of cars in the United States. Chrysler once again energetically began to cut costs by closing plants and firing employees, by selling its 50 percent share in its strategic alliance with Mitsubishi Motors, and by modifying its operating systems. For instance, Chrysler began assigning engineers to teams that design a single car rather than continuing to place them in functional groups (such as engine design). This change cut product development time from $4\frac{1}{2}$ to $3\frac{1}{2}$ years. Chrysler also began implementing ways to cut the delivery time of cars to dealers. As a result, Chrysler had record profits in 1994 of $3.7 billion, and its cash position in 1994 and 1995 was enviable in the auto industry. This firm's superior performance continued through the latter 1990s.

Divestment

When a corporation sells or "spins off" one of its business units, as Chrysler did, it is engaging in **divestment.** Divestment usually occurs when the business unit is performing poorly or when it no longer fits the corporation's strategic profile. The business unit may be sold to another company, to its managers and employees, or to an individual or group of investors. Such sales are fairly common. For instance, General Electric, Westinghouse, and Singer have all sold their computer businesses. Singer also sold its original core business unit that produced sewing machines and began to concentrate on high-technology electronics.

Note that divestment may be necessary in a number of situations—where a business unit drains resources from more profitable units, where the business unit is not as efficient as alternatives in the marketplace, or where the unit's interdependence with other units is not synergistic. Divestments in the 1980s and the 1990s have been motivated by the underperformance of many of the business units acquired in the 1960s and the 1970s. Moreover, select authors have suggested that the underperformance of some corporations has been due to the unrelatedness of their units.[23] Consequently, the takeovers of the 1980s and the 1990s have often been characterized as acquisitions that were followed by sell-offs of previously acquired unrelated businesses or leveraged takeovers by the managers themselves that were then pruned by substantial sell-offs of assets.[24]

As suggested above, divestment can also occur through a spin-off. In this case, shares of stock in the business unit that is to be spun off are distributed. The stock of the parent corporation and the spun-off business unit then begin to trade separately. For example, the Adolph Coors Company has spun off business units that sell ceramic multilayer computer boards, packages for soaps and dog food, vitamins for animal feed, and automobile parts in order to concentrate more fully on the highly competitive beer industry.

Liquidation

A strategy of last resort is **liquidation.** When neither a turnaround nor a divestment seems feasible, liquidation occurs through termination of the business unit's existence by sale of its assets. Most stakeholder groups suffer in liquidations. Stockholders and creditors lose, some of the managers and employees lose their jobs, suppliers lose a customer, and the community suffers an increase in unemployment and a decrease in tax revenues.

S U M M A R Y

In choosing a strategy, top management may adopt any one of three general corporate profiles: The firm may compete in a single business, in several related businesses, or in several unrelated businesses. A recent phenomenon related to the corporate profile decision is corporate restructuring. The purpose of corporate restructuring is to enhance the wealth of the shareholders through the satisfaction of needs of various stakeholders. Corporate restructuring has organizational, financial, and portfolio dimensions.

Given the corporate portfolio, top managers have three corporate-level strategies available: growth, stability, or retrenchment. Growth can be attained through internal growth or the creation of new businesses. New businesses can be created horizontally or vertically. Growth is also possible through horizontal integration—acquiring other companies in the same line of business.

Diversification (acquiring another company through a payment of cash and/or stock) can be either horizontal or vertical. Horizontal diversification may take the form of horizontal related diversification, or horizontal unrelated diversification. Vertical integration may be related or unrelated. Mergers involve the voluntary combination of two or more firms into one through an exchange of stock. A final form of growth is the strategic alliance—a partnership in which two or more independent firms carry out a specific project or cooperate in a selected area of business.

Some firms adopt a stability strategy in which they attempt to maintain their size and current lines of business. Firms in less satisfactory competitive positions are forced to adopt a retrenchment strategy. Retrenchment may take one of three forms: turnaround (transforming the organization into a leaner and more effective business), divestment (selling or spinning off one or more business units), or liquidation (terminating a business unit's existence by sale of its assets).

TAKE IT TO THE NET

We invite you to visit the Wright page on the Prentice Hall Web site at:

http://www.prenhall.com/wright

for this chapter's World Wide Web exercise.

KEY CONCEPTS

Combination of horizontal scope economies and scope innovations   When a firm's multiple business units share or transfer competencies at a lower total cost than would be available if the business units did not share or transfer and, at the same time, they share or transfer improvements or innovations.

Combination of vertical chain economies and chain innovations   When a firm, within its vertical distribution channel, is able to attain economies through its internal supplier-customer relationships while sharing or transferring improvements or innovations among its multiple vertical business units.

Complementary core competencies   When one firm's competency (such as strength in the research and development area) fits, in a complementary fashion, with another firm's core competency (such as strength in manufacturing).

Conglomerate diversification   See Horizontal unrelated diversification.

Core competency   A major strength of an organization—present or potential.

Corporate-level strategy   The strategy that top management formulates for the overall company.

Corporate restructuring   A process that may include a broad set of decisions and transactions, such as changing the organization of work itself in the firm, reducing the amount of cash under the discretion of senior executives, and acquiring or divesting business units.

Diversification   A corporate-level growth strategy in which one company acquires another company in an industry outside of its present scope of operations through a payment of cash or stock or some combination of the two.

Divestment   A corporate-level retrenchment strategy in which a firm sells one or more of its business units.

Financial restructuring   Reducing the amount of cash available to senior executives so that they will not be tempted to waste shareholders' wealth on unprofitable projects that may be personally appealing to them.

Growth strategy   A corporate-level strategy designed to increase profits, sales, and/or market share.

Horizontal integration   A form of acquisition in which a firm expands by acquiring other companies in its same line of business.

Horizontal internal growth   A type of internal growth strategy in which a firm creates new companies that operate in the same business as the original firm, in related businesses, or in unrelated businesses.

Horizontal related diversification   A form of diversification in which a firm expands by acquiring a business that is in an industry outside of its present scope of operations but is related to its core competencies.

Horizontal scope economies   Economies that occur when a firm's multiple business units are able to share functional activities at a lower total cost than would be available if they did not share.

Horizontal scope innovations   Improvements or innovations that can be transferred or shared across a corporation's business units.

Horizontal unrelated diversification   A form of diversification in which a firm expands by acquiring a business in an unrelated industry.

Internal growth   A corporate-level growth strategy in which a firm expands by internally increasing its size and sales rather than by acquiring other companies.

Liquidation   A corporate-level retrenchment strategy in which a firm terminates one or more of its business units by the sale of their assets.

Merger   A corporate-level growth strategy in which a firm combines with another firm through an exchange of stock.

Organizational restructuring   A change in the organization of work in the corporation to improve effectiveness and efficiency.

Portfolio restructuring   The acquisition or divestment of business units in order to enhance corporate value.

Retrenchment strategy   A corporate-level strategy undertaken by a firm when its performance is disappointing or when its survival is at stake. A retrenchment strategy tends to reduce the size of the firm.

Similar core competencies   When one firm's core competency or resource strengths (such as strength in the research and development area) is the same as another firm's core competency.

Stability strategy   A corporate-level strategy intended to maintain a firm's present size and current lines of business.

Strategic alliance   A corporate-level growth strategy in which two or more firms form a partnership to carry out a specific project or to cooperate in a selected area of business.

Turnaround   A corporate-level retrenchment strategy intended to transform the firm into a leaner and more effective business by reducing costs and rethinking the firm's product lines and target markets.

Vertical chain economies   Scale economies in a firm's distribution channel that result from eliminating production steps, reducing overhead costs, and coordinating distribution activities to attain greater synergy.

Vertical chain innovations   Improvements or innovations that may be transferred or shared among a firm's business units in the distribution channel.

Vertical chain/horizontal scope economies   Scale economies that occur when a firm's horizontally related or unrelated business units purchase from one of the firm's business units that serves as a supplier in sufficiently large quantities to improve the supplier's economies of scale while reducing purchasing costs for the horizontal business units.

Vertical integration   Merging into a functional whole various stages of activities backward into sources of supply or forward in the direction of final consumers.

Vertical integration of related businesses   A form of integration in which a firm expands by acquiring a company with similar or complementary core competencies in the distribution channel.

Vertical integration of unrelated businesses   A form of integration in which a firm expands by acquiring a company that will provide limited synergy in its distribution channel.

Vertical internal growth   A type of internal growth strategy that generally takes the form of supplier-customer relationships within the firm's channel of distribution.

DISCUSSION QUESTIONS

1. Explain the distinction between horizontal and vertical internal growth.

2. What do you believe are the advantages that internal growth has over growth through mergers and acquisitions? What particular advantages might mergers and acquisitions have over internal growth?

3. Explain the distinction among horizontal integration, horizontal related diversification, and horizontal unrelated diversification.

4. Discuss the major advantages and disadvantages of horizontal related diversification.

5. Explain the following statement: "While diversifying into related industries is strategically driven, diversifying into unrelated industries is largely financially driven."

6. Discuss the major advantages and disadvantages of vertical integration of related businesses.

7. Why would a firm prefer to engage in a strategic alliance over a more permanent arrangement?

8. Why would management adopt a stability strategy? Do you feel that such a strategy is viable over a lengthy period of time? Why or why not?

9. When is a retrenchment strategy appropriate? Identify some criteria that will help determine what particular retrenchment strategy should be used.

STRATEGIC MANAGEMENT EXERCISES

1. Using information in your library, identify three firms: one that is in a single business, one that is in two or more related businesses, and one that is in unrelated businesses. Now, insofar as information permits, explain the advantages and disadvantages of the corporate profile that each company has selected.

2. Identify a particular type of business that you might wish to start, assuming that you have the necessary financial resources. Furthermore, assume that after some period of time during which the business is successful, you wish to adopt a growth strategy for your company. Explain how your firm might expand through each of the following strategies: internal growth, horizontal integration, horizontal related diversification, horizontal unrelated diversification, merger, and strategic alliance.

3. Identify a well-known company with which you are reasonably familiar. Explain how it might expand either through vertical integration of related businesses or vertical integration of unrelated businesses. What are the potential benefits and risks associated with the form of growth that you have selected for this particular company?

NOTES

1. G. Donaldson, "Voluntary Restructuring: The Case of General Mills," *Journal of Financial Economics* 27 (1990): 117–141.

2. J. E. Bethel and J. Liebeskind, "The Effects of Ownership Structure on Corporate Restructuring," *Strategic Management Journal* 14 (1993): 15–31; E. H. Bowman and H. Singh, "Corporate Restructuring: Reconfiguring the Firm," *Strategic Management Journal* 14 (1993): 5–14.

3. A. D. Chandler, *Strategy and Structure*, Cambridge: MIT Press, 1962.

4. E. J. Zajac and M. S. Kraatz, "A Diametric Forces Model of Strategic Change: Assessing the Antecedents and Consequences of Restructuring in the Higher Education Industry," *Strategic Management Journal* 14 (1993): 83–102.

5. M. C. Jensen and K. J. Murphy, "Performance Pay and Top-Management Incentives," *Journal of Political Economy* 98 (1990): 225–264.

6. M. Lubatkin and S. Chatterjee, "Extending Modern Portfolio Theory into the Domain of Corporate Diversification: Does It Apply?" *Academy of Management Journal* 37 (1994): 109–136.

7. B. O'Brian, "American Air Expands into Three Continents, Flexing Its U.S. Muscle," *Wall Street Journal*, 8 June 1990, p. A1.

8. L. Therrien, "ConAgra Turns Up the Heat in the Kitchen," *Business Week*, 2 September 1991, p. 59.

9. B. Kelley, "A Day in the Life of a Card Shark," *Journal of Business Strategy*, March/April (1994): 36–39.

10. M. Lubatkin and S. Chatterjee, "Extending Modern Portfolio Theory into the Domain of Corporate Diversification: Does It Apply?" *Academy of Management Journal* 37 (1994): 109–136.

11. M. S. Salter and W. S. Weinhold, "Diversification Via Acquisition: Creating Value," *Harvard Business Review* 56, no. 4 (1978): 166–176.

12. M. Lubatkin, "Merger Strategies and Stockholder Value," *Strategic Management Journal* 8 (1987): 39–53; J. B. Barney, "Returns to Bidding Firms in Mergers and Acquisitions: Reconsidering the Relatedness Hypothesis," *Strategic Management Journal* 9 (1988): 71–78.

13. G. Samuels, "Learning by Doing," *Forbes*, 14 March 1994, pp. 51–54.

14. L. Zweig, "Who Says the Conglomerate is Dead?" *Business Week*, 23 January, 1995, p. 92.

15. R. Davis and L. G. Thomas, "Direct Estimation of Synergy: A New Approach to the Diversity-Performance Debate," *Management Science* 39 (1994): 1334–1346.

16. K. Kelly, "Learning from Japan," *Business Week*, 27 January 1992, p. 53.

17. R. D. Buzzell, "Is Vertical Integration Profitable?" *Harvard Business Review* 61 (January–February 1994): 92–102.

18. R. A. D'Aveni and A. Y. Ilinitch, "Complex Patterns of Vertical Integration in the Forest Products Industry: Systematic and Bankruptcy Risks," *Strategic Management Journal* 35 (1992): 596–625.

19. B. B. Pray, "Types of Vertical Acquisitions and Returns to Acquiring Firms," unpublished manuscript, University of Memphis, 1992.

20. R. D. Buzzell, "Is Vertical Integration Profitable?" *Harvard Business Review* 61 (January–February 1994): 92–102; M. Gort, *Diversification and Integration in American Industry*, (Princeton: Princeton University Press, 1962); G. J. Stigler, "The Division of Labor Is Limited by the Extent of the Market," *Journal of Political Economy* (June 1951): 185–193.

21. J. Mohr and R. Spekman, "Characteristics of Partnership Success: Partnership Attributes, Communication Behavior, and Conflict Resolution Techniques," *Strategic Management Journal* 15 (1994): 143–152; A. A. Lado, "The Role of Strategic Intent in the Choice of Modes of Cross-Border Alliances: An Investigation of Select U.S. Multinational Companies," unpublished manuscript, University of Memphis, 1992.

22. See M. Garry, "A&P Strikes Back," *Progressive Grocer,* February 1994, pp. 32–38.

23. A. Shleifer and R. W. Vishny, "Takeover in the '60's and the '80's: Evidence and Implications," *Strategic Management Journal* 12 (1991): 51–59.

24. S. N. Kaplan, "The Staying Power of Leveraged Buyouts," Working Paper, 1990, University of Chicago.

STRATEGIC MANAGEMENT MODEL

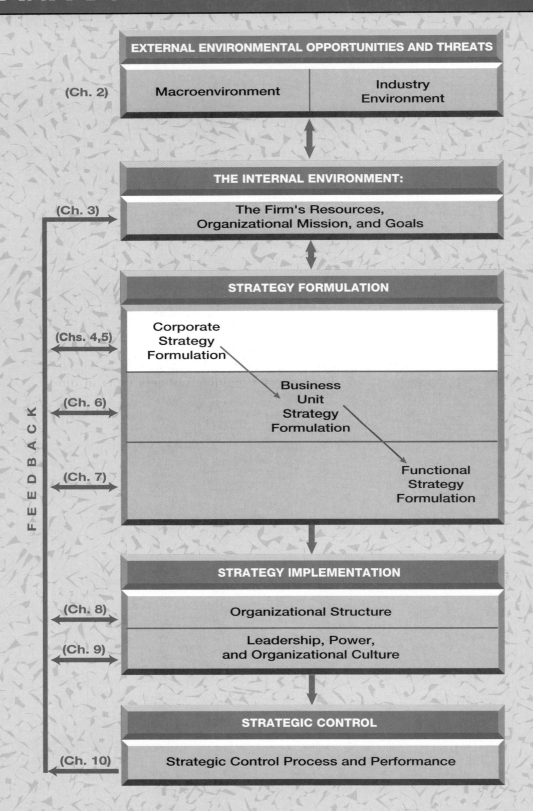

EXTERNAL ENVIRONMENTAL OPPORTUNITIES AND THREATS

(Ch. 2)

Macroenvironment	Industry Environment

THE INTERNAL ENVIRONMENT:

(Ch. 3)

The Firm's Resources, Organizational Mission, and Goals

STRATEGY FORMULATION

(Chs. 4,5) — Corporate Strategy Formulation

(Ch. 6) — Business Unit Strategy Formulation

(Ch. 7) — Functional Strategy Formulation

STRATEGY IMPLEMENTATION

(Ch. 8) — Organizational Structure

(Ch. 9) — Leadership, Power, and Organizational Culture

STRATEGIC CONTROL

(Ch. 10) — Strategic Control Process and Performance

FEEDBACK

5 Corporate Portfolio Management and Related Issues

M any firms operate multiple business units in different industries. Such firms may often use portfolio frameworks as a guide to corporate strategy formulation. This chapter will initially examine a number of corporate portfolio frameworks. Then, discussion will focus on corporate involvement in business unit operations and on the financial returns associated with corporate-level strategies. Finally, the role that top managers' motives may play in corporate acquisitions is discussed.

CORPORATE PORTFOLIO FRAMEWORKS

It is essential to note, as the various corporate portfolio frameworks are presented, that although each provides useful guidelines for the strategist, unique firm-specific conditions may require exceptions to the guidelines. This section examines select analytical frameworks that can be used in corporate management: our S.W.O.T. portfolio framework, the original and revised Boston Consulting Group frameworks, and the General Electric (GE) framework. Discussion then turns to the extent to which corporate-level top management may be involved in managing the firm's business units.

■ S.W.O.T. Portfolio Framework

Our **S.W.O.T. portfolio framework** is designed along two dimensions: the competitive status of the corporation's business units (their resource strengths and weaknesses relative to those of competitors, as discussed in chapter 3) and

113

the state of the external environment (environmental opportunities and threats). By external environment we mean the macroenvironmental or industry factors discussed in chapter 2. From this perspective, the corporation's business units can be classified as having strong, average, or weak competitive status, and the environment of the corporation's business units can contain critical threats, moderate opportunities and threats, or abundant opportunities. The resultant matrix, showing the competitive status of the corporation's business units on the horizontal axis and the state of the environment on the vertical axis, is presented in Figure 5.1.

Recall that corporate, business unit, and functional strategies are intertwined. Hence, the strengths and weaknesses of each of these strategies can enhance or inhibit the organization's overall effectiveness. For instance, lower costs may be attained at the corporate level through scope economies, as discussed in the preceding chapter. Then the business unit level may further reduce costs by adopting its own low-cost strategy, discussed in the following chapter, and by adopting appropriate functional strategies (e.g., mass purchasing and mass production), as presented in chapter 7. The strengths or weaknesses of strategies at any level, then, will affect the organization's overall performance. Thus, while the discussion that follows emphasizes the corporation's business units, it should be evident that the firm's strengths and weaknesses evolve collectively from corporate, business unit, and functional levels.

Understanding of the matrix in Figure 5.1 can be enhanced by looking at some examples. A corporation's business unit may be categorized to be in compartment A, for instance, if it has impressive competitive strengths with few weaknesses and competes in an environment with abundant opportunities and relatively few threats. On the other hand, a corporation's business unit may be categorized to be in compartment F if it has average competitive strengths and weaknesses and operates in an environment full of critical threats and few opportunities. And a firm's business unit that is categorized to be in compartment H possesses more weaknesses than strengths and does business in an environment with moderate opportunities and threats.

Our S.W.O.T. portfolio framework offers strategy guidelines for the corporation's business units that are categorized to be in any one of the framework's nine compartments. Each of these compartments will now be examined.

Compartment A

Compartment A is obviously a desirable category. The corporation's business units that are evaluated to be in this compartment possess impressive competitive strengths and few weaknesses and operate in an environment with abundant opportunities and few significant threats. In such a setting, a number of strategies may be appropriate. Internal growth can be an effective strategy if top management believes that it would best preserve the business unit's organizational culture, efficiency, quality, and image. Vertical integration of related businesses may be more suitable for business units that wish to assure themselves of predictable sources of supply or of outlets for their outputs, especially in stable environments.[1] This strategy may also be appropriate if management feels that it will help reduce systemwide costs or improve output innovations. Mergers or horizontal integration may be appropriate, provided antitrust laws do not impede those strategies, if the business unit desires a larger market share and increased competitive clout.

Figure 5.1

ask about

S.W.O.T. Portfolio Framework

Competitive Status of the Corporation's Business Units

	Strong	Average	Weak
Abundant environmental opportunities	**Compartment A** 1. Internal growth 2. Vertical integration of related businesses 3. Mergers 4. Horizontal integration	**Compartment D** 1. Mergers 2. Horizontal integration 3. Strategic alliances	**Compartment G** 1. Turnaround 2. Divestment
Moderate environmental opportunities and threats	**Compartment B** 1. Vertical integration of related businesses 2. Horizontal related diversification	**Compartment E** 1. Stability 2. Mergers 3. Horizontal integration 4. Strategic alliances 5. Divestment	**Compartment H** 1. Turnaround 2. Divestment
Critical environmental threats	**Compartment C** 1. Horizontal related diversification 2. Horizontal unrelated diversification (conglomerate) 3. Vertical integration of unrelated businesses 4. Divestment	**Compartment F** 1. Divestment 2. Horizontal related diversification 3. Horizontal unrelated diversification 4. Stability	**Compartment I** 1. Liquidation

State of the External Environment

Corporate growth need not always result in an expanding business unit. An alternative method is to divide the business unit into smaller, semiautonomous business units, with each concentrating on a growing, but narrower, market. For example, Johnson & Johnson (J&J) divides any of its business units that grow beyond what top management believes is optimal. As a result, J&J now has 166 highly decentralized businesses, each concentrating on a specific market for health and personal care products. Because the optimal size for a J&J business unit differs from one market to another, J&J's businesses range in size from $100,000 in annual sales to $1 billion.[2]

Compartment B

The corporation's business units that possess significant competitive strengths and that operate in environments with moderate opportunities and threats may find that a vertical integration of related businesses or horizontal related diversification strategy is appropriate. Because the environment is only moderately promising, a compartment B firm may enhance its success by diversifying into a related industry that has better prospects.

Consider PepsiCo as an example. The soft-drink industry at one time presented only moderate opportunities. Although this industry has reasonable growth prospects, particularly outside the United States, this opportunity was dampened by the immense competitive threat posed by Coca-Cola. By diversifying into a related industry, fast-food restaurants, PepsiCo reduced its

Gaylord Entertainment's TNN and CMT: Operating in Compartment B

Gaylord Entertainment—once primarily entrenched in the publishing industry—presently operates businesses in entertainment, cable television, and broadcasting, including Opryland U. S.A. Theme Park. In recent years, Gaylord's strategy of growth through related diversification has proven successful, due in part to the country music phenomenon. Gaylord's cable television business consists of TNN—The Nashville Network—and CMT—Country Music Television.

The Nashville Network, launched in 1983, is an advertiser-supported cable television network focusing on Nashville-type entertainment that is on the air eighteen hours a day and is available throughout the United States and Canada. Its programming focuses on country music entertainment, variety and talk shows, news, and sports. Popular TNN shows include Nashville Now, Crook and Chase, On Stage, Country Kitchen, and American Music Shop. Currently, TNN is the tenth-largest cable network in terms of subscribers, serving approximately 57 million subscribers (approximately 93 percent of all cable households and 61 percent of all television households in the United States).

Country Music Television was acquired in partnership with Group W Satellite Communications, a Westinghouse subsidiary. Country music's answer to MTV, CMT is a 24-hour country music video channel with approximately 20 million subscribers. Gaylord provides a satellite uplink (or alternative means of transmission) to the cable systems.

The Nashville Network and Country Music Television are performing very well as Gaylord management develops expertise in its relatively new line of business. Although competition for cable adoption is intense, few cable alternatives exist in the country/western niche. According to published reports, Gaylord is presently considering further expansion in this area. Hence, the future for this firm appears promising.

SOURCES: "Gaylord Entertainment Names E. K. Gaylord II Vice Chairman," *Dow Jones News Services,* 8 May 1996; M. Burgi, "Cable's Promised Land: Networks Discover Original Programming Can Achieve Broadcast-Quality Ratings," *Mediaweek,* 27 March 1995, pp. 26–34; R. Brown, "The Nashville Network," *Broadcasting and Cable,* 20 February 1995, pp. 34–35; B. Battle, "Gaylord CEO: We are Going to Grow," *Nashville Banner,* 16 April 1994, p. A1; A. Sharpe, "Country Music Finds New Fans and a Firm in Nashville Prospers," *Wall Street Journal,* 19 January 1994, pp. A1, A8; "Opryland Music Has Fertile Roots," *Nashville Banner,* 26 June 1993; P. Stark, "Country Ratings Streak Ends as Format Reaches Plateau," *Billboard,* 15 June 1993, pp. 87–89; D. A. Fox, "Gaylord is Stretching Its Muscles," *Tennessean,* 30 May 1993, p. A1.

dependence on the soft-drink industry. Simultaneously, PepsiCo used its core competence in marketing to expand its fast-food business units. This growth, in turn, helped protect an increasing amount of PepsiCo's soft-drink sales, because Taco Bell, KFC, and Pizza Hut served only soft drinks produced by PepsiCo. (Recall that the preceding chapter suggested that PepsiCo's purchase of fast-food businesses can be considered both horizontal related diversification and vertical integration of related businesses.) Subsequently, PepsiCo spun-off these businesses to again concentrate on soft drinks.

Compartment C

A business unit in compartment C has distinct competitive strengths but faces critical environmental threats. For some firms, the appropriate strategy may be to diversify into more attractive related industries. Some tobacco firms, for instance, perceive that increasing social and political-legal threats reduce their opportunities for profit and growth. Philip Morris, as one example, has diversified into such related businesses as brewing (Miller) and consumer foods (Kraft General Foods). Such diversification has benefited from Philip Morris's core competence in consumer marketing.

In other cases, the desirable strategy could be to diversify horizontally into unrelated industries, or, by vertical integration of unrelated businesses, to enter into more promising opportunities, or to adopt a divestment strategy. Philip Morris's purchase of a packaging company for its tobacco and food products represents a vertical integration of unrelated businesses. On the other hand, Primerica at one time manufactured containers and packaging materials. Declining opportunities in those industries caused Primerica to diversify horizontally into such unrelated businesses as financial services and specialty retailing. Eventually, it divested itself entirely of its manufacturing businesses and became heavily involved in service industries.

Compartment D

In compartment D, abundant opportunities face a business unit that has average competitive strengths and weaknesses. In such a situation, management generally prefers to remain in the industry, because of its rich opportunities, but attempts to improve the business unit's competitive strengths.

Moderate competitive strength can take either of two forms: The business unit may have only moderate core competencies, or its strengths may be offset by equivalent weaknesses. In either case, a firm can try to improve its competitive prospects by adopting strategies—merger, horizontal integration, and/or strategic alliance—that link the business unit to organizations that can provide synergistic core competencies. For example, both Nike and Reebok are considered to possess strengths in design and marketing but weaknesses in manufacturing. Consequently, both have forged strategic alliances with low-cost, high-quality manufacturers in Southeast Asia.[3]

Compartment E

Compartment E business units—those with average strengths and weaknesses that face environments with moderate opportunities and threats—have several strategic alternatives available to them. If the business is reasonably profitable, it may elect a stability strategy. Alternatively, it may attempt to improve its competitive position through a strategy of merger, horizontal integration, or strategic alliance. Should the business unit not become more competitive, the firm might consider divestment, which is also an option for firms that cannot find compatible partners for a merger, horizontal integration, or strategic alliance. Some leading corporations, such as General Electric, for example, divest any business unit that does not become one of the top two performers in its industry within a reasonable period of time.

Compartment F

Although a business unit in compartment F has moderate competitive strengths, it faces critical environmental threats. If the threats are anticipated to be relatively permanent, divestment may be an appropriate strategy for the

---

S T R A T E G I C   I N S I G H T

Delta Air Lines: Operating in Compartment E

By many standards, Delta Air Lines, Inc.'s airline business has been one of the most successful airlines since the deregulation process began in 1978. During the 1980s, the number of passengers served by the airline increased twentyfold while revenues quadrupled to approximately $13 billion. Some possible explanations for Delta's success include its informal corporate culture, its strong service orientation, and the high commitment to its employees.

But regardless of its historically solid competitive position, not all is currently well at Atlanta-based Delta. The carrier lost more than $1.2 billion over three years in the early 1990s. Low-cost airlines such as Southwest have chipped away at Delta's business for a decade. Delta's pilots earn about $100,000 more per year than do pilots at some of the upstart low-cost airlines.

In an effort to become more cost-competitive by making the carrier more efficient, CEO Ronald W. Allen is slashing everything from advertising budgets to fuel expenses. Delta plans to reduce its work force by 20 percent or 15,000, cut annual labor costs by $640 million, and trim marketing expenses by $400 million by the late 1990s. Allen projects that with these changes, Delta will become profitable.

Allen expects the periodic price competition to continue into the foreseeable future. He believes that the airline can become cost-competitive. Although some analysts are skeptical about Delta's prospects, most agree that Delta will improve and survive as a carrier into the twenty-first century.

SOURCES: "U. S. Okays Delta Air Lines, Korean Air Code-Sharing Pact," *Dow Jones Business News*, 29 May 1996; A. Bryant, "Three Airlines Chart Austerity Course; Delta and Two Small Carriers Are Thriving by Cutting Costs," *New York Times*, 14 June 1995, p. D1; "Delta Achieves Strong Results in Cost-Cutting," *New York Times*, 28 July 1995, p. C4; D. Greising, P. Dwyer, and W. Zellner, "A Destination, But No Flight Plan," *Business Week*, 16 May 1994, pp. 74–75; P. M. Swiercz, "Delta Airlines, Inc.: Taking the Family Global," in P. Wright, J. A. Parnell, and M. Kroll (eds.), *1993 Edition of Cases in Strategic Management* (Boston: Allyn & Bacon, 1993), pp. 53–68.

---

firm because transforming a business unit into a top performer is extremely challenging in the face of critical threats. Alternatively, a firm may diversify out of the present industry into horizontally related or unrelated industries with more promising opportunities. If the environmental threats are deemed temporary, a stability strategy can be appropriate. For instance, some financial institutions with savings and loan businesses chose stability in the latter 1980s and early 1990s because the environmental threats of economic recession and intense competition were expected to be relatively short-lived.

Compartment G

A turnaround strategy is particularly appropriate for business units in compartment G. They have few strengths and many weaknesses and operate in an environment with plentiful opportunities. The firm might eliminate or outsource any activities in which it lacks competence. Simultaneously, management should attempt to cultivate the business unit's potential strengths. In some cases, granting the business unit significant autonomy from the corporate bureaucracy can unleash latent strengths.

Another alternative is to divest the business through a spin-off. For example, when Lexmark was a business unit of giant IBM, its needs were often neglected. Its printer and typewriter business was represented by IBM salespeople who were more interested in selling computers that brought higher sales commissions; typewriters and printer sales were no more than afterthoughts. Eventually, Lexmark was spun off by IBM. After eliminating 2,000 jobs, Lexmark's management divided the business into small, semiautonomous units, with each concentrating on one product line such as printers, keyboards, printer supplies, or typewriters. Operating procedures were also modified. For instance, Lexmark's CEO, who had been the business unit's top manager when it was under IBM's centralized control, indicated that, whereas IBM had encouraged managers to acquire large budgets and then spend every cent of them, Lexmark would reward managers for coming in under budget.[4]

Divestment can be an appropriate strategy for firms operating business units in compartment G for another reason. Because the environment's opportunities are ample, a business already in the industry can be attractive to other firms desiring to enter the industry on the belief that the business can be turned around. The proceeds from the divestment can be used to strengthen the corporation's remaining business units. Although other strategies—such as mergers, horizontal integration, and strategic alliance—are possible, they are unlikely choices. Other firms are rarely desirous of becoming partners with a business unit that has critical weaknesses.

Compartment H

A business unit in compartment H has critical competitive weaknesses and faces moderate environmental opportunities. In this case, the turnaround and divestment strategies seem most appropriate, although they are more challenging to implement than in compartment G, where opportunities are more prevalent. A turnaround would take more time and effort, and divestment would be more difficult because fewer potential buyers are interested in acquiring a business in a less-promising industry. Even if divestment were possible, the proceeds from the business's sale would be relatively small.

Compartment I

The worst case scenario exists for a business unit in compartment I, where the business's critical weaknesses are overwhelmed by extreme environmental threats. In such situations, liquidation is usually the most feasible strategy. Neither a turnaround nor a divestment strategy is practicable because the business's precarious position provides a poor foundation for either strengthening its operations or attracting outsiders.

Because liquidation is distasteful to virtually all of the firm's stakeholders, top management may delay in closing the business. Unfortunately, a delay can jeopardize the health of the entire corporation because the profits of some business units must be used to offset the losses of the business unit that should already have been liquidated. If overall losses exceed profits, the entire firm may have to declare bankruptcy. With some forms of bankruptcy, a firm can continue operating under the supervision of the courts in return for the settlement of the firm's financial obligations.

LTV Corporation is an example of such a firm. For years, its defense and aerospace business subsidized its unprofitable steel business. By 1986, its corporate operating loss amounted to $3 billion. In declaring bankruptcy, LTV's top management indicated that the corporation would liquidate its steel business to concentrate on its more attractive defense and aerospace business.[5]

The following three sections present other portfolio frameworks—two developed by the Boston Consulting Group and one by General Electric.

■ Original BCG Framework

The framework discussed in this section was developed in 1967 by the Boston Consulting Group (BCG), a firm that specializes in strategic planning. Originated by Alan J. Zakon of BCG and William W. Wommack of Mead Corporation, the framework has since been elaborated upon by Barry Hedley, a director of BCG.

The **original BCG framework** is illustrated by the matrix shown in Figure 5.2. The market's rate of growth is indicated on the vertical axis, and the firm's share of the market is indicated on the horizontal axis. Each of the circles represents a business unit. The size of the circle reflects the business unit's annual sales, the horizontal position of the circle indicates its market share, and its vertical position depicts the growth rate of the market in which it competes. For instance, the circle in the lower left corner of the matrix symbolizes a business unit with relatively large sales and a very high share of its market. Its market, however, is stagnant, exhibiting little growth. Using this framework, management can categorize each of its different businesses as stars, question marks, cash cows, or dogs, depending upon each business unit's relative market share and the growth rate of its market.[6]

Figure 5.2   **The Original BCG Framework**

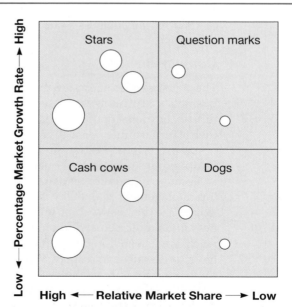

Source: Reprinted from *Long Range Planning*, Vol. 10, B. Hedley, "Strategy and the 'Business Portfolio,'" pp. 9–15, Copyright (1977), with permission from Pergamon Press Ltd., Headington Hill Hall, Oxford OX3 OBW, UK.

A star is a business unit that has a large share of a high-growth market (one with an annual growth rate of 10 percent or more). Although stars are profitable businesses, they usually must consume considerable cash to continue their growth and to fight off the numerous competitors that are attracted to fast-growing markets. Question marks are business units with low shares of rapidly growing markets. Many question marks are new businesses just entering the market. If they are able to grow and become market leaders, they evolve into stars; but if they are unable eventually to command a significant market share despite heavy financial support from corporate headquarters, they will usually be divested or liquidated.

Turning to the lower half of the matrix, a cash cow is a business unit that has a large share of a slow-growth market (one growing at an annual rate of less than 10 percent). Cash cows are normally highly profitable because they often dominate a market that does not attract many new entrants. Because they are so well established, they need not spend vast resources for advertising, product promotions, or consumer rebates. The excess cash that they generate can be used by the corporation to support its stars and question marks. Finally, dogs are business units that have small market shares in slow-growth (or even declining) industries. Dogs are generally marginal businesses that incur either losses or small profits.

Ideally, a corporation should have mostly stars and cash cows, some question marks (because they represent the future of the corporation), and few, if any, dogs. To attain this ideal, corporate-level managers can use any of the four alternative strategies described in the following paragraphs.

STRATEGIC INSIGHT

Neglecting a Cash Cow at Diamond International

From the perspective of the original BCG portfolio framework, U. S. Playing Card was a cash cow for its parent company, Diamond International. Although cash cows do not require vast expenditures for advertising or product promotions, they must still be managed carefully so that they will generate as much excess cash as possible to invest in stars and promising question marks. But Diamond International neglected its U. S. Playing Card subsidiary by allowing the number of highly paid unionized employees to grow without corresponding increases in productivity and by failing to maintain and replace aging machinery and equipment.

Over time, the cash cow became a dog and was divested by Diamond International. The business, however, continued to perform poorly until it was purchased in 1986 by Ronald Rule. Rule engaged in a successful turnaround through such actions as cutting labor costs by one-third, replacing the company's union labor with nonunion employees, and purchasing state-of-the-art machinery and equipment. Today, U. S. Playing Card produces 220,000 decks of cards daily and holds a 70 percent share of the U. S. market and a worldwide market share of 45 percent. Its annual sales amount to $83 million.

U. S. Playing Card is now owned by the Jesup Group of Stamford, Connecticut, although Rule remains its CEO. It accounts for over a quarter of Jesup's annual revenues and serves as a cash cow for some of Jesup's other product lines: laminated plastics, plastic materials and resins, adhesives and sealants, and synthetic rubber.

Build Market Share

One of the strategies is to build market share. To accomplish this end, managers must identify promising business units that currently fall into the question mark category. Management then attempts to transform these businesses into stars. This process of increasing market share may involve significant price reductions, even if that means incurring losses or marginal profitability in the short run. The underlying assumption of this strategy is that once market share leadership is attained, profitability will follow.

Hold Market Share

Another strategy is to hold market share. In this situation, cash cows are managed so as to maintain their market shares, rather than to increase them. Holding a large market share generates more cash than building market share does. Hence, the cash contributed by the cash cows can be used to support stars and selected question marks.

Harvest

Harvesting means milking as much short-term cash from a business as possible, usually while allowing its market share to decline. The cash gained from this strategy is also used to support stars and selected question marks. The businesses harvested are usually dogs, question marks that show little promise of growth, and perhaps some weak cash cows.

Divest

Divesting a business unit usually provides some cash to the corporation (from the sale) and stems the cash outflow that would have been spent on the business in the future. As dogs and less promising question marks are divested, the cash provided is reallocated to stars and to question marks with the potential to become stars.

As is evident, the BCG framework heavily emphasizes the importance of market share leadership. Cash cows and stars are market share leaders. Some question marks are cultivated to become leaders as well, but less promising question marks and dogs are usually targeted either for harvesting or divestiture. This emphasis on market share has been heavily criticized, leading the BCG to reformulate its portfolio framework.

■ Revised BCG Framework

The **revised BCG framework** is illustrated in Figure 5.3. In place of the star, question mark, cash cow, and dog categories are volume, specialization, fragmented, and stalemate business units. Only the volume business is targeted for market share leadership. The volume business generates high profitability through large market share and its accompanying economies of scale. Business units denoted by specialization, however, are those able to yield high profits even though they have a low market share. Because they have selected a market niche in which to operate, they are able to distinguish themselves from their

Figure 5.3   **The Revised BCG Framework**

Maintain and Support	Divest
Volume (emphasize market share leadership)	Stalemate (regardless of relative market share)
Specialization (emphasize maintenance of low market share)	Stalemate (regardless of relative market share)
Profitable fragmented (do not emphasize market share)	Unprofitable fragmented (regardless of relative market share)

competitors in the market. The appropriate strategies for these two types of business units, according to the BCG, are for the volume business unit to attempt to gain an even greater market share and for the specialization unit to maintain its low market share.

The next category is fragmented businesses. This term refers to business units operating in fragmented industries. A fragmented industry is one in which numerous firms, perhaps even thousands, exist. Examples include the motel, restaurant, and retail clothing industries. Fragmented industries are characterized by low barriers to entry. (By contrast, a consolidated industry, such as the U. S. automobile manufacturing industry, has high barriers to entry, and, therefore, contains only a few very large competitors.) Businesses in this category can be highly profitable—or unprofitable—regardless of their market share. A local motel or restaurant, for example, can be quite successful, as can Holiday Inn or McDonald's. So fragmented business units should be cultivated for profitability while the importance of market share is de-emphasized. The BCG recommends that profitable fragmented business units be maintained and supported and that unprofitable units be divested.

In the final category, a stalemate business is one that has low, or no, profitability because its industry offers poor prospects. Again, market share is not a consideration in this category. The recommendation for stalemate businesses is that they be divested.

These strategic recommendations are reflected in Figure 5.3. Business units shown on the left side of the figure should be maintained and supported, but those on the right side should be divested.

■ GE Framework

Another well-known framework was developed by GE with the help of McKinsey and Company, a consulting firm. As shown in Figure 5.4, the **GE framework** categorizes business units according to industry attractiveness (low, medium, or high) and business unit strength (weak, average, or strong). The ideal business unit is one that is strong relative to its competitors and operates in an industry that is attractive. Some of the criteria used to determine industry attractiveness and business strength are shown in Table 5.1.

Table 5.1   **Criteria for Determining Industry Attractiveness
                        and Business Unit Strengths**

Industry Attractiveness Criteria	*Business Unit Strength Criteria*
Annual industry growth rate	Market share
Cyclicality of the industry	Firm profitability
Historical profitability of the industry	Per-unit cost of operation
Macroenvironmental opportunities and constraints particularly relevant to the industry	Process research and development performance
Overall industry size	Product quality
Seasonality of the industry	Managerial and personnel talent
Intensity of competition	Market share growth
Industry predisposition to unionization	Operation capacity
Rate of innovation in the industry	Technological know-how
	Product research and development performance
	Brand reputation

As shown in Figure 5.4, a corporation's most successful business units fall in the top left section of the diagram, and its least successful ones are in the bottom right section. Average business units fall in between. Strategically, the corporation should divest itself of the business units in the bottom right section while supporting those in the top left area. The average business units will receive less support than those in the upper left unless they are perceived as candidates that have the potential for becoming highly profitable operations.

Figure 5.4   **The GE Framework**

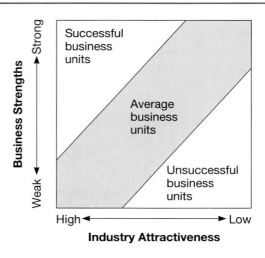

The S.W.O.T., BCG, and GE frameworks may be used by corporate-level management to evaluate each of their business units, to make strategic decisions, and to reallocate resources. Although our discussion has focused on large firms with multiple business units, some small, privately held companies are also active in a number of businesses. These frameworks may be used by their top managers to evaluate their businesses as well.

■ Corporate Involvement in Business Unit Operations

We have seen that corporations may have multiple business units in related or unrelated industries. How closely corporate-level managers become involved in the strategy formulation and operation of those business units varies from one firm to another. Historically, corporations that have diversified into unrelated businesses operate in a relatively decentralized fashion.[7] In **decentralization,** firms tend to employ small corporate staffs and allow the business unit managers to make most strategic and operating decisions. These decisions involve functional areas such as purchasing, inventory management, production, finance, research and development, and marketing. Examples of decentralized corporations are Viacom, Litton Industries, and Textron.

Alternatively, corporations whose business units are in the same industry or in related industries usually operate in a relatively centralized fashion. Under **centralization,** many major decisions affecting the business units are made at corporate headquarters, so these companies have larger corporate staffs. Examples include GE and Daimler-Benz.

Corporate involvement in business unit operations can be conceptualized as shown on the continuum below. Involvement can range from being highly centralized to being almost completely decentralized.

Centralized corporations ◄─────────► Decentralized corporations

Corporations, of course, may be found at literally any point on this continuum. Decisions regarding centralization and decentralization are not of the either-or variety. Instead, a firm's decision-making processes are termed *relatively centralized* or *relatively decentralized*. Most companies, therefore, are not located at either of the extreme ends of the continuum.

Companies that are relatively centralized make many functional decisions—such as those in purchasing, marketing, finance, and production—at the corporate level. The more commonality in those functional activities across the firm's business units, the greater the tendency is to coordinate those activities at the corporate level. Such centralized decisions can result in efficiencies and consistencies across all business units.

For instance, quantity discounts are larger if the same products are purchased at the corporate level for all business units than if each business unit purchases them separately. As another example, a corporation can borrow more funds at a lower interest rate than separate business units can. Also, central coordination can encourage business units to buy components, if possible and economically feasible, from other business units within the same corporation instead of buying them from outside the company.

Centralization, however, also incurs costs. As the organization grows, larger and larger corporate staffs are required. As the staff increases, so does the distance between top corporate management and the business units. Top managers are forced to rely increasingly on their staff for information, and they communicate downward to the business units through their staff. These processes result in obvious problems in communication and coordination and in the proliferation of bureaucratic procedures.

Decentralized corporations are able to eliminate these problems since highly decentralized firms maintain only skeletal corporate staffs. But they are seldom able to benefit from coordinated activities across their business units, since each operates as at least a semi-independent entity. Therefore, synergy may be lower in a decentralized organization than in one that is centralized.

CORPORATE STRATEGIES AND RETURNS

In the preceding chapter, we discussed the advantages and disadvantages of various growth strategies. Because most corporations adopt growth strategies of one or more types, considerable research has been conducted on the financial returns associated with these strategies. In this section, we examine the returns generated by corporate growth strategies that involve acquisitions (The following chapter will look at the returns associated with businesses that confine their activities to a single industry.)

Despite the volume of research on this topic, little consensus has been reached. Although numerous studies have concluded that the stockholders of target businesses (those being acquired) benefit financially from the takeover,[8] to what extent the acquiring firms' shareholders benefit is not clear.

One reason for this lack of clarity may be that if competitive rivalry erupts among several acquirers for bidding on a target company, the price of the target company may rise until all above normal profits are eliminated for the corporation that ultimately wins the bidding war. On the other hand, when private and unique synergistic potentials exist between an acquirer and a target company, other bidders may not enter into a competitive bidding for the target company.[9] Thus, in this situation, above normal profits may accrue to the acquiring corporation. Whether competitive bidding occurs or not may explain why the evidence is not clear on the benefits of acquisitions to the shareholders of the acquiring firms.

Another reason for lack of clarity might be that sources of synergy may change over time. What will yield a positive synergy between a bidder and a target company at one point in time may yield a negative synergy at another point in time.[10] Yet another reason may hinge on whether stock ownership of an acquiring corporation is concentrated or diffused.[11] In a diffusely held firm, no one shareholder may find it worthwhile to monitor the corporate executives to make sure that they manage the target company efficiently. Moreover, whether the acquisition is made with cash or stock (or a combination) may influence returns given that cash offerings normally have more positive impacts in financial markets.[12]

Adding a final note to the confusion is the different theoretical paradigms that drive empirical investigations. This is discussed next.

▪ Acquisitions Are Not Beneficial

In microeconomics—as well as in one of its research streams, industrial organization—and in select financial theories, it is suggested that acquisitions do not benefit the shareholders of acquiring firms. According to the microeconomics perspective, markets are characterized by perfect competition. (A perfectly competitive market contains a large number of firms, none of which can affect price or supply on its own; each firm has complete knowledge of the activities of all the other firms, including their profitability; there are many customers, none of whom can affect price on their own; all customers have complete knowledge of all products and prices; all of the industry's products are homogeneous; there are many identical potential acquiring firms, none of which on its own can affect the share price of target companies; all shareholders possess perfect information; and no shareholder alone can affect stock prices.) If there were such a setting, all of the firms in a single industry would be identical in their attributes and strategies because, as soon as one attempted to differentiate its product or lower its price to attract more customers, the others would follow suit.

In such a setting, acquisitions could offer only above average returns to the shareholders of the target companies. The acquiring firm's stockholders would receive only "normal returns" because, when the acquiring firm made a bid for another company, its competitors would also recognize the value of the target company and, hence, would engage in competitive bidding to drive up the price of the target company's stock until only normal returns could be realized. Within this context, firms should not make acquisitions because such takeovers will not benefit the shareholders of the acquiring firms. Scholars influenced by this perspective have generally found empirical support for their theories.

In traditional organization theory it is pointed out that the external environment determines the firm's strategy and returns. According to this theory, industry environments differ in their potential returns.[13] Firms that operate business units in favorably industry environments will have higher returns than those operating in unfavorable industry environments.

Select financial theories also emphasize the financial market environment rather than the firm. Because these theories assume that markets are competitive, acquiring attractive target companies would be costly. Therefore, the acquisition strategies of potential acquiring firms would be identical, and the market would set the price of any acquisition. Under such circumstances, these theories do not necessarily recommend acquisitions because they are not thought to be particularly beneficial to the acquiring firms' shareholders.

All of these streams of thought attribute importance to environmental or external factors rather than to the relative strategic strengths and weaknesses of the corporation and its business units. In summary, because acquisitions are viewed as identical strategies that yield only normal returns in competitive markets, scholars in these areas do not consider acquisitions to be advantageous to the shareholders of acquiring firms.

■ Acquisitions May Be Beneficial

Advocates of contingency theory and of resource-based theory suggest that acquisitions may benefit the acquiring firms' shareholders. Contingency theorists argue that returns are influenced not only by the environment but also by the strategic fit between the firms' business units and their environments. This school of thought more realistically views markets as imperfectly competitive (markets in which individual suppliers and/or customers can influence price or supply, where firms do not have complete knowledge of all products and prices, where products are differentiated, and where potential acquiring firms may benefit differentially from purchasing a target company so that they would submit dissimilar bids for the same company). Under this scenario, corporations may pursue different acquisition strategies and, hence, would earn different returns.

Implicit in contingency theory is the assumption that related acquisitions may create shareholder value. Related acquisitions are those in which the acquiring and target firms are in related industries and have similar core competencies (such as both in research and development) or complementary core competencies (such as one in manufacturing and one in marketing). The results of research on acquisitions, relevant to this field of thought, are mixed. Some studies show that related acquisitions may be associated with relatively high returns to the acquiring firm's stockholders.[14] Other studies, however, have questioned the value of relatedness in acquisitions. Some have found no significant differences in the returns to the acquiring firm's shareholders whether the acquisition was related or unrelated. Others have found that unrelated acquisitions are associated with higher returns to the acquiring firm's owners than are related acquisitions.[15]

According to advocates of resource-based theory, although the environmental opportunities and threats do matter, they are not the prime influences on an organization's performance, because they change so frequently. A more stable basis for developing strategy would be the firm's unique attributes or strengths. Resource-based theory, therefore, gives less emphasis to the externally imposed bounded opportunities for the firm than does the previously discussed contingency theory. Hence, from this perspective, the firm can behave in a highly proactive fashion. Similar to contingency theory, this school of thought also views markets as imperfectly competitive.

Implicit in resource-based theory is the assumption that related acquisitions might create shareholder value due to the synergies created by similar or complementary core competencies. Although few empirical investigations are based strictly on resource-based theory, the contention that synergies are possible due to similarities or complementarities in core competencies does have empirical support.[16]

So we have seen that, although the stockholders of target companies generally benefit from acquisitions, the evidence is mixed on the extent to which the shareholders of acquiring firms benefit. The question arises, therefore, as to why corporations continue to acquire other businesses in the face of this mixed evidence. Some researchers have argued that top managers may be motivated to acquire other companies because of certain benefits that may accrue to themselves, but not necessarily to the firm's owners.

MANAGERS' MOTIVES FOR ACQUISITIONS

Although, ideally, the interests of top management and the firm's owners should be congruent, they often are not.[17] In fact, according to numerous studies, the compensation of top-level managers appears unrelated to the financial success of their organizations.[18] Since their compensation often is not closely tied to bottom line results, top managers may select corporate strategies that could enrich them without necessarily benefiting their stockholders. This potential for conflict of interest is termed an **agency problem**—that is, a situation in which the owners' agents, the corporation's top managers, fail to act in the best interests of the owners.

Agency problems may be particularly prevalent in acquisition situations. Since an acquisition immediately increases the size of the acquiring firm and since higher compensation for top management can be related to the size of the firm,[19] top managers may well be encouraged to acquire other companies. However, increased firm size is not always beneficial to shareholders. Acquisitions often involve taking on significant amounts of debt to finance the purchase, which can, at least for several years, depress profits. Depressed profits generally translate into lower stock prices and sometimes even reduced dividends.

Additionally, acquisitions of companies in other industries may also benefit the acquiring firm's top management but not its stockholders. Diversification may reduce the risk that top executives will lose their jobs[20] because it reduces the firm's overall risk by spreading risk across more than one industry. But, as suggested earlier, shareholders can better reduce their financial risk by diversifying their own investments (through buying stocks in companies in different industries or purchasing mutual funds) rather than by having top management do it for them.

SUMMARY

Because managing several businesses concurrently is quite complex, a number of corporate portfolio frameworks are available to assist top managers. The S.W.O.T. portfolio framework helps corporate-level managers assess the strengths and weaknesses of each of their business units in light of the opportunities and threats presented by the business unit's environment. Based upon the relative match between the environment and the business unit, this framework suggests which corporate-level strategy or strategies are appropriate for each of the firm's business units.

Other frameworks, by the Boston Consulting Group and by General Electric, can assist corporate-level managers to evaluate the performance of each of their business units, to make strategic decisions for each unit, and to reallocate resources from one unit to another.

Corporate-level managers must decide on the extent to which they will be involved in strategic and operational decision making at the business unit level. Usually, corporations that have diversified into related businesses remain fairly centralized, whereas conglomerates operate in a relatively decentralized fashion.

Because of the prevalence of growth strategies, considerable research has been conducted on the financial returns associated with these strategies. To date, studies indicate that, in general, the stockholders of target businesses benefit financially from the takeover, but the extent to which shareholders of the acquiring firm benefit is not entirely clear. In some cases, acquisitions appear to yield no benefits, whereas in other cases, they do. Yet, even when takeovers do not benefit the acquiring firm's shareholders, top managers are often encouraged to acquire other firms because, by so doing, they can reduce the risk of losing their jobs while they increase their compensation.

TAKE IT TO THE NET

We invite you to visit the Wright page on the Prentice Hall Web site at:

http://www.prenhall.com/wright

for this chapter's World Wide Web exercise.

KEY CONCEPTS

Agency problem   A situation in which a corporation's top managers (who serve as the agents of the firm's owners, the stockholders) fail to act in the best interests of the owners.

BCG portfolio framework (original)   A corporate portfolio framework developed by the Boston Consulting Group that categorizes a firm's business units by the market share that they hold and the growth rate of their respective markets.

BCG portfolio framework (revised)   The more recent framework developed by the Boston Consulting Group that categorizes a firm's business units as volume (generates high profitability through large market share), specialization (yields high profits by operating in a market niche), fragmented (operates in a fragmented industry in which market share is unrelated to profitability), and stalemate (incurs low or no profits because its industry offers poor prospects).

Centralization   An organizational decision-making process in which most strategic and operating decisions are made by managers at the top of the organization structure (at corporate headquarters).

Decentralization   An organizational decision-making process in which most strategic and operating decisions are made by managers at the business unit level.

GE portfolio framework   A corporate portfolio framework developed by General Electric Company that categorizes a corporation's business units according to industry attractiveness and business unit strength.

S.W.O.T. portfolio framework   Our corporate portfolio framework that categorizes each of a corporation's business units according to its strengths and weaknesses and its environment's opportunities and threats. It goes on to provide guidelines as to which corporate strategies may be appropriate under particular situations.

DISCUSSION QUESTIONS

1. Explain the purpose of corporate portfolio framework analysis.

2. Discuss how the S.W.O.T. portfolio framework can help corporate-level managers develop strategies for multiple business units.

3. Which corporate-level strategies are most viable for a business unit operating in compartment E in the S.W.O.T. portfolio framework? Under what circumstances might each of these strategies be appropriate? Which ones would you recommend for a corporation of your own choosing and its business units?

4. Which corporate-level strategies are most viable for a business unit operating in compartment G of the S.W.O.T. portfolio framework? Under what circumstances might each of these strategies be appropriate?

5. Compare and contrast the S.W.O.T. portfolio framework with the original BCG portfolio framework.

6. What are the differences and similarities between the original and revised BCG frameworks?

7. Explain the differences and similarities between the original BCG framework and the GE framework.

8. What types of organizations are likely to operate in a relatively centralized (versus a relatively decentralized) fashion? Why?

9. When one firm acquires another, which group of stockholders—those of the acquiring firm or those of the target firm—is more likely to benefit financially? Why?

10. Even though the evidence is mixed on the extent to which the stockholders of acquiring firms benefit from acquisitions, the top managers of many firms continue to engage in acquisitions. Why?

STRATEGIC MANAGEMENT EXERCISES

1. Choose a real corporation that has multiple business units (either related or unrelated). Attempt to place each of the firm's business units into the appropriate compartment (A, B, C, etc.) in the S.W.O.T. portfolio framework.

2. Now place each business unit (Exercise 1) into the appropriate category in the original BCG framework (star, cash cow, question mark, or dog).

3. Place each of the business units (Exercise 1) into the appropriate category in the revised BCG portfolio framework (volume, specialization, fragmented, or stalemate).

4. Place each of the business units (Exercise 1) into the appropriate category in the GE portfolio framework (successful, average, or unsuccessful).

5. Now take one of these business units (Exercise 1) and compare the strategies that are recommended for it by the S.W.O.T. framework, the

original BCG framework, the revised BCG framework, and the GE framework. Discuss why different frameworks have recommended different strategies for the same business unit (if they have).

NOTES

1. R. A. D'Aveni and A. Y. Ilinitch, "Complex Patterns of Vertical Integration in the Forest Products Industry: Systematic and Bankruptcy Risks," *Strategic Management Journal* 35 (1992), 596–625.

2. B. Dumaine, "Is Big Still Good?" *Fortune*, 20 April 1992, p. 51.

3. Ibid., p. 53.

4. P. B. Carroll, "Story of an IBM Unit That Split Off Shows Difficulties of Change," *Wall Street Journal*, 23 July 1992; Dumaine, "Is Big Still Good?" p. 56.

5. M. Schroeder and A. Bernstein, "A Brawl with Labor Could Block LTV's Rebirth," *Business Week*, 16 March 1992, p. 40.

6. B. Hedley, "Strategy and the Business Portfolio," *Long Range Planning*, 10, no. 2 (1977): 9–14.

7. D. K. Datta and J. H. Grant, "Relationships Between Type of Acquisition, the Autonomy Given to the Acquired Firm, and Acquisition Success: An Empirical Analysis," *Journal of Management* 16 (1990): 29–44.

8. J. B. Barney, "Returns to Bidding Firms in Mergers and Acquisitions: Reconsidering the Relatedness Hypothesis," *Strategic Management Journal* 9 (1988): 71–78.

9. Ibid.

10. R. Davis and L. G. Thomas, "Direct Estimation of Synergy: A New Approach to the Diversity-Performance Debate," *Management Science* 39 (1993): 1334–1346; S. Huddart, "The Effect of a Large Shareholder on Corporate Value," *Management Science* 39 (1993): 1407–1421.

11. S. Huddart, "The Effect of a Large Shareholder on Corporate Value," *Management Science* 39 (1993):1407-1421.

12. O. Nodoushani, "The Legitimacy of Management," *Scandinavian Journal of Management* 9 (1993): 225–240; A. A. Lado, N. G. Boyd, and P. Wright, "A Competency-Based Model of Sustainable Competitive Advantage: Toward a Conceptual Integration," *Journal of Management* 18 (1992): 77–91; J. B. Barney, "Returns to Bidding Firms."

13. L. Everett, "Past Returns, Acquisition Strategies and Returns to Bidding Firms," unpublished manuscript, the University of Memphis, 1992; R. P. Rumelt, *Strategy, Structure, and Economic Performance* (Cambridge: Division of Research, Graduate School of Business Administration, Harvard University Press, 1974); C. K. Prahalad and R. A. Bettis, "The Dominant Logic: A New Linkage Between Diversity and Performance," *Strategic Management Journal* 7 (1986): 485–501; R. M. Grant, "On Dominant Logic, Relatedness, and the Link Between Diversity and Performance," *Strategic Management Journal* 9 (1988): 639–642; C. K. Prahalad and G. Hamel, "The Core Competence of the Corporation," *Harvard Business Review* 68, no. 3 (1990): 79–91.

14. R. A. Bettis and W. K. Hall, "Diversification Strategy, Accounting Determined Risk, and Accounting Determined Return," *Academy of Management Journal* 25 (1982): 254–264; M. Lubatkin, "Merger Strategies and Stockholder Value," *Strategic Management Journal* 8 (1987); 39–53.

15. P. T. Elgers and J. J. Clark, "Merger Types and Stockholder Returns: Additional Evidence," *Financial Management* 9 (1980): 66–72; P. Dubofsky and P. Varadarajan, "Diversification and Measures of Performance: Additional Empirical Evidence," *Academy of Management Journal* 30 (1987): 597–608.

16. J. S. Harrison, M. A. Hitt, R. E. Hoskisson, and R. D. Ireland, "Synergies and Post-Acquisition Performance: Differences versus Similarities in Resource Allocations," *Journal of Management* 17 (1991): 173–190; H. Singh and C. A. Montgomery, "Corporate Acquisition Strategies and Economic Performance," *Strategic Management Journal* 8 (1987): 377–386.

17. P. Wright, S. P. Ferris, A. Sarin, and V. Awasthi, "Impact of Corporate Insider, Blockholder, and Institutional Equity Ownership on Firm Risk Taking," *Academy of Management Journal* 39 (1996): 441–463; G. P. Baker, M. C. Jensen, and K. J. Murphy, "Compensation and Incentives: Practice vs. Theory," *Journal of Finance* 43 (1988): 593–616; M. C. Jensen and K. J. Murphy, "CEO Incentives—It's Not How Much You Pay, But How," *Harvard Business Review* 14, no. 3 (1990): 138–153.

18. Jensen and Murphy, "CEO Incentives—It's Not How Much You Pay, But How."

19. M. Kroll, P. Wright, L. Toombs, and H. Leavell, "Form of Control: A Critical Determinant of Acquisition Performance and CEO Rewards," *Strategic Management Journal*, 18 (1997): 85–96.

20. Y. Amihud and B. Lev, "Risk Reduction as a Managerial Motive for Conglomerate Mergers," *Bell Journal of Economics* 7 (Autumn 1981): 605–617.

STRATEGIC MANAGEMENT MODEL

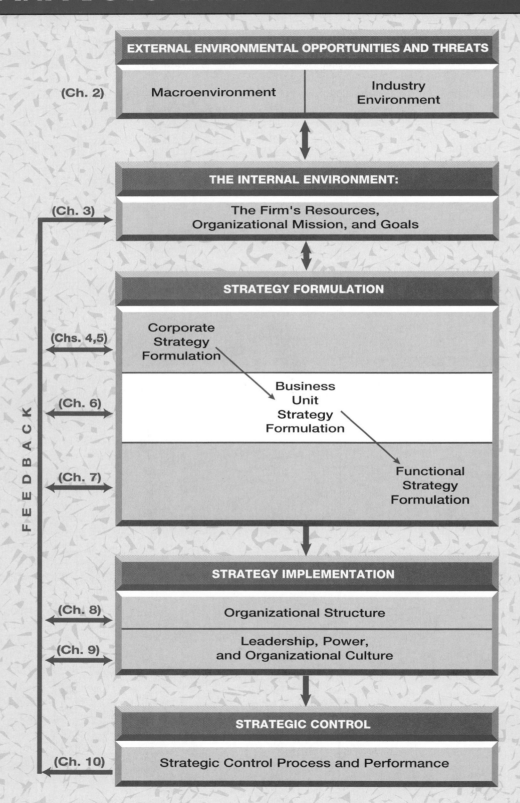

EXTERNAL ENVIRONMENTAL OPPORTUNITIES AND THREATS

(Ch. 2)

| Macroenvironment | Industry Environment |

THE INTERNAL ENVIRONMENT:

(Ch. 3)

The Firm's Resources, Organizational Mission, and Goals

STRATEGY FORMULATION

(Chs. 4,5)

Corporate Strategy Formulation

(Ch. 6)

Business Unit Strategy Formulation

(Ch. 7)

Functional Strategy Formulation

STRATEGY IMPLEMENTATION

(Ch. 8)

Organizational Structure

(Ch. 9)

Leadership, Power, and Organizational Culture

STRATEGIC CONTROL

(Ch. 10)

Strategic Control Process and Performance

FEEDBACK

6 Business Unit Strategies

W hile the strategic question at the corporate level is, In what industries or businesses should we be operating?, the appropriate question at the business unit level is, How should we compete in the chosen industry or business? A **business unit** is an organizational subsystem that has a market, a set of competitors, and a mission distinct from those of the other subsystems in the firm. The concept of the strategic business unit was pioneered by General Electric Company (GE). At GE, for example, one business unit manufactures and markets major appliances such as ranges, refrigerators, dishwashers, and clothes washers and dryers. Another business unit is responsible for producing and selling jet engines to airplane manufacturers. In total, GE contains more than 200 strategic business units. Each of these business units adopts its own strategy consistent with the organization's corporate-level strategy. Because each business unit serves a different market and competes with different companies than do the firm's other business units, it must operate with its own mission, goals, and strategy.

A single company that operates within only one industry is also considered a business unit. For instance, an independent company that builds and sells swimming pools is considered a business unit. In such an organization, corporate-level strategy and business unit strategy are the same. Hence, the focus of this chapter is on organizational entities that contain their own functional departments, such as production and sales, and operate within a single industry.

Managers of these business units can choose from a number of **generic strategies** to guide their organizations. These strategic alternatives are termed *generic* because they can be adopted by any type of business unit, whether it be a traditional manufacturing company, a high-technology firm, or a service organization. Of the seven strategies available and discussed in this chapter, three are most appropriate for small business units; the remaining four are used by large business units.

GENERIC STRATEGIES FOR SMALL BUSINESS UNITS

This section presents the generic strategies that are most appropriate for small business units: the niche–low cost, niche–differentiation, and niche–low-cost/ differentiation strategies.

▪ Niche–Low-Cost Strategy

The **niche–low-cost strategy** emphasizes keeping overall costs low while serving a narrow segment of the market. Business units that adopt this strategy produce no-frills products or services for price-sensitive customers in a market niche. The no-frills outputs of one business differ little from those of competing businesses, and market demand for these outputs is elastic.

Depending upon the prevailing industry forces, customers generally are willing to pay only low to average prices for no-frills products or services. Hence, it is essential that businesses using this strategy keep their overall costs as low as possible. Therefore, they emphasize keeping their initial investment low and holding operating costs down. For instance, these organizations will purchase from suppliers who offer the lowest prices, and they will emphasize the function of financial control. Research and development efforts will be directed at improving operational efficiency, and attempts will be made to enhance logistical and distribution efficiencies. Such businesses will de-emphasize the development of new or improved products or services that might raise costs, and advertising and promotional expenditures will be minimized.

Figure 6.1   **A Business Competing with the Niche–Low-Cost Strategy**

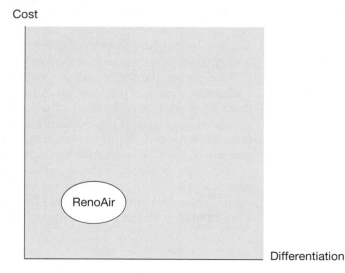

Figure 6.1 portrays the strategic position of a business unit (Reno Air) that competes using the niche–low-cost strategy. Its location on the chart reflects its strategy of low costs and minimal product/service differentiation.

Ideally, the small business unit that adopts the niche–low-cost strategy competes only where it enjoys a cost advantage relative to large low-cost competitors. For example, small short-line railroads are able to make a profit by serving shippers whose business is too insignificant for the large railroads. The small railroads do not have to hire union labor, so their wage rates are lower and they can use smaller crews than their larger rivals.[1]

Businesses that compete using the niche–low-cost strategy might deliberately avoid creating successively new outputs for fear of increasing their costs.

S T R A T E G I C   I N S I G H T

Reno Air's Niche–Low-Cost Strategy

Reno Air, Inc. is a Reno-based, publicly held short-haul passenger carrier. It offers daily jet service to destinations throughout the western United States and Canada for low fares. The company is led by airline veteran Robert Reding, president and CEO. Reno Air, which began operations in 1992, employs a niche–low-cost strategy. The company appeals to price-sensitive and time-conscious travelers, and, management places a heavy emphasis on intensive aircraft use and high employee productivity.

By keeping its costs low, Reno Air is price-competitive not only with other airlines but also with such alternative modes of transportation as personal automobiles and rental cars. For instance, Reno Air once charged $39 for a flight from Reno to Seattle, less than half the fare of its competitors. Moreover, Reno Air does not require that passengers purchase round-trip tickets. Fares are based on advance purchase only. It is not surprising that a U. S. Department of Transportation study found that 48 million new passengers took to the skies in 1996 because of low-cost airlines such as Reno Air.

Although Reno Air has adopted some of the successful strategies of Southwest Airlines, there are some fundamental strategic differences as well. Unlike Southwest, which is committed to increasing its market share nationally, Reno Air management intends to pursue controlled growth while keeping the airline fairly small and limiting flights to its twenty or so destinations, primarily located in the western United States. Further, whereas some low-cost carriers like Southwest attempt to dominate the routes they serve with more than ten daily flights, Reno Air has chosen to concentrate on few departures between cities, partly to avoid head-on competition with the large carriers.

Reno Air's niche–low-cost strategy is not without its challenges. In the airline industry, low-price firms are under constant scrutiny by the media, organized labor, and larger airlines concerning pilot training, flight hours, and safety issues. After the May 1996 ValuJet crash near Miami that killed more than 100 people, larger airlines and government officials called for federal investigations into safety standards. Safety records released after the crash revealed that small, low-cost airlines experience four times as many accidents as major airlines, although the Federal Aviation Administration's subsequent investigation of low-cost airlines revealed a spotless record for Reno Air.

SOURCES: J. Stearns, "Winning Industry Respect," *Reno Gazette-Journal*, 25 February 1996, pp. 1E, 2E; H. Robertson, "Boss Pilots Reno's Inaugural Flight to Fairbanks," *Fairbanks Daily News-Miner*, 5 April 1996, pp. B1, B2; E. deLisser, "Low-Fare Airlines Mute Their Bargain Message," *Wall Street Journal*, 22 May 1996, pp. B1, B7; "Conditions Are Ideal for Starting an Airline, and Many Are Doing It," *Wall Street Journal*, 1 April, 1996, pp. A1, A7; J. Stearns, "Federal Report Shows Reno Air with Flawless Record for Safety," *Reno Gazette-Journal*, 25 May 1996, pp. 1A, 5A; A. Bryant, "Three Airlines Chart Austerity Course; Delta and Two Small Carriers Are Thriving by Cutting Costs," *New York Times*, 14 June 1995, p. D1; G. Delaplane, "Flyin' High on Low Fares," *Reno Gazette-Journal*, 11 July 1996, pp. 1C, 6C; *Reno Air 1995 Annual Report*.

Such businesses may value technological stability in their organizations. Stable technologies enable them to produce no-frills outputs at low costs.

An important vulnerability of the niche–low-cost strategy is that intense price competition periodically occurs in markets with no-frills outputs. For instance, several years ago Laker Airways used the niche–low-cost strategy successfully by providing a first in the airline industry: no-frills, low-priced trans-Atlantic passenger service. However, the major airlines eventually responded by offering virtually identical service. The resulting price war drove Laker Airways out of business. The large competitors, because of their greater financial resources, were able to survive the shakeout even though many of them incurred financial losses.

Another important vulnerability of this strategy may be technological obsolescence. Businesses that may value technological stability, and consequently might avoid responding to new product and market opportunities, may eventually find that their products have become obsolete and are no longer desired by their customers.

■ Niche-Differentiation Strategy

The **niche-differentiation strategy** is appropriate for business units that produce highly differentiated, need-fulfilling products or services for the specialized needs of a narrow range of customers or a market niche. Because these outputs are intended to fulfill a deeper set of customer needs than either no-frills goods or differentiated goods (discussed later under the differentiation strategy), and because the market demand for these outputs tends to be inelastic, these goods or services can command high prices. Hence, cost reduction efforts are not often emphasized by businesses competing with the niche-differentiation strategy.

In fact, these businesses may be deliberately inefficient because they continuously attempt to create new product and market opportunities or to respond to them. Both actions are costly. Therefore, they may highly value technological and organizational fluidity in order to create or keep pace with new developments in their industries.

Broadly speaking, high prices are acceptable to certain customers who need product performance, prestige, safety or security. For instance, some customers may be willing to pay high prices for state-of-the-art stereo component systems that perform at a wide range of frequencies and low sound distortions (performance needs). Another cluster of customers will pay very high prices for designer clothes (prestige needs). Yet another group of industrial buyers will pay significantly more to suppliers who continuously improve the reliability of the nuts and bolts they produce to fasten the wings of an airplane to its body (safety or security needs). Figure 6.2 shows the strategic position of a business unit (Bijan) that serves the specialized needs of select customers. Note that high costs and high product/service differentiation characterize the niche-differentiation strategy.

The exclusive Beverly Hills retailer Bijan demonstrates this strategy. Bijan buys specialized, quality products only for customized needs that tend to change frequently and carries one-of-a-kind, costly merchandise. Shopping at Bijan is done only through personal appointment.

The chief vulnerability of this strategy is that competitors who also emphasize lowering of costs may in some situations be able to offer similar products

Figure 6.2 — **A Business Competing with the Niche-Differentiation Strategy**

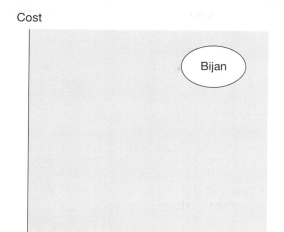

Cost

Bijan

Differentiation

at predatory prices. In fact, using niche–differentiation in conjunction with lower costs can be a particularly effective strategy for a number of, but not all, small business units in select industries.

■ Niche–Low-Cost/Differentiation Strategy

Business units that compete using the **niche–low-cost/differentiation strategy** produce highly differentiated, need-fulfilling products or services for the specialized needs of a select group of customers or of a market niche while keeping their costs low. Figure 6.3 on page 140 reflects the strategic position of a business unit (Porsche) that has adopted this strategy. Note that this business has low costs relative to Rolls-Royce, for instance, while offering a high degree of output differentiation.

How can a business simultaneously differentiate its products or services and lower its costs? The following discussion presents several ways these dual goals can be attained. These methods are listed in Table 6.1. (Note that although these routes are discussed in the context of small business units, they also pertain to large business units that adopt the low-cost–differentiation strategy, which is discussed later in this chapter.)

Table 6.1 — **Ways Organizations Can Simultaneously Differentiate Their Products/Services and Lower Their Costs**

Dedication to quality

Process innovations

Product innovations

Leverage through organizational expertise and image

Figure 6.3   **A Business (Porsche) Competing by Using the Niche–Low-Cost/Differentiation Strategy and Another Business (Rolls-Royce) Competing by Using the Niche-Differentiation Strategy**

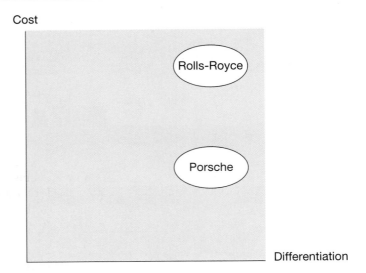

Dedication to Quality

A consistent, continual dedication to quality throughout the business not only improves outputs but also reduces costs involved in scrap, warranty, and service after the sale. **Quality** is defined as "the totality of features and characteristics of a product or service that bear on its ability to satisfy stated or implied needs."[2] Hence, a high-quality product or service conforms to a predetermined set of specifications and satisfies the needs of its users. In this sense, quality is a measure of customer satisfaction with a product over its lifetime, relative to customer satisfaction with competitors' product offerings.[3] Note that the customer's perception of quality is the key criterion. While conformance to a predetermined set of specifications is necessary, perceived quality by the buyer provides the sufficient condition.

Quality consultant Philip B. Crosby states that building quality into a product does not cost a company more, because the costs of rework, scrap, and servicing the product after the sale are reduced, and the business benefits from increased customer satisfaction and repeat sales. Simultaneous emphasis on quality and low costs is feasible not only in manufacturing but also in service businesses.[4] For example, improved information systems allow banks to offer higher-quality services to their customers at lower costs.

In a broader sense, numerous companies in recent years have adopted **total quality management (TQM)** programs. Such approaches attempt to improve product and service quality and increase customer satisfaction by modifying a company's management practices. An essential attribute of TQM programs is that the customer is the final arbiter of quality. A U. S. General Accounting Office study of twenty companies that adopted TQM programs concluded that, in most cases, quality improved, costs fell, customer satisfaction increased, and profitability grew.[5]

Process Innovations

Activities that increase the efficiency of operations and distribution are termed **process innovations.** Although these improvements are normally thought of as lowering costs, they can also enhance product or service differentiation.

> A computer manufacturer invested $20 million in a flexible assembly system. The investment made good operational sense because it paid for itself in less than a year. Strategically, the investment was even more attractive. Production time was cut by 80%, and product quality improved tenfold.[6]

In this case, costs were lowered, and the significant increase in product quality helped differentiate the product from those of the organization's competitors.

Product Innovations

Although it is common to think of **product innovations** in the context of enhancing differentiation, such improvements can also lower costs. For instance, over the years Philip Morris developed a filter cigarette and then, later, cigarettes with lower tar and nicotine levels. Although these innovations differentiated its product, they also helped lower its costs. The techniques used to produce these cigarettes (freeze drying and reconstituted tobacco sheets) allowed the company to use less tobacco per cigarette to produce a product perceived as higher quality at a dramatic reduction in per-unit costs.[7]

Leverage Through Organizational Expertise and Image

There are other ways to lower costs and heighten differentiation. For instance, small manufacturers normally suffer from a disadvantage in purchasing relative to their larger competitors, because big firms can obtain quantity discounts and often receive substantial engineering support from their suppliers. However, Porsche, a relatively small manufacturer of sports cars, has overcome this problem.

> Even though Porsche purchases small quantities of goods for its operations, it gets competitive prices and significant technical support from its suppliers. The reason is that Porsche does quite a bit of outside engineering for giants such as General Motors, Ford, Volkswagen, etc. Suppliers wish to be a part of Porsche's outside engineering developments in order to have the inside track for future orders forthcoming from those larger companies. Hence, it is to the benefit of suppliers to keep Porsche a very satisfied customer.[8]

Porsche, then, is able to use its **organizational expertise**—a business's ability to do something particularly well in comparison with its competitors—in engineering to persuade its suppliers to discount their prices, which lowers Porsche's costs. At the same time, Porsche has obtained high-quality supplier support.

Porsche has also creatively lowered its costs and heightened its differentiation in the area of promotion. Rather than spend substantial sums on mass advertising, Porsche has concentrated its efforts on public relations. Knowing that automobile enthusiasts perceive a certain image or mystique associated with Porsche cars, the company has used this leverage (organizational image) to cultivate a close relationship with such magazines as *Road and Track, Motor Trend,* and *Car and Driver.* These magazines report extensively on Porsche cars, at no cost to Porsche.

GENERIC STRATEGIES FOR LARGE BUSINESS UNITS

This section presents the generic strategies that are most appropriate for large business units. These are the low-cost, differentiation, and low-cost–differentiation strategies. Finally, in some instances, large business units may employ some combination of generic strategies. This approach is termed *multiple strategies*[9] and is discussed subsequently.

■ Low-Cost Strategy

Large businesses that compete by using a **low-cost strategy** produce no-frills products and services industrywide. That is, they address a mass market comprised of price-sensitive customers. The outputs of one business differ little from those of other businesses, and the market demand for the outputs is elastic. Consequently, companies using this strategy attempt to lower their costs in their functional areas. For instance, purchases are made from suppliers that offer quantity discounts and the lowest prices. Mass production is pursued whenever possible to lower production costs per unit. Finance plays an influential role since cost control is a high priority. Research and development efforts are directed at improving operational efficiency, and attempts are made to improve logistical and distribution efficiencies. Such businesses de-emphasize the development of new or improved products or services that may raise costs, and advertising and promotional costs are minimized. Figure 6.4 portrays the

---

Figure 6.4   **A Business (Wal-Mart) Competing by Using the Low-Cost Strategy and Another Business (Nieman-Marcus) Competing by Using the Differentiation Strategy**

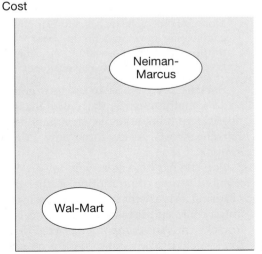

strategic position of a large business unit (Wal-Mart) that competes with the low-cost strategy. As may be seen, Wal-Mart offers low-differentiated services at low costs relative to Neiman-Marcus, for instance. Wal-Mart's purchasing costs are generally the lowest in the industry, and as in other discount department stores, its services are minimal.

Pursuing a low-cost strategy is consistent with acquiring a large share of the market.[10] A large market share allows scale economies in such areas as purchasing (quantity discounts), manufacturing (mass production), financing (lower interest rates are usually available to large firms), and distribution (mass wholesaling and merchandising).

Small business units using the niche–low-cost strategy keep their costs down through a low initial investment and low operating expenses, but large business units that pursue a low-cost strategy rely on large market shares and scale economies. For example, a small bank offering no-frills services benefits from operating in a small, unpretentious building (low initial investment). Its fixed and variable costs are relatively low because it operates with few employees and limited assets relative to large banks with head offices, bank branches, and many employees. By contrast, a large bank offering no-frills services benefits from the economies of scale that can be gained through large-volume operations. So even though both the niche–low-cost strategy and the low-cost strategy rely on keeping costs down, the means of attaining this goal are different.

Examples of companies that compete by pursuing the low-cost strategy can be found in the commodities industries, where firms produce and sell no-frills products. As a case in point, Hanson PLC's business units compete with the low-cost strategy. For instance, one of Hanson's business units—Peabody—produces coal, another one—Quantum Chemical—is a maker of polyethylene, used in packaging, and yet another one—Cavenham—is in the forest products and lumber business. A well-known historical example in the manufacturing arena is the Ford Motor Company, which used to compete using the low-cost strategy. The Model T, a no-frills automobile, was mass-produced and sold at a low price to a large and growing market.

Some manufacturers that choose to use a low-cost strategy, however, may be vulnerable to intense price competition, which drives profit margins down.[11] Under these circumstances, their ability to improve outputs, augment their products with superior services, or spend more on advertising and promotion may be severely limited.[12] If they begin to lose customers to competitors with superior products, they might, in response, lower their prices, which would put even more pressure on their profit margins. The prospect of being caught in this vicious cycle keeps many manufacturers from adopting the low-cost strategy.

Another important vulnerability of this strategy may be technological obsolescence. Manufacturers that value technological stability, and consequently avoid responding to new product and market opportunities, may eventually find that their products have become obsolete and are no longer desired by their customers.

■ Differentiation Strategy

Businesses that employ the **differentiation strategy** produce distinct products or services industrywide. That is, they address a large market with a relatively inelastic demand. Their customers are generally willing to pay average to high prices for distinct outputs. Because customers are relatively price-insensitive, businesses emphasize quality in each of their functional areas. For instance, purchases are made from suppliers that offer high-quality raw materials, parts, and components, even if the cost is relatively high. The production department emphasizes quality over cost considerations. Research and development activities focus on developing new or improved products and services, and the company's sales efforts are generously supported with advertising and promotion. Although the finance function is important, it does not dominate organizational decision making.[13] If a business suddenly finds itself faced with a competitor's superior products, it may well borrow money immediately to improve its products, even if the prevailing interest rate is high.

Businesses that compete by pursuing the differentiation strategy attempt to create new product and market opportunities or respond to them,[14] although these actions are costly. Such organizations value technological fluidity so that they may create or keep pace with new developments in their industries.[15]

Figure 6.5 portrays the strategic position of a business unit (Sony Engineering and Manufacturing, maker of televisions, video and audio hardware) that uses the differentiation strategy; note its high costs and high differentiation. Such a company requires a large market share so that it may establish a distinct image throughout the industry. To attain this end, the business may either acquire patent protection or develop strong brands that create consumer loyalty. Sony is an example of a successful differentiator.

Others have not been as fortunate and have had to change their strategy. Xerox is an example of such a business. For years, Xerox copiers were made with costly, internally produced components, and they were heavily advertised and promoted. And for years, the company was able to pass along its high costs to its customers in the form of high prices.[16] However, Xerox, like other businesses using a differentiation strategy, found itself vulnerable to new competitors with similar products at lower costs and prices.[17] As Japanese competitors began to offer high-quality copiers that were produced more efficiently and priced significantly lower than Xerox products, Xerox saw its earnings and

---

Figure 6.5   **A Business Competing by Using the Differentiation Strategy**

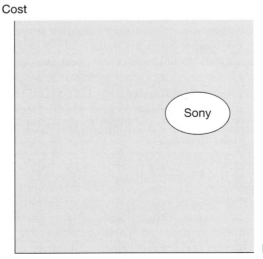

market share decline significantly. To rebound, it cut its manufacturing costs by 30 percent, reduced the time needed to develop new products by 50 percent, and greatly improved the quality of its copiers.[18] Xerox now follows the generic strategy, discussed next.

■ Low-Cost–Differentiation Strategy

Organizations that compete by pursuing a **low-cost–differentiation strategy** serve, for the most part, the same large, relatively price-insensitive market for distinct products or services that was already discussed. This strategy is illustrated in Figure 6.6. The business (Anheuser-Busch) shown in the figure maintains low costs while offering differentiation.

This particular strategy is relatively controversial. Some theorists believe that competing simultaneously with low costs and differentiation is inconsistent. That is, a business that emphasizes differentiation cannot also maintain low costs, and a business that keeps costs low cannot produce differentiated outputs.[19] However, a growing volume of theoretical and empirical work demonstrates that a dual emphasis on low costs and differentiation can result in high performance.

We believe that the low-cost–differentiation strategy is possible to attain and can be quite effective. This strategy begins with an organizational commitment to quality products or services. Thus, the organization is active technologically in order to improve output quality. By providing high-quality outputs, the business differentiates itself from its competitors. Because customers for particular products or services are drawn to high quality, the business unit that offers such quality will experience an increasing demand for its outputs. This increasing demand results in a larger market share, providing economies of scale that permit lower per-unit costs in purchasing, manufacturing, financing, research and development, and marketing. Such businesses as Wrigley, Campbell Soup,

---

Figure 6.6   **A Business Competing by Using the Low-Cost–Differentiation Strategy**

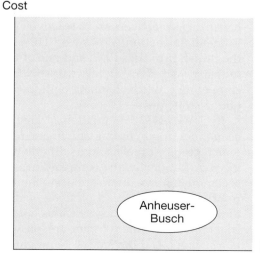

Cost

Anheuser-Busch

Differentiation

and many of the large business units of GE differentiate their outputs through high quality while they simultaneously maintain low per-unit-cost operations.

For instance, Anheuser-Busch is the largest producer of beer in the United States, with a market share of 42 percent. Because of its size, the company benefits from quantity discounts in purchasing and from other scale economies in its processing operations, its research and development activities, and its marketing functions. Even with its low costs, however, Anheuser-Busch differentiates itself through its taste and its advertising ("This Bud's for you" and "The night belongs to Michelob") and by emphasizing its high-quality raw materials ("choicest hops, rice and best barley") and its production process ("brewed by our original process"). Additionally, this business keeps pace with market developments and introduces new products periodically, with Ice Draft being a recent example.

In the service area, Federal Express used the differentiation strategy to create the overnight delivery industry two decades ago. But, as competitors entered the industry and began to duplicate Federal Express's superb service, customers began shopping for companies with lower prices. By 1992, Federal Express was rapidly adopting the low-cost–differentiation strategy to stay competitive. It shut down many of its European operations, purchased more efficient aircraft, and developed new technology and productivity methods to lower its costs. Simultaneously, it differentiated its services by offering just-in-time shipments for customers' manufacturing and distribution processes and by installing computer terminals in large customers' offices so that they could track their own shipments.[20]

■ Multiple Strategies

In some cases, large business units employ **multiple strategies,** or more than one of the strategies identified in the preceding sections. For instance, a business that uses the differentiation strategy or the low-cost–differentiation strategy may also adopt one of the niche strategies used by small companies. Figure 6.7 on page 148 portrays the strategies of two hotels: Hyatt uses both the differentiation strategy and the niche-differentiation strategy; Holiday Inn employs a combination of low-cost–differentiation and niche-differentiation strategies.

Large business units may compete with multiple strategies for either proactive reasons (attempting to modify some segment of their operations to enhance their effectiveness) or reactive reasons (reacting to environmental change to maintain their effectiveness). For example, Holiday Inn, a business unit of the British firm Bass PLC, and one of the largest companies in the hotel/motel industry with 1,600 hotels worldwide, maintains its preeminent position by competing proactively using both low-cost–differentiation and niche–differentiation strategies.

Its low-cost–differentiation strategy is revealed through its use of scale economies in purchasing and financing and its nationwide reservation system, which keeps cost low, and its differentiation through its quality rooms and services. Additionally, the company heavily advertises and promotes its quality accommodations. But to appeal to more than one customer group, this business reserves a small section of some of its inns for the more discriminating customer. In these sections, spacious suites with plush furnishings, wet bars, refrigerators, and hair dryers are provided, along with complimentary food, newspapers, and beverages. As might be expected, the price that Holiday Inn

STRATEGIC INSIGHT

The Low-Cost–Differentiation Strategy: A Giant Success at Giant Foods

Perhaps no business has used the low-cost–differentiation strategy with more success than the $3.3 billion Giant Foods supermarket chain, one of the largest retailing companies in the nation. The chain has differentiated itself by being among the first to offer gourmet meals to go, fresh pizza made in-house, and a "frequent-buyer" program that rewards customer loyalty with credits toward future shopping trips. Further differentiation efforts include offering more Asian goods in areas with substantial Vietnamese and Thai populations and stocking extensive lines of vegetarian foods in neighborhoods where many Seventh-Day Adventists live.

Yet Giant has managed to keep its costs at rock bottom through such innovations as providing its own house brands, milk, soda, ice cream, ice cubes, and plastic packaging; pioneering efficient replenishment technology that uses point-of-sale scanning data to reorder merchandise automatically when needed; employ-

ing electronic article surveillance (EAS) systems to reduce shoplifting; developing many of the shopping centers in which its stores are located; producing its own television ads; and even doing its own pest exterminating. These operations make Giant one of the nation's more versatile supermarket chains.

The chain, whose after-tax profit margins are triple the industry average, is highly competitive. When Safeway restructured, Giant responded by cutting its own prices further and by increasing its coupon offerings. When wholesale clubs invaded Giant's territory, the supermarket initiated its own "club pack" program for health and beauty care items, dog food, laundry detergents, frozen foods, and other grocery items.

Few cost-saving possibilities are overlooked. When its shopping center construction crews are not building the chain's own centers, they are earning more than $20 million annually from outside contracts.

SOURCES: M. Garry, "Efficient Replenishment: The Key to ECR," *Progressive Grocer*, December 1993, pp. 5–8; M. Garry, "The Electronic Cop," *Progressive Grocer*, August 1993, pp. 113–118; S. Bennett, "Niche Jumping," *Progressive Grocer*, June 1993, pp. 97–100; K. Swisher, "Giant Plans 1st Expansion Outside Local Sales Region," *Washington Post*, 28 January 1993; "The Service 500: The 50 Largest Retailing Companies," *Fortune*, 1 June 1992, p. 188; R. A. Pyatt Jr., "Giant's Expansion Plans Made with Refreshing Optimism," *Washington Post*, 29 November 1990; D. Foust, "Why Giant Foods Is a Gargantuan Success," *Business Week*, 4 December 1989, p. 80.

charges for these suites is significantly higher than its price for ordinary rooms. This niche-differentiation strategy requires a higher initial investment per suite and higher operating costs. By using multiple strategies, Holiday Inn appeals to different groups of customers.

Likewise, Hyatt offers special suites in each of its hotels to elite customers. However, even its regular rooms are advertised to discriminating customers who are willing to pay higher-than-average prices for a hotel room.

R. J. Reynolds provides an example of a large business that reactively competes with multiple strategies. For years, Reynolds employed a low-cost–differentiation strategy for its cigarette brands. But as the Liggett Group and other smaller firms began to produce generic (no-brand) cigarettes in the early 1980s, Reynolds responded by also adopting a niche–low-cost strategy. The company positioned its otherwise slow-selling and lackluster-performing brand, Doral, against generic cigarettes by reducing its costs of production and its price.[21]

Figure 6.7   **Businesses Competing by Using Multiple Strategies: Hyatt Uses the Differentiation and Niche-Differentiation; Holiday Inn Uses the Low-Cost–Differentiation and Niche-Differentiation**

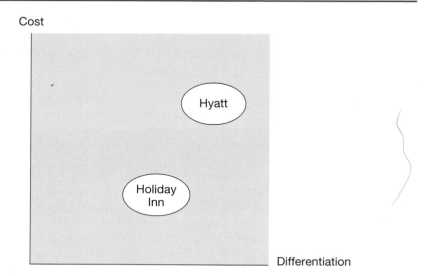

It is important to note several exceptions to the preceding discussion. First, a large business unit that uses a low-cost strategy is unlikely to employ multiple strategies. A combination of the low-cost strategy with a niche–low-cost strategy is redundant, since both strategies concentrate on no-frills outputs at low costs. Combining the low-cost strategy with either of the other niche strategies is probably unworkable because it is difficult for an organization to operate primarily on the foundation of a no-frills philosophy (and all that it implies) while simultaneously producing highly differentiated products.[22]

Additionally, a large business unit that competes by pursuing a differentiation strategy is unlikely to employ a niche–low-cost strategy or a niche–low-cost/differentiation strategy because low costs are not emphasized by its managers.

Also, large business units will not adopt as their sole strategy any of the three niche strategies identified earlier as being appropriate for small business units. A small market share with relatively low sales figures cannot justify sizable expenditures on research and development, operations, and marketing.[23] Of course, enlightened managers of small business units and entrepreneurs are well aware of these restrictions on the operations of large business units. Hence, small enterprises are often strategically buffered from head-to-head competition with large firms. The market that small companies have carefully chosen is simply too small to attract large organizations as major competitors.

The seven generic strategies that have been discussed in this chapter are summarized in Table 6.2. The emphasis of each strategy, its market coverage, the characteristics of its products and services, its market demand, and its pricing are all identified.

Table 6.2   **Generic Business Unit Strategies and Their Ramifications**

Generic Business Unit Strategy	Emphasis of Business Unit	Market Coverage	Characters of Products and Services	Market Demand	Pricing
Niche–low-cost	Lower overall costs	Market niche	No frills	Elastic	Depending on industry forces, low to average
Niche–differentiation	Fulfilling specialized customer needs	Market niche	Highly differentiated	Inelastic	High
Niche–low-cost/ differentiation	Fulfilling specialized customer needs and low costs	Market niche	Highly differentiated	Inelastic	High
Low-cost	Lower overall costs	Marketwide	No frills	Elastic	Depending on industry forces, low to average
Differentiation	Higher quality	Marketwide	Differentiated	Relatively inelastic	Depending on industry forces, average to high
Low-cost–differentiation	Higher quality and low cost	Marketwide	Differentiated	Relatively inelastic	Depending on industry forces, average to high
Multiple strategies	Mixed	Mixed	Mixed	Mixed	Mixed

(Handwritten annotations: "Healthcare" near Niche–low-cost; "Niche" circled; "4 discipline of engineering services", "NEEDS services when they" near Highly differentiated; "standard Engineering" near High pricing.)

SELECTING A GENERIC STRATEGY

In theory, an industry progresses through certain stages during the course of its life cycle: embryonic, growth, shakeout, maturity, and decline. If so, then the appropriate generic strategy for a business unit would depend, at least to some extent, upon the particular stage of its industry's life cycle.

Of course, not all industries follow these exact stages. For instance, some industries, following their decline, may be revitalized into new growth because of changes in the macroenvironment. For example, the bicycle industry fell into decline some years ago. It has now, however, been rejuvenated by society's interest in health and physical fitness.

The following paragraphs will demonstrate how generic strategies for business units are related to industry life cycle stages.[24] This discussion is appropriate for those industries that follow the traditional life cycle, but it can also be useful for business units operating in industries that deviate from the traditional life cycle. First, we will examine the industry life cycle stages and then present a framework that integrates the business generic strategies with these life cycle stages.

STRATEGIC INSIGHT

A Change in Strategy at Compaq Computer

Founded in 1982 by three ex-employees of Texas Instruments, Compaq Computer quickly rose to prominence by adopting the niche–differentiation strategy. Its personal computers (PCs) were characterized by innovative technology, high quality, and premium prices. Compaq's corporate culture was one of "sparing no expense to launch only the very best PCs on the market."

But by the late 1980s Compaq's industry environment was changing. New low-cost clone producers such as Dell Computers and AST Research entered the market, driving prices down. At first Compaq took little notice of these changes, continuing to operate in its customary fashion. But financial losses, a decline in its market share, and a fall in Compaq's stock price roused the company's board of directors. Cofounder and CEO Rod Canion was ousted and replaced by Eckhard Pfeiffer, the company's chief operating officer, who had been pressing for cost and price cuts.

Less than a year later Compaq introduced a new line of desktop and laptop PCs to the market. Priced to compete directly with Dell and AST, these machines were to be marketed, not through the traditional network of Compaq dealers, but through mass merchandise outlets, computer stores, and direct mail.

Supporting these new products was a massive cost-cutting program. Compaq eliminated 25 percent of its work force, forced suppliers to engage in competitive bidding, replaced some in-house production of components with outside contractors, shifted some production from Texas to Singapore, and even abolished its tradition of offering free soft drinks to employees. At the same time Compaq increased its U. S. advertising by 60 percent and set up a toll-free telephone number for its customers. Compaq managed to lower prices while raising margins by squeezing excess from its once-bloated infrastructure.

Although Compaq has lowered prices, its products are still priced higher than its rivals because they are more innovative. Compaq had switched to a niche–low-cost/differentiation strategy.

In 1994 Compaq built up an estimated $1 billion worth of inventory in anticipation of industry growth. The gamble paid off. In 1995 Compaq became the market leader for personal computers in the United States and has moved aggressively to restructure its operations and remain customer-focused. In 1996 Compaq continued to expand volume.

SOURCES: "H-P and Compaq to Invest in Silicon Video, a Start-Up," *Wall Street Journal Interactive Edition*, 14 May 1996; "Compaq Continues Strategy of Chopping Computer Prices," *Dow Jones News Service*, 7 May 1996; N. Templin, "Compaq Watches Its Users to Improve Their Computers," *Wall Street Journal Interactive Edition*, 8 May 1996; M. Fitzgerald, "Compaq Refocuses on Customers," *Computerworld*, 15 May 1995, p. 32; D. McGraw and A. Bernstein, "A Hard Drive to the Top: Compaq Is Now the U. S. Leader in Personal Computers," *U. S. News and World Report*, 9 January 1995, pp. 43–44; L. Zuckerman, "Compaq Cuts Its Prices in Effort to Widen Its Lead," *New York Times*, 17 August 1995, p. C3; P. Burrows, "Where Compaq's Kingdom Is Weak: In Laptops and Home PCs, the Monarch Doesn't Rule," *Business Week*, 8 May 1995, pp. 98–99; C. Arnst, S. A. Forest, K. Rebello, and J. Levene, "Compaq: How It Made Its Impressive Move Out of the Doldrums," *Business Week*, 2 November 1992, pp. 146–151.

■ Industry Life Cycle Stages

The traditional stages in an **industry's life cycle** are shown in Figure 6.8. A young industry that is beginning to form is considered to be in the *embryonic stage*. Consumer demand for the industry's outputs is low at this time because many consumers are not yet aware of these products or services. Virtually all purchasers are first-time buyers. At this stage in the industry's development, choice of technology is often not yet settled. For instance, at the beginning of the automobile industry, various small manufacturers experimented with electric, steam, and internal combustion technologies.

Normally, once the choice of technology is made and increasing numbers of consumers begin to desire the industry's outputs, the industry enters the *growth stage*. In the car industry, this stage began when the internal combustion engine became the accepted technology. Simultaneously, Henry Ford installed the assembly line to produce a single model car that many customers could afford. At this stage, most buyers are still first-time purchasers of the industry's outputs.

Over time, growth of the industry begins to slow as market demand approaches saturation. Fewer first-time buyers remain; most purchases are now for replacement purposes. As growth in demand begins to slow, some of the industry's weaker competitors may go out of business. This stage, therefore, is known as the *shakeout stage*. In the U. S. auto industry, the shakeout stage resulted in the demise of such independent car producers as Hudson, Packard, Studebaker, and American Motors, leaving General Motors, Ford, and Chrysler as survivors.

When the market demand for the industry's outputs is completely saturated, the *maturity stage* has been reached. Virtually all purchases are limited to replacement demand, and industry growth may be low, nonexistent, or even negative. The U. S. car industry is currently in the maturity stage.

Finally, market demand begins to fall steadily. This *decline stage* is often ushered in when consumers begin to turn to the products or services of substitute industries. These substitutes may have lower costs or greater convenience (such as mass transportation over car travel), they may be safer (such as chewing gum over tobacco products), or they may be technologically superior (such as the personal computer over the typewriter).

Figure 6.8   **Industry Life Cycle Stages**

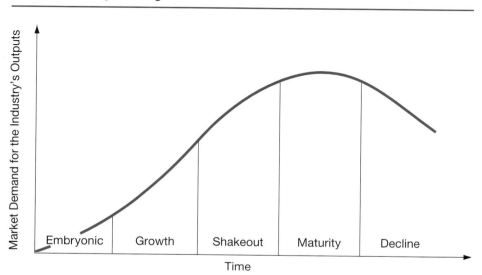

■ An Integrative Framework

How appropriate a generic strategy is for a given business unit depends upon the business's competitive status and the external forces in its industry life cycle stage. Recall that a business unit's competitive status is derived from the combined strengths and weaknesses of corporate-level, business unit, and functional-level strategies. For instance, a business unit's ability to differentiate its outputs may depend upon corporate scope innovations (discussed in chapter 4) and functional strength in research and development (discussed in the following chapter).

Figure 6.9 presents general guidelines for choosing a generic strategy in light of a business unit's particular industry life cycle stage. The vertical axis represents the life cycle stage, and the size of the business unit is shown on the horizontal axis.

Figure 6.9   **Generic Strategies in the Context of Industry Life Cycle and Size of Businesses**

Size of Businesses

	Smaller Businesses	Larger Businesses
Decline	**Cell 5** Niche–low-cost Niche–low-cost/differentiation	**Cell 9** Low-cost Low-cost–differentiation Multiple
Maturity	**Cell 4** Niche–low-cost Niche-differentiation Niche–low-cost/differentiation	**Cell 8** Low-cost Differentiation Low-cost–differentiation Multiple
Shakeout	**Cell 3** Niche–low-cost Niche-differentiation Niche–low-cost/differentiation	**Cell 7** Low-cost Differentiation Low-cost–differentiation Multiple
Growth	**Cell 2** Niche–low-cost Niche-differentiation Niche–low-cost/differentiation	**Cell 6** Low-cost Differentiation Low-cost–differentiation Multiple
Embryonic	**Cell 1** Niche-differentiation	

Stage of Industry Life Cycle

Cell 1

Virtually all businesses are small during an industry's embryonic stage since there has not yet been much opportunity for growth.[25] In this situation, the niche-differentiation strategy is appropriate because businesses in cell 1 are attempting to create new product or market opportunities. Their costs tend to be high and the number of first-time buyers to whom their outputs appeal is limited. Such businesses value organizational and technological fluidity so that they can either create or keep pace with state-of-the-art developments in the new industry. Those customers who purchase the industry's outputs are willing to pay high prices because these products or services fulfill their particular needs.

Cells 2 and 6

As the industry grows, some businesses grow with it (those in cell 6) while others remain relatively small (those in cell 2). In cell 2, any of the generic strategies for smaller businesses may be appropriate, depending upon the particular business's strengths and weaknesses and the external opportunities and threats its management identifies. If a business can keep its costs down while serving price-sensitive customers, the niche–low-cost strategy can be appropriate. For instance, while the personal computer industry grew quickly during the 1980s, Kaypro remained small by serving the no-frills needs of certain price-sensitive customers.

Businesses that can produce highly differentiated, need-fulfilling outputs, however, may use the niche-differentiation strategy. For example, the industry for stereophonic products has grown significantly during the last three decades, but small companies such as Ampax have thrived by producing exclusive, top-of-the-line products. Likewise, a small business that is able to control its costs while producing highly differentiated outputs may use the niche–low-cost/differentiation strategy.

Similarly, among those businesses that choose to grow along with the industry, any of the strategies available to larger businesses may be appropriate. A company can choose to grow at a rapid pace by emphasizing low costs and no-frills outputs, by differentiating its outputs to a large market, by simultaneously emphasizing low costs and differentiated outputs, or by employing multiple strategies.

Cells 3 and 7

The same strategies that were appropriate in the two preceding cells would also be suitable as the industry begins to "shake out" its less effective competitors. Although the growth in market demand is slowing, the industry is still expanding, and well-managed companies can thrive by following any of the generic strategies that best suit their strengths and weaknesses and their environment's opportunities and threats.

Cells 4 and 8

As the industry approaches zero or even negative growth, emphasis is placed on cutting costs and/or differentiating products/services to maintain sales levels. Without market expansion, competing successfully with high costs becomes increasingly difficult. Hence, the more viable smaller companies can normally be expected to adopt either the niche–low-cost or niche–low-cost/differentiation strategy in cell 4, and most viable larger businesses are likely to adopt either the low-cost or low-cost–differentiation strategies in cell 8.[26] Some businesses with unique products or services may still be able to compete successfully with either the niche-differentiation or differentiation strategies, but there will be fewer of them than in cells 3 and 7.

Cells 5 and 9

As demand for the industry's outputs declines significantly, high-cost businesses find themselves unable to compete as companies slash prices to try to maintain their market shares. Virtually all surviving smaller business units will have adopted the niche–low-cost or niche–low-cost/differentiation strategies, whereas those larger companies that remain will be following the low-cost, low-cost–differentiation, or multiple strategies.[27]

■ Generic Strategies and Business Unit Size

The preceding sections identified generic strategies appropriate for small and large business units. Midsized business units were not discussed because these organizations normally perform poorly in comparison with small or large competitors.[28] The reason is that midsize businesses often do not possess the advantages of their smaller or larger counterparts. Whether the business unit is considered small, midsize, or large, of course, depends upon its size relative to the size of its competitors in the industry.

The competitive superiority that small businesses enjoy over midsize business units includes their flexibility in meeting specific market demands and their potentially quicker reaction to environmental changes. Additionally, because of their lower investments, they can pursue small orders that would be unprofitable for midsize businesses. Finally, they can capitalize on their small market shares by creating an image of exclusivity. Customers who buy products for prestige purposes do so only if the market has relatively few of those products.[29] For instance, consumers who purchase Rolls-Royce automobiles would be alienated if they began to see a Rolls-Royce on every block, because the prestige of exclusivity is the primary reason for their purchase. Management at Rolls-Royce is satisfied with this situation, because nearly three months is required to build each car. The company's image is enhanced by the fact that 60 percent of the 115,000 cars it has produced can still be driven.[30]

The crucial advantage that a large business has over the midsize company lies in its ability to translate its economies of scale into lower costs per unit. Also, larger businesses may be better able to bargain with their suppliers or customers.

Therefore, since midsize business units may not have the advantages of either small or large firms, they have two strategic options to increase their effectiveness. First, they may, over time, expand their operations to take advantage of scale economies. Second, they may retrench in order to avail themselves of the advantages possessed by small companies. The feasibility of expansion or retrenchment depends upon various competitive and industry forces.[31]

VALUE CHAINS AND BUSINESS UNIT RECONFIGURATION

Traditionally, each business unit has been conceived as a link in a **value chain.** That is, an enterprise receives inputs from suppliers of resources, transforms them into outputs (thus adding value to the inputs through their transformation), and channels the outputs to buyers (whether the buyers are other enterprises or the final consumers). Each enterprise, then, serves as a link in the value chain, in which raw materials are provided (by some enterprises); these are subsequently transformed into semifinished goods and components (by other companies); and these semifinished goods and components are then transformed into finished goods and services (by yet other businesses).

Moreover, each business unit has been viewed as having its own internal value chain. That is, the business unit is conceived as a progression of activities that incrementally add value in the context of an organizational continuum. For example, purchasing and materials management, production and operations management, and marketing all add incremental value in the organization's transformation of inputs into outputs. [32]

Each business unit has its own vulnerabilities and core competencies. Recall that core competencies are the major resource strengths (human, organizational, and physical) of a firm. In creating and delivering value to customers, business units with a competitive advantage are those that undertake functional or process activities that are based on their core competencies while leaving to others those functions or processes in which they do not excel. Thus, executives need to analyze the value chain by looking at the firm internally as well as assessing outside suppliers, potential partners (strategic allies), and customers in order to structure a superior system of value creation and delivery.

As shown in Figure 6.10, supplier organizations create and deliver value in terms of provision of goods or services. These goods and services are subsequently purchased by another organization as inputs. More specifically, purchasing and materials management plans and coordinates the procurement of these inputs, thus adding and delivering further value (by locating and contracting appropriate suppliers). As shown, other functions are also involved in this process of value creation and delivery. However, although a business may perform the functions of managing purchasing and materials, production/operations, finance, human resources, and marketing (because of its own strengths in these functions), it may leave to other organizations the functions of information systems management as well as research and development (in which the outside firms excel).

Value chain examination should be undertaken periodically because conditions tend to change over time. For instance, in the past numerous firms found it more economical to perform many functions internally. More recently, however, a number of companies have switched to outsiders for some of their functions because the outsiders are more efficient in those functions. Indeed, some firms, such as Reebok, only design and market their outputs, leaving such functions as purchasing and materials management and production/operations management to outsiders.

The value chain may be perceived as a series of internal and external agency relationships. An **agency relationship** exists when an individual, group, or organization, called an **agent,** acts on behalf of another individual, group, or organization, identified as a **principal,** to increase the value of the principal's

Figure 6.10   **A Chain of Creating and Delivering Value**

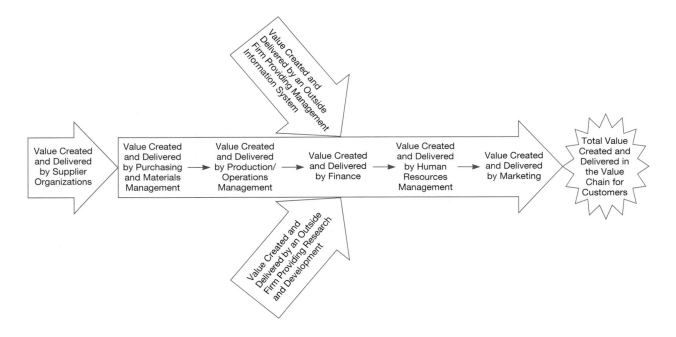

resources or activities. For instance, production/operations management may act as a principal and the purchasing and materials management as an agent within a firm. An agency relationship may also exist between the firm and an outside organization. Note that the business in Figure 6.10, as the principal, has contracted outside agents to perform the functions of managing information systems and research and development. By performing these functions, the outside agents add value to the overall value chain of the principal organization.

We emphasize that functions do not necessarily determine who is the principal and who is the agent. A manufacturer may be a principal and a marketing organization an agent in one situation. (Ford, for instance, is a principal and its dealers are agents.) In another situation, however, a marketer may be the principal and the manufacturer the agent. (Recall that Reebok is a marketer and the principal, leaving manufacturing to an outside agent.)

The value chain and its examination is meant to improve the effectiveness and efficiency of the system of value creation and delivery. In the preceding discussion, the value chain is portrayed as a point-to-point process of value creation. A periodic examination of this process is normally necessary for incremental and continuous improvements. Although in some situations this conception of value chain may be appropriate, in other situations it may be limiting.

Management consultants Richard Normann and Rafael Ramirez have criticized the concept of a value chain, calling it "as outmoded as the old assembly line that it resembles."[33] Hammer and Champy have argued that none of the business fads in the last two decades, including value chain analysis, has reversed the deterioration of competitiveness of U. S. businesses.[34] We emphasize that some of the winning enterprises base their strategic advantage on **re-configuring** their business practices around nontraditional options to create and deliver value, rather than on using value chain analysis, which focuses on predetermined, point-to-point, incremental improvements. Simply put, reconfiguring the business is the fundamental changing of business activities and relationships internally or externally to achieve desired performance outcomes.

Reconfiguring the business unit is motivated by the idea that many existing enterprises are locked into predetermined, point-to-point sequencing of activities that deliver value, when in fact their commitment to the conventional value chain may be their competitive vulnerability. Other businesses can attack this vulnerability by reconfiguring the way value is created and delivered, thus significantly improving their competitive prospects. Reconfiguring the business unit involves making radical changes in conventional business practices. Radical change may be needed internally or in the way the enterprise interacts with external variables. Also referred to as reengineering or process redesign, reconfiguring the business starts with a clean sheet of paper on which alternative answers to the following question may be explored: "How do we better satisfy the needs and expectations of the buyers through reconfiguring our business internally and perhaps changing its relationships with outsiders, such as suppliers and even the customers themselves?"

When businesses perform poorly, asking this question becomes necessary and meets with less resistance from an organization's personnel. As explained by John Thorbeck, CEO of the Geo E. Keith shoe company, "One of the few good things about companies in trouble is that they're nervous about the status quo and primed for change."[35] The same question, however, may need to be asked periodically by executives whose businesses are currently performing well. In this scenario, the managers may face more opposition from personnel. That is, the personnel may subscribe to the notion that "if it ain't broke, don't fix it!" According to John Welch, GE's CEO, a business that is performing well simply cannot maintain the status quo: "Somebody's always coming from another country with another product, or consumer tastes change, or the cost structure does, or there's a technology breakthrough."[36] The following are a number of examples of business reconfigurations. Note that in every case reconfiguration of the business unit involves adopting business practices that are substantially different from "business-as-usual" norms prevalent in the industry. This radical change is what may enable an enterprise to turn competitive disadvantages into advantages or to build on the competitive advantage the business unit already possesses.

■ Southwest Airlines

Southwest began its operations in 1971 as a small, short-haul airline between the older in-town airports of Dallas and Houston. At the time, leading airlines had a number of strategic advantages in the industry, including, for example, ownership of their computer reservation systems, meals-on-board service, and the capability to transfer baggage to other carriers. Southwest reconfigured the conventional way of doing business in the airline industry, turning what might have been competitive disadvantages into advantages. First, its city-to-city, short-haul flight strategy made a computer reservation system unnecessary. Not owning a computer reservation system saved Southwest $25 million annually, contributing to its strategy of keeping costs down. Second, since serving a meal on short-haul flights was not considered crucial by customers, a no-frills airline did not have to provide meals. This helped Southwest maintain its low costs and undercut fares offered by competitors. Finally, being a city-to-city, short-haul airline, Southwest did not have to provide baggage transfer, again contributing to its cost savings and its capability of offering low prices relative to its rivals.

■ Savin Business Machines

This company has reconfigured the conventional approach to competing in the office products industry. The major players are vertically integrated; thus they manufacture their own components and parts. They then mass produce the office products and market them through their own sales representatives. Moreover, they offer lease options to their customers. Contrarily, Savin Business Machines purchases components and parts from reliable suppliers that offer low prices. It has developed a more efficient and flexible method of manufacturing its products. Rather than hiring a costly sales force to parallel that of its rivals, it has entered into long-term contracts with select office products dealers, some of whom offer their own lease options to the customers.

■ IKEA

Furniture retailing has traditionally consisted of stores purchasing finished furniture from manufacturers or wholesalers and displaying it in their retail outlets. What the customers purchase is ordinarily delivered to them. IKEA, a Swedish furniture retailer, has become the largest firm of its kinds in the world, with operations across Europe, the Far East, and North America, through reconfiguring the way value is created and delivered. Note that its reconfiguration represents a radical change from the conventional practice in furniture retailing. The radical change is evident by observing IKEA's internal operations as well as its interactions with external variables, such as suppliers and customers.[37]

IKEA enables its suppliers to gain access to the world marketplace by selling the goods of the suppliers in the global arena. Moreover, IKEA provides technical and research and development assistance to the suppliers and even leases needed equipment to them. The purpose of providing such supplier support is to ensure that IKEA's goods will keep pace with world standards in design and efficiencies that will then assure IKEA of a low cost structure.

In order to provide items for as much as 50 percent below competitors' prices, IKEA links its customers to its operations by helping them become partners in furniture assembly and distribution. That is, customers purchase furniture kits that can easily be assembled at home and are often provided in smaller packings that can be transported by the customers themselves. Finally, the company's internal operations are fundamentally different, offering a unique experience to the customer that varies from what is normally associated with a furniture store. The buyers not only are provided with notepaper, pencils, and tape measures to facilitate their purchases, but also with such augmented services as supervised child care as well as playgrounds for the children. Reconfiguration has also enabled management to further empower personnel while flattening the organizational structures not only at IKEA, but at other organizations.[38]

We emphasize that corporate and business unit mission and strategy tend to influence how the business is reconfigured. For instance, if the mission of a corporation is to be in high-technology, innovative businesses, corporate strategy may answer the question, "In what high-technology businesses should we be operating?" Business unit strategy, in this context, may emphasize select differentiation dimensions instead of, or in conjunction with, low cost considerations. In this situation, reconfiguration of the business may be explored with the intention of enhancing differentiation through innovations.

Contrarily, the mission may emphasize being in commodity businesses in which low costs are important. For instance, Union Carbide's mission emphasizes commodity chemicals as opposed to specialty, high-technology chemicals. Union Carbide's business units, consequently, have adopted the low-cost strategy and emphasize efficiencies as opposed to differentiation dimensions. This firm has reconfigured its businesses so that the entire corporation can "seek its competitive advantage in the lowest possible manufacturing costs."[39] Union Carbide's polyethylene business unit, as an example, developed a low-cost process in the early 1970s and has continued to improve upon it. Polyethylene is the most widely used basic plastic. Not only does this company receive fees from licensing others to use its patented technology, it also maintains its competitive edge by a series of reconfigurations, yielding further enhancements and keeping "some enhancements all to itself—a still cheaper way of making polyethylene . . . or low-cost extensions of the technology to make plastic for TV and phone casings."[40]

VALUE ANALYSIS AND STRATEGIC GROUPS

This concluding section of the chapter analyzes how generic strategies are related to what customers value and strategic groups. First, the strategies that are most likely to provide value to buyers are discussed. Then the concept of strategic groups is examined.

■ Generic Strategies and Value Analysis

The marketplace rewards business units that are able to offer better **value** to buyers, which is the worth of a good or service in terms of its perceived usefulness or importance to consumers in relation to its price. The ultimate judge of value is the customer. Customers compare the price and quality of any one business unit's outputs with the price and quality of competitors' outputs. Business units that offer poor value to their customers in the form of relatively high prices and relatively low quality face negative prospects. If they hold to their price level, they will lose market share and profitability. Likewise, if they maintain their market share by discounting their prices, they will also suffer lower profits. In either case, they will be hard-pressed to generate the necessary funds to increase their product quality so that their value might be maintained or improved.

On the other hand, business units that offer good value (competitive prices and high quality) to their customers face bright prospects. If they increase their prices, they may be able to maintain their market share if consumers perceive that the new price–quality relationship is still fair relative to competitors' outputs. The worst that can happen is that they will lose market share but will be able to maintain or even increase their overall profits on the reduced sales through their higher prices. Alternatively, these businesses may reduce their prices, which will increase their market share and allow them to lower their costs through economies of scale. The result will be increased profitability.

Depending on the strengths and weaknesses of a business and the opportunities and threats in the external environment, any of the generic strategies may be associated with creating and delivering value, particularly if the strategy involves reconfiguration of the business unit, discussed in the previous section. For instance, Reno Air, competing with a niche–low-cost strategy, delivers value through the adoption of a set of business practices substantially different from what is prevalent in the airline industry—as did Southwest Airlines when it was a start-up company. Likewise, IKEA, while competing with the low-cost strategy, nonconventionally creates and delivers value in the furniture retailing industry.

■ Generic Strategies and Strategic Groups

Most industries are comprised of a number of business units that compete more directly with certain businesses in the industry than with others.[41] Groups of direct competitors are identified by the similarity of their strategic profiles, and each collection of direct competitors is termed a **strategic group.**

Figure 6.11   **Groups of Business Units in an Industry Competing by Using Different Generic Strategies**

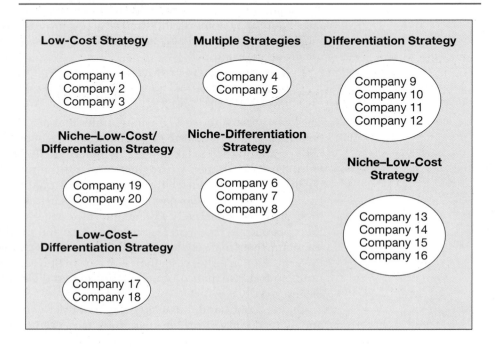

As an example, assume that an industry contains many businesses, each of which employs one of the seven generic strategies that has been discussed. Such an industry can be portrayed as shown in Figure 6.11. All twenty business units in this industry compete with one another. But business units within each strategic group engage in more direct and intense competition with one another.

Businesses normally experience difficulty in moving from one strategic group to another. In fact, strategic groups are quite stable and remain distinct from one another because of this relative immobility. Group-specific mobility barriers arise because the businesses in each group make strategic decisions that cannot easily be duplicated by enterprises outside the group. Such decisions require "outsiders" to incur significant costs, elapsed time, and/or uncertainty about the outcome of their decisions.[42] Thus, businesses in a lower-performing strategic group find it difficult and costly to switch to a higher-performing strategic group.

Note should be taken that controversy exists over the strategic group concept. For instance, strategic groups have been identified in ways that differ from our definition,[43] and some observers even question the existence of strategic groups.[44]

SUMMARY

While the strategic question at the corporate level is, In what industries or businesses should we be operating?, the appropriate question at the business unit level is, How should we compete in the chosen industry or business? Three generic strategies are available for small business units: the niche–low-cost strategy, the niche-differentiation strategy, and the niche–low-cost/differentiation strategy. Large business units may choose from among the low-cost strategy, differentiation strategy, low-cost–differentiation strategy, and multiple strategies.

While the niche-differentiation strategy is most appropriate for businesses in the embryonic stage of an industry's life cycle, any of the three generic strategies for smaller businesses or any of the four generic strategies for larger businesses may be appropriate during the growth, shakeout, or maturity stages of the industry life cycle. The choice of a particular strategy depends upon the strengths and weaknesses of each company and the environment's threats and opportunities. In the decline stage of the industry's life cycle, however, the industrywide emphasis on price competition renders the niche-differentiation and differentiation strategies ineffective.

Analysis of these strategies leads to the conclusion that either small or large business units are likely to be more effective than midsize business units. Small businesses have the advantages of flexibility and/or the ability to produce outputs that fulfill customers' particular needs for prestige, performance, or safety, and large companies possess the advantage of economies of scale.

Some of the winning enterprises base their strategic advantage on reconfiguring their business practices around nontraditional options in creating and delivering value. Reconfiguring the business is the fundamental changing of activities and relationships to achieve desirable performance outcomes.

The marketplace rewards business units that are able to offer better value to buyers. The ultimate judge of value is the customer.

Within most industries, certain business units compete more directly with some businesses than with others. Businesses that engage in very direct and intense competition with one another are considered to be a strategic group. Most industries contain several strategic groups, each of which is composed of members possessing similar strategic profiles.

TAKE IT TO THE NET

We invite you to visit the Wright page on the Prentice Hall Web site at:

http://www.prenhall.com/wright

for this chapter's World Wide Web exercise.

KEY CONCEPTS

Agency relationship A relationship that exists when an individual, group, or organization, called an agent, acts on behalf of another individual, group, or organization, identified as a principal, to increase the value of the principal's resources or activities.

Agent The individual, group, or organization in an agency relationship that acts on behalf of another individual, group, or organization, identified as a principal, to increase the value of the principal's resources or activities.

Business unit An organizational subsystem that has a market, a set of competitors, and a mission distinct from those of the other subsystems in the firm.

Differentiation strategy A generic business unit strategy in which a larger business produces distinct products or services industrywide for a large market with a relatively inelastic demand.

Generic strategies Strategies that can be adopted by business units to guide their organizations.

Industry life cycle The temporal stages (embryonic, growth, shakeout, maturity, and decline) through which many—but not all—industries pass.

Low-cost–differentiation strategy A generic business unit strategy in which a larger business unit maintains low costs while producing distinct products or services industrywide for a large market with a relatively inelastic demand.

Low-cost strategy A generic business unit strategy in which a larger business produces, at the lowest cost possible, no-frills products and services industrywide for a large market with a relatively elastic demand.

Multiple strategies   A strategic alternative for a larger business unit in which the organization simultaneously employs more than one of the generic business strategies.

Niche-differentiation strategy   A generic business unit strategy in which a smaller business produces highly differentiated, need-fulfilling products or services for the specialized needs of a narrow range of customers or a market niche. Because the business's outputs are intended to fulfill a deep set of customer needs, prices are high and demand for the outputs tends to be inelastic.

Niche–low-cost/differentiation strategy   A generic business unit strategy in which a smaller business produces highly differentiated, need-fulfilling products or services for the specialized needs of a select group of customers or a market niche while keeping its costs low.

Niche–low-cost strategy   A generic business unit strategy in which a smaller business keeps overall costs low while producing no-frills products or services for a market niche with elastic demand.

Organizational expertise   An organization's ability to do something particularly well in comparison with its competitors.

Principal   In an agency relationship, an individual, group, or organization on whose behalf an agent acts to increase the value of the principal's resources or activities.

Process innovations   A business unit's activities that increase the efficiency of operations and distribution.

Product innovations   A business unit's activities that enhance the differentiation of its products or services.

Quality   The totality of features and characteristics of a product or service that bear on its ability to satisfy stated or implied needs.

Reconfiguring the business unit   Fundamentally changing businesses' practices and relationships to achieve desirable performance outcomes.

Strategic group   Within an industry, a select group of direct competitors who have similar strategic profiles.

Total quality management (TQM)   A broad-based program designed to improve product and service quality and to increase customer satisfaction by modifying a company's management practices.

Value   The worth of a good or service in terms of its perceived usefulness or importance to a consumer. Value is usually judged by comparing the price and quality of one business's outputs with those of its competitors.

Value chain   The notion that an enterprise receives inputs from suppliers of resources, transforms them into outputs, and channels the outputs to buyers, adding value at each point in the process.

DISCUSSION QUESTIONS

1. How does a business unit strategy differ from a corporate-level strategy?

2. Small business units have a choice of three generic strategies. Explain each of these strategies and give an example of a business unit that competes with each strategy.

3. Large business units have a choice of four generic strategies. Explain each of these strategies and give an example of a business unit that competes with each strategy.

4. Explain the difference between a niche–low-cost/differentiation strategy and a low-cost–differentiation strategy.

5. How is it possible for a business to differentiate its outputs and, simultaneously, lower its costs?

6. What strategy or strategies are most appropriate for business units in the embryonic stage of an industry's life cycle? Now identify the strategies that are most effective in the decline stage of an industry's life cycle. Explain why.

7. Why might we expect the performance level of midsize business units to be lower than the performance level of either small or large business units?

8. What does reconfiguring the business unit mean?

9. What is a strategic group? Select an industry and identify, by name, some of the business units that comprise two of the strategic groups within that industry.

STRATEGIC MANAGEMENT EXERCISES

1. Assume that you have conducted market research that indicates the need for a bookstore close to your campus. Further assume that you believe that either of two generic strategies could be successful for the bookstore: the niche–low-cost strategy or the niche–differentiation strategy. Respond to the following questions for *each* of these two strategies. Note that your responses for the two strategies will be quite different.

   • What type of physical store should you create?
   • What kinds of books would you carry in your inventory?
   • What in-store services would you provide?
   • Would you generally charge low, average, or high prices?

   Now, answer these same questions for a small business and a generic strategy of your own choosing.

2. Assume that you have the financial resources to own a national chain of video stores. Further assume that you believe that either of two generic strategies could be successful for this chain: the low-cost strategy or the differentiation strategy. Describe the physical aspects of your stores, their services, their advertising programs, and so on, for *each* of these two strategies.

3. Select an actual business and analyze its strategic profile (i.e., which generic strategy has it adopted?). Please justify your answer.

NOTES

1. S. D. Atchison, "The Little Engineers That Could," *Business Week*, 27 July 1992, p. 77.

2. ANSI/ASQC, *Quality Systems Terminology, American National Standard* (1987), A3-1987.

3. D. A. Garvin, *Managing Quality* (New York: Free Press, 1988).

4. M. Helms, M. Ahmadi, and R. Driggans, "Quality and Quantity Goals in Service Industries: Compatible or Conflicting Strategies," *Journal of Business Strategies* 7 (1990): 120–133; S. Cappel, P. Wright, M. Kroll, and D. Wyld, "Competitive Strategies and Business Performance: An Empirical Study of Select Service Businesses," *International Journal of Management* 9 (1992): 1–11.

5. United States General Accounting Office, "Management Practices: U. S. Companies Improve Performance Through Quality Efforts," GAO/NSIAD-91-190, May 1991.

6. E. A. Haas, "Breakthrough Manufacturing," *Harvard Business Review* 65, no. 2 (1987): 76.

7. A. Farnham, "America's Most Admired Companies," *Fortune*, 7 February 1994, pp. 50–54; R. H. Miles, *Coffin Nails and Corporate Strategies* (Englewood Cliffs, NJ: Prentice Hall, 1982).

8. P. Wright, "Winning Strategies for Small Manufacturers," *Planning Review* 14 (1986): 20.

9. K. Kelley, "Suddenly, Big Airlines Are Saying: 'Small Is Beautiful,'" *Business Week*, 17 January 1994, p. 37.

10. H. Rudnitsky, "The King of Off-Price," *Forbes*, 31 January 1994, pp. 54–55; J. A. Parnell, "New Evidence in the Generic Strategy and Business Performance Debate: A Research Note," *British Journal of Management*, in press.

11. W. J. Abernathy and K. Wayne, "Limits of Learning Curve," in Harvard Business School, eds., *Survival Strategies for American Industry* (New York: Wiley, 1983), pp. 114–131; R. Luchs, "Successful Businesses Compete on Quality–Not Costs," *Long Range Planning* 19, no. 1 (1986): 12–17.

12. R. D. Buzzell and B. T. Gale, *The PIMS Principles* (New York: Free Press, 1987).

13. N. Paley, "Post These Notes," *Sales & Marketing Management*, February 1994, pp. 49–50.

14. J. Trout and A. Ries, "Don't Follow the Leader," *Sales & Marketing Management*, February 1994, pp. 25–26; P. Wright, "A Refinement of Porter's Strategies, *Strategic Management Journal* 8 (1987), 93–101.

15. P. Wright, M. J. Kroll, C. D. Pringle, and J. A. Johnson, "Organization Types, Conduct, Profitability, and Risk in the Semiconductor Industry," *Journal of Management Systems* 2 (1990): 33–48.

16. R. Buaron, "New Games Strategies," *The McKinsey Quarterly* 3 (1981): 24–40.

17. W. D. Vinson and D. F. Heany, "Is Quality Out of Control?" *Harvard Business Review* 55, no. 6 (1977): 114–122.

18. C. Willis, "Wall Street," *Money*, April 1992, p. 70.

19. M. E. Porter, *Competitive Advantage: Creating and Sustaining Superior Performance* (New York: Free Press, 1985).

20. C. Hawkins, "FedEx: Europe Nearly Killed the Messenger," *Business Week*, 25 May 1992, pp. 124–126.

21. Wright, "A Refinement of Porter's Strategies."

22. P. Wright, "The Strategic Options of Least Cost, Differentiation and Niche," *Business Horizons* 22 (1986): 21–26.

23. Wright, "A Refinement of Porter's Strategies."

24. Industry and organizational life cycles may not be correlated. For a discussion of organizational life cycles, see H. R. Dodge, S. Fullerton, and J. E. Robbins, "Stage of the Organizational Life Cycle and Competition as Mediators of Problem Perceptions for Small Businesses," *Strategic Management Journal* 15 (1994): 121–134.

25. L. R. Watts, "Degrees of Entrepreneurship and Small Firm Planning," *Journal of Business and Entrepreneurship* 2, no. 2 (1992): 59–67.

26. Many brewers attempt to differentiate while keeping their costs down. See E. Sfiligoj, "Ice Beers Give Stroh Another Excuse to Keep Coming Out with New Brews," *Beverage World*, 31 January 1994, p. 3.

27. See L. Zinn, "The Smoke Clears at Marlboro," *Business Week*, 31 January 1994, pp. 76–77.

28. S. Schoeffler, R. Buzzell, and D. Heany, "Impact of Strategic Planning on Profit Performance," *Harvard Business Review* 52 (1974): 137–145; M. E. Porter, *Competitive Strategy* (New York: Free Press, 1980); Wright, "A Refinement of Porter's Strategies"; L. Feldman and J. Stephenson, "Stay Small or Get Huge—Lessons from Securities Trading," *Harvard Business Review* 66, no. 3 (1988): 116–123; M. T. Hannan and J. Freeman, "The Population Ecology of Organizations," *American Journal of Sociology* 82 (1977): 946–947.

29. P. Wright, "Systematic Approach in Finding Export Opportunities," in Harvard Business School, eds., *Managing Effectively in the World Marketplace* (New York: Wiley, 1983), pp. 331–342.

30. T. Aeppel, "Rolls-Royce Tries to Restore Luster as Car Sales Fade," *Wall Street Journal*, 26 May 1992.

31. P. Chan and T. Sneyoski, "Environmental Change, Competitive Strategy, Structure, and Firm Performance: An Application of Data Development Analysis," *International Journal of Systems Science* 22 (1991): 1625–1636.

32. The concept of value chain was developed by McKinsey and Company and refined by Professor Michael Porter.

33. R. Normann and R. Ramirez, "From Value Chain to Value Constellation: Designing Interactive Strategy," *Harvard Business Review* 71 (1993): 65.

34. M. Hammer and J. Champy, *Reengineering the Corporation* (New York: Harper Business, 1993).

35. J. Thorbeck, "The Turnaround Value of Values," *Harvard Business Review* 69 (1991): 54.

36. J. E. Davis, "A Master Class of Radical Change," *Fortune*, 13 December 1993, p. 82.

37. Normann and Ramirez, "From Value Chain to Value Constellation: Designing Interactive Strategy," p. 65.

38. R. Heygate and G. Breback, "Corporate Reengineering," *McKinsey Quarterly* 2 (1991): 44–55; R. B. Kaplan and L. Murdock, "Core Process Redesign," *McKinsey Quarterly* 2 (1991): 27–43.

39. T. A. Stewart, "Reengineering: The Hot New Managing Tool," *Fortune*, 23 August 1993, p. 43.

40. M. Magnet, "Let's Go for Growth," *Fortune*, 7 March 1994, p. 62.

41. W. T. Jackson, L. R. Watts, and P. Wright, "Small Businesses: An Examination of Strategic Groups," *Journal of Business and Entrepreneurship* 5, no. 1 (1993): 86–96.

42. J. McGee and H. Thomas, "Strategic Groups: Theory, Research and Taxonomy," *Strategic Management Journal* 7 (1986): 141–160.

43. Ibid.

44. J. B. Barney and R. E. Hoskisson, "Strategic Groups: Untested Assertions and Research Proposals," *Managerial and Decision Economics* 11 (1990): 187–198.

STRATEGIC MANAGEMENT MODEL

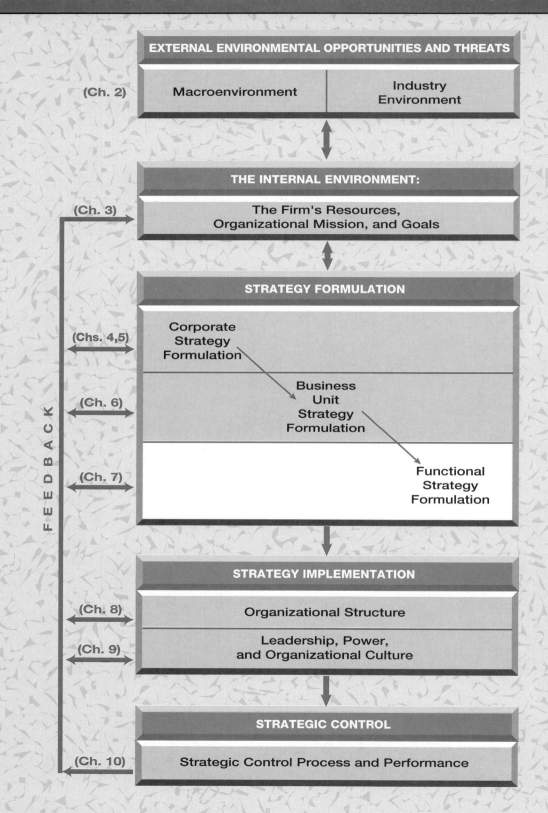

EXTERNAL ENVIRONMENTAL OPPORTUNITIES AND THREATS

(Ch. 2)

| Macroenvironment | Industry Environment |

THE INTERNAL ENVIRONMENT:

(Ch. 3)

The Firm's Resources, Organizational Mission, and Goals

STRATEGY FORMULATION

(Chs. 4,5) Corporate Strategy Formulation

(Ch. 6) Business Unit Strategy Formulation

(Ch. 7) Functional Strategy Formulation

STRATEGY IMPLEMENTATION

(Ch. 8) Organizational Structure

(Ch. 9) Leadership, Power, and Organizational Culture

STRATEGIC CONTROL

(Ch. 10) Strategic Control Process and Performance

FEEDBACK

7 Functional Strategies

Recall from the previous chapter that the marketplace rewards businesses that are able to offer value to buyers, that is, the perceived usefulness or importance of a good or service to customers in relation to its price. In fact, the ultimate judge of value is the customer. To create and deliver value to customers, all businesses rely on the performance of certain functions—production, finance, research and development, marketing, and so on. Moreover, proper use of generic strategies (chapter 6) requires that considerable attention be given to the business unit's functional areas.

In formulating **functional strategies**—the strategies pursued by the functional areas of a business unit—managers must be aware that these functions are interrelated. Each functional area, in attaining its purpose, must mesh its activities with the activities of the other functional departments, as shown in Figure 7.1. A change in one department will invariably affect the way other departments operate. Hence, the strategy of one functional area cannot be viewed in isolation; rather, the extent to which all of the business unit's functional tasks mesh smoothly determines the effectiveness of the unit's generic strategy.

Unfortunately, in some companies, personnel in each functional area tend to view their operations introspectively and independently of other functions. If the ultimate judge of value is the customer, such a view is unlikely to result in customer satisfaction, since the needs and expectations of the customer are ordinarily fulfilled through the interaction of a number of functional areas. Many companies are learning this lesson. Boeing's unsettling experience, for instance, with discontinuities among its production, human resources, and marketing functions in the manufacture and delivery of its 747-400 airline has resulted in

Figure 7.1   **Interrelationships among Functions**

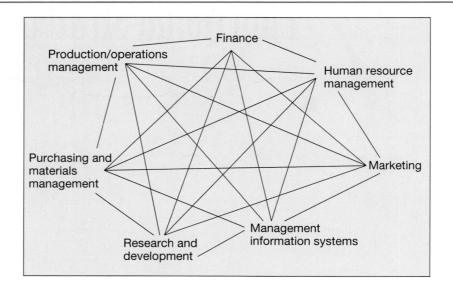

significant changes. Its new 777 airplane is designed and built by teams of marketing, engineering, manufacturing, finance, and service representatives so that each functional area will always know what the other is doing.[1]

This chapter examines functional strategies in the areas of purchasing and materials management, production/operations, finance, research and development, human resources, information systems, and marketing. Then the ways in which these functional strategies can be integrated are analyzed.

PURCHASING AND MATERIALS MANAGEMENT

All organizations have a purchasing function. For example, in manufacturing companies, the purchasing department buys raw materials and/or parts so that the production department may process them into a finished product for the marketing department to sell. In retailing organizations, individual buyers purchase clothing, toys, furniture, and other items from manufacturers for resale to the ultimate consumer. The tasks of purchasing are to identify potential suppliers, evaluate them, invite bids and price quotations, negotiate prices and terms of payment, place orders, follow up on those orders, inspect incoming shipments, and pay suppliers.

A business unit's purchasing strategy will differ, depending upon which generic strategy it adopts. Companies that use either the niche–low-cost strategy or the low-cost strategy emphasize purchasing at the lowest costs possible. Large organizations are able to purchase at low costs through their ability to demand quantity discounts. [The terms *large* and *small* are relative ones referring to an organization's size (usually measured in annual sales or total assets) in relation to the size of its competitors in the industry.] And buyers that are larger than their suppliers and whose purchases represent a significant percentage of their suppliers' sales also possess considerable negotiating clout.

Small companies, however, must attain low-cost purchasing in other ways. A recent purchasing trend for small business is to form industry networks—that is, to band together with other small businesses in the same industry—to pool their purchasing requirements. Such a network is able to wield as much power as a single large business in demanding quantity discounts and exerting negotiating clout. Other small businesses may attempt to develop contacts with domestic and foreign suppliers that are able to offer limited supplies at low prices. In many cases, an extensive search can locate such suppliers.

We wish to emphasize that low costs are not the only consideration in purchasing activities. It is more accurate to state that businesses using niche–low-cost or low-cost generic strategies should seek out the "best cost." The best cost is as low as possible consistent with the quality of the purchased good or service. A low price is useless if the item breaks in the production process or fails to perform for the customer. On the other hand, excessive quality unnecessarily raises costs and prices.[2]

Organizations that use the generic strategy of niche-differentiation or differentiation emphasize the procurement of high-quality inputs, even if they cost more than alternative offerings. In these cases, the quality of the parts or products takes precedence over cost considerations.

When management pursues a niche–low-cost/differentiation or low-cost–differentiation generic strategy, however, emphasis is placed on buying high-quality inputs at low costs. As pointed out in the preceding chapter, even small businesses that adopt niche–low-cost/differentiation may be able to attain this purchasing goal through the development of organizational expertise and image, as Porsche has done.

Using multiple strategies, of course, requires a mixture of purchasing plans. At Holiday Inn, for instance, cost is a consideration in purchasing furnishings and accessories for the Inn's regular rooms. But the company buys higher-quality items—at higher costs—for its top-of-the-line suites. These suites feature more expensive linens, towels, soaps, shampoos, and beverages, which are provided free of charge.

The purchasing function is the first step in the materials management process. From the materials management perspective, purchasing, the operation of storage and warehouse facilities, and the control of inventory are interrelated functions;[3] consequently, they can only be efficiently and effectively conducted if they are viewed as parts of a single task.[4]

As an example of how these functions are interrelated, consider the **just-in-time inventory system (JIT).** This system of inventory management was popularized by Japanese manufacturers to reduce materials management costs. Using this technique, the purchasing manager asks suppliers to ship parts just at the time they are needed by the company to use in its production process. Such a system, of course, holds inventory, storage, and warehousing costs to a minimum.

Although American manufacturers are turning to this system in growing numbers, it is important to realize that just-in-time deliveries work particularly well in Japan because large Japanese manufacturers buy many of their inputs from small local companies. Hence, the giant buyers have considerable bargaining power over their much smaller suppliers. (In fact, some Japanese manufacturers own controlling interests in their suppliers, giving them even more power to control deliveries.) Such a system is likely to work well in the United States when the manufacturer has greater bargaining power than its suppliers. However, in the reverse situation, a just-in-time system is unlikely to evolve. Another hindrance to its use is that some suppliers, owing to the high demand for their products, are occasionally late in their deliveries by weeks or even months. However, most American-based suppliers are small concerns, with under $5 million in annual sales and fewer than thirty employees.[5]

Another potential difficulty with the JIT system is the possibility that labor strikes can shut down a supplier. A few years ago, for example, one of the plants that supplies parts to GM's Saturn manufacturing operations shut down—fortunately, for a short time—due to a local labor dispute. Saturn, which uses the JIT system, suddenly found itself unable to produce cars—in a time of overwhelming consumer demand—because it had no inventory of the more than 300 metal parts that it purchased exclusively from the supplier whose plant was struck.[6]

Most large U.S. manufacturers are currently reducing the number of suppliers they use from a dozen or more to two or three to control delivery times and quality.[7] These companies then attempt to build strong and enduring relationships with their suppliers and provide them with detailed knowledge of their requirements and specifications. Buyers and suppliers work together to improve the quality and lower the costs of the purchased items.

> This involves taking a *long* term view of the buyer/supplier relationship and also involves commitment to building an enduring cooperative relationship with individual suppliers where information is readily shared and both organizations work to meet shared goals.[8]

PRODUCTION/OPERATIONS MANAGEMENT

Business unit Strat

Although production/operations management (POM) is most often associated with manufacturing processes, operations management is crucial to all types of organizations.[9] Credit card companies, for instance, must satisfy customers' desires for timeliness, accuracy, and company responsiveness. Hospitals must diagnose medical problems and attempt to heal patients. Prisons must house prisoners and try to rehabilitate them. Insurance companies must meet their clients' demands for fast, responsible, thorough coverage. Each of these POM examples from service organizations requires a careful analysis of their operations.

The following sections describe POM strategies for small and large business units and discuss the quality considerations emerging currently in POM.

▪ Production/Operations Management Strategies for Small Business Units

Strategies for POM differ, of course, depending upon which generic strategy the business unit adopts. Small business units that compete with the niche–low-cost strategy emphasize low initial investments in their plants, equipment, and outlets to hold their fixed costs down, and they attempt to keep their variable operations costs as low as possible. Because of technological in-

STRATEGIC INSIGHT

Improving Supplier Quality Across Several Industries

Never before has there been such emphasis on the purchasing and materials management function. The primary impetus for this movement is the increasing intensity of foreign competition. The results to date have been a reduction in the number of suppliers used by most companies and growing pressure on those that remain to meet high-quality, cost, and delivery time standards.

As a buyer begins to pressure its suppliers, they, in turn, must convince their own suppliers to improve. For example, Ford influenced its suppliers to improve their quality and cost levels. One of those suppliers, Motorola, has lowered its defect rate from 3,000 per million parts to fewer than 200 per million parts as a result. In fact, Motorola's emphasis on "doing it right the first time" has cut its waste, inspection time, and warranty costs by $250 million in two years. Now Motorola has urged its 3,000 suppliers (down from 10,000) to improve their quality by asking them to enter the competition for the Malcolm Baldrige National Quality Award (won by Motorola in 1988). Those that have

chosen not to enter have been dropped as suppliers by Motorola.

Although more is being demanded from suppliers, the best ones become "partners" with their buyers. Their employees may receive training in new manufacturing and quality techniques from buyers, may become involved in the design of the buyers' new products, may receive free consulting assistance from their buyers, and may become privy to the strategic plans of the buyers. In some cases, such suppliers are even able to become the sole supplier of a particular part to a buyer.

These principles have been adopted by retail organizations as well as manufacturers. Dillard's, a fast-growing and highly profitable department chain in the South, Southwest, and Midwest, works closely with its venders and is amazingly loyal to them. The company has discovered, like many others, that building stronger relationships and improving dialogue with fewer suppliers can serve its needs more effectively in the long run.

SOURCES: A. L. Adler, "Ford Suppliers Take On More Design, Engineering Costs," *Automotive News*, 7 August 1995, pp. 3–4; J. Carbone, "Improving Delivery Performance," *Electronic Business Buyer*, February 1994, p. 79; T. Stundza, "More Dialogue, Fewer Suppliers," *Purchasing*, 13 January 1994; J. R. Emshwiller, "Suppliers Struggle to Improve Quality As Big Firms Slash Their Vendor Rolls," *Wall Street Journal*, 16 August 1991; A. Gabor, "The Front Lines of Quality," *U. S. News and World Report*, 27 November 1989, pp. 57–59; S. Camaniti, "A Quiet Superstar Rises in Retailing," *Fortune*, 23 October 1989, pp. 167–174.

novations, some industries, such as steel manufacturing and film developing, can create small physical plants that are cost-competitive with much larger companies.

An example of this comparison is shown in Figure 7.2. The graph on the left depicts the per-unit production cost of a small business; the graph on the right shows the per-unit production cost of a large company. Note that the small business has achieved low per-unit costs similar to those of the larger organization because of its use of modern technology. Because the emphasis of business units that compete with the niche–low-cost generic strategy is on holding costs down, production/operations strategies are continuously scrutinized to make them more efficient. In some cases, production facilities may even be moved abroad to lower costs significantly.

Figure 7.2   **Per-Unit Cost of Production in a Small and in a Large Firm**

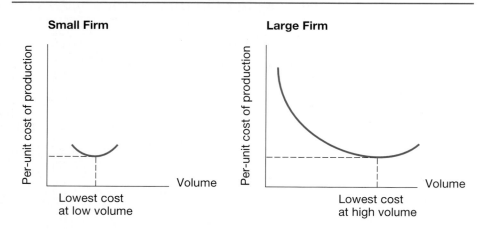

Small business units that compete with the niche-differentiation strategy stress POM strategies that yield superior quality. In some instances, such strategies may involve hand-crafting processes versus the mass production operations of much larger businesses. Rolls-Royce, for example, stresses the hand crafting of many automobile components, and each component can be traced to the individual worker who took part in its creation. As is evident, low costs are not the primary concern of this niche-differentiation strategy.

Small business units competing with the niche–low-cost/differentiation strategy emphasize POM strategies that simultaneously lower costs and heighten differentiation. This strategy may initially involve higher costs, but over time, cost savings and quality improvements evolve. For instance, one American manufacturer of electronic products realized that moving its metal production processes overseas would result in a 15 percent cost reduction. But switching to plastics in place of metal would lower costs by 20 percent and could be accomplished in the United States. In addition, plastic materials would offer better value for electronic products because of their lighter weight. Elizabeth Haas, a consultant in manufacturing strategy and advanced technology, has documented businesses in a variety of industries that have managed both to lower costs and heighten differentiation.[10]

■ Production/Operations Management Strategies for Large Business Units

Large business units can take advantage of a number of factors that accompany their larger size. Each factor falls under the concept of the **experience curve:** the reduction in per-unit costs that occurs as an organization gains experience producing a product or service. The Boston Consulting Group has popularized this concept, noting that production/operations costs may be systematically reduced through larger sales volume.[11] That is, each time a company's output doubles, POM costs decline by a specific percentage, which varies from one industry to another. For instance, with a sales volume of 1 million units, per-unit costs may be $100 in a particular industry. With a doubling of volume to 2 million units, per-unit costs may decline by 30 percent. Another doubling of volume to 4 million units may lower per-unit costs another 30 percent. In other industries, however, each doubling of volume will reduce costs by other amounts. The experience curve has been observed in a wide range of industries, including automobiles, long-distance telephone calls, airlines, and life insurance. Note that both manufacturing and service industries are represented.

The experience curve concept is based on three underlying variables: learning, economies of scale, and capital-labor substitution possibilities. Learning refers to the idea that the more an employee performs a task, the more efficient he or she should become at the job. Increases in volume, therefore, permit the employee to perform the task more often, resulting in greater expertise. This reasoning holds for all jobs—line and staff, managerial and nonmanagerial—and at all levels—corporate, business unit, and functional. Learning does not occur automatically, however. For instance, as experience is gained with a particular product, production managers, operative employees, and design engineers have the opportunity to learn more about how to redesign the product for manufacturing and assembly. By taking advantage of this opportunity, a business is able to conserve material, gain greater efficiencies in the manufacturing process, and substitute less costly materials, while simultaneously improving the product's performance. Such techniques, for example, allowed Ford Motor Company's business units to trim their manufacturing costs significantly. For instance, Ford plants can manufacture such midsize models as the Taurus and Mercury Sable in fewer than 17.2 hours, whereas such comparable models as the Chevrolet Lumina and Pontiac Grand Prix require 32.2 to 36.3 hours.[12]

Economies of scale at the business unit level refer to reductions in per-unit costs as volume increases. Capital-labor substitution means that as volume increases, an organization may be able to substitute labor for capital, or capital for labor, depending upon which combination produces lower costs and/or greater effectiveness. For example, a car manufacturer may operate highly automated factories in economically advanced nations because of the high cost of labor. But the same manufacturer may employ more labor and less automation in its factories located in developing nations to take advantage of the lower cost of labor in those areas.

Putting all three of these variables together, Figure 7.3 portrays how the overall experience curve promotes lower unit costs as volume increases. Hence, as a business gains greater market share, its per-unit costs can decrease as it takes advantage of the experience curve. However, investing in greater plant capacity is not necessarily an automatic route to lower unit costs. As can be seen from the curve in Figure 7.3, the experience curve flattens at point A on the graph. Production beyond that point will not lower unit costs any further.

Although large business units benefit from the experience curve, the particular generic strategy adopted by a given business unit will have different ramifications for success. For instance, many (but not all) businesses that compete with the low-cost strategy tend to buy their way to lower costs. In other words, they sell their products or services at low prices, even if those prices are initially below their costs. The low prices increase their volume, thereby permitting them to lower their costs through use of the experience curve. These businesses, however, are particularly vulnerable to business units that are also able to attain low costs but offer better-quality products and services.[13]

A different approach is taken by business units that compete with the differentiation and low-cost–differentiation generic strategies. Instead of charging

Figure 7.3   **Experience Curve**

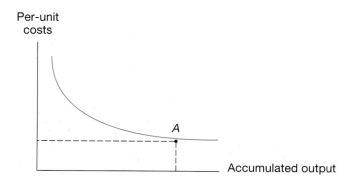

average or low prices, they charge average to high prices, seeking to gain market share by offering higher-quality outputs. The increase in sales may also allow them to lower their costs. But the managers of the business units that adopt differentiation as their strategy do not actively capitalize on the opportunities presented by low costs, whereas managers of businesses that compete with low-cost–differentiation do.[14] Hence, adopters of differentiation as a generic strategy are vulnerable to competitors that offer alternative products, but at lower, or even predatory, prices. The low-cost–differentiation adopter is less vulnerable than businesses using either of the preceding strategies, however, because this strategy emphasizes lower costs (as protection against low-cost companies) and high-quality outputs (to protect against differentiated businesses).

Regardless of the generic strategy adopted, large business units that use the experience curve take a significant risk. Increases in volume often involve substantial investments in plant and equipment and a commitment to the prevailing technology. However, if technological innovations should make the plant's production processes obsolete, millions of dollars in capital equipment may have to be written off. How may this need to invest in plant and equipment be balanced against the risk that technology will change? History provides a partial answer.

Virtually any technology is improved upon over time. But at some point, further improvement becomes prohibitively expensive.[15] At such times, emphasis should be placed on developing innovations, even at the risk of rendering obsolete the company's prevailing technology. A major vulnerability in using the experience curve is that managers become psychologically dependent upon the organization's technology both because they are familiar with it and because they have committed so much in resources to it. Consequently, when a competitor develops a new technology, the company can quickly become technologically obsolete.

As an example, consider NCR, a business that once had the lowest costs (through the experience curve) in the mechanical cash register industry. When Burroughs and other competitors developed a fully integrated electronic cash register that was superior in performance, the market demand quickly shifted from the technologically obsolete mechanical cash register to the new product. As a result, NCR lost its competitive edge.

▪ Quality Considerations

An issue of increasing importance in production/operations management in recent years is quality or total quality management (TQM). This concept, introduced in chapter 6, refers to the totality of features and characteristics of a product or service that bear on its ability to satisfy stated or implied needs. Historically, quality has been viewed largely as a controlling activity that takes place somewhere near the end of the production process, an after-the-fact measurement of production success. Over the years, however, more and more managers have come to realize that quality is not something that is measured at, or near, the end of the production process but is an essential ingredient of the product or service being provided. Consequently, quality is part of the overall approach to doing business and becomes the concern of all members of the organization. When quality comes to be viewed in this way, the following conditions prevail:

- Making a quality product decreases the quantity of defects, which causes yield to increase.
- Making a product right the first time reduces the number of rejects and time spent on rework.
- Making the operative employees responsible for quality eliminates the need for inspection.

These conditions also apply to service quality, whether the service is performed for the customer or for some other department in the same organization. The ultimate result is that quality is viewed as reducing, rather than increasing, costs.[16] As quality consultant Philip B. Crosby points out:

> Every penny you don't spend on doing things wrong, over, or instead of, becomes . . . [a savings] right on the bottom line. . . . If you concentrate on making quality certain, you can probably increase your profit by an amount equal to 5% to 10% of your sales.[17]

W. Edwards Deming, the world-renowned consultant, argued that improvement of quality converts the waste of employee hours and machine time into the manufacture of good product and better service. Management in some Japanese companies observed as early as the late 1940s that improvement of quality naturally and inevitably begets improvement of productivity.[18] This process is illustrated in Figure 7.4. As you can see, such a process is essential to businesses that use the niche–low-cost/differentiation or low-cost–differentiation generic strategies. If below-average industry prices are charged, the business benefits because it may increase its market share and, subsequently, may reduce its costs. If average or above-average industry prices are charged, the business benefits from greater profit margins. Even companies that adopt differentiation as their strategy can develop a distinct competitive advantage by focusing on the quality of their products and services.

In fact, quality improvements in virtually any type of company seem to yield attractive results. A U.S. General Accounting Office study of twenty companies—including both large and small businesses in manufacturing and service industries—that had adopted TQM programs concluded that quality improvements enhanced profitability, increased market share, decreased customer complaints, and improved customer satisfaction. These results occurred on average two and a half years after the TQM programs were adopted.[19] Although the

Figure 7.4   **The Deming Chain Reaction**

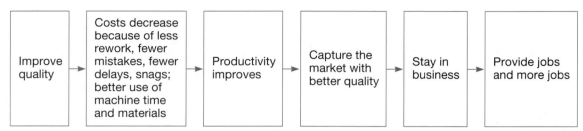

exact form of each program differed from one company to another, these programs did contain the following common features:

- Corporate attention was focused on meeting customer requirements.
- Top management took the lead in emphasizing quality.
- All employees were trained, empowered, and involved in organizational efforts to improve quality and to reduce costs.
- Systematic processes were integrated throughout the organization to foster continuous improvement.[20]

FINANCE

The finance function encompasses not only cash management but also the use of credit and decisions regarding capital investments. Ideally, each business would like to have a surplus of internally generated cash, beyond what is needed for expenditures, to allow it to reinvest the cash back into the business. In this way, the future viability of the enterprise is assured. However, a company resorts to borrowing funds when strategic decisions require cash beyond what can be generated from operations. Long-term capital investment decisions focus on the allocation of resources and, hence, are linked to corporate and business unit strategies in an obvious fashion.

Business units that use niche–low-cost or low-cost generic strategies pursue financial strategies that are intended to lower their financial costs. Insofar as possible, they attempt to keep their costs within the limits of the funds they are able to generate from operations. If borrowing becomes necessary, they try to borrow during times when credit costs are relatively low. If they sell common stock to generate additional funds, they time the sale carefully to coincide with a bull market (a market in which stock prices, on the average, are rising). Their capital investment decisions center on plant and equipment, technology, and research and development efforts that can lower their cost positions even more. Furthermore, they attempt to time major equipment purchases from foreign producers when the dollar is strong relative to the foreign currency.

Business units that adopt the niche-differentiation or differentiation generic strategies pursue financial strategies that fund quality enhancements. To stay in step with their competitors' product improvements or innovations, they direct their financial efforts toward upgrading their present and future outputs. If internal funds are insufficient, then they will attempt to raise money either through selling common stock or borrowing funds. Stock may be sold even though stock prices in general are relatively low, and funds may be borrowed even if interest costs are relatively high. In other words, these business units place the highest strategic priority on quality maintenance and enhancement rather than on financial considerations.

Finally, those business units that compete with the niche–low-cost/differentiation, low-cost–differentiation, or multiple strategies use their financial function, on the one hand, to lower costs and, on the other hand, to promote quality enhancements. Because such business units ordinarily perform well, they tend to have stronger financial positions than other business units, which allow them greater flexibility. These business units often have cash surpluses, can borrow funds at competitive rates, and are able to command high prices for new stock offerings. Hence, their investment strategies revolve around financial considerations that attempt to lower costs and heighten differentiation simultaneously. Further specifics on financial considerations are offered in Exhibit 1 of "Strategic Management Case Analysis."

RESEARCH AND DEVELOPMENT

Research and development (R&D) has two basic components: product/service R&D and process R&D. **Product/service R&D** refers to efforts that ultimately lead to improvements or innovations in the company's outputs. **Process R&D** aims at reducing the costs of operations and making them more efficient. The more dynamic the industry environment, the more important R&D efforts of both kinds become.

Business units that compete with the niche–low-cost and low-cost strategies emphasize process R&D to reduce their operations costs. However, those business units that use the niche-differentiation and differentiation strategies place more importance on product/service R&D to produce improved and innovative outputs. Finally, adopters of the niche–low-cost/differentiation, low-cost–differentiation, and multiple strategies simultaneously stress both product/service R&D and process R&D efforts.

Organizations with effective R&D departments are, in essence, lowering their risks by making themselves more competitive. Product/service R&D focuses on market competitiveness, and process R&D emphasizes cost competitiveness. But R&D efforts also involve risks of another kind.

Process innovations, for instance, may be too technologically sophisticated to be implemented effectively, or they may not even be used at all. For example, consider the U.S. Postal Service's experience with expensive, high-technology mail sorting machines. The use of these machines achieved only about a third of the expected productivity improvements. At 91 percent of the post office sites reviewed by the Postal Inspection Service, mail that was supposed to have been processed by the new machines was still being processed in the traditional way.[21]

Product/service innovations also involve risks. Once they are introduced, new products or services may find little market demand. RJR Nabisco, for example, spent millions of dollars to develop and produce its "smokeless" cig-arette, Premier. Although introduced to the market with considerable fanfare, smokers refused to switch to the new product, and it was canceled within a few weeks of its introduction.

This example illustrates the problems inherent in **technology transfer,** the process whereby a company transforms its scientific discoveries into mar-ketable products. Some companies accomplish this transfer exceedingly well. Hewlett-Packard, for example, estimates that about 60 percent of its research results in product applications. In fact, over 50 percent of its sales come from products developed within the past three years. This remarkable record results from a two-tier arrangement in which corporate R&D operations work on pro-jects with three-to-seven-year time horizons, while each business unit has its own R&D function that concentrates on shorter-range product applications.[22] But no one method is best. General Electric, another highly innovative firm, op-erates through a corporate-level R&D department that then demonstrates its inventions to each of its business units. This system has resulted in some unex-pected applications; for instance, a device that was invented to protect coal-spraying nozzles in a locomotive was subsequently used to create a new gener-ation of energy-saving light bulbs. Likewise, a medical diagnostic instrument invented for human body imaging is now also used as a cost-saving tool for in-specting jet engines.[23]

Noted management consultant Peter Drucker emphasizes the importance of both process and product R&D. He stresses that Japanese companies "aban-don" their new products as soon as they reach the market. This decision to min-imize the life cycle of each new product forces the Japanese to develop new products immediately to replace the ones currently on the market. Such a swift cycle, they believe, gives them a considerable advantage.[24] U.S. companies are responding by increasingly forming direct research links with their domestic competitors (GM, Ford, and Chrysler, e.g., are jointly developing new battery technology for electric automobiles), asking their suppliers to participate in new-product design programs, and taking ownership positions in small start-up companies that have promising technologies.[25]

HUMAN RESOURCE MANAGEMENT

The human resource management functions include such major activities as planning for future human resource needs, recruiting personnel, placing peo-ple in jobs, compensating them, evaluating their performance, developing them into more effective employees, and enhancing their work environment. Overall, the aim is to build a work force that enables the organization to achieve its goals.[26] Moreover, the human resource function may facilitate the development and utilization of organizational competencies.[27]

One of the major detriments to effective human resource management prac-tices over the past decade was an unprecedented wave of mergers and acquisi-tions. This massive restructuring of American business resulted in widespread layoffs and disillusioned formerly loyal employees. Before this time, many workers assumed that as long as they performed well, they would have a job for as many years as they wished. The past decade not only ended that dream for those who were laid off but also created anxiety among those who survived

STRATEGIC INSIGHT

Importance of Human Resources at Merck and Motorola

Merck, the New Jersey-based pharmaceutical company that has topped *Fortune*'s "Most Admired Corporations" list for several consecutive years, attributes its success to "attracting, developing, and keeping good people." And, indeed, companies in virtually every industry are becoming increasingly aware of the importance of their human resources.

Perhaps the biggest change in attitude has occurred in American factories. The unskilled, single-task job that typified factory work for most of this century is rapidly disappearing. Its replacement is a position on an empowered cross-functional team in which each member must be a generalist who is able to participate in a variety of decisions. Many of these decisions are technical, involving computer-operated machinery and other manufacturing processes.

This need for technically sophisticated employees clashes with the public school system in the United States, where 27.8 percent of the students over the age of 15 drop out before finishing high school and students who have not yet mastered the skills in their current grade are routinely promoted. Examples of this conflict abound. For instance, several years ago, as Motorola was beginning to use empowered teams,

management discovered that only half of its work force could solve the equation $4 + x = 10$. Programs to remediate this deficit cost Motorola $30 million over a five-year period—a cost, its management points out, that did not have to be borne by its major competitors in Japan and Sweden.

A National Association of Manufacturers poll revealed that 50 percent of the 360 companies surveyed reported serious deficiencies among their employees in fundamental math and reading skills. As *Business Week* concludes, "The issue is one of a growing gap between the skills people have and the skills that jobs demand."

Although the root of the problem may be in America's educational system, businesses— and American competitiveness—suffer from it. Consequently, many companies that are upgrading their technological processes or are moving to empowered cross-functional teams are investing sizable amounts of money in remedial math, reading, and writing programs. Observers report that employees tend to pay more attention to their teachers than they did in junior high or in high school because what they are learning is directly relevant to their continued employment.

SOURCES: "Enter the 'New Hero': A Boss Who Knows You Have a Life," *Wall Street Journal Interactive Edition*, 8 May 1996; K. Ludeman, "Motorola's HR Learns the Value of Teams Firsthand," *Personnel Journal*, June 1995, pp. 117–120; K. Kelley and P. Burrow, "Motorola: Training for the Millenium," *Business Week*, 28 March 1994, pp. 158–162; C. Milloy, "Teaching Failure By Example," *Washington Post*, 17 March 1993; F. Swoboda, "A New Breed on the Line," *Washington Post*, 2 August 1992; T. Segal, K. Thurston, and L. Haessly, "When Johnny's Whole Family Can't Read," *Business Week*, 20 July 1992, pp. 68–70; K. Ballen, "America's Most Admired Corporations," *Fortune*, 10 February 1992, p. 43.

the cutbacks. It is difficult for a company to eliminate as much as 20 percent of its work force and still retain a commitment among those who remain.

Hence, a priority for business units, regardless of their particular generic strategy, is to develop commitment among their employees to the organization and to the job. Companies that wish to foster that commitment and develop a strong, competitive work force must create—and maintain—certain working conditions for their employees. And progressive organizations consider human resources their most precious asset. Consequently, such companies give their employees' needs for customized benefits, child day care, parental leave, and flexible working hours equal consideration with such traditional needs as training and development, job enrichment, and promotional opportunities.

The modern work force is frequently characterized as "diverse." In rapidly increasing numbers, women, African Americans, Hispanic Americans, Asian Americans, and disabled persons are transforming the traditional white, male image of many American corporations. As a result, managers must learn to help persons of diverse backgrounds and perceptions to work closely together. This necessity for teamwork, of course, is further impelled by the need for closer cooperation among the employees of the organization's functional areas. The success of such cooperative endeavors as cross-functional teams, quality circles, and just-in-time inventory systems requires a unity of action that can be achieved only through the mutual respect and understanding of others.

This increased diversity in today's work force requires changing organizational policies and practices to mesh with its needs. Attracting the best from the new work force is a prerequisite for reducing costs and/or heightening differentiation. Valuable human resources may contribute to efficiencies through cost-cutting ideas and by lower absenteeism and turnover. Likewise, valuable human resources could promote differentiation via their innovative ideas and excellence in job performance.

In a more narrow sense, a business unit's generic strategy also influences specific components of its human resource program. Take, for example, a company's reward system. Rewards—in the usual sense of recognition, pay raises, and promotions—should be tied to employee behavior that helps the business attain its goals. Hence, business units that follow a niche–low-cost strategy or a low-cost strategy must reward employees who help reduce operating costs. Businesses adopting the niche-differentiation or differentiation strategy should establish reward systems that encourage output improvements or innovations. Finally, those companies that use the niche–low-cost/differentiation strategy or a low-cost–differentiation strategy should have broad-based reward programs that foster activities that either lower costs or promote output improvements or innovations.

INFORMATION SYSTEMS MANAGEMENT

A well-designed information system can benefit all of a business unit's functional areas. A computer-based decision support system can permit each functional area to access the information it needs and to communicate electronically with the other functional departments to enhance interdepartmental coordination.

This advantage is not the only benefit of an effective information system, however. Such a system can cut internal costs (essential to business units pursuing the niche–low-cost, niche–low-cost/differentiation, low-cost, or low-cost–differentiation strategy) while promoting differentiation and quality through a faster response to the market's needs (vital to companies that follow the niche-differentiation, niche–low-cost/differentiation, differentiation, or low-cost–differentiation strategy). In fact, some businesses owe their high performance to their information systems. In the overnight package delivery industry, for example, the chairman and CEO of United Parcel Service (UPS), Kent Nelson, believes that "the leader in information management will be the leader in international package distribution—period."[28] Hence, UPS and such competitors as Federal Express use their core competencies in managing information to keep their costs low while giving their customers superb service (differentiation).

Leading retailers, such as The Limited, have also developed sophisticated information systems to manage their vertically integrated distribution channels. The Limited's system links its hundreds of retail stores throughout the United States to its Columbus, Ohio, headquarters and to its textile mills in Hong Kong. Sales information from each of the stores is gathered and analyzed in Columbus. Based on that analysis, within a few days, the Hong Kong textile mills are producing more fast-selling items and fewer slow-turnover goods.[29]

Because of the rapidity of change in information technology, some companies are increasingly *outsourcing*, or farming out, their information systems function. Kodak, for instance, has turned over to IBM its information processing through 1999. Kodak's management believed that it should concentrate on its core competencies and concluded that running computers was not one of those competencies. Enron, the Houston-based natural gas producer, likewise outsourced its information processing to EDS (the world's largest provider of information services) in order to focus on its goal to become the leading natural gas company in the nation. Says its CEO, "Nothing in [our mission] says we want to be a provider of information systems."[30]

Although other functional areas—such as marketing, human resources management, or POM—may be outsourced, contracting out the information systems management function is more prevalent because many companies simply are unable to keep up with the frequent technological information changes in this area. Additionally, outsourcing can lower a company's information costs because such information systems providers as EDS, IBM, or Andersen Consulting can process data from several client companies through a single mainframe, thereby passing along the lower costs achieved through economies of scale.[31]

Whether it is conducted in-house or farmed out, an information system is effective not because of its sophisticated nature but because it helps the business carry out its strategy. Far too many companies emphasize the hardware and software components of their functional system rather than the system's ability to satisfy customer needs.[32] For that reason, some managers oppose outsourcing of information systems. Computer programmers, these managers maintain, are the key to creating software that can set a company apart from its competitors. They recommend that a business outsource only standard tasks, such as payroll processing or accounts receivable or payable, while retaining technologically creative information systems experts.[33]

MARKETING

Marketing consists of four dimensions: products/services, pricing, channels of distribution/location of outlets, and promotion. The particular generic strategy adopted by the business unit influences how these various dimensions are planned and executed.

As we saw in the preceding chapter, business units that compete using the niche–low-cost and low-cost generic strategies produce no-frills products/ services. Although these outputs are undifferentiated or minimally differentiated with respect to those of their competitors, they are by no means unreliable or shoddy. For example, Motel 6 Inc. offers no-frills rooms. They are clean and contain comfortable, but low-priced, furniture and beds. Motel 6 offers few services; for instance, it has no restaurants or conference rooms. Its simple brand name, Motel 6, is intended to convey the impression of economy services.

Consistent with its no-frills outputs, Motel 6 normally charges low prices. In particular circumstances, it may be able to charge average prices, but only when competitors are either few or far removed. Because it is a service company, channels of distribution are not relevant, but geographic location is. Motel 6 has been successful in choosing locations, primarily near interstate highway exit ramps. Promotion efforts are undertaken at low costs and attempt to convey to the traveling public that Motel 6 offers satisfactory economy lodging.

Different marketing strategies are pursued by businesses that use the generic strategies of differentiation and low-cost–differentiation. Marketing quality products and services that are distinguishable from the outputs of rivals requires approaches considerably at variance from those described in the preceding two paragraphs.[34] For example, Holiday Inn offers larger rooms with better-quality furnishings than Motel 6. Holiday Inns also contain such

---

S T R A T E G I C   I N S I G H T

The Importance of Distribution and Production Capacity at Colgate-Palmolive and Compaq Computer

The role of distribution is often overlooked amid the more glamorous marketing activities of advertising, selling, and designing products and packages. Although less visible, distribution is certainly as important as these other aspects of marketing.

Consider a company that has used distribution to its distinct advantage: Colgate-Palmolive. This multiunit company's most profitable business is not toothpaste or soap; it is, surprisingly, pet food. Part of the secret to the success of its Hill's Pet Products division is distribution. Unlike better-known and much larger competitors such as Ralston Purina, Hill's sells its pet food almost exclusively through veterinarians. Its premium-priced product (a single can of dog food costs about $2) comes in several formulations, ranging from diet food for overweight pets to low-sodium meals for animals with heart conditions. Although Ralston Purina has

similar products, it faces considerable difficulty breaking into Hill's long-established distribution channel.

On the one hand, a good product can be ruined by limited production capacity. Compaq Computer at one time developed an additional computer line called ProLinea. This entry into the inexpensive, low-profit-margin market was enormously successful at building consumer demand. However, Compaq greatly underestimated demand, leading to widespread shortages of the much-desired ProLinea computer within a month of its introduction. While it took Compaq over a year to add shifts at manufacturing plants in order to meet the influx of demand, disappointed consumers turned to such competitors as Dell and Hyundai. Compaq has secured the production capacity necessary and is now also performing well with this product line.

SOURCES: H. W. Jenkins Jr., "That Old-Time Religion," *Wall Street Journal Interactive Edition*, 23 April 1996; "Helping Two Companies Form a Third," *Personnel Journal*, January 1994, p. 63; R. Blackburn and B. Rosen, "Total Quality and Human Resources Management: Lessons Learned from Baldridge Award-Winning Companies," *Executive*, August 1993, pp. 49–66; C. Milloy, "Teaching Failure by Example," *Washington Post*, 17 March 1993; F. Swoboda, "A New Breed on the Line," *Washington Post*, 2 August 1992; K. Ballen, "America's Most Admired Corporations," *Fortune*, 10 February 1992, p. 43.

features as restaurants, shops, swimming pools, and conference rooms. The brand name Holiday Inn is intended to give the impression of quality. Average to high prices are charged for Holiday Inn rooms, depending upon the competitive situation, and promotional efforts convey a differentiated quality image.

Still other marketing strategies are followed by business units that adopt the niche-differentiation and niche–low-cost/differentiation generic strategies. These businesses tend to offer specialized, highest-quality products and services to meet the particular needs of a relatively small market. Holiday Inn Suites, featured in some Holiday Inns, offer spacious rooms, wet bars, hair dryers, and complimentary food, beverages, and newspapers. The brand name attempts to convey the impression that in addition to having access to Holiday Inns' restaurants, shops, swimming pools, and conference rooms, customers will be further pampered by these extra features. High prices are charged for these suites, and promotional campaigns address the relatively few potential customers who desire the suites' extra features.

A summary of our discussion to this point is shown in Table 7.1 (see pages 186–87). The entries in the left column represent the generic strategy that a given business unit is following. The horizontal entries to the right indicate the particular strategy that should be used by each of the business unit's functional areas.

BENCHMARKING

Buyers everywhere look for value. In Lima, Peru, Coke is preferred to the locally produced Inca Cola. Customers across Latin America, Europe, Africa, Asia, and Australia demand Levis and Toyotas. What is the ramification of creating and delivering value for the functional areas? The answer is that in order to provide value to buyers, the business must have superior functional and cross-functional performance. **Benchmarking,** in this context, refers to the comparison of functional and cross-functional performance of one business relative to desirable standards.

Traditionally, U.S. businesses benchmarked their performance relative to superior rivals in the same American industry. This worked well particularly during the post–World War II years when the plants of overseas competitors were struggling to emerge from being bombed into rubble. During the 1970s, however, the game changed dramatically as "lean and mean" European and Japanese competitors began to challenge U.S. businesses not only globally but also in the American market. By the latter 1970s and throughout the 1980s, U.S. companies began to benchmark against the best global competitors in the same industry. This allowed many of the American enterprises to achieve competitive parity with their global rivals.

What is emerging during the 1990s and what will drive superior performance into the next century is the realization that achieving competitive parity (or even a marginal advantage) is not enough and will not last long. According to McKinsey and Company, a leading global consulting firm, a business and its functional areas must strive not for competitive parity but for "stimulating new ways of competing that dramatically surpass competitors' capabilities."[35] This involves benchmarking functional and cross-functional performance of one business against the best in any industry anywhere in the world. Indeed, each

The Link Between Business Unit Strategies and Functional Strategies

	Purchasing & Materials Management	Production/ Operations Management	Finance
Niche–low-cost	Purchase at low costs through networks and contacts with domestic and foreign suppliers. Operate storage and warehouse facilities and control inventory efficiently.	Emphasize low initial investments in plants, equipment, and outlets. Emphasize low operation costs.	Lower financial costs by borrowing when credit costs are low, selling common stock during a bull market, etc.
Niche-differentiation	Purchase high-quality inputs, even if they cost more. Conduct storage, warehouse, and inventory activities with utmost care, even if at higher costs (e.g., fine wine must be kept in high-cost storage with correct lighting and air-conditioned space).	Emphasize specialized quality in operations even at high cost, such as the hand crafting of products.	Emphasize obtaining resources and funding output improvements or innovations. Emphasize innovations even when financial costs may be high.
Niche–low-cost/ differentiation	Purchase high-quality inputs, if possible, at low costs. This may be done through the development of organizational expertise, as Porsche has done. Conduct storage, warehouse, and inventory activities with utmost care, if possible, at low costs.	Emphasize specialized quality of operations, if possible, at low costs.	Emphasize obtaining resources and funding output improvements or innovations, if possible, at low costs.
Low-cost	Purchase at low costs through quantity discounts. Operate storage and warehouse facilities and control inventory efficiently.	Emphasize operation efficiencies through learning, economies of scale, and capital-labor substitution possibilities.	Lower financial costs by borrowing when credit costs are low, selling common stock during a bull market, etc.
Differentiation	Purchase high-quality inputs, even if they cost more. Conduct storage, warehouse, and inventory activities when extensive care, even if at higher costs.	Emphasize quality in . operations, even if at high cost.	Emphasize obtaining resources and funding output improvements or innovations. Emphasize innovations even when financial costs may be high.
Low-cost– differentiation	Purchase high-quality inputs, if possible, at low costs. Conduct storage, warehouse, and inventory activities with care, if possible, at low costs.	Emphasize quality in operations, if possible, at low costs.	Emphasize obtaining resources and funding output improvements or innovations, if possible, at low costs.
Multiple	Mixed	Mixed	Mixed

Research & Development	Human Resource Management	Information Systems	Marketing
Emphasize process R&D aimed at reducing costs of operations and distribution.	Emphasize reward systems that encourage lowering of costs.	Emphasize timely and pertinent information on costs of operations.	Emphasize low-cost distribution and low-cost advertising and promotion.
Emphasize product and service R&D aimed at enhancing the outputs of the business.	Emphasize reward systems that encourage output improvements or innovations.	Emphasize timely and pertinent information on the ongoing specialized processes that yield highly differentiated outputs.	Emphasize specialized distribution and targeted advertising and promotion.
Emphasize product and service R&D as well as process R&D.	Emphasize reward systems that encourage lowering of costs and output improvements or innovations.	Emphasize timely and pertinent information on costs of operations and on the ongoing specialized processes that yield highly differentiated outputs.	Emphasize specialized distribution and targeted advertising and promotion, if possible, at low cost, as Porsche has done.
Emphasize process R&D aimed at reducing costs of operations and distribution.	Emphasize reward systems that encourage lowering of costs.	Emphasize timely and pertinent information on costs of operations.	Emphasize low-cost distribution and low-cost advertising and promotion.
Emphasize product and service R&D aimed at enhancing the outputs of the business.	Emphasize reward systems that encourage output improvements and innovations.	Emphasize timely and pertinent information on the ongoing processes that yield differentiated outputs.	Emphasize differentiated distribution and emphasize advertising and promotion on a broad scale.
Emphasize product and service R&D as well as process R&D.	Emphasize reward systems that encourage output improvements or innovations and the lowering of costs.	Emphasize timely and pertinent information on costs of operations and and on the ongoing improvement or innovation processes that are meant to yield differentiated outputs.	Emphasize differentiated distribution and emphasize advertising and promotion, on a broad scale, if possible, at low costs.
Mixed	Mixed	Mixed	Mixed

business and its functional personnel need to answer the question, Are we as good as the best in the world marketplace? According to one expert, "If you're not better than the best on a worldwide basis, you're not going to make a living."[36] Although benchmarking may start with competitor analysis, it should be extended to other businesses outside the industry. Benchmarking only against the rivals tends to encourage personnel to "fight the last war" or to develop competencies to beat competitors "as they exist today, rather than as they will exist tomorrow."[37]

INTEGRATING THE FUNCTIONS

For a business unit's generic strategy to be successful, each functional area must do more than simply operate effectively. Overall strategic success requires that all functional activities be tightly integrated so that their operations mesh smoothly with one another. Those businesses that are best able to achieve functional integration are those most likely to attain the competitive advantages detailed in the following paragraphs.

■ Superior Product Design

Although product design has been recognized as an important competitive dimension for years, only in the past few years has it received increased attention. Until recently, design was primarily associated with product appearance. But now, the concept is being broadened to include such features as designing a product for easy manufacturability so that fewer parts have to be purchased. Additionally, increased emphasis is being put on improving the product's functionality (its ability to perform its purpose) and quality. Overall, today good design addresses aesthetics as well as "the consumer's every concern—how a product works, how it feels in the hand, how easy it is to assemble and fix, and even, in this era of environmental concern, whether it can be recycled."[38]

Gaining a competitive advantage through superior product design involves all functional areas. Even in those companies where POM has been the dominant function, the revised emphasis is on the interrelationships of all functional areas. For instance, when Caterpillar reorganized so that it could compete more effectively with heavy-equipment manufacturers from Japan, it first "intended to move only its design engineers to the plants to work more closely with the production people. . . . [Then the question became] why just the manufacturing and the engineering people . . . so marketing and pricing folks [also moved] into the plants."[39]

A well-designed product is attractive and easy to build, market, use, and maintain. Simplicity drives the best-designed products. But superior product design alone is not sufficient to gain a substantial competitive edge; design must be combined with superior service.

■ Superior Customer Service

Developing and maintaining the quality of customer service is often more challenging than improving product quality.[40] The reason is that the consumer perceives service value primarily at the time the service is either rendered or not rendered. As one manager put it:

S T R A T E G I C   I N S I G H T

Concurrent Engineering at Chrysler and Caterpillar

Impressive increases in manufacturing productivity in Japan and in Germany over the past twenty years and the deepening U. S. trade deficit have placed growing pressure on U. S. factories to become more efficient. Although there are a number of ways to increase industrial productivity, the process of concurrent engineering seems to hold particular promise.

During the 1980s, American manufacturers spent billions of dollars on factory automation, with no dramatic increase in productivity. Some experts believe the poor result was due to misplaced priority: The emphasis should have been on product design rather than on the production process. Even the most sophisticated automation equipment cannot compensate for a poorly designed product, in that design decisions "lock in" up to 90 percent of production costs long before the first item is ever produced. As a result, U. S. manufacturers are beginning to adopt concurrent engineering, a technique in which the product and its production processes are designed simultaneously.

Traditionally, an organization's R&D department came up with a new product idea. Then the idea went to design engineers who built a prototype, which was then turned over to the production department. Production had to develop a process for manufacturing the product, which usually meant that they had to give the blueprints back to design for revision. Further transfer of the blueprints back and forth between design and production could occur several times. Finally, purchasing would get copies of the finalized plans and ask for bids from suppliers. Then eventually, actual production of the product would begin. If problems occurred during the production process, the product might have to be reworked in each of the preceding departments.

By contrast, concurrent engineering brings together personnel from R&D, design engineering, purchasing, production, and marketing, as well as from the company's suppliers, to work side by side and compare notes constantly from the very inception of the project. Using concurrent engineering, Chrysler was able to bring its Viper, Neon, Intrepid, and Grand Cherokee models to market in only three years—versus Chrysler's normal five-year development time. And adoption of concurrent engineering has helped Caterpillar cut its new product development time in half. One expert estimates that the use of concurrent engineering can save a company anywhere from 20 to 90 percent of its usual time to market, while its quality improves by 200 to 600 percent and its return on assets increases from 20 to 120 percent.

SOURCES: "Caterpillar: Exports to Make Up 75% of Sales within 10 Years," *Dow Jones News Service*, 13 May 1996; K. Jackson, "Chrysler's Next Task: Update the Product," *Automotive News*, 21 August 1995, pp. 18–19; F. AitSahlia, E. Johnson, and P. Will, "Is Concurrent Engineering Always a Sensible Propositions?" *IEEE Transactions on Engineering Management*, May 1995, pp. 166–170; E. Raia, "IH Story," *Purchasing*, 18 February 1993; K. Kelley, A. Bernstein, and R. Neff, "Caterpillar's Don Fites: Why He Didn't Blink," *Business Week*, 10 August 1992; O. Port, Z. Schiller, and R. W. King, "A Smarter Way to Manufacture," *Business Week*, 30 April 1990, pp. 110–117.

You can tell me how awful someone's behavior was, but there is nothing for me to go back and look at. There aren't any artifacts, like broken gizmos I can go back and test.[41]

All functional areas must work together to provide the customer with product and service value. For example, a supermarket must fulfill several customer needs. First, it must offer value to customers in their shopping. Carrying the products that customers desire, at competitive prices, means that the purchasing, inventory, information systems, and finance functions must communicate with one another and cooperate closely. Next, the store must make certain that its employees are able to respond to customer inquiries. This capability requires effective human resource management practices in hiring and training. Then, the supermarket must ensure that it stocks sufficient quantities of the items that it advertises. Meeting this objective requires interaction among the purchasing, inventory, information systems, and marketing functions. Finally, the store must provide the means for customers to check out their purchases accurately and quickly, requiring the close cooperation of information systems and human resource management.

The importance of service cannot be overemphasized. In a recent survey, over one-third of the respondents indicated that they choose businesses that charge high prices but provide excellent service over companies that offer low prices but mediocre service.[42] As one observer points out:

> Despite all the talk these days about quality and customer satisfaction, most companies provide more lip service than customer service. Companies that really do provide service can command premium prices for their products. . . . [For example,] at Premier's [a business that provides hard-to-find fasteners and other related items] . . . charges are typically between 10% and 15% more than competitors' prices—and sometimes as much as 200% higher.[43]

Personal attention is an important way that some businesses provide superior service. Personal attention involves paying heed to details, addressing customers' concerns, answering technical questions, and providing service after the sale.[44] Such attention often plays an important psychological role as well. For example, the top managers of one industrial products supplier routinely visit plants to which the company has sold its products. In speaking of the psychological aspect of those visits, one manager indicated:

> We know our machine products are reliable and do not require visits. But when our clients see us physically inspecting their machines, sometimes merely dusting them off, they derive a sense of security and comfort that our products are in their plants, albeit at higher costs to them. When they are asked for a reference on suppliers, they usually suggest our firm.[45]

Recall that TQM not only involves producing a high-quality product, but it also implies quality in all of the services that accompany the product. In this regard, a TQM orientation means that a company must be willing to perceive the world from the customer's viewpoint and that the company can move quickly to satisfy the customer.[46] Consequently, we now examine the importance of superior speed.

■ Superior Speed

Speed in developing, making, and distributing products and services can give a business a significant competitive advantage.[47] In fact, a survey of fifty major U.S.-based companies revealed that speed (alternatively referred to as "time-based strategy") was a top priority.[48] To illustrate the point, consider the comments of two managers:

> We can design, produce, and deliver before our big competitors get the paperwork done.

> We have a lock on our customers. You see, it may take some of our big buyers several weeks [to complete a purchase order], during which time their engineers request an order, their purchasing department receives the request and commu-

nicates it to the suppliers. We are in constant touch with the plant engineers, and normally we know what their next purchases are before their own purchasing departments. Consequently, we can normally deliver their needs overnight or within a few days.[49]

Some companies have taken these lessons to heart. Motorola, for instance, cut the time it takes to produce a cellular radio telephone from 14 hours to 90 minutes. Concomitantly, the retail price of the phone dropped from $3,000 to $600 in three years.[50] Today, Coleman Company can produce and ship an order of camping stoves or lanterns in a week, versus two months just a few years ago. At the same time, it significantly reduced new product development time. Citibank estimates that Coleman's increased speed has enhanced the company's value by about $100 million.[51]

The importance of superior speed in serving customers cannot be exaggerated. For example, Premier, the fastener company mentioned earlier, received a call one day from one of its customers, Caterpillar. A $10 electrical relay had malfunctioned, bringing one of Caterpillar's assembly lines to a halt. A Premier representative located a replacement part in a Los Angeles warehouse and had it placed immediately on a plane bound for St. Louis. When it arrived, a Premier employee picked the part up and delivered it to Caterpillar. As might be expected, Caterpillar and other firms are willing to pay significantly higher prices for Premier's products because of the speed and superior service they receive.[52]

■ Superior Guarantee

Even in the best-managed businesses, problems occasionally arise that result in less-than-acceptable product or service quality. Hence, companies must take steps to guarantee an acceptable level of quality. Highly successful companies often go to great lengths to back their guarantees. For example, the famous retailer and mail-order house L. L. Bean accepts customer returns of its products for any reason, even after several years. A pair of hunting boots that was returned after ten years would be immediately replaced by a new pair with no questions asked.[53]

Many companies, however, ignore this competitive advantage. Often, guarantees lapse after a very short time period or contain too many exceptional conditions to be effective competitive weapons. For instance, some companies guarantee their electronic products for only ninety days; others are sufficiently confident of their product quality to offer one-year guarantees. Some airlines guarantee that their passengers will make connecting flights on time if no delays are caused by air traffic control problems or poor weather conditions. Unfortunately for the passengers, the majority of flight delays are due to these two factors.

Because of its intangible nature, a service guarantee is even more challenging to provide than a product guarantee. Christopher W. L. Hart, a business researcher and consultant, suggests that the following five desirable characteristics be included in service guarantees.[54]

- The guarantee should be unconditional, with no exceptions.
- It should be easily understood and written in simple language.
- The guarantee should be meaningful by guaranteeing what is important to the customer and making it worth the customer's time and effort to invoke the guarantee, should he or she be dissatisfied.

- The guarantee should be convenient to invoke and not require the customer to appeal to several layers of bureaucracy.
- The customer should be satisfied promptly, without a lengthy waiting period.

These characteristics, of course, should also be included in product guarantees.

CROSS-FUNCTIONAL TEAMS AND PROCESS MANAGEMENT

Satisfying the customer may require that instead of functional managers, the organization adopt **process managers** who supervise teams of people representing various functional areas. Consequently, the parameter of activities would shift from independent functions to key processes containing interdependent functions. This may not only improve operations, but also permit the flattening of the organizational structure (further discussed under horizontal structure in chapter 8).

The advantage of process management and cross-functional teams over independently operating functions can be demonstrated by a product-improvement example. Traditionally, the marketing manager could authorize market research studies. The market research group may ask customers through a number of methods what they might desire in products and services. When the results of the market research are brought back, they are submitted to the marketing manager, who may discuss the results with a vice president. Once the vice president gives her approval, the results are typically presented to the production manager. This manager normally asks the production engineers to develop a prototype for testing. If the prototype is acceptable to marketing, the manager of purchasing is contacted and asked for an analysis of costs associated with the procurement of parts and components necessary for the product. The personnel in purchasing are subsequently charged with determining such costs through their interaction with various suppliers. If supplier prices are too high, then the production people may be asked to revise product specifications that might permit the use of less costly components and parts. The revised product specification must then be approved by the marketing personnel.

As is evident, much effort (going up and down as well as laterally in the organization) is expended in the above product improvement example to coordinate activities among independently operating functional areas. Note that if a process manager were in charge of the same activities, while having in her group personnel from the various functions, that effectiveness and efficiency might improve. As an example, let us scrutinize how Thermos developed its breakthrough product for the charcoal barbecue grill market[55] through a cross-functional team.

Thermos assigned the job to develop a superior grill to its product development process manager. The members of this process group were composed of people from various functional areas. This enabled the group to simultaneously consider multiple functional issues (such as marketing, production, and purchasing issues) relevant to the product development effort rather than in sequence. The process group members, similar to many people, presumed that the barbecue grill was typically used by men. Moreover, they assumed that grilling might be an enjoyable alternative to cooking in the kitchen. In order to gather further information, Thermos's cross-functional team made trips to various parts of the country attending and videotaping barbecues at home.

Several surprising conclusions were drawn. First, cooks were often found to be women rather than men. Second, grilling seemed to require substantial effort. That is, the charcoal must be purchased and brought to the house, where it has to be put into the grill and lighted. After the cookout, cleaning the grill is arduous and time consuming. Third, rather than being an enjoyable experience, the cooks were visibly uncomfortable with the dirty chores involved in preparing, grilling, and cleaning afterwards. Fourth, barbecuing seemed to take place on expensive decks in attractive backyards, and a dirty, ash-ridden grill detracted from the appearance of the residence.

The cross-functional team members decided on the development of a nontraditional product in response to their first-hand observations. The consensus was that the product needed to be attractive and low maintenance while producing a charcoal taste. This meant that the product must use electricity and have a nonstick cooking grid (for easy cleaning). Moreover, the warm-up time had to be less than for charcoal.

To produce a charcoal taste with conventional electrical grill models was not possible because they used heat rods built several inches away from the grill surface, which baked the meat instead of grilling it. To obtain a cookout taste, it was necessary to sear the meat with electricity. Consequently, electrical heat rods needed to be structured within the surface of the grill. Also, a double-walled insulated dome was necessary to keep moisture, smoke, and the heat inside. The parts and components needed for manufacture of such a new product were determined to be reasonably priced by select suppliers.

This is how Thermos developed its thermal electric grill. The grill preheats within five minutes and produces the barbecue lines on the surface of the meat. Moreover, the meat tastes as if it were prepared on charcoal. The grill is not only attractive but it also is easy to clean.

SUMMARY

Once corporate-level and business unit generic strategies are developed, management must turn its attention to formulating strategies for each business unit's functional areas. Here, the manager should not view the strategy of one functional area in isolation, because it is the extent to which all of the functional tasks mesh smoothly that determines the effectiveness of the unit's generic strategy.

A business unit's purchasing strategy will differ depending upon which generic strategy it adopts. Companies that use the niche–low-cost strategy or the low-cost strategy emphasize purchasing at the lowest costs possible. Those that use niche-differentiation or differentiation stress the procurement of high-quality inputs, even if they cost more than alternative offerings. Organizations that pursue niche–low-cost/differentiation or low-cost–differentiation attempt to buy high-quality inputs at low costs, and those that employ multiple strategies use a mixture of purchasing plans. Purchasing is the first step in the materials management process, followed by storage and warehousing functions and inventory control. The latest trend in materials management, the just-in-time inventory system, ties these functions together.

The next functional strategic area is POM. Small business units that compete with the niche–low-cost strategy emphasize low initial investments in their plants, equipment, and outlets to hold their fixed costs down, and they attempt to keep their variable operations costs as low as possible. Small businesses competing with niche–differentiation stress POM strategies that yield superior quality, and those that use niche–low-cost/differentiation emphasize POM activities that simultaneously lower costs and heighten differentiation. Large business units, on the other hand, are able to take advantage of the experience curve by using learning, economies of scale, and capital-labor substitution possibilities to their advantage. To gain market share so that they may enjoy the experience curve, large business units that compete with the low-cost strategy may sell at low prices to increase volume. Large enterprises that use differentiation or low-cost–differentiation may attempt to gain market share by offering higher-quality outputs. But using the experience curve entails risks, such as becoming wed over time to an obsolete technology.

One of the primary considerations in any POM strategy is product or service quality. Businesses that build quality in, rather than attempt to inspect for quality after production has occurred, are able to enhance both productivity and profitability. Well-designed TQM programs, in particular, have yielded positive results.

In the finance function, business units that compete with the niche–low-cost and low-cost strategies pursue financial strategies intended to lower their financial costs. Companies that adopt niche–differentiation and differentiation strategies develop financial strategies that fund quality enhancements. And those that use niche–low-cost/differentiation, low-cost–differentiation, and multiple strategies use their financial function both to lower costs and to promote quality enhancements.

Research and development (R&D) has two basic components: product/service R&D and process R&D. Business units competing with the niche–low-cost and low-cost strategies emphasize process R&D to reduce their operations costs; those that use niche-differentiation or differentiation place greater importance on product/service R&D; and adopters of niche–low-cost/differentiation, low-cost–differentiation, and multiple strategies simultaneously stress both types of R&D.

Effective organizations will manage their human resource function so as to maintain a strong, competitive work force. This goal requires attention to personnel needs and the development of strategies that strengthen organizational and job performance commitment and teamwork across functional areas.

Tying all of these functions together is the organization's information system. Well-designed information systems are capable of cutting internal costs while they promote differentiation and quality through faster responses to the market's needs.

In marketing, the particular generic strategy adopted by a business unit influences the types of products or services the business offers, its prices for those products or services, the channels of distribution it uses, the location of its outlets, and its advertising and promotional policies. The key is to strive for consistency among these elements.

How well the functional areas perform may be evaluated through benchmarking. This involves the comparison of functional performance of one business relative to desirable standards.

Finally, it is essential that the business's functional activities be tightly integrated. An organization that is able to mesh its functional strategies smoothly is more likely to gain a competitive advantage based on superior product design, customer service, speed, and/or guarantee. In some situations, satisfying the customer may require that instead of functional managers, the organization adopt process managers who supervise teams of people representing various functional areas.

TAKE IT TO THE NET

We invite you to visit the Wright page on the Prentice Hall Web site at:

http://www.prenhall.com/wright

for this chapter's World Wide Web exercise.

KEY CONCEPTS

Benchmarking   The comparison of functional and cross-functional performance of one business relative to desirable standards.

Experience curve   The reduction in per-unit costs that occurs as an organization gains experience producing a product or service. The experience curve concept is based on three underlying variables: learning (the more an employee performs a task, the more efficient he or she should become at the job), economies of scale (the decline in per-unit costs of a product or service as the absolute volume of production increases per period of time), and capital-labor substitution possibilities (as volumes increase, the organization may be able to substitute labor for capital, or capital for labor, depending upon which combination produces lower costs and/or greater effectiveness).

Functional strategy   The strategy pursued by each functional area of a business unit. Functional areas are usually referred to as "departments" and include purchasing/materials management, production/operations, finance, research and development, marketing, human resources, information systems, and marketing. Their strategies may take various forms, depending upon which generic strategy the business unit adopts.

Just-in-time inventory system (JIT)   An inventory system, popularized by the Japanese, in which suppliers deliver parts just at the time they are needed by the buying organization to use in its production process. Used properly, such a system holds inventory, storage, and warehousing costs to a minimum.

Process managers   Managers who supervise teams of people representing various functional areas.

Process R&D   Research and development activities that concentrate upon reducing the costs of operations and making them more efficient.

Product/service R&D   Research and development activities that are intended to lead to improvements or innovations in the firm's products or services.

Technology transfer   The process whereby a company transforms its scientific discoveries into marketable products.

DISCUSSION QUESTIONS

1. What is the relationship among corporate-level, business unit, and functional strategies?

2. Explain the linkage that a just-in-time inventory system provides between the purchasing and production functions. What are the implications for quality?

3. Production/operation management concepts are equally applicable to manufacturing and service organizations. Explain the POM process at a university.

4. What are some of the more important relationships among the POM, finance, and R&D functions?

5. What sorts of POM strategies might a small business unit adopt to compete effectively with a large business unit?

6. Relate the concept of the experience curve to the production operations of an automobile assembly plant.

7. Explain the relationship between quality and productivity.

8. What is the linkage between long-term capital investment decisions and the organization's corporate and business unit strategies?

9. Give, and explain, an example of (a) a business that emphasizes product/service R&D, and (b) another business that emphasizes process R&D.

10. What are some of the major relationships among marketing, information systems, and human resources management?

STRATEGIC MANAGEMENT EXERCISES

1. Assume that two groups of investors are each planning to start a restaurant in the same city. The first group wishes to appeal to family meal needs, and the second wants to appeal to the needs of people who prefer gourmet food in particularly nice surroundings on special occasions. As is evident, different functional strategies will need to be adopted by the two restaurants. How would you suggest that each restaurant plan and implement its functional strategies? Be specific in your suggestions. If you need further information, either conduct relevant research or make reasonable assumptions.

2. Assume that you are asked to consult for a top-of-the-line restaurant in New York City that competes with the niche-differentiation strategy. While attending management's strategic-planning session, you learn that the managers would like to broaden their appeal in the New

York City market. One way of doing that, they believe, is to reduce their prices. To attain that end, they must cut costs. Therefore, one manager suggests that to reduce costs, they should make some of their purchases locally instead of purchasing from the highest-quality suppliers worldwide. (Currently, the restaurant flies in certain foods from foreign countries at considerable cost.) Another manager believes that the restaurant should use less expensive tablecloths and napkins. Finally, another wishes to cancel the restaurant's live musical entertainment to save money. Through these cost-cutting measures, the managers believe that they can reduce their prices and become more competitive.

What advice would you give these managers regarding their functional strategies?

3. Contrast the functional strategies that are followed by two automobile manufacturers: (a) Ford, which, as one of the world's largest producers, competes with the low-cost–differentiation strategy, and (b) Rolls-Royce, a relatively small company, which uses the niche-differentiation strategy. Specifically, how might you expect these two companies to differ in carrying out each of the following functional strategies: purchasing/materials management, production/operations, finance, research and development, human resources, information system, and marketing?

4. Select a specific company on which you will be able to obtain information.

   a. Determine which generic business unit strategy this company has adopted.
   b. Analyze the company's functional strategy in purchasing/materials management, production/operations, finance, research and development, human resources, information systems, and marketing.
   c. Analyze the extent to which these functional strategies mesh smoothly with one another and with the business's generic strategy.
   d. Make suggestions for improvements in the company's functional strategies.
   e. If you were asked to form cross-functional teams and have process managers for these teams, what would be your suggestions?

NOTES

1. J. Cole, "Boeing's Dominance of Aircraft Industry Runs into Bumpiness," *Wall Street Journal*, 10 July 1992; D. J. Yang, M. Oneal, S. Toy, M. Maremont, and R. Neff, "How Boeing Does It," *Business Week*, 9 July 1990, pp. 46–50.

2. E. E. Scheuing, *Purchasing Management* (Englewood Cliffs, N. J.: Prentice Hall, 1989), p. 4.

3. T. H. Hendrick and F. G. Moore, *Production/Operations Management*, 9th ed. (Homewood, Ill.: Irwin, 1985), p. 336.

4. J. G. Miller and P. Gilmour, "Materials Managers: Who Needs Them?" *Harvard Business Review* 57, no. 4 (1979): 145.

5. S. P. Galante, "Distributors Bow to Demands of 'Just-in-Time' Delivery," *Wall Street Journal*, 30 June 1986.

6. F. Swoboda, "GM's Saturn Plant Closed by Strike," *Washington Post*, 28 August 1992.

7. J. Dreyfuss, "Shaping Up Your Suppliers," *Fortune*, 10 April 1989, p. 116.

8. J. Browne, J. Harhen, and J. Shivnan, *Production Management Systems: A CIM Perspective* (Workingham, England: Addison-Wesley, 1988), pp. 158–159.

9. W. T. Neese, "Food for Thought: Should We Teach More about Operations?" *Marketing News*, 17 January 1994, p. 4.

10. E. A. Haas, "Breakthrough Manufacturing," *Harvard Business Review* 65, no. 2 (1987): 75–81.

11. See Boston Consulting Group, *Perspectives on Experience* (Boston: The Boston Consulting Group, 1976); G. Hall and S. Howell, "The Experience Curve from an Economist's Perspective," *Strategic Management Journal* 6 (1985): 197–212.

12. A. Taylor III, "Can GM Remodel Itself?" *Fortune*, 13 January 1992, p. 33.

13. T. Peters and N. Austin, *A Passion for Excellence* (New York: Random House, 1985), p. 53.

14. R. D. Buzzell and B. T. Gale, *The PIMS Principles* (New York: Free Press, 1987), chap. 6.

15. B. Saporito, "Behind the Tumult at P & G," *Fortune*, 7 March 1994, pp. 74–82.

16. R. Johnson, W. O. Winchell, and P. B. DuBose, *Strategy and Quality* (Milwaukee: American Society for Quality Control, 1989); B. Jones, "Formula for Success," *Progressive Grocer*, February 1994, pp. 117–118.

17. P. Crosby, *Quality Is Free* (New York: McGraw-Hill, 1979), p. 1.

18. W. E. Deming, *Out of the Crisis* (Cambridge, Mass.: Massachusetts Institute of Technology, Center for Advanced Engineering Study, 1986).

19. United States General Accounting Office, "Management Practices: U.S. Companies Improve Performance Through Quality Efforts," GAO/NSIAD-91-190, May 1991.

20. Ibid., p. 4.

21. M. Lewyn, "The Post Office Wants Everyone to Pay for Its Mistakes," *Business Week*, 5 March 1990, p. 28.

22. G. Bylinsky, "Turning R&D into Real Products," *Fortune*, 2 July, 1990, pp. 72–73; J. Benson, "A Far Different Competitive Landscape," *Directors and Boards* (Winter 1994): 12–13.

23. A. K. Naj, "GE's Latest Invention: A Way to Move Ideas from Lab to Market," *Wall Street Journal*, 14 June 1990.

24. P. F. Drucker, "Japan: New Strategies for a New Reality," *Wall Street Journal*, 2 October 1991.

25. K. Kelly, O. Port, J. Treece, G. DeGeorge, and Z. Schiller, "Learning from Japan," *Business Week*, 27 January 1992, p. 53.

26. P. M. Wright and G. C. McMahan, "Theoretical Perspectives for Strategic Human Resource Management," *Journal of Management* 18 (1992): 298.

27. A. A. Lado and M. C. Wilson, "Human Resource Systems and Sustained Competitive Advantage: A Competency Based Perspective," *Academy of Management Review* 19 (1994): 699–727; J. A. Parnell, "Functional Background and Business Strategy: The Impact of Executive Strategy Fit on Performance," *Journal of Business Strategies* 11, no. 1, pp. 49–62.

28. P. Coy, "The New Realism in Office Systems," *Business Week*, 15 June 1992, p. 128.

29. R. B. Chase and D. A. Garvin, "The Service Factory," *Harvard Business Review* 67, no. 4 (1989): 67.

30. J. W. Verity, "Let's Order Out for Technology," *Business Week*, 13 May (1996), p. 47.

31. Ibid.

32. P. Coy and C. Hawkins, "UPS: Up from the Stone Age," *Business Week*, 15 June 1992, p. 132; Coy, "The New Realism in Office Systems," pp. 129–130.

33. Kirkpatrick, "Why Not Farm Out Your Computing?", p. 112.

34. M. McCarthy, "Mazda Earmarks $30 Million to Ring in Millenia," *Brandweek*, 7 March 1994, pp. 1, 6.

35. A. S. Walleck, J. D. O'Halloran, and C. A. Leader, "Benchmarking World-Class Performance," *The McKinsey Quarterly* 1 (1991): 8, 9.

36. S. Sherman, "Are You as Good as the Best in the World?" *Fortune*, 13 December 1993, p. 95; B. Dumaine, "Design That Sells and Sells and . . . ," *Fortune*, 11 March 1991, p. 86.

37. Walleck, O'Halloran, and Leader, "Benchmarking World-Class Performance," pp. 8, 9.

38. Dumaine, "Design That Sells and Sells and . . . ," p. 86.

39. J. Main, "Manufacturing the Right Way," *Fortune*, 21 May 1990, p. 54.

40. A. G. Perkins, "Manufacturing: Maximizing Service, Minimizing Inventory," *Harvard Business Review* 72, no. 2: 13–14.

41. A. Bennett, "Making the Grade with the Customer," *Wall Street Journal*, 12 November 1990.

42. A. Bennett, "Many Consumers Expect Better Service and Say They Are Willing to Pay for It," *Wall Street Journal*, 12 November 1990.

43. D. Milbank, "Service Enables Nuts-and-Bolts Supplier to Be More Than Sum of Its Parts," *Wall Street Journal*, 16 November 1990.

44. L. Dube, L. M. Renaghan, and J. M. Miller, "Measuring Customer Satisfaction for Strategic Management," *Cornell Hotel and Restaurant Administration Quarterly* (February 1994): 39–47.

45. P. Wright, "Competitive Strategies for Small Businesses," in A. A. Thompson Jr., A. J. Strickland III, and W. E. Fulmer, eds., *Readings in Strategic Management* (Plano, Tex.: Business Publications, 1984), p. 90.

46. F. Rose, "New Quality Means Service Too," *Fortune*, 22 April 1991, pp. 97, 100.

47. W. M. Bulkeley, "Pushing the Pace," *Wall Street Journal*, 23 December 1994, pp. 1, 5.

48. B. Dumaine, "How Managers Can Succeed Through Speed," *Fortune*, 13 February 1989, p. 54.

49. Wright, "Competitive Strategies for Small Businesses," p. 89.

50. J. D. Burge, "Motorola's Transition to a High Performance Workforce," an Executive Lecture at James Madison University, 20 February 1992.

51. B. Dumaine, "Earning More by Moving Faster," *Fortune*, 7 October 1991, pp. 89, 94.

52. S. Phillips, A. Dunkin, J. Treece, and K. Hammonds, "King Customer," *Business Week*, 12 March 1990, p. 88.

53. B. Uttal, "Companies That Serve You Best," *Fortune*, 7 December 1987, p. 98.

54. C. W. L. Hart, "The Power of Unconditional Service Guarantees," *The McKinsey Quarterly* (Summer 1989): 75–76.

55. B. Dumaine, "Payoff from the New Management," *Fortune*, 13 December 1993, pp. 103–104.

STRATEGIC MANAGEMENT MODEL

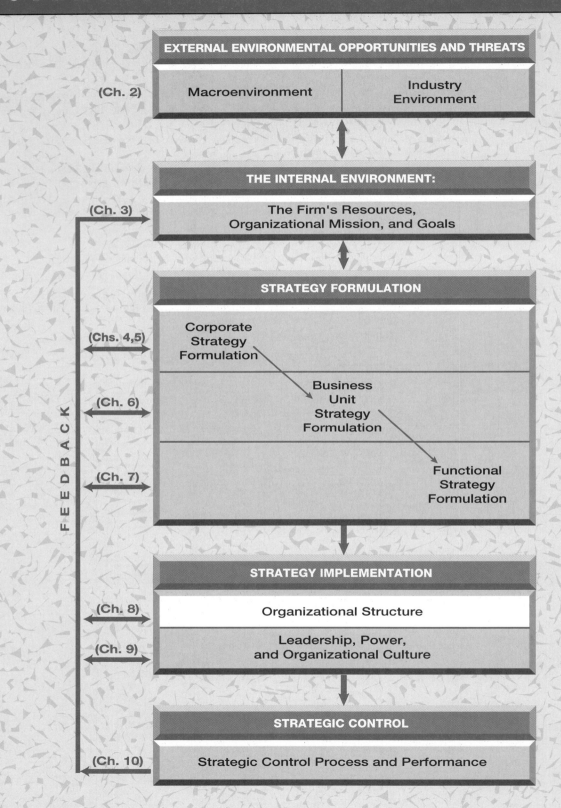

EXTERNAL ENVIRONMENTAL OPPORTUNITIES AND THREATS

(Ch. 2)

| Macroenvironment | Industry Environment |

THE INTERNAL ENVIRONMENT:

(Ch. 3)

The Firm's Resources, Organizational Mission, and Goals

STRATEGY FORMULATION

(Chs. 4,5) Corporate Strategy Formulation

(Ch. 6) Business Unit Strategy Formulation

(Ch. 7) Functional Strategy Formulation

STRATEGY IMPLEMENTATION

(Ch. 8) Organizational Structure

(Ch. 9) Leadership, Power, and Organizational Culture

STRATEGIC CONTROL

(Ch. 10) Strategic Control Process and Performance

FEEDBACK

8 Strategy Implementation: Organizational Structure

The four preceding chapters dealt with strategy formulation at the corporate, business unit, and functional levels. This chapter and the following one address the implementation of these strategies. Successful strategies not only must be well formulated but also must be carried out effectively.

Effective strategy implementation requires managers to consider a number of key issues. Chief among them are how the organization should be structured to put its strategy into effect and how such variables as leadership, power, and organizational culture should be managed to enable the organization's employees to work together in carrying out the firm's strategic plans. This chapter deals with the first of these key issues—structuring the organization. Leadership, power, and organizational culture will be addressed in the following chapter.

ORGANIZATIONAL GROWTH

Organizational structure refers to the ways that tasks and responsibilities are allocated to individuals and the ways that individuals are grouped together into offices, departments, and divisions. The structure, which is reflected in an organization chart, designates formal reporting relationships and defines the number of levels in the hierarchy.[1]

Normally, when small businesses are started, they consist of an owner-manager and a few employees. Neither an organization chart nor formal assignment of responsibilities is necessary at this stage. Structure is fluid, with each employee often knowing how to perform more than one task and with the owner-manager involved in all aspects of the business. If the organization survives those crucial first years and becomes successful, it is because of the increased demand that it has created for its products or services. To meet this increased demand, the business must grow. With growth, the organization of the business begins to evolve from fluidity to a status of more permanent division of labor. The owner-manager, who once was involved in all functions of the enterprise on a hands-on basis, now finds that his or her role is becoming more managerial and less operational. As new employees are recruited, each is assigned to perform a specialized function.

As Figure 8.1 illustrates, growth expands the organization's structure, both vertically and horizontally. In this figure, the owner-manager's hands-on activities have been taken over by managers who specialize, respectively, in manufacturing and marketing. Each of them manages employees who work only in one specialized functional area. The organization has now added one vertical level—a managerial one—and has expanded horizontally into two separate departments. The following sections discuss these two types of organizational growth.

■ Vertical Growth

Vertical growth refers to an increase in the length of the organization's hierarchical chain of command. The **hierarchical chain of command** represents the company's authority-accountability relationships between managers and employees. Authority flows down the hierarchy from the highest levels in the organization to those at the bottom, and accountability flows upward from bottom to top. In Figure 8.1, the organization on the right has three levels in its hierarchy. Employees at each level report to the manager who is in charge of their specific operations. The number of employees reporting to each manager represents that manager's **span of control.**

Figure 8.2 illustrates two extremes in organizational configuration. At the left is a **tall organization,** comprised of many hierarchical levels and narrow spans of control. The other structure is a **flat organization,** which has few levels in its hierarchy and a wide span of control from top to bottom. It is important to note that each of these configurations represents an extreme. Rather than being at either extreme, many organizations fall somewhere in between. Hence, we speak of organizations as being "relatively tall" or "relatively flat."

Figure 8.1   **Organization of the Enterprise at Start-up and with Growth**

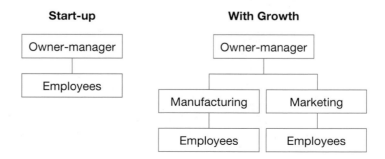

Figure 8.2   **Tall and Flat Organizational Structures**

Tall organization, with nine levels   Flat organization, with three levels

According to John Child, a management researcher, the average number of hierarchical levels for an organization with 3,000 employees is seven.[2] Consequently, we might consider an organization with about 3,000 employees and four hierarchical levels to be relatively flat, but another of similar size with nine levels to be relatively tall.

Because relatively tall organizations have a narrow span of control, the managers in such organizations have a relatively high degree of control over their subordinates. The opposite, of course, is true in relatively flat structures. Because managers in tall organizations have more control readily available to them and because almost everyone in the company is a specialist, authority in tall organizations is usually centralized at the top of the hierarchy. Only at that level are there individuals who deal with and understand all parts of the organization's operations.

Conversely, authority is more decentralized in relatively flat structures. This is because a manager with a broad span of control must grant more authority to his or her employees, as the manager is unable to keep up sufficiently with all developments to make the best decisions. Decisions are more likely to be made by the employee who is on the scene and is most familiar with the situation. As might be expected, employees in flat organizations are less specialized than those in taller ones.

Strategically speaking, both organizational types have certain advantages.[3] The relatively tall, centralized organization allows for better communication of the business's mission, goals, and objectives to all employees. It also enhances coordination of functional areas to ensure that each area works closely with the other functions and that all work together to attain the business's goals and objectives. Finally, in these organizations, planning and its execution are relatively easy to accomplish since all employees are centrally directed. Tall organizational structures are well suited for environments that are relatively stable and predictable.

Relatively flat structures also have their advantages. Administrative costs are usually less than those in taller organizations, because fewer hierarchical levels require fewer managers, which, in turn, means fewer secretaries, offices, and fringe benefits. A second advantage is that decentralized decision making allows managers at various levels to have more authority, which may increase their motivation to assume responsibility for their area's performance. Third, because of the greater freedom in decision making, innovations are encouraged. Flat structures, therefore, are appropriate for more dynamic environments.

For example, Alcoa, the world's largest producer of aluminum, recently flattened its structure in an attempt to lower costs and to speed up decision making in its increasingly competitive environment. The company eliminated two levels of top management—including the offices of president and three group vice presidents, and twenty-four staff positions—and granted considerable autonomy to its twenty-five business unit managers. Each business unit manager, for instance, now has authority to spend up to $5 million without higher-level approval, an increase of 400 percent over the previous spending limit, and reports directly to the chief executive officer (CEO) rather than to a group vice president.[4]

■ Horizontal Growth

Returning to our earlier illustration of a small business with an owner-manager, recall that success necessitates growth. This growth is not only vertical, as just discussed, but also horizontal. **Horizontal growth** refers to an increase in the breadth of an organization's structure. In Figure 8.1, the small business segmented itself horizontally into two departments—manufacturing and marketing. If the company continues to grow, it will eventually need specialists in such areas as personnel, accounting, and finance. Right now, the owner-manager is carrying out those functions, but with growth, his or her expertise will be increasingly needed for strategic management. Individuals will need to be hired to manage the personnel, accounting, and finance activities. Thus, with growth, the structure of an organization is broadened to accommodate the development of more specialized functions.

As an example, consider the comments of T. J. Rodgers, founder of Cypress Semiconductor Corporation. Using a niche-differentiation strategy, this enterprise grew to a $135 million company in five years by developing superfast memory chips. With such rapid growth, however, Rodgers quickly found himself overextended.

> At about $50 million in revenues, I felt I could run it. . . . I could name everybody in the company. But as it grew larger, I found myself stretched. One Friday night at 11 P.M., I realized that if there wasn't a change, I'd have to stop sleeping within six months to keep up the pace.[5]

In other words, a new business may originally have its owner-manager and its few employees performing multiple functions on a daily basis. With growth, however, each function expands so that ultimately no one individual can be intimately involved—either physically or intellectually—in all of the company's functions. This is the point at which various key functional areas are formally set apart as departments, and existing employees and new hires are each assigned to one of these newly formed functional units.

This functional structure, elaborated upon in the following section, is the way small businesses typically organize as they experience growth. This structure, of course, is not the only form available to management. After the functional structure is discussed, other forms are also presented. But, in all cases, growth involves both vertical and horizontal elaboration. It is the strategic direction of the firm that determines the specific type of structure that is most appropriate.

ORGANIZATIONAL STRUCTURE

As an enterprise grows to become an established business, it will adopt one of a number of different organizational structures to implement its strategy. Over time, as its situation changes, the enterprise may shift to another structure. Many large, well-known companies change structures several times in a decade in order to carry out their strategy more effectively. This section discusses seven major types of structures that are available to organizations: functional, product divisional, geographic divisional, multidivisional, strategic business unit, matrix, and horizontal.

■ Functional Structure

As suggested in the preceding section, the initial growth of an enterprise often requires it to organize by functional areas. The **functional structure** is characterized by the simultaneous combination of similar activities and the separation of dissimilar activities on the basis of function. This structure is by no means limited to small businesses. Companies of any size that have a single product line or a few similar product lines are well suited to the functional organizational structure. Small businesses, however, are likely to have only a few functional departments; larger organizations may be quite differentiated, both horizontally and vertically. Figure 8.3 shows a large business that has experienced both vertical and horizontal growth.

Figure 8.3   **A Functional Structure with Vertical and Horizontal Growth**

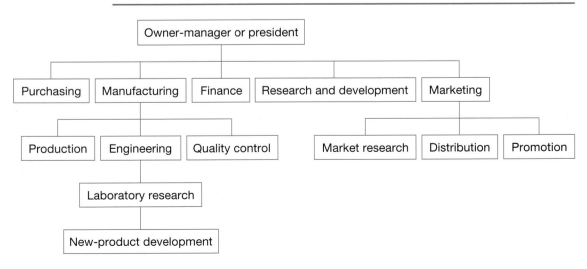

Comparing this business with the one shown in Figure 8.1, we can see that growth brings about more extensive horizontal expansion. Rather than simply dividing its employees into manufacturing and marketing functions, this organization has grown so that it also needs specialists in purchasing, finance, and research and development. Furthermore, its growth has resulted in vertical extensions. Manufacturing has become so complex that it has had to segment itself into the functions of production, engineering, and quality control. Engineering contains two additional levels—laboratory research and new-product development. Likewise, marketing has been divided into market research, distribution, and promotion functions.

A functional structure has certain strategic advantages and disadvantages. On the plus side, this structure emphasizes the functions that the organization must carry out. Specialization by function is encouraged, with the resulting benefits that specialization brings. For instance, when functional specialists interact frequently, they may realize synergies that increase their department's efficiency and effectiveness. Furthermore, their interaction can result in improvements and innovations for their functional area that may not have occurred had there not been a critical mass of specialists organized within the same unit. On the psychological side, working closely on a daily basis with others who share one's functional interests is likely to increase job satisfaction and, hence, contribute to lower turnover.

In addition, the functional organization facilitates the processes of planning, organizing, motivating, and controlling groups of personnel. Translating the organization's mission, goals, and objectives into action is easier when each functional area is activated to plan, organize, motivate, and control within its own boundaries. Finally, the training and development of personnel is often more efficient than in other structures because the training centers on standard types of functional skills.

This structure, however, is accompanied by some disadvantages. Because the business is organized around functions rather than around products or geographic regions, it is difficult to pinpoint the responsibility for profits or losses. If an organization's sales have declined, is the problem due to purchasing, research and development, manufacturing, or marketing? In a functional structure, such problem analysis can be quite ambiguous.

Along these same lines, a functional structure often creates a narrow perspective of the organization among its members. Marketing personnel, for instance, are likely to view the organization totally from a marketing perspective, because they have little experience with other functional areas. The same is true for employees in manufacturing, finance, and other functions. Problems and opportunities are perceived more in terms of the interests of each functional area than in the way they affect the overall organization. Consequently, different solutions to the same problem or different strategies to take advantage of an environmental opportunity are advanced as desirable by the various functional departments.

Finally, communication and coordination across functional areas are often difficult. For instance, employees in manufacturing view their function as central to organizational success and attribute operational problems to other functional areas. Marketing, meanwhile, views increased sales as primarily attributable to its efforts but sees slow sales as manufacturing's fault. It should be clear that as functional departments begin to proliferate, coordination becomes increasingly difficult. Functional differentiation presents management with the

S T R A T E G I C   I N S I G H T

Removing the Blinders at Ford

One of the potential weaknesses in a functional structure is that it can encourage employees to take a narrow perspective of their organization. It is easy for functional managers and operative employees to look at problems from the standpoint of marketing or production or some other functional specialty rather than see them from the viewpoint of the company as a whole.

Ford Motor Company has devised a program to reduce this problem. In a $5\frac{1}{2}$-day session for middle managers, the managers are first grouped by their functional specialties. Then they are asked to "think about how their function works within the company, how others perceive it, and how it ought to work."

As they discuss their thoughts with managers from other functional areas, they begin to realize how narrow their perspective is. That is, they tend to view Ford primarily as a manufacturing company or a finance company or a company that specializes in personnel. As a result of the session, they learn to take a broader view of the organization, realizing that their particular function is only one of many interrelated activities that must be accomplished for Ford to attain its goals. Ford terms this process "chimney-breaking."

In a broader sense, Ford's strategic alliance with Mazda to develop several cars and sport-utility vehicles jointly has helped Ford engineers expand their perspective. Ford has learned to emphasize quality over price in purchasing parts. Mazda has learned how to better control emissions, measure noise and vibration, and improve its marketing skills. Both firms have improved their operations by taking a broader view of their organizations rather than focusing on functional activities in isolation of total organizational needs.

SOURCES: O. Suris, "Ford Hopes to Set Pattern for Contract with Union," *Wall Street Journal Interactive Edition*, 10 May 1996; D. K. Rigby and R. W. T. Buchanan, "Alliances the Corning Way," *Directors & Boards*, Winter 1994, p. 18; T. Sasaki, "What the Japanese Have Learned from Strategic Alliances," *Long Range Planning* 26(6) (1994): pp. 41–53; J. B. Treece, K. L. Miller, and R. A. Melcher, "The Partners," *Business Week*, 10 February 1992, pp. 102–107.

challenging task of coordinating disparate activities so that a unified, logical whole may be attained.

Whenever an organization begins to expand its product lines significantly or grow geographically, the functional structure begins to lose its strategic usefulness. Management then faces the issue of changing its organization's structure to one more appropriate to its strategy.

■ Product Divisional Structure

The product divisional structure is well suited for businesses with several product lines. Rather than organizing the firm around functions, the **product divisional structure** focuses on the company's product categories. Figure 8.4 illustrates this structure for a firm that manufactures and sells home appliances. Its activities and personnel are grouped into three product divisions: refrigerators and ranges, washers and dryers, and small appliances. Each product division will contain its own functional areas. The small-appliances division, for instance, may have its own manufacturing and marketing departments because the products that it makes and sells may require different manufacturing methods and channels of distribution from those of the other two divisions. Other functions, however, such as finance, may be centralized at the

Figure 8.4   **Product Divisional Structure**

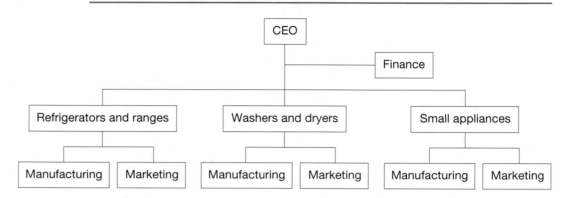

top of the organization because they benefit the organization as a whole and because economies can be realized. For example, the corporation as a whole can obtain more favorable interest rates when borrowing money than could the small-appliances division alone.

This structure is also widely used in nonmanufacturing organizations. For instance, supermarkets typically have a number of product managers (e.g., produce manager, meat manager, dairy manager, and bakery manager) who report to the store manager; and department stores are divided into product areas such as women's sportswear, men's shoes, children's wear, furniture, and appliances. Universities, being service organizations, are also usually organized by "product" divisions: history, mathematics, computer sciences, marketing, art, and so on.

The advantages of the product divisional structure are several. Rather than emphasize the functions that the organization performs, the structure emphasizes product lines. The result is a clear focus upon each individual product category and a greater orientation toward customer service. Also, the ability to pinpoint the responsibility for profits or losses is greatly enhanced, since each product division becomes a profit center to which profits and losses can be directly attributed. A **profit center** is an organizational unit charged with a well-defined mission and is headed by a manager accountable for the center's revenues and expenditures. Thus, it is clear to upper management which divisions are operating profitably and which are incurring losses. Furthermore, the product divisional structure is ideal for training and developing managers, since each product manager is, in effect, running his or her "own business." Hence, product managers develop general management skills—an end that can be accomplished in a functional structure only by rotating managers from one functional area to another.

Even relatively small companies can use a product divisional structure. A few years ago Stryker Corporation, with annual revenues of $281 million, converted from a functional structure to one with several semiautonomous product divisions. Now, Stryker employs a highly trained sales force for each division to market a specialized product—such as hospital beds, hip implants, medical video cameras, or surgical power tools—rather than use one companywide sales force to sell all of these products. As its president says, "It's achieving focus through decentralization."[6]

Of course, the product divisional structure also has its disadvantages. In some ways, it can be more expensive to operate than a functional structure, because more functional personnel may be required. In Figure 8.4, for example, because the firm has three manufacturing departments rather than only one, the total personnel expense for manufacturing is likely to be higher than if only one department were necessary. Such extra expenses raise the firm's break-even point. Second, the coordination of activities at headquarters becomes more difficult. Top management finds it harder to ensure that all of the firm's marketing personnel, for instance, are following the same policies and procedures when serving customers. This problem can become fairly significant when an organization has forty or fifty product divisions, which is fairly common among large firms. In addition, the customer can be confused by being called on by different sales representatives from the same firm. Third, because each product manager emphasizes his or her own product area, what may be in the best interests of the firm may be overlooked as product managers compete for resources such as money, physical space, and personnel.

In fact, disadvantages like these led Nestlé's U.S.-based subsidiary to convert its product divisional structure to a functional structure in 1991. By consolidating such product lines as Carnation, Stouffer Foods, Quik, and Taster's Choice under one manager, Nestlé saved at least $30 million in overhead and administrative expenses. It also allowed the business unit to benefit from increased scale economies.[7]

■ Geographic Divisional Structure

When a firm operates in various geographical areas, an appropriate structure may be the **geographic divisional structure,** in which activities and personnel are grouped by specific geographic locations. This structure may be used on a local basis (a city may be divided into sales regions), on a national basis (northeast region, mid-Atlantic region, midwest region), or on an international basis (North American region, Latin American region, Western European region, Middle Eastern region). Figure 8.5 illustrates a national company (at the top) and an international company (at the bottom) organized by geographic divisions.

There are a number of advantages to organizing geographically. First, products and services may be better tailored to the climatic needs of specific areas. For example, retailers may stock heavier clothing for their outlets in northern states and lighter clothes in southern stores. Second, a geographic divisional structure allows a firm to respond to the technical needs of different international areas. For instance, in many parts of the world, the electrical system is different from that in the United States; the geographic structure allows firms to accommodate these geographic differences. Third, producing or distributing products in different national or global locations may give the organization a competitive advantage. Many firms, for example, produce components in countries that either have a labor cost advantage or are located close to essential raw materials. The final product may then be assembled in still another location that is more appropriate for the advanced technology required or that is closer to the final consumer. Fourth, a geographic organization may better serve the consumer needs of various nations. For instance, the

Figure 8.5   **Geographic Divisional Structures**

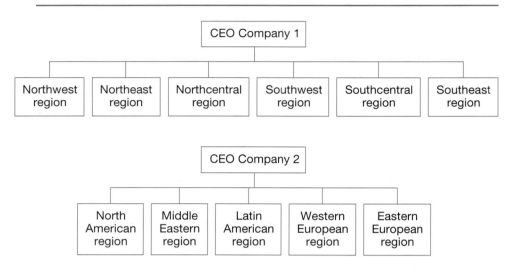

need for hair-grooming products differs from one society to another, and the geographic structure allows firms to respond to these differing needs. Fifth, organizing along geographic lines enables a company to adapt to varying legal systems. Automobile insurance companies within the United States, for example, often have a geographic division because no two states have the same insurance regulations. Finally, geographic divisions allow firms to pinpoint the responsibility for profits or losses, because each division is a profit center.

The disadvantages of a geographic divisional structure are similar to those identified earlier for the product divisional structure. Often, more functional personnel are required than would be the case for a functional structure, because each region has its own functional departments. Coordination of companywide functions is more difficult than in a strictly functional organization, and regional managers may emphasize their own geographic areas to the exclusion of a companywide viewpoint.

■ Multidivisional Structure

As a firm continues to expand by adding more and more product lines, it may outgrow all of the preceding structures. At this stage, firms with multiple product lines may adopt the **multidivisional structure,** in which the company is partitioned into several divisions, with each division responsible for one or more product lines.

Consider Maytag as an example. At one time in its history, this appliance firm had a fairly simple structure with three product divisions—gas range products, laundry products, and electric range products. But it continued to expand its product lines by acquiring Magic Chef (a producer of air conditioners, refrigerators, and furnaces), Toastmaster (a manufacturer of small appliances), and Hoover (a maker of vacuum cleaners and European major appliances).

Figure 8.6   **Multidivisional Structure of Maytag**

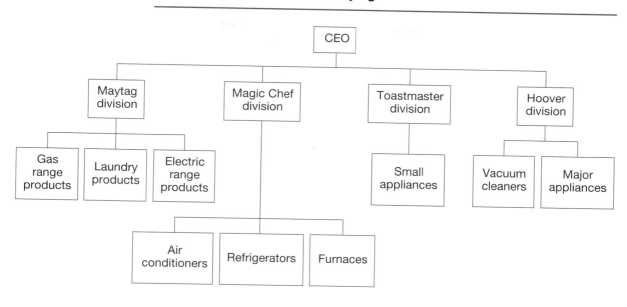

Maytag's current structure is depicted in Figure 8.6. As you can see, the multidivisional structure encompasses several divisions, with each division comprised of one or more product lines.

The multidivisional structure has several advantages. First, continued growth is facilitated. As new product lines are created or acquired, those lines may be integrated into an existing division or may serve as the foundation for a newly developed division. Second, since each division has its own top-level strategic managers, the workload of the CEO's headquarters staff is lightened. This gives the CEO more time to analyze each division's operations and to decide on resource allocations on the basis of the portfolio analysis techniques discussed in chapter 5. Third, authority is delegated downward to each division and, within each division, to each product line. This decentralization allows for a better alignment of each division and product line with its unique external environment. Fourth, accountability for performance can be logically evaluated at the product line level as well as at the divisional level.

As is true with each structure discussed, however, the multidivisional structure has certain disadvantages. First, the distribution of corporate overhead costs across the divisions is difficult and relatively subjective. Inevitably, the distribution results in some divisional managers feeling that their divisions have received too heavy an allocation. Second, dysfunctional divisional rivalries often emerge as each division attempts to secure a greater share of the firm's resources. Third, when one division makes components or products that another division needs, conflicts can arise in setting transfer prices. *Transfer pricing* refers to the price that one division charges another division for its products or parts. The selling division normally prefers to charge a relatively high transfer price to increase its profits, but the purchasing division prefers to pay a relatively low transfer price to lower its costs.

ITW's Multidivisional Structure

Illinois Tool Works (ITW), headquartered in a Chicago suburb, is a low-profile manufacturer of 90 product lines and almost 100,000 products, including nails, screws, bolts, strapping, wrapping, valves, capacitors, filters, adhesives, tools and machines, plastic buckets, plastic loops that hold six-packs together, Zip-Pak resealable food packages, and Kiwi-Lok nylon fasteners. ITW is a member of the Fortune 200, with annual sales of about $3 billion and 17,000 employees. Its primary markets are the construction, automotive and truck, electronics, agricultural, and telecommunications industries. Half of its revenues come from foreign sales.

The company searches for market niches and often dominates those in which it operates. At the corporate level, the firm follows a growth strategy, with most of its business units pursuing a niche–low-cost/differentiation strategy.

In addition to focusing on internal growth, ITW pursues a strategy of horizontal integration and diversification by regularly acquiring smaller companies that complement ITW's core businesses. Its ninety product lines are grouped into nine divisions. ITW's businesses are relatively small, with about $30 million in annual revenue. Each product line manager controls manufacturing, marketing, and R&D. When a new product with commercial possibilities is developed, it is often split off to form a new business unit.

ITW seeks to keep costs as low as possible. Its largest division, the construction products group, generates $420 million a year but has only three headquarters employees: a president, a controller, and a shared secretary.

According to corporate chairman W. James Farrell, ITW's success is linked to its decentralized structure, enabling it to remain close to its customers and minimize costs. These efforts may explain why ITW has been noted for its unique ability to prosper during recessionary times. Its carefully formulated strategy and appropriate structure have helped ITW to rank consistently toward the top in the metals products industry in *Fortune's* annual survey of "Most Admired Corporations."

SOURCES: "Illinois Tool Names Farrell Chairman, CEO," *Dow Jones News Service,* 7 May 1996; H. S. Byrne, "A New Chapter," *Barron's,* 11 December 1995, p. 18; "Illinois Tool Works, Inc." *Wall Street Journal,* 8 August 1995, p. B2; C. Willis, "Wall Street," *Money,* April 1992, pp. 69–70; H. S. Byrne, "Illinois Tool Works," *Barron's,* 16 November 1992, pp. 51–52.

■ Strategic Business Unit Structure

Organizational growth may ultimately require that related product lines be grouped into divisions and that the divisions themselves then be grouped into strategic business units. This **strategic business unit structure** is particularly well suited to very large, diversified firms. An example of such a firm is illustrated in Figure 8.7.

The major advantage of the strategic business unit structure is that it reduces corporate headquarters' span of control. Rather than managers at the corporate level having to control many divisions, they need control only relatively few strategic business units. This reduction in span of control also lessens the chance that headquarters will experience information overload as the various organizational units report on their operations. Another advantage is that this structure permits better coordination among divisions with similar missions, products, markets, or technologies.

The strategic business unit structure, however, has a number of disadvantages. First, corporate headquarters becomes more distant from the division and product levels with the addition of another vertical layer of management. Second, rivalry among the strategic business unit managers for greater shares of corporate resources can become dysfunctional and can negatively affect the corporation's overall performance. Third, this structure complicates portfolio analysis. For instance, a strategic business unit may be considered a poor performer overall, but some of its divisions may be stars.

Note that it is important not to confuse the concept *strategic business unit* with that of *strategic business unit structure*. When we are discussing strategy formulation, the term *strategic business unit* may be used in more than one way.[8] A single company that operates within a single industry (e.g., a business that builds swimming pools) is a strategic business unit. But a product division or geographic division of a large multidivisional firm is also a strategic business unit. *Strategic business unit* may even be used to refer to the large firm's multidivisional level that combines several product divisions or geographic divisions. More specifically, a strategic business unit is an organization or a division, product line, or profit center of an organization that produces a set of products/services for well-defined markets or customers in competition with identifiable competitors.

When our reference point is strategy implementation, however, the term *strategic business unit structure* is used to identify the organizational structure type discussed in this section of the chapter. That is, a strategic business unit structure is one in which related product lines are grouped into divisions and those divisions are then grouped into larger entities referred to as strategic business units, as shown in Figure 8.7.[9]

- ## Matrix Structure

Up until this point, each of the organizational structures discussed has possessed a single chain of command. That is, each employee in those structures reports to only one manager. The structure discussed in this section, however, is unique in that it possesses a dual chain of command. The **matrix structure** is

Figure 8.7   **Strategic Business Unit Structure**

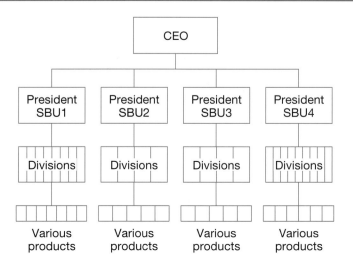

one in which both functional and project managers exercise authority over organizational activities. Hence, personnel within the matrix have two supervisors—a project manager and the manager of their functional department.

The matrix structure is most commonly used in organizations that operate in industries where the rate of technological change is very fast. For example, firms such as TRW and Boeing use a matrix structure. As shown in Figure 8.8, a matrix structure contains literally two organizations—a functional organization (shown horizontally across the top) and a project organization (shown vertically at the left of the chart). In project A, for example, the project manager has brought together some members of the organization's functional departments to work on a specific project. In a construction company, for instance, that project might be the building of a refinery in Thailand. When it is completed, the personnel in project A will return to their functional departments. As another example, in the computer industry, project A might be the development of a new, more powerful personal computer. During the time they are assigned to the project, the employees are accountable not only to the project manager but also to the manager of the functional department from which they came.

Some companies use a matrix even though the rate of technological change in their industry is not extremely fast. For example, Toyota used the matrix structure to develop the Lexus, its entry into the top-of-the-line luxury-car market. A number of engineering, marketing, research and development (R&D), and finance personnel were brought together to work on developing an automobile that would compare favorably with the best offered by the German, British, and U.S. automakers.[10]

A variation on the traditional project form of the matrix structure is reflected in Procter & Gamble's (P&G) use of this system. Although many people associate the matrix structure most closely with high-technology enterprises, P&G actually pioneered this form of organization in 1927. At P&G, rather than a project manager being in charge of a temporary project, each of

Figure 8.8   **Matrix Structure**

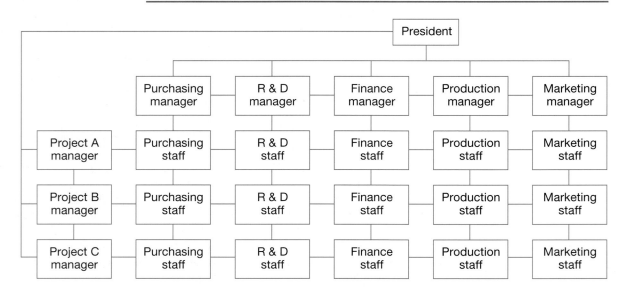

P&G's individual products has a brand manager. The brand manager pulls various specialists, as they are needed, from their functional departments. For instance, if a detergent, such as Tide, is experiencing slowing sales, the brand manager for Tide might call together members of the R&D department to develop a new additive, members of the advertising staff to create ads for "new, improved Tide," members of the packaging department to design a new container for the detergent, and so on. Each brand manager reports to one of twenty-six category managers, an individual who is in charge of all related products in a single category (e.g., detergents such as Tide, Cheer, and Ivory Flakes). It is this manager's responsibility to coordinate the advertising and sales of related products so that competition among the products is minimized.[11] As we can see, then, P&G uses a mixture of a matrix structure and a multidivisional (category) structure.

In whatever form it is used, the matrix structure offers certain advantages. First, by combining both the functional structure and the project (or product) structure, a firm can enjoy the advantages of both forms. Second, the matrix is a cost-efficient structure because project managers pay only for the services of functional personnel when they need them. The remainder of the time, these functional employees are working in their own departments and are not on the payroll of any particular project. By contrast, in a strictly project form of organization, the functional employees are employed full-time within a single project or product division.

Third, a matrix organization has considerable flexibility. Employees may be transferred with ease between projects, a flexibility that is greatly reduced in a more permanent form of structure. Fourth, a matrix permits lower-level functional employees to become intimately involved in a project. They are responsible for making and implementing many of the decisions at the project level. Hence, their motivation may be enhanced, and their job satisfaction is also likely to be relatively high.

Fifth, the matrix structure is an excellent vehicle for training and developing general managers. Each project manager, in a sense, is running his or her "own business." The skills developed at this level are essential skills for higher-level positions in the organization. Finally, top management in a matrix is freed from day-to-day involvement in the operations of the enterprise and is, therefore, able to concentrate on strategic problems and opportunities.

Although the matrix has numerous advantages, it is also accompanied by some significant disadvantages. First is the greater administrative cost associated with its operation. Because coordination across functional areas and across projects is so important, matrix personnel spend considerable time in meetings exchanging information. Although this communication is essential, it consumes valuable time that could otherwise be spent on actual project implementation. Second, matrix structures are characterized by considerable conflict, which takes two forms. One is conflict between project and functional managers over budgets and personnel. The other is conflict among the project managers themselves over similar resource allocation issues.

Finally, working in a matrix can be a source of considerable stress for some functional employees. Reporting to two managers can create significant amounts of role ambiguity and role conflict for an individual. As might be expected, some organizations, such as PepsiCo and Digital Equipment, have found managing a matrix to be so complicated that they have reverted to more traditional structures.

■ **Horizontal Structure**

As American firms have grown in size, many of them have also grown in their organizational layers, with ensuing increases in their bureaucracy. This has made some of them less efficient as well as less capable of meeting the needs and expectations of their customers. These problems have had to be confronted by management. Senior executives have ordinarily responded by instituting a more **horizontal structure**—one with fewer hierarchies.

Recall from chapter 4 that a phenomenon has been in vogue in the 1980s and the 1990s—corporate restructuring, which means changing the way work is done in organizations (changing activities and relationships). Throughout the 1980s and the 1990s, organizational restructuring has often involved forming a more horizontal structure through **downsizing,** which refers to two related changes.

The first is eliminating one or more hierarchical levels from the organization's structure. Most frequently, the levels eliminated are those staffed by vice presidents or other middle managers, although the headquarters' staff positions are also common targets. Additionally, some employees temporarily or permanently lose their jobs. The goal is to cut costs (and thereby improve the corporation's ability to compete) and to abolish some of the bureaucratic maze and red tape that invariably accompany multiple organizational layers.

The first change must necessarily be accompanied by the second: a pushing of decision making downward in the organization. That is, by removing one or more hierarchical levels, an organization reduces the number of individuals in the chain of command who must approve decisions. Because fewer levels result in a broader span of control for upper-level executives, more decisions must be made by lower-level personnel who are closer to the customer. Otherwise, continuing to refer most decisions upward would quickly overload top management.

What is anticipated from the horizontal structure through downsizing is the achievement of higher efficiencies as well as customer responsiveness. In some situations, as discussed in the previous chapter, substantial decision-making authority is transferred to cross-functional teams who are in charge of key processes.

The horizontal organization may take various unconventional forms. As shown in the top part of Figure 8.9, a horizontal organization may have a president and three vice presidents. Each vice president may be in charge of several key organizational processes. For instance, vice president 1 is in charge of process A and B. Each of these processes has its own manager whose group is comprised of cross-functional personnel.

As shown in the bottom part of Figure 8.9, a horizontal organization may be circular. Similar to Eastman Chemical's structure, the organization may have a president connected to various cross-functional teams. According to Ernest Deavenport, president of Eastman Chemicals, "Our organizational chart is now called the pizza chart because it looks like a pizza. . . We did it in circular form to show that everyone is equal in the organization"[12]

ASSESSMENT OF ORGANIZATIONAL STRUCTURE

The key issue in this chapter is how an organization can implement its strategy by designing its structure appropriately. In this section, we wish to examine how managers can assess the effectiveness of their organization's current

Figure 8.9   **Horizontal Structure**

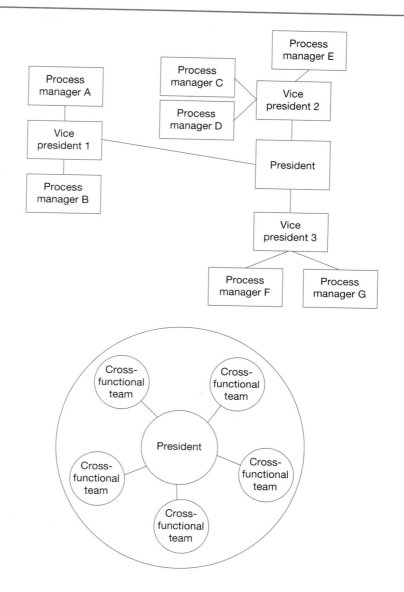

structure in that regard. There are, unfortunately, no hard-and-fast rules for evaluating the appropriateness of an organization's structure. However, the extent to which a structure is—and will continue to be—effective in helping the organization implement its strategy can be at least partially assessed by answering the following questions. These questions are highlighted in Table 8.1.

- *Is the structure compatible with the corporate profile and the corporate strategy?* Recall that at the corporate level, a firm may be in one business, several related businesses, or several unrelated businesses. Although the one-business company may effectively adopt the functional struc-

Table 8.1   **Checklist for Determining Appropriateness of Organizational Structure**

1. Is the structure compatible with the corporate profile and the corporate strategy?
2. At the corporate level, is the structure compatible with the outputs of the firm's business units?
3. Are there too few or too many hierarchical levels at either the corporate or business unit level of analysis?
4. Does the structure promote coordination among its parts?
5. Does the structure allow for appropriate centralization or decentralization of authority?
6. Does the structure permit the appropriate grouping of activities?

ture, this form of specialization may be inappropriate for one in multiple businesses. In the situation of a multiple business firm, a product divisional or multidivisional structure can more appropriately emphasize the corporation's products and services rather than its functions. Hence, an organization's structure should be compatible with its corporate profile.

Its structure should also be compatible with its corporate-level strategy. For instance, if the corporation intends to grow continuously, it may find its growth eventually stymied by a product divisional or geographic divisional structure. The reason is that horizontal expansion places an ever-increasing burden on corporate-level management owing to the widening span of control. At some point, it is not humanly possible to keep up with the activities of all of the firm's product or geographic divisions. Hence, continued growth may eventually require adopting the multidivisional or strategic business unit structure.

- *At the corporate level, is the structure compatible with the outputs of the firm's business units?* A product divisional structure, for instance, may be more appropriate than a geographic divisional structure for a corporation with business units that produce fasteners, cutting tools, and hand tools. The reason is that the demand for these products is based on their technical specifications and perceived quality. Each product division can, therefore, concentrate on producing and marketing its own product line. However, a geographic divisional structure may be better suited to a corporation with business units that sell retail clothing and shoes. These items are sold together, and demand for them will differ from one geographic region to another depending on climate, culture, and tradition. Hence, they can be marketed more effectively through specialization based on geographic location.

- *Are there too few or too many hierarchical levels at either the corporate or business unit level of analysis?* It is important that an organization's structure match the nature of the environment in which it operates. Normally, flatter organizations with relatively fewer hierarchical levels and wider spans of control may be better suited for dynamic, fast-changing environments than taller structures. Conversely, taller organizations with relatively more hierarchical levels and narrower spans of control may operate more effectively in stable, more predictable environments than flatter ones do. Recall that the trend has been to reduce the number of hierarchies in firms, although some organizations will remain taller relative to others even after they are downsized.

Corporate-level managers must also realize that the firm's business units need not necessarily have the same structures. Some business units may operate in relatively dynamic environments, and others may compete in relatively stable environments, necessitating differences in their structures.

Overall, in answering this particular question, a manager may find it helpful to compare the configuration of his or her organization with those of its competitors.

- *Does the structure promote coordination among its parts?* Varying degrees of coordination among an organization's parts may be necessary, depending upon the particular situation. For instance, firms with multiple unrelated business units that operate fairly autonomously may find that relatively little coordination among the business units' operations is required. However, within each business unit, management may find it essential to coordinate closely the activities of functional departments potentially through process management. Firms with multiple related businesses usually require greater coordination of their business units' activities, and companies that operate in only one business generally concentrate on coordinating their functional processes.

As a rule, the more complex an organization, the more difficult coordination is to achieve. This problem is especially evident in organizations with related businesses. Very complex businesses may have to establish special, permanent coordinating units that integrate, for example, the activities of research and development, production, and sales.

- *Does the structure allow for appropriate centralization or decentralization of authority?* The extent to which decision making should be systematically delegated downward in an organization depends upon a number of factors. One, obviously, is organizational size. In general, very large organizations tend to be more decentralized than very small ones, simply because it is difficult for the CEO of a very large company to keep up with all of the organization's operations.

Another factor is the number and type of businesses a firm is in. Firms with large numbers of unrelated businesses tend to be relatively decentralized, allowing the heads of the diverse business units to make most of the decisions affecting those units. In such cases, corporate-level management's primary responsibility is to determine the overall corporation's mission, goals, and strategy and to leave the actual operating decisions to those on the scene. By contrast, organizations in only one business can more easily be managed in a centralized fashion.

The type of environment affects the need for decentralization. Organizations in rapidly changing environments must be relatively decentralized so that decisions can be made quickly by those who are closest to the situation. At the other end of the spectrum, organizations in relatively stable environments can be managed effectively through centralized decision making, since change is relatively slow and fairly predictable. In such cases, the majority of decisions follow a routine pattern, and procedures can be established in advance for many decision-making situations.

- *Does the structure permit the appropriate grouping of activities?* The extent to which organizational activities are appropriately grouped affects how well strategy is implemented. For instance, related product lines should be grouped together. Customers are confused when they are called on by one sales representative for personal computers but have to contact another sales representative from the same company to purchase a printer for the computer. Likewise, some department stores insist on selling men's suits in one department, but ties and dress shirts in another department down the aisle. As another type of example, it is difficult to hold a product divisional manager fully responsible for sales of a product when he or she had no control over either the development or the production of the product.

KEIRETSU AND OTHER POSSIBLE STRUCTURES

The organizational structures discussed so far are Western conceptions. A Japanese form of organization that has received increasing attention is the **keiretsu,** which represents a horizontally and vertically connected group of businesses with interlocking board members who are senior managers of member companies. The member companies also have mutual ownerships in each other. Keiretsu members often engage in joint ventures with each other and sign reciprocal purchase agreements. Some knowledgeable observers have argued that to compete effectively in the global economy may require forming European and American keiretsus in the future.[13]

The keiretsu normally includes twenty to forty-five businesses anchored to a major manufacturer or a bank. The businesses cooperate in research and development and share technological and market information with each other.

Some of today's Japanese keiretsus are capitalizing on the digitalization of technology, relating to each other what may have been previously unrelated businesses, according to Ferguson, an expert in high-technology industries. He asserts, with respect to keiretsus, that previously unrelated businesses—"cameras, computers, stereos, photocopiers"—are converting to form a related and "unified information technology sector, itself based on common digital components and standard interfaces."[14]

Other knowledgeable observers alternatively believe that the wave of the future will be a structure variously termed the "modular corporation," the "virtual corporation," or the "network pattern."[15] In this configuration, an organization "outsources," or contracts with other companies for all of its functions except for its core competencies. For instance, a company might concentrate on designing and marketing a product while letting other companies manufacture the product, deliver it, and bill customers for their purchases. Such a system allows a company to concentrate on those processes in which it possesses a particular competence, without having to divert its resources to other activities. The amount of capital investment is obviously much lower than it would be if the company itself handled all of the functions, and this lowered-investment level means that the company has considerable flexibility to change with its environment.

For instance, neither Reebok nor Dell Computer owns a manufacturing plant. Both outsource all manufacturing functions to contractors. This system, of course, has had precedence. Construction companies and publishing houses have been structured in this fashion for decades. But it is clear that organizations in other industries are increasingly interested in shedding fixed assets and gaining flexibility by adopting elements of a modular structure.

A Structural Revolution at IBM

One of the world's largest and most successful firms of the past fifty years found itself floundering as it entered the 1990s. In 1991, IBM's sales dropped 6.1 percent, to $64.8 billion, its first decline in revenue since 1946. And, for the first time in its history, IBM incurred a loss—$2.8 billion. That loss grew to $5 billion in 1992.

Its problem? IBM was operating as it always had, but its environment had changed dramatically. The computer industry today is one of continually accelerating change. For instance, the life cycle of a notebook computer may be as short as three months. Many of IBM's competitors, moreover, are aggressive, flexible, and extremely quick, garnering the rewards that accrue to those who are first to the market with new technology.

At the center of this dynamic environment stood huge, bureaucratic, centralized IBM—a company still dominated by its mainframe computer division. As it always had, IBM required that all major decisions be made at corporate headquarters at Armonk, New York. Those decisions were guided by policies that virtually forbade any internal competition with the mainframe division, subjected new product plans to endless discussion, and kept IBM divisions from competing unfettered with their more nimble competitors. As a result, IBM introduced its personal computer four years after Apple did, entered the PC-compatible laptop market five years behind Toshiba, and followed Digital Equipment into the minicomputer market only after an eleven-year lag.

To turn the corporation around, top management unveiled an extensive structural reorganization. Some of the major changes being implemented are:

- The creation of semiautonomous business units, each with profit and loss responsibility, but also able to make its own manufacturing and pricing decisions. Every business unit manager must sign an annual contract with corporate management agreeing to goals and objectives in such areas as growth, profit, return on assets, quality, and customer satisfaction. Each business unit decides for itself how it will meet those goals and objectives.
- A drastic reduction in work force. After avoiding involuntary layoffs for more than 70 years, IBM has pruned its work force by 160,000 and its payroll by about 40 percent. Most—but not all—of this reduction has been accomplished by voluntary buyout and early retirement programs. By design, the majority of these cuts were primarily in managerial and staff positions.
- Reorganization of the research and development function. Insiders have complained that IBM takes too long to get products outside the door, testing them repeatedly and delaying delivery. As a result, top managers, engineers, and customer-service representatives worked together to create a leaner department that emphasizes speed and eliminates useless paperwork and excessive product testing.

Several obstacles to effective implementation of the restructuring remain. One is the ongoing attempt to change IBM's culture, which, historically, has not encouraged autonomy. A recent survey of many of the firm's top managers revealed that many still do not accept the need for changing the "old IBM." Another is the challenge to maintain high-quality standards while improving customer responsiveness and speed to market. IBM officials have always boasted that their products have always met or exceeded quality standards. But IBM must now pursue quality with speed.

SOURCES: B. Ziegler, "IBM Is Growing Again; 'Fires Are Out', Chief Says," *Wall Street Journal Interactive Edition,* 1 May 1996; L. Hayes, "Gerstner Is Struggling as He Tries to Change Ingrained IBM Culture," *Wall Street Journal,* 13 May 1994, pp. A1, A8 (quotation from p. A1); "IBM Will Raise Number of Jobs It Plans to Trim," *Wall Street Journal,* 11 February 1993; J. Main, "Betting on the 21st Century Jet," *Fortune,* 20 April 1992, pp. 102–117 (quotation from p. 102); D. Moreau, "From Big Bust to Big Blue: IBM and Its Vigorous Rebirth," *Kiplinger's Personal Finance Magazine,* July 1995, pp. 34–35.

SUMMARY

Implementing strategy requires management to consider how the organization should be structured. In new, small companies, structure is fluid, with each employee often knowing how to perform more than one task and the owner-manager being involved in all aspects of the business. Success leads to growth, however—both vertical and horizontal. With growth comes a more permanent division of labor.

Vertical growth refers to an increase in the length of an organization's hierarchical chain of command. Organizations in stable, predictable environments often become relatively tall, with many hierarchical levels and narrow spans of control. Conversely, companies in dynamic, rapidly changing environments usually adopt flat structures with few hierarchical levels and wide spans of control.

Horizontal growth refers to the segmentation of the organization into departments or divisions. The first formal structure usually adopted by a growing business is the functional structure, an organizational type that forms departments along functional lines—manufacturing, marketing, finance, research and development, personnel, and so on. Its strengths are that it emphasizes the functions that the organization must carry out, which results in a number of advantages; it facilitates the processes of planning, organizing, motivating, and controlling; and it is an efficient structure for the training and development of personnel. Its weaknesses, however, are that it makes pinpointing the responsibility for profits or losses difficult; it creates a narrow perspective of the organization among its members; and it inhibits communication across functional areas and coordination of their disparate activities. Whenever an organization begins to expand its product lines significantly or grow geographically, the functional structure begins to lose its strategic usefulness.

The product divisional structure is well suited for a business with several product lines because the firm is structured around its product categories. This structure's strengths are that it emphasizes the firm's product lines; it makes coordination of functions easier because each product division has its own functions; it allows responsibility for profits or losses to be pinpointed since each product division is a responsibility center; and it encourages development of general managers. Its weaknesses are that it may be more expensive to operate than a functional structure because more functional personnel are required; it inhibits coordination of activities at the corporate level; and it creates dysfunctional competition among division managers for corporate resources.

The geographic divisional structure is used by firms that operate in various geographic areas. Structuring around location provides such advantages as tailoring products/services to climatic needs of specific areas, responding to the technical needs of different international locations, gaining a competitive advantage by producing or distributing products in different locations, serving the consumer needs of various nations better, adapting to varying legal systems, and pinpointing the responsibility for profits or losses. The disadvantages of this structure are the same as those for the product divisional structure.

As a firm adds more product lines, it may eventually adopt the multidivisional structure, in which similar product lines are organized into divisions. This structure facilitates continued growth, frees corporate management for strategic planning, decentralizes authority to individual divisions and product lines so that decision making is quicker, and enables management to pinpoint responsibility for profits and losses. Its unique weaknesses are that distribution of corporate overhead costs is subjective and difficult to make, dysfunctional divisional rivalries often occur, and transfer pricing from one division to another can become a source of contention.

Further growth may lead an organization to adopt the strategic business unit structure. In this case, divisions with similar missions, products, markets, or technologies are combined under a strategic business unit. This structure further reduces corporate headquarters' span of control and permits better coordination. However, it also distances corporate headquarters from the product level, can create dysfunctional rivalries among strategic business units, and complicates portfolio analysis.

The matrix structure is a combination of the functional structure and the product/project structure. The matrix enjoys the advantages of both structural types, it is cost-efficient for each individual project or product, it is flexible, it permits lower-level employees to become highly involved in projects, it helps train and develop general managers, and it frees top-level management for planning. But the matrix also is associated with greater administrative costs, greater conflict, and higher stress.

The horizontal structure has been developed in response to the increasing bureaucracy associated with growth of some firms. Throughout the 1980s and 1990s, organizational restructuring has involved forming a more horizontal structure through downsizing. Downsizing refers to the elimination of one or more hierarchical levels accompanied by a pushing of decision making downward in the organization.

To determine whether an organization's structure is appropriate for implementing the organization's strategy, a manager must analyze how compatible the structure is with such features as the organization's corporate profile, corporate strategy, business unit strategy, need for coordination, number of hierarchical levels, degree of decentralization, and grouping of activities. Other structures, such as the keiretsu and the "modular corporation," are structures that American firms may adopt in increasing numbers.

TAKE IT TO THE NET

We invite you to visit the Wright page on the Prentice Hall Web site at:

http://www.prenhall.com/wright

for this chapter's World Wide Web exercise.

KEY CONCEPTS

Downsizing   A means of organizational restructuring that includes the elimination of one or more hierarchical levels from the organization and a pushing of decision making downward in the organization.

Flat organization   An organization characterized by relatively few hierarchical levels and a wide span of control.

Functional structure   A form of organizational structure in which jobs and activities are grouped on the basis of function—for example, manufacturing, marketing, and finance.

Geographic divisional structure   A form of organizational structure in which jobs and activities are grouped on the basis of geographic location—for example, northeast region, midwest region, and far west region.

Hierarchical chain of command   The authority and accountability chain that links managers and employees in an organization.

Horizontal growth   An increase in the breadth of an organization's structure.

Horizontal structure   An organizational structure with fewer hierarchies designed to improve efficiency by reducing layers in the bureaucracy.

Keiretsu   A horizontally and vertically connected group of businesses with interlocking board members who are senior managers of member companies.

Matrix structure   A form of organizational structure that combines a functional structure with some form of divisional structure (usually product or project divisions). It contains a dual chain of command in which the functional manager and the project/product manager exercise authority over the same employees.

Multidivisional structure   A form of organizational structure that contains several divisions, with each division comprised of one or more product lines.

Organizational structure   The formal ways that tasks and responsibilities are allocated to individuals and the ways that individuals are formally grouped together into offices, departments, and divisions.

Product divisional structure   A form of organizational structure whereby jobs and activities are grouped on the basis of types of products or services—for example, automobiles, computer services, and electronics.

Profit center   An organizational unit charged with a well-defined mission and headed by a manager who is accountable for the unit's revenues and expenditures.

Span of control   The number of employees reporting directly to a given manager.

Strategic business unit structure   A form of organizational structure in which related product lines are grouped into divisions and those divisions are then grouped into larger entities referred to as strategic business units.

Tall organization   An organization characterized by relatively many hierarchical levels and a narrow span of control.

Vertical growth   An increase in the length of the organization's hierarchical chain of command.

DISCUSSION QUESTIONS

1. Why does organizational growth require greater formalization of roles within the organization?

2. Why does organizational growth require both vertical and horizontal expansion?

3. Explain why a relatively tall organizational structure is not appropriate for a dynamic, rapidly changing environment.

4. Why is a functional structure often appropriate for small businesses?

5. As an organization that is structured functionally begins to add new products to its original product offerings, it often changes its structure to a product divisional form. Explain why.

6. What is the rationale underlying the geographic divisional structure?

7. Explain the difference between a multidivisional structure and a strategic business unit structure.

8. A matrix structure is a combination of which two forms of organizational structure? Explain.

9. Of all of the forms of organizational structure discussed—functional, product divisional, geographic divisional, multidivisional, strategic business unit, matrix, and the horizontal structure—which is the most flexible? Explain why.

STRATEGIC MANAGEMENT EXERCISES

1. Assume that you have started a pizza restaurant in your town. Furthermore, assume that your restaurant has become very successful and that you eventually expand on a national basis. Draw an organization chart that portrays your business at the very beginning. Then, draw two more organization charts that show the vertical growth and the horizontal growth of your company as it grows to become a nationwide business.

2. Assume that you own a business that produces casual furniture. Draw a functional organization chart for your business. Now, assume that your business expands into furniture retailing. Draw a product divisional structure that encompasses your manufacturing and retailing operations.

3. Choose a company and examine its latest annual report. Sometimes, an explicit organization chart is contained in the report. Other times, a

summary chart is provided. In still other cases, there may be no structure depicted, but there is sufficient information for you to draw a rough sketch of the structure. Once you have determined the organization's structure, identify what type it is (functional, product divisional, geographic divisional, multidivisional, strategic business unit, matrix, or a combination of two or more of these). Explain your reasoning.

4. Select a business that has existed for at least ten years. Detail how its organizational structure has evolved over time. Explain why it changed from one structure to another at certain junctures. Or, if it has maintained the same structure during its life, explain why. Can you offer suggestions for improving its present structure?

5. From library research, identify an organization that is using a corporate growth strategy (discussed in chapter 4). Analyze how this organization's strategy has influenced its structure. Is its current structure the optimal structure for this enterprise? If not, what structure might be more appropriate?

6. From library research, identify an organization that is using a corporate retrenchment strategy (chapter 4). Analyze how this organization's strategy has influenced its structure. Is its current structure the optimal structure for this enterprise? If not, what structure might be more appropriate?

NOTES

1. J. Hagel, "Fallacies in Organizing Performance," *The McKinsey Quarterly* 2 (1994): 97–108. Also see J. Child, *Organization: A Guide for Managers and Administrators* (New York: Harper & Row, 1977), p. 10.

2. Ibid., pp. 50–70.

3. P. R. Lawrence and J. W. Lorsch, *Organization and Environment: Managing Differentiation and Integration* (Homewood, Ill.: Irwin, 1969); R. Duncan, "What Is the Right Organizational Structure?" *Organizational Dynamics* 7 (Winter 1979): 59–80.

4. M. Schroeder, "The Recasting of Alcoa," *Business Week,* 9 September 1991, pp. 62–64.

5. J. A. Byrne, "Is Your Company Too Big?" *Business Week,* 27 March 1989, p. 90.

6. Z. Sawaya, "Focus Through Decentralization," *Forbes,* 11 November 1991, pp. 242–244 (quotation from p. 244).

7. Z. Schiller and L. Therrien, "Nestlé's Crunch in the U.S.," *Business Week,* 24 December 1990, pp. 24–25.

8. See C. W. Hoffer, "Toward a Contingency Theory of Business Strategy," *Academy of Management Journal* 18 (1975): 784–810.

9. R. P. Rumelt, *Strategy, Structure, and Economic Performance* (Cambridge: Harvard University Press, 1974).

10. A. Taylor, "Here Comes Japan's New Luxury Cars," *Fortune,* 14 August 1989, pp. 62–66.

11. B. Dumaine, "P&G Rewrites the Marketing Rules," *Fortune,* 6 November 1989, pp. 34–48; A. Swasy, "In a Fast-Paced World, Procter & Gamble Sets Its Store in Old Values," *Wall Street Journal,* 21 September 1989, p. 1; Z. Schiller, "No More Mr. Nice Guy at P&G—Not by a Long Shot," *Business Week,* 3 February 1992, pp. 54–56.

12. J. A. Byrne, "The Horizontal Corporation," *Business Week,* 20 December 1993, p. 81.

13. M. Anchordoguy, *Computers, Inc.: Japan's Challenge to IBM* (Cambridge: Harvard University Press, 1989).

14. C. H. Ferguson, "Computers Are the Coming of the U.S. Keiretsu," *Harvard Business Review* , 68 p. 56 (1990).

15. S. Tully, "The Modular Corporation," *Fortune,* 8 February 1993, pp. 106–116; J. A. Byrne, R. Brandt, and O. Port, "The Virtual Corporation," *Business Week,* 8 February 1993, pp. 98–103; J. Wilson and J. Dobrzynski, "And Now the Post-Industrial Corporation," *Business Week,* 3 March 1986, pp. 64–71; and M. Piore and C. Sabel, *The Second Industrial Divide* (New York: McGraw-Hill, 1984).

STRATEGIC MANAGEMENT MODEL

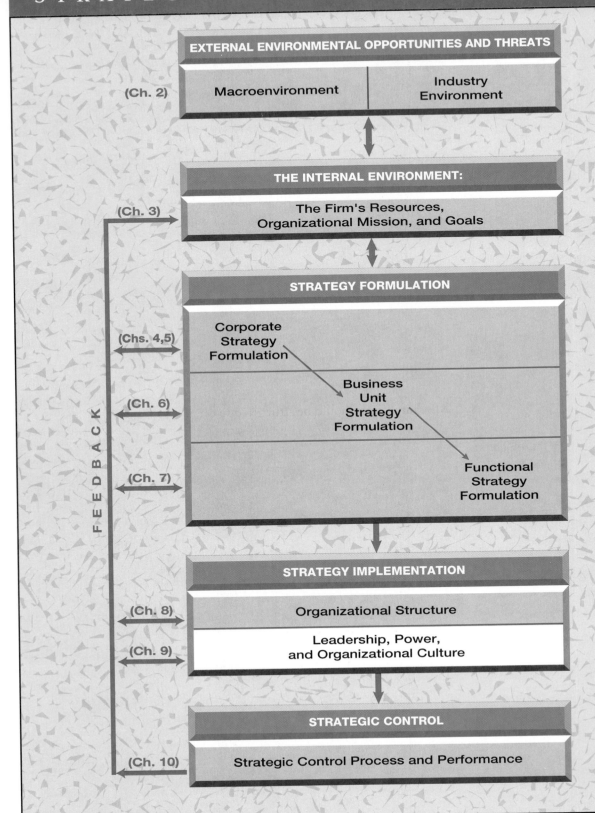

EXTERNAL ENVIRONMENTAL OPPORTUNITIES AND THREATS

(Ch. 2)

| Macroenvironment | Industry Environment |

THE INTERNAL ENVIRONMENT:

(Ch. 3)

The Firm's Resources, Organizational Mission, and Goals

STRATEGY FORMULATION

(Chs. 4,5) Corporate Strategy Formulation

(Ch. 6) Business Unit Strategy Formulation

(Ch. 7) Functional Strategy Formulation

STRATEGY IMPLEMENTATION

(Ch. 8) Organizational Structure

(Ch. 9) Leadership, Power, and Organizational Culture

STRATEGIC CONTROL

(Ch. 10) Strategic Control Process and Performance

FEEDBACK

9

Strategy Implementation: Leadership, Power, and Organizational Culture

Any strategy, no matter how well conceived, is doomed to failure unless it is effectively implemented. The preceding chapter examined how an organization should be structured to carry out its strategy. This chapter analyzes implementation from another perspective. Our interest here is in how an organization's chief executive officer (CEO) as well as other top managers can use their office and influence to ensure that the organization's members are implementing strategies effectively.

The top management team has several means at its disposal to encourage managers and other employees to put their full efforts into strategy implementation. The first resource is leadership. The CEO is recognized as the organization's principal leader, one who sets the tone for the members of the firm. The second resource is power. By influencing the behavior of others through formal and informal means, the CEO and other top managers attempt to ensure that organizational members channel their efforts into appropriate directions. The third resource is organizational culture. All organizations have a culture; the key for the CEO and other top managers is to understand and manage the culture in such a way that it facilitates—rather than hinders—the firm's strategic actions.

LEADERSHIP

Although some people equate *leadership* with *management*, the two concepts are not synonymous. For example, over time, a manager plays many roles. Several of them are not directly related to leadership. For instance, as a *resource allocator*, the manager determines the distribution of organizational resources such as money, time, and equipment. As a *monitor*, he or she receives information and analyses related to internal operations and external events. As a *disseminator*, the manager transmits information received from the external environment to members of the organization. All of these roles are part of the manager's job. Another role is that of *leader*.[1] A manager exhibits **leadership** when he or she secures the cooperation of others in accomplishing a goal. Hence, it is evident that the term *manager* is considerably broader than the term *leader*.

Although this chapter emphasizes the role of the CEO as the organization's leader, it is important not to overlook the fact that leadership is required at all organizational levels and in all functional areas. Strategies cannot be implemented through the CEO's efforts alone.

The need for organizational leadership has never been more important. As John P. Kotter, a management researcher, points out, in the relatively stable and prosperous 1950s and 1960s, the saying "If it ain't broke, don't fix it" prevailed. Under this axiom, it was clear that too much leadership "could actually create problems by disrupting efficient routines."[2] But as has been emphasized throughout this book, today's world is too dynamic and turbulent for an organization to compete effectively by simply continuing—no matter how efficiently—to do what it did in past years.

Our concern in this chapter is with strategic leadership, which differs from leadership at the middle-management and supervisory levels in a number of ways. **Strategic leadership** is concerned with both the external environment and with the firm's internal operations (rather than primarily with the latter); the process is characterized by greater ambiguity, complexity, and information overload; it involves the complicated task of integrating multiple functional areas rather than managing only one or a few functions; and it requires managing through others rather than directly supervising operations.[3] The job of strategic leadership is to establish the firm's direction—by developing and communicating a vision of the future—and to motivate and inspire organization members to move in that direction.[4] Not surprisingly, a review of leadership research concludes that top-level managers have a substantial impact on organizational performance.[5]

Just as strategic leadership is more important now than in past decades, it most surely will become even more essential in the coming years. Frequent environmental change and the growing complexity of organizations are trends that are likely to accelerate. Figure 9.1 portrays how external environmental changes and internal organizational complexity increase the importance of competent leadership.

It is important to remember throughout this chapter that good leadership is a necessary, but not sufficient, condition for organizational effectiveness. Although research demonstrates that leadership is an important determinant of organizational performance, it is clear that organizational effectiveness also depends on factors beyond the leader's control.[6] As we saw in chapter 2, such factors as economic conditions, industry structure, international developments, governmental policies, and technological innovations influence organizational results.

This section examines the concept of leadership. First, the formal role, or office, of the strategic leader is explored. Then the focus turns to the leader's style of leadership—the way the leader behaves in exercising authority and making decisions. Finally, how the leader works with other managers as a member of the top management team is analyzed.

Figure 9.1   **External and Organizational Changes that Present Challenges for Leadership**

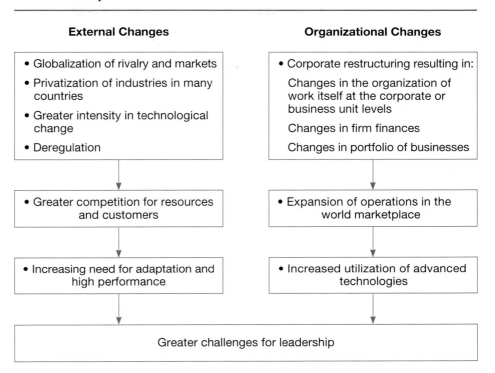

External Changes

- Globalization of rivalry and markets
- Privatization of industries in many countries
- Greater intensity in technological change
- Deregulation

↓

- Greater competition for resources and customers

↓

- Increasing need for adaptation and high performance

Organizational Changes

- Corporate restructuring resulting in:

  Changes in the organization of work itself at the corporate or business unit levels

  Changes in firm finances

  Changes in portfolio of businesses

↓

- Expansion of operations in the world marketplace

↓

- Increased utilization of advanced technologies

↓

Greater challenges for leadership

■ The Office of the Leader

Anyone who occupies the office of the CEO has the right to influence the behavior of the organization's members. In the case of a corporation, the CEO has been granted **formal authority** by the board of directors to influence specific aspects of employees' behavior. In a small entrepreneurial company, the CEO's authority may stem from the ownership of the firm.

Why do employees follow the direction of the CEO? Their motivation may be "an internalized value, such as obedience to authority figures, loyalty to the organization, respect for law, reverence for tradition, or merely the recognition that submission to authority is a necessary condition for membership in the organization."[7]

In any case, the chief mechanism for wielding formal authority is through the CEO's control over resources and rewards. These elements can cover a broad spectrum, including pay and bonuses, career progress, budgets, delegation of authority and responsibility, formal recognition of accomplishments, and status symbols.[8] The effective leader ensures that the organization's reward systems are consistent with its strategic direction. For instance, a company that wants to emphasize product innovation must allocate sufficient budget resources to research and development personnel, reward risk-taking behaviors, and not reward actions that are designed to maintain the status quo. For example, at 3M, pay raises and promotions are tied to innovative results. Managers and employees simply are not rewarded for standing still.

■ The Style of the Leader

Every leader has a distinctive **leadership style**—the characteristic pattern of behavior that a leader exhibits in the process of exercising authority and making decisions. Some leaders are flamboyant; others are quiet and contemplative. Some seek broad-based participation when making decisions; others arrive at decisions primarily on their own with little input from others. Whatever the style, an organization's leader sets the tone for the firm's members. His or her style is a matter of considerable interest to employees at virtually all levels, and it is an important variable in determining how committed the employees are to the firm's mission and goals and how much effort they will put into implementing the company's strategies.[9]

The most appropriate leadership style is a matter of some controversy and, in any case, is partially constrained by the personality of the leader. Because the bulk of research in this area focuses upon the styles of leaders of relatively small groups, the usefulness of that research for our purposes is limited. Here, our concern is with leaders of entire organizations or business units. As we have already emphasized, upper-level leadership is qualitatively different from leadership at lower levels.[10] From this perspective, the most pertinent body of knowledge available is the recent work on transformational and transactional leadership styles.[11] These styles and how they are used in practice are discussed in the paragraphs that follow.

Transformational and Transactional Leadership Styles

With **transactional leadership**, managers use the authority of their office, much as we just described, to exchange rewards such as pay and status for employees' work efforts. By contrast, with **transformational leadership**, managers inspire involvement in a mission, giving followers a "dream" or "vision" of a higher order than the followers' present reality. In effect, the transformational leader motivates followers to do more than they originally expected to do by stretching their abilities and increasing their self-confidence.[12] Organizational members are "transformed" by becoming more aware of the importance of their tasks and by being helped to transcend their own self-interest for the sake of the organization's mission.

Steven Jobs, the founder of Apple Computer, serves as an example of a transformational leader. In the company's early days, he was able to inspire his employees with his vision of making computing power accessible to a wide range of customers. Without his employees' willingness, and even enthusiasm, to put in long hours of work and to generate innovative ideas, Apple would never have been able to revolutionize the computer industry. By contrast, transactional leaders are less interested in inspiring followers than in ensuring that their organizations operate effectively and efficiently. The typical transactional leader is often concerned with increasing sales, market share, and profits incrementally rather than with "transforming" the organization.

Management researcher Bernard M. Bass proposes that most leaders exhibit both transactional and transformational styles, although they do so in different amounts.[13] Ultimately, the distinction between the two leadership styles is that leaders who are largely transactional continue to move their organizations in

Leadership Style at Southwest Airlines

Herb Kelleher has built Southwest Airlines into one of the most profitable and fast-growing airlines in the country through an emphasis on low-cost operations. In doing so, he has also managed to win the trust and respect of the personnel.

Now the nation's seventh-largest airline, Southwest has grown from a local carrier in Texas that specialized in no-frills flights between Dallas and Houston to one that offers service throughout the Southwest, Midwest, Southeast, and West Coast. It has expanded profitably even though it offers no on-board meals, no assigned seating, no interairline baggage transfers, and no listings on computer reservation systems. In some areas, standby tickets can be purchased through automated teller machines in convenience stores.

The market for this bare-bones service is short-haul passengers who desire low prices and frequent departures. To serve these passengers efficiently, Southwest's planes are able to arrive at an airport gate, unload baggage and passengers, load new baggage and passengers, and leave within ten minutes. How? By having employees who are considerably more productive than those in the rest of the airline industry. High productivity, combined with the airline's lack of frills, give Southwest a 43 percent cost advantage over the huge American Airlines. Under Kelleher's leadership, productivity, sales, and profits have soared in the 1990s. Some analysts have suggested that Kelleher may be America's best CEO.

Why are employees this dedicated? One pilot says that "it's not a Mary Kay-type atmosphere where we're all starry-eyed. It's mutual respect." This respect starts at the top with CEO Kelleher. He has established excellent rapport with the personnel and seems to be able to work out amenable agreements with which all sides are happy, unlike the bitter negotiations that have characterized labor contracts at several other airlines. Through profit-sharing plans, cross-utilization of workers, and Kelleher's concern for employees, the company has managed to forge an atmosphere of trust and loyalty.

Kelleher, for instance, is highly visible. He often takes Southwest flights and frequently visits the service areas where the planes are maintained. The visits are invariably upbeat and optimistic, with Kelleher dressing in a casual fashion (often in a Southwest Airlines shirt) and kidding with the crew. He knows individuals' names and sends birthday and Valentine's Day cards to each employee.

Most of all, though, he seems to care. As he puts it: "If you don't treat your own people well, they won't treat other people well." His actions support his words. He and all the other top managers of Southwest Airlines work at least once every three months as baggage handlers, ticket agents, and flight attendants. The point is to create an understanding of what each employee encounters on his or her job. As Kelleher explains, "When you're actually dealing with customers, and you've done the job yourself, you're in a better position to appraise the effect of some new program or policy."

His words are reinforced by the head of Southwest's mechanics and cleaners union: "How many CEOs do you know who come into the cleaners break room at 3 A.M. on a Sunday passing out doughnuts or putting on a pair of overalls to clean a plane?"

SOURCES: A. Q. Nomani, "Eastern Airports Are Still Out of Reach to Start-Ups," *Wall Street Journal Interactive Edition*, 25 April 1996; M. A. Verespej, "Flying His Own Course," *Industry Week*, 20 November 1995, pp. 22–24; "Southwest Airlines' Herb Kelleher: Unorthodoxy at Work," *Management Review*, 84(1) (1995):9–12; K. Labich, "Is Herb Kelleher America's Best CEO?" *Fortune*, 2 May 1994, pp. 44–52; P. O'Brian, "Southwest Airlines Is a Rare Air Carrier: It Still Makes Money," *Wall Street Journal*, 26 October 1992, p. A1 (source of fourth quotation); R. S. Teitelbaum, "Southwest Airlines: Where Service Flies Right," *Fortune*, 24 August 1992, p. 116 (source of second quotation); A. Farnham, "The Trust Gap," *Fortune*, 4 December 1989, pp. 56–78 (source of third quotation, p. 78); F. Gibney Jr., "Southwest's Friendly Skies," *Newsweek*, 30 May 1988, p. 49 (source of first quotation).

line with historical tradition, resulting in incremental improvements. Transformational leaders, however, lead their organizations toward a future that may result in significantly different processes and levels of performance.[14] This proposed difference is illustrated in Figure 9.2.

Note that transactional leadership is hypothesized to enhance an organization's performance steadily, but not dramatically. The proponents of transformational leadership, on the other hand, suggest that it can make significant changes in organizational performance. Also note that we propose that an organization's performance declines somewhat shortly after the transformational leadership process begins. Dramatic changes in the way an organization operates often result in short-term declines in performance, because organizational members may initially resist changing from the status quo and may experience difficulty in rising to the new expectations.

Both transactional and transformational leaders can exhibit all of the leadership styles identified in the well-known leadership theories. These include such commonly studied styles as task-oriented leadership (emphasizing task effectiveness) or relationship-oriented leadership (emphasizing the building of relationships with employees), as well as those styles that emphasize directing employees, encouraging employee participation in decision making, or setting goals. But even as these two types of leaders engage in the same style, their intent may be quite different. For instance, the transactional leader may delegate responsibility to an employee as a reward for fulfilling an agreement, but a transformational leader may delegate for the purpose of developing employee skills.[15]

Leadership Style in Practice

When is a transactional style needed, and when might a transformational style be required? As we have already seen, most leaders will exhibit both behaviors, although one may predominate. In general, we can propose that organizations that are meeting or exceeding their objectives and that do not foresee signifi-

Figure 9.2   **Hypothesized Results of Transactional and Transformational Leadership Styles**

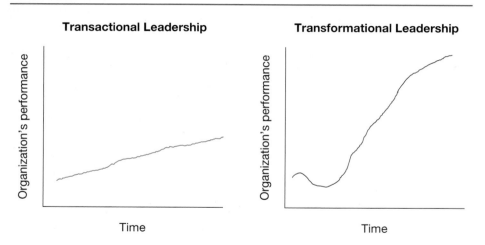

Henry Ford: Transactional and Transformational Leadership

Henry Ford (1863–1947) illustrates a leader who combined both transactional and transformational leadership styles:

> In 1914, he made a deal that workers found hard to resist. He offered them the unusually high wage for that time of $5 a day in exchange for their accepting rigid control of their behavior both inside and outside the plant. No idle time was to be tolerated. Internal spies were employed to enforce disciplinary rules. Yet, it was this same Henry Ford who revolutionized the automobile industry, making possible the mass production of the cheap, affordable automobile for the mass market.

How did Henry Ford transform the automobile industry? The transformation began with an argument between Ford and his partner Alexander Y. Malcolmson in 1905. Ford wanted to produce a simple, inexpensive car, but Malcolmson favored a more expensive and exclusive line. Malcolmson lost the argument and subsequently sold his interest in the company, leaving Ford to concentrate on the Model T—a sturdy, black automobile with a four-cylinder, twenty-horsepower engine. Introduced in 1908, the car sold for $825.

The Model T clearly met the needs and the financial resources of American consumers. More than 10,000 cars were sold the first year. Within five years, annual unit sales reached about a half-million. When production of the car ceased in 1927, 15 million Model Ts had been sold by Ford Motor Company.

By concentrating on one type of affordable automobile, Henry Ford created a mass market for the Model T. In turn, the huge demand for the car gave rise to the use of assembly line production with standardized parts. The volume enabled Ford to reduce the price of the car without decreasing profits. By 1913, the car's selling price had dropped to $500. It fell to $390 two years later and sold for $260 in 1925. Meanwhile, the time required to produce the car declined from $12\frac{1}{2}$ worker-hours in 1912 to $1\frac{1}{2}$ worker-hours in 1914.

This single car literally transformed not only the automobile industry but also the lifestyle and work habits of an entire nation. The impact of Henry Ford's transformational leadership continues to this day.

SOURCES: Arthur M. Johnson, "Henry Ford," in *The Encyclopedia Americana, International Edition*, Vol. 11 (Danbury, Conn.: Grolier, 1990), pp. 566–567; Robert Sobel, "Henry Ford," in *The World Book Encyclopedia*, Vol. 7 (Chicago: World Book, 1990), p. 380; B. M. Bass, *Leadership and Performance Beyond Expectations* (New York: Free Press, 1985), p. 27 (source of quotation).

cant changes in their environment can be well led through a transactional style. Increasingly, however, because of the intensity of domestic and foreign competition and dramatic environmental changes, many organizations require transformational leadership. Even casual perusal of such publications as the *Wall Street Journal, Business Week*, and *Fortune* will illustrate the strategic difficulties that many firms are facing.

Consider, for instance, the different strategic directions taken by IBM and Canon when they entered the copier business in the 1970s. Pursuing a transactional style, IBM's top management concentrated on developing products that were similar to those of the market leader—Xerox—and they imitated Xerox's service, pricing, and distribution. IBM's efforts were such a failure that it withdrew from the copier market. By contrast, Canon's top management used a transformational approach. Rather than duplicating Xerox's strategy, Canon concentrated on smaller copiers and taught its sales force to make presentations directly to department managers and secretaries who desired decentralized copying facilities rather than a centralized copy center. This approach contrasted dramatically with the traditional route of selling to the head of the duplicating department. Today, Canon is a major player in the copier industry.

Because transformational leadership is of considerable importance and is likely to take on even more significance, we will examine the process in detail at this point. Researchers Tichy and Devanna, who studied twelve CEOs, propose a three-stage process of transformational leadership.[16] Each stage will now be described.

Recognize the Need for Change.   First, the transformational leader must recognize the need for change and be able to persuade key managers in the organization of that need. This task may be difficult when changes in the environment are gradual and the organization is still meeting its objectives. As Peter F. Drucker, a management theorist and consultant, emphasizes, the best time to cast off the past is when the organization is successful—not when it is in trouble. When an organization is successful, its resources are allocated "to the things that *did* produce, to the goals that *did* challenge, to the needs that *were* unfulfilled."[17]

To overcome this tendency, Tichy and Devanna suggest that leaders measure the performance of their organizations against that of their competitors and not just against last year's performance. Additionally, measures of organizational performance must include more than the typical economic indicators, such as earnings per share, market share, and return on investment or assets. They should also include such measures as customer satisfaction, product quality as compared with competitors', new-product innovations, and other similar indicators.

Managers of troubled organizations more readily recognize the need for change. Increasingly, such firms are replacing their CEOs with managers from other corporations. For example, in recent years, Hughes Aircraft hired its CEO away from IBM, the CEO of Gulfstream Aerospace came from Xerox, and Campbell Soup's CEO was recruited from Gerber Products. An outsider can sometimes make the hard decisions, such as to initiate mass layoffs, that an insider might be reluctant to make. Outsiders, of course, also bring a fresh perspective to the firm and its problems. On the other hand, outsiders may have to spend months just learning the business and industry and trying to develop a network of contacts before they are able to take any decisive actions. Furthermore, hiring an outsider generally sends a message to the firm's vice presidents and other top managers that they were not considered worthy of promotion. For that reason, the act of hiring an outsider is often followed by an exodus of some of the company's top managerial talent.[18]

Create a Shared Vision.   Once the need for change is recognized, the leader must inspire organizational members with a "vision" of what the organization can become. In entrepreneurial ventures, this vision may be developed by the leader; but in large corporations, the vision is more likely to evolve through a participative process involving the CEO and key managers in the firm.[19] But Andrall E. Pearson, former CEO of PepsiCo, makes it clear that it is the leader's role to "spearhead" this effort, not just preside over it.[20] He also emphasizes that no strategic vision is permanent: "Lasting competitive edges are hard to generate."[21] Therefore, the transformational process is ongoing and not a one-time event.

An important part of the vision is high performance standards. From observation, it is clear that transformational leaders stretch their followers' abilities. High-performing organizations rarely pursue moderate goals or performance standards. Pearson observes, "This doesn't mean arbitrary, unrealistic goals that are bound to be missed and motivate no one, but rather goals that won't allow anyone to forget how tough the competitive arena is."[22] In such cases, the CEO must provide a role model for the organization's members. Transformational CEOs must "set a personal example in terms of the long hours they work, their obvious commitment to success, and the consistent quality of their efforts."[23] Furthermore, their public behavior should reflect their own excitement and energy, and the more contact they have with employees at all levels, the more contagious their excitement is likely to be.[24]

Besides serving as role models, transformational leaders must communicate their vision clearly and completely to all members of the organization. Management researchers Warren G. Bennis and Burt Nanus reinforce the importance of this suggestion by stating that the lack of a clear vision is a major reason for the declining effectiveness of many organizations in recent years. Clear communication of a vision creates a focus for the employees' efforts, and it is important that this vision be repeated over and over and not be allowed to fade away.[25] Few suggestions are more timely. The consulting firm Booz, Allen & Hamilton has reported that only 37 percent of senior managers think that other key managers completely understand new organizational goals, and only 4 percent of the senior managers believe that middle managers totally understand those goals.[26]

The common conception of the transformational leader as a dynamic, charismatic personality is only occasionally true.[27] Many CEOs have effectively led their organizations through major transformations without being charismatic figures. Undoubtedly, charisma helps a leader influence others, but it is hardly a requirement for a transformational leader.

Institutionalize the Change. Finally, the transformational leader must institutionalize the changes that have been created. The CEO must first ensure that the change is proceeding as planned. David A. Nadler, a management researcher, points out that all too many CEOs have learned, to their chagrin, that the changes they ordered never occurred. The reason is usually a lack of feedback mechanisms. Those mechanisms that were effective during stable periods often break down during turbulent change periods. In such situations, top management must develop multiple and highly sensitive feedback devices.[28] Feedback through multiple channels is essential, because change programs, even though successful, often have side effects such as the creation of new problems.

The CEO must also realize that the institutionalization of significant change (i.e., making the new ways of behaving a regular and normal part of organizational life) takes time. Encouraging organizational members to work and interact in different ways requires a new reward system. Because people are likely to behave in ways that lead to the rewards they desire, rewards such as pay increases and promotions should be linked to the types of behavior that are required to make the organization change effective. Management researcher Aaron J. Nurick recommends that if the organization benefits financially from the change program, its members should share in the gains. The connection between organizational improvement and the employees' well-being thus becomes clear. Without such rewards, employees are unlikely to see involvement as worthy of their efforts.[29]

At all three of these stages identified by Tichy and Devanna, it is essential that the CEO have clear, accurate, and timely information. Bennis makes a number of suggestions, based on his own experience and research, for ensuring that such information reaches the CEO.[30] These suggestions include that the CEO not rely exclusively on his or her assistants and intimate associates for information. Thus, the CEO should be accessible to the members of the organization and to its customers and should read more than staff summaries for information on the environment. Second, he proposes that CEOs rotate their key assistants every two years to ensure continuing openness. He also recommends that these assistants be in contact with the organization's constituent groups so that they will understand their obligations and the limits of their power. Finally, he believes that CEOs should actively encourage their advisers to act as devil's advocates so that "groupthink" (the situation that results when group members emphasize the importance of solidarity over critical thinking) does not prevail.

■ The Leadership Team

Although this chapter focuses primarily upon the CEO, no single individual can possibly lead a complex organization alone. Therefore, most CEOs spend considerable amounts of time and effort developing a team of top-level managers. Typically, the **top management team** is headed by the CEO and is comprised of executives immediately below the CEO's level on the organization chart. However, such teams may also include middle managers, depending upon the desires of the CEO and the situation facing the particular company. A group of compatible managers who work well together and complement one another's abilities can provide a very powerful sense of direction for a company.

Why are many organizations today emphasizing team building at the top management level? There are a number of excellent reasons:[31]

- The CEO has a complex integrative task and cannot possibly be effective at that task without working closely with the individuals who are in charge of the organization's major activities (functions, products, regions, etc.).
- Subordinate managers usually possess greater expertise about the operating components of the organization and their own fields than the CEO does.
- The outcomes of a team's deliberations—versus the decisions of a single manager—are more likely to be innovative, because they come from a group of individuals possessing different skills, perspectives, and information.
- Team members, and their divisions or departments, should be more understanding and supportive of organizational decisions because they have a voice in shaping those decisions.
- Communication among top managers is enhanced because of their regular, frequent meetings.
- The lower-level managers on the team receive valuable developmental experience.

Furthermore, a recent study of top management teams in 460 midwestern banks revealed that technical and administrative innovations were more likely to occur when the team members represented diverse functional areas. Cross-functional communication was considered essential to organizational innovation.[32]

One well-known firm that has used its top management team advantageously is UAL Corporation. Chairman and CEO Stephen M. Wolf works closely on a daily basis with the executives in charge of such areas as finance, marketing, employee relations, public relations, and the legal department. The successful turnaround that UAL has achieved since Wolf took over in 1987 is partially attributed to his ability to assemble a talented top management team.[33]

Some corporations have gone even further, replacing their chief operating officer (COO) with an executive team—or committee—that reports directly to the CEO. For example, Xerox has a six-person executive team, Nordstrom (the Seattle-based department store) is run by four "co-presidents," and Microsoft's three-person "office of the president" reports directly to Chairman William Gates III. Such arrangements, of course, can sometimes prove unwieldy. Their success often depends upon the interpersonal compatibility of the executives and the extent to which each is willing to be a "team player."[34]

POWER

To influence the behavior of others, a leader must possess power. This section examines the need to acquire power and then explores the ways a leader can use power to implement strategy.

■ The Role of Power

Although the popular conception of a CEO is of an individual who wields great amounts of power, this perception is far from correct. In fact, each time a manager climbs to a higher rung on the hierarchical ladder within an organization, he or she becomes more, not less, dependent upon other people.[35] In some sense, the CEO is the most dependent of the managers in an organization, because how well or how poorly the CEO (and, consequently, the organization) performs depends upon the performance of all of the organization's members. This is not to say that a CEO does not have formal authority to influence the behavior of employees, because he or she does. But we do wish to emphasize that trying to control the behavior of others solely through formal authority has its limitations.

The first of these limitations is that CEOs soon find out that not everyone in today's organizations passively accepts and enthusiastically carries out a constant stream of orders from above. Subordinates may resist orders, subtly ignore them, blatantly question them, or even quit. As Robert H. Miles, a management researcher, points out: "The raw use of power doesn't have the acceptance it did 25 years ago. People aren't willing to put up with it."[36]

Second, CEOs are always dependent upon some individuals over whom they have no formal authority.[37] Common examples include members of the board of directors, customers, and influential members of government regulatory agencies.

Hence, effective implementation of strategy requires the CEO to influence the behavior of others in ways that rely upon formal authority but also in ways that do not. In the latter sense, the CEO must acquire power over those individuals upon whom he or she is dependent. By **power** we refer to the ability—apart from formal authority or control over resources and rewards—to influence the behavior of other people. The following section explains how top managers can use power to implement strategies.

■ Techniques of Using Power

Top managers can wield power in a number of ways, as illustrated in Figure 9.3. This section discusses these common techniques, which CEOs and other top-level managers employ to implement organizational strategies.

Expertise

A major source of power for many top managers is expertise.[38] Managers generally establish this power base through visible achievement. The greater the achievement, the more power the manager is able to accumulate.[39]

Expertise refers to a manager's ability to influence the behavior of others because these individuals believe that their manager is more knowledgeable about a problem, an opportunity, or an issue than they are. Managers who reach the CEO's office by rising through the firm's ranks will often be viewed as experts because it is clear to the organization's members that their CEO mastered a variety of jobs on the way to the top and, hence, is familiar with the employees' tasks. An executive who is hired from outside the firm to become its CEO may or may not enter that job with expert power, however. If the individual is from a company in the same industry, though, he or she is more likely to be viewed as an expert.

For example, Lee Iacocca was probably perceived as an expert by Chrysler's employees when he was hired as that firm's CEO, because he had spent most of

Figure 9.3   **Techniques of Using Power**

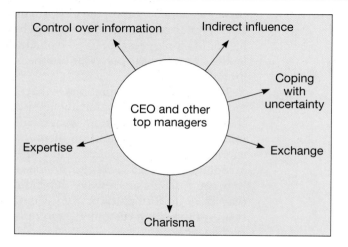

his career prior to that time at Ford, where he had successfully held a variety of jobs. On the other hand, when John Sculley became CEO of Apple Computer, his expertise was as a marketing whiz at PepsiCo. Although much of his marketing experience could be transferred to the personal-computer business, one could have predicted that his expert power would be constrained by his limited knowledge of computers. To overcome this constraint, Sculley attempted to learn all that he could about computers after being hired at Apple.

Management researcher Gary A. Yukl suggests that leaders who possess expert power must take care in how they communicate that expertise to others. He cautions such leaders to avoid acting superior to others who possess less expertise and not to speak in an arrogant, condescending manner. As he points out, sometimes expert leaders who are trying to sell their proposals to others "fire a steady stream of arguments, rudely interrupt any attempted replies, and dismiss any objections or concerns without serious consideration."[40]

Control over Information

Control over information refers to a manager's access to important information and control over its distribution to others.[41] Henry Mintzberg's research indicates that the CEO is normally the single best-informed member of an organization. He or she is formally linked to all of the organization's key managers. Because each of these managers is a specialist relative to the CEO, the CEO is the person who best sees the totality of the organization and is most knowledgeable about its internal activities. He or she also has a number of external contacts—in other companies, in regulatory agencies, and so on—which provide excellent sources of information. Although the CEO may not know everything, he or she usually knows more than anyone else.[42]

Because the CEO has more information than anyone else, he or she is able to interpret information in order to influence the perceptions and attitudes of others.[43] If the leader's information is more complete than that of any other individual, no one will be able to question his or her decisions effectively. Even the board of directors may prove impotent, because its power, based on legal standing, can be overcome by the CEO's power of information and knowledge.[44]

Exchange

The use of exchange as a power base is very common. In **exchange**, a leader does something for someone else and can then expect that person to feel a sense of obligation toward the leader. Hence, when the leader makes a special request of that person later, the person will usually feel obligated to carry out that request. CEOs may even develop friendships with others in terms of exchange, knowing that friendship carries with it certain obligations.

For instance, a top manager's relationship with the corporation's CEO or board of directors can add to—or detract from—the manager's power. As an extreme example, take the case of one COO who supported higher pay for his chairman, insisted that the chairman's country club dues be paid by the firm, deferred in public to the CEO, invariably addressing him as "Mr. Chairman," and even donated $250,000 in company funds to a university to honor the chairman. This manager, not surprisingly, was later named CEO by the chairman.[45]

Quite often, building reciprocal relationships with organizational members requires the ability to submerge one's ego. Those who set aside their status and power are more likely to be viewed favorably by those who are either above or below them in the organization's hierarchy. Such managers, of course, are more able to secure the enthusiastic cooperation of others.[46]

Indirect Influence

Top managers can often get others to implement the organization's strategies through **indirect influence**—that is, by modifying the situation in which individuals work. One variation of this technique involves making permanent changes in the organization's formal reward systems. In such cases, only those individuals who correctly carry out the organization's strategy will receive bonuses, pay raises, or promotions. For example, each of the six persons on the executive team that runs Xerox has a specific area of responsibility. However, to encourage the executives to work closely together, Xerox's board of directors has developed a compensation system for the executive team members that rewards overall company results—not simply the results of each person's own area.[47] Carrying this concept further, a manager can modify the organization's structure or even the physical layout of offices and departments to weaken groups or individuals who oppose certain aspects of the strategy.

Opposition to an organization's strategy is not unusual. Strategic change often reduces the status and power of some individuals while enhancing that of others. Those who believe that their status will be diminished often oppose the new strategy, if not openly, then through delaying tactics and other quiet forms of noncompliance.

In another type of indirect influence, the CEO may place only those individuals who are supporters in responsible positions. A loyal supporter, for instance, can be placed in charge of an important task force or committee to ensure that the group's recommendation coincides with the strategic direction set by the manager. Obviously, this technique must be used with care. If the CEO is surrounded only by loyal supporters, strategic decisions can become characterized by groupthink, and questions and objections that should be voiced may never arise.

Charisma

Another highly effective power base for influencing the behavior of others is charisma. **Charisma** refers to a leader's ability to influence others through his or her personal magnetism, enthusiasm, and strongly held convictions. Often, leaders are able to communicate these convictions and their vision for the future through a dramatic, persuasive manner of speaking.[48] As Yukl points out, charismatic leaders attempt to create an image of competence and success. Their aura of success and personal magnetism makes them role models for their employees. The more that followers admire their leaders and identify with them, the more likely they are to accept the leaders' values and beliefs. This acceptance enables charismatic leaders to exert considerable influence over their followers' behaviors.[49]

The more success the charismatic leader has, the more powerful he or she becomes. This combination of charisma and expertise can be extremely potent in influencing the behavior of others. Hence, charismatic leaders who set high standards of performance that are realistic are likely to have highly motivated and committed organization members.[50]

As some researchers have pointed out, charismatic leaders are most likely to be effective during periods of organizational crisis or transition.[51] Times of stress are more likely to encourage employees to respond to a leader who appears to have the answer to the problems that the organization is facing. If the leader's strategy results in early successes and if organizational performance begins to improve, the leader's power base will increase dramatically.

Coping with Uncertainty

Every organization faces environmental contingencies; these may consist of various trends or developments, such as competition, governmental regulations or laws, cost pressures, new technologies, and so on. The relative importance of these many contingencies will vary from one organization and industry to another. But when a development or trend has an important implication for any particular organization at a specific time, it can be termed a **critical contingency**.[52]

For example, in the highly competitive and rapidly changing financial services industry, the critical contingency is developing new financial products. Those companies that are most effective at anticipating and meeting the market's needs are more likely to be profitable. Thus managers in those companies who create popular new financial products are able to amass significant amounts of power to influence organizational decisions. Likewise, in an industry whose critical contingency is efficiency/cost control—such as in the airline industry—managers who lower their organization's cost structure can gain considerable amounts of power.[53]

Relating these ideas to the business unit strategies presented in chapter 6, we can surmise that, in industries in which the critical contingency is external product/market trends or events, companies that adopt either the niche-differentiation strategy or the differentiation strategy are more likely to be profitable. In those companies, most of the power therefore will likely be held by managers in marketing, advertising, and/or product research and development (R&D). Similarly, in environments in which the efficiencies of processing or delivering products/services comprise the critical contingency, those businesses that adopt the niche–low-cost strategy or the low-cost strategy will be most effective. Hence, their operating decisions are most likely to be influenced by managers in accounting, production/operations, or process R&D. Finally, in environments in which both operating efficiencies and product/service differentiation are the critical contingencies, executives in any—or all—of these areas are likely to wield power.

ORGANIZATIONAL CULTURE

Organizational culture refers to the values and patterns of belief and behavior that are accepted and practiced by the members of a particular organization.[54] Because each organization develops its own unique culture, even organizations within the same industry and city will exhibit distinctly different ways of operating. The following sections discuss the evolution of organizational culture, the impact of culture on an organization's strategy, and the methods leaders use to shape organizational culture.

■ The Evolution of Culture

The purpose of organizational culture is to enable a firm to adapt to environmental changes and to coordinate and integrate its internal operations.[55] But how do appropriate values, behaviors, and beliefs develop to enable the organization to accomplish these ends?

For many organizations, the first—and major—influence upon their culture is their founder. His or her assumptions about success form the foundation of the firm's culture.[56] For instance, the primary influence upon McDonald's culture was the fast-food company's founder, Ray A. Kroc, who died in 1984. His philosophy of fast service, assembly line food preparation, wholesome image, and devotion to the hamburger are still reflected in McDonald's operations today. Kroc's influence is the primary reason why McDonald's did not diversify outside the fast-food industry, did not specialize in made-to-order hamburgers, prohibited franchisees from being absentee owners, encouraged franchisees to experiment with new products, targeted advertisements and sales promotions to both adults and children, and opened Ronald McDonald Houses near major medical centers to provide low-cost housing to families of sick children.

As Yukl points out, the set of beliefs about the distinctive competence of the organization (i.e., what differentiates it from other organizations) is one of the most important elements of culture in new organizations. These beliefs directly affect organizational strategies and operations. For example, a company that owes its success to developing innovative products is likely to respond to a decline in sales with new-product introductions; a company that offers a common product at a low price would respond with attempts to lower costs even further.[57]

However, as time passes, Yukl notes, "segments of the culture that were initially functional may become dysfunctional, preventing the organization from adapting successfully to a changing environment."[58] McDonald's, for instance, has departed from some of Kroc's precepts in order to continue its success under changing conditions. As customers have become more interested in a diversified menu, McDonald's has expanded from hamburgers to fish and chicken sandwiches and even pizza. Increasing societal emphasis on healthy diets has led to new products such as salads, cereal, and low-fat hamburgers and yogurt as well as to modifications in the food preparation process. The company even made its first departure from fast food to take advantage of its strong brand name by licensing Sears, Roebuck & Company to sell children's clothing with the McDonald's name emblazoned on it.[59]

So, in general, we can say that the foundation of an organization's culture reflects the values and beliefs of its founder. But the culture is modified over time as the environment changes. Environmental change renders some of the firm's culture obsolete and even dysfunctional. New elements of the culture must be added as the old are discarded in order for the organization to maintain its success. But as Figure 9.4 illustrates, a given organization's culture may also change to reflect the powerful influence of a transformational leader other than the founder.[60]

Figure 9.4　　　　　　　　**Evolution of Organizational Culture**

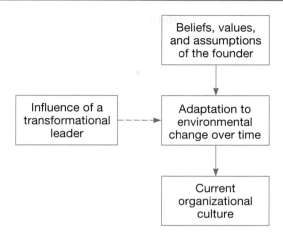

For example, in recent years, the culture of Walt Disney Company has changed significantly. The founder's influence on the conservative family entertainment company was such that for years after his death, executives would wonder "What would Walt have done?" before making decisions. As the company lost ground to its competitors by releasing an outdated line of family movies, its newly hired CEO, Michael Eisner, brought in a new team of managers who had never known Disney. By freeing its top management of the elements of the past, which had become dysfunctional, Eisner has produced the types of movies that are popular with today's moviegoers.[61]

▪ Impact of Culture on Strategy

Organizational culture can facilitate or hinder the firm's strategic actions. One study showed that firms with "strategically appropriate cultures"—such as PepsiCo, Wal-Mart, and Shell—outperformed selected other corporations with less appropriate cultures over an eleven-year period. The successful firms experienced an average revenue increase of 682 percent (versus 166 percent for the other organizations), their stock prices rose by 901 percent (versus 74 percent), and growth in their net income outpaced the other firms by 756 percent to 1 percent. These successful firms had developed cultures that emphasized three key groups of stakeholders—customers, stockholders, and employees. Note that the point is *not* that these corporations have strong cultures, for many less successful firms—such as Sears, General Motors, and Citicorp—possess strong cultures. The point, rather, is that the culture of a successful firm must be appropriate to—and supportive of—that firm's strategy. Furthermore, the culture must contain values that can help the firm adapt to environmental change.[62]

STRATEGIC INSIGHT

Leadership and Organizational Culture at Wal-Mart

Wal-Mart's culture cannot be separated from the beliefs of its founder, Sam Walton, who died in 1992. During his career, "Mr. Sam" provided the guiding vision that took his company from a single store in Arkansas in 1962 to the position of world's largest retailer by 1990. This meteoric growth was not due simply to low prices or store location. Many retailers that offered low prices, such as Korvette's and Woolco, no longer exist; and, if location were the primary key to success, Sears and Macy's would be highly profitable. Rather, to a great extent, the biggest difference between Wal-Mart and other retailers was Sam Walton himself.

From the beginning, Walton realized that retailing begins with the customer. The concepts of customer service and customer satisfaction are ingrained into every one of Wal-Mart's 400,000 "associates" (the firm's term for employees). Each week, Wal-Mart's regional vice presidents follow in Walton's footsteps by spending three or four days visiting stores in their region, talking to customers and associates and comparing Wal-Mart's prices and merchandise with those of such competitors as Kmart. Each Saturday, all of Wal-Mart's top managers meet to compare findings and decide what changes are needed in their stores during the coming week. Some even say that the first lesson Walton instilled in his associates was a "bias for action," so that change in the stores is constant.

As the company grew, Walton realized that empowering associates was the most efficient way of keeping in touch with the customer. Hence, associates are kept informed weekly about their store's—and even their own department's—performance. All associates know their products' cost, markup, overhead, and profit. Walton believed that the more associates understand about their business, the more interested they'll be in serving their customers. Each department manager acts as an entrepreneur, running his or her own business, and each is encouraged to experiment. Those whose experiments are successful are invited to the Saturday meeting at company headquarters in Bentonville, Arkansas, to explain their ideas to top management.

Finally, Sam Walton realized that giving motivational speeches and leading associates in the "Wal-Mart cheer" ("Give me a W! Give me an A! Give me an L! Give me a squiggly! . . .") could only go so far in helping them identify with the organization. So, early on, he decided to make associates a real part of the company by making every associate who has been with Wal-Mart for at least a year eligible for profit sharing. Wal-Mart contributes about 6 percent of each associate's salary to the plan, and associates can take their share in cash or in Wal-Mart stock whenever they leave the company. As a typical example, one Wal-Mart truck driver related that, after driving for thirteen years, he received only $700 when he resigned. But, in nineteen years with Wal-Mart, he had already accumulated $707,000 in profit sharing.

CEO David Glass is continuing Walton's commitment to cost control, innovation, greater emphasis on the upscale market, and a customer-centered culture. He is convinced that there is no other company where 400,000 people work so closely together as true partners.

SOURCES: T. Agins, "Queen-Sized Women Find Fashion in Upscale Label," *Wall Street Journal Interactive Edition*, 8 May 1996; L. Lee, "Discounter Wal-Mart Is Catering to Affluent to Maintain Growth," *Wall Street Journal*, 7 February 1996, pp. A1, A8; R. Halverson, "David Glass," *Discount Store News*, 4 December 1995, pp. 55–56; T. Andreoli, "Bud Walton: Vision and Spirit: Wal-Mart's Co-Founder Dies at Age 73," *Discount Store News*, 3 April 1995, pp. 1–2; D. Longo, "New Generation of Execs Lead Wal-Mart into the Next Century," *Discount Store News*, 5 December 1994, pp. 45–48; A. Markowitz, "Wal-Mart Charts Future in Mexico, Canada," *Discount Store News*, 21 February 1994, pp. 1, 87; B. Saporito, "A Week Aboard the Wal-Mart Express," *Fortune*, 24 August 1992, pp. 77–84; S. Walton and J. Huey, *Sam Walton: Made in America* (New York: Doubleday, 1992).

Because culture reflects the past, periods of environmental change often require significant modification of the organization's culture.[63] It is essential that changes in strategy be accompanied by corresponding alterations in organizational culture; otherwise, the strategy is likely to fail. Conservative organizations do not become aggressive, entrepreneurial firms simply because they have formulated new goals and plans.[64]

A firm caught in changing environmental conditions may devise a new strategy that will make sense from a financial, product, or marketing point of view. Yet the strategy will not be implemented because it requires "assumptions, values, and ways of working" that are at variance with the organization's culture.[65] An organization can change its strategy and its structure, but may find its employees reverting to their prior ways of operating if it does not confront the assumptions underlying its culture.[66]

As an example of a company modifying both its culture and its strategy, consider Electronic Data Systems (EDS).[67] Founded in the early 1960s by H. Ross Perot, EDS exemplified a powerful "can-do, anything-is-possible" entrepreneurial spirit. Strongly nonunion, the company had an extremely stringent hiring process followed by a grueling trial and training period. Those who survived displayed unusually high morale and a devotion to doing whatever was required to accomplish the task. By the early 1980s, EDS possessed a culture that could be described as "gung ho."

But in the mid-1980s EDS was acquired by General Motors, and Perot left the company within two years. In a brief period of time, EDS found itself without its strong leader, without its independence, and with a work force that had expanded almost overnight from several thousand to 60,000 employees. To compound its identity crisis, EDS failed to win an important contract with Kodak, leading its top management to reassess both its strategy and its culture.

EDS is now undergoing some material changes under chairman and CEO Les Alberthal. His vision for EDS is that it be recognized "as the premier provider of information technology services based on its contributions to the success of its customers."[68] Toward that end, Alberthal emphasizes that EDS must help its customers succeed by understanding their needs. To accomplish that goal, EDS's structure is being transformed from that of a big company to an organization of many smaller companies (multiple business units with decentralized decision-making authority). Because each business unit focuses upon a specific segment of the market, this move puts EDS employees in closer contact with customers and their needs. At the same time, EDS is transforming its historical "trust us" type of customer service to one that is more characterized by listening and cooperation.

To support this strategy/structure transformation, EDS modified its culture. Employees are viewed as "volunteers" who may, if their needs are not fulfilled, leave EDS for other employment. Managers are evaluated not only on revenue and profit figures but also on the extent to which they motivate and empower their employees. Managerial training programs have been altered to help managers become more involved with their employees and to learn to serve as mentors to them. Overall, the manager's role has changed from that of "taskmaster" to one of "servant" to the employee. Alberthal saw these shifts as essential to attracting talented employees in an increasingly diverse work force.

S T R A T E G I C   I N S I G H T

PepsiCo's Distinctive Culture

Surely one of the most distinctive U.S. corporate cultures is PepsiCo's. New managers are put through a rigorous training program likened to Marine Corps boot camp, with those who can't meet the standards washing out. Once through the program, each manager is given considerable freedom. Risk taking is encouraged, and second guessing is rare. Even after PepsiCo lost $16 million on its ill-fated Grandma's Cookies venture, the executive who designed the project was subsequently promoted.

An important value is winning. Not surprisingly, the typical managerial work week is sixty hours. In fact, when an internal survey revealed that some employees at headquarters were disturbed that they didn't have sufficient time to do their laundry at home, the company installed dry cleaning equipment rather than reduce the workweek.

PepsiCo may take management development more seriously than almost any other corporation. CEO Roger Enrico spends about half of his time reviewing the performance of the firm's top 600 managers. He also personally interviews all applicants for positions of vice president and president. He expects those below him to spend about 40 percent of their time on personnel development and performance evaluation.

The managers who survive the intense atmosphere are rewarded with first-class air travel, stock options, bonuses that can reach 90 percent of salary, fast promotions, and fully loaded company cars. Those who don't meet the firm's expectations are out.

These values are consistent with PepsiCo's strategic direction—growth. Managers are given considerable autonomy and are encouraged to "love change" and move quickly to take advantage of opportunities.

Capitalizing on growth opportunities is of paramount importance in consumer products and has made PepsiCo one of the premier firms in the world. When growth slows, PepsiCo is not afraid to change, as shown by its spin-off of its fast-food restaurants.

SOURCES: M. Wallin and D. Lytle, "PepsiCo Moves to Shore Up S. American Bottler," *Dow Jones News Service*, 9 May 1996; R. Frank, "Pepsi to Take Control of Latin American Bottler," *Wall Street Journal Interactive Edition*, 10 May 1996; P. Sellers, "PepsiCo's New Generation," *Fortune*, 1 April 1996, pp. 110–118; J. M. Graves, "Wayne Calloway's Gift and Curse," *Fortune*, 6 February 1995, pp. 14–15; S. Sherman and A. Hadjian, "How Tomorrow's Best Leaders Are Learning Their Stuff," *Fortune*, 27 November 1995, pp. 90–96; D. Anfuso, "PepsiCo Shares Power and Wealth with Workers," *Personnel Journal*, June 1995, pp. 42–48; M. Magnet, "Let's Go for Growth," *Fortune*, 7 March 1994, pp. 64–66; "Pepsi's Old Boy Wins Lead Post," *Marketing*, 27 January 1994; A. Rothman, "Can Wayne Calloway Handle the Pepsi Challenge?" *Business Week*, 27 January 1992, pp. 90–98.

■ How Leaders Shape Culture

CEOs other than the founder can be influential in shaping the organization's culture so that it becomes more appropriate for its present or anticipated environment. Transactional leaders are less likely to modify the firm's culture than transformational leaders. Bass points out: "The transactional leader works within the organizational culture as it exists; the transformational leader changes the organizational culture."[69]

How can a leader change the organization's culture? Management researcher Edgar H. Schein advocates five "primary embedding mechanisms" for altering culture.[70] The first mechanism is systematically paying attention to certain areas of the business. This goal may be accomplished through formally measuring and controlling the activities of those areas or, less formally, through the CEO's comments or questions at meetings. For instance, a top manager can direct the attention of organizational members toward controlling costs or to serving customers effectively. By contrast, those areas that the leader does not react to will be considered less important by employees.

The second mechanism involves the leader's reactions to critical incidents and organizational crises. The way a CEO deals with a crisis—such as declining sales, new governmental regulation, or technological obsolescence—can emphasize norms, values, and working procedures or even create new ones. For instance, some companies have reacted to declining profits by cutting compensation across the board; all employees, including top management, take the pay cut. This action emphasizes a belief that "we are a family who will take care of one another." Other firms, by contrast, lay off operative employees and middle managers, while maintaining (or even increasing) the salaries of top management. Nonadaptive cultures frequently reflect top management's values of arrogance and insularity. Self-interest takes precedence over concerns about customers, stockholders, or employees.[71]

The third mechanism is to serve as a deliberate role model, teacher, or coach. As we have seen earlier in the chapter, the visible behavior of the leader communicates assumptions and values to subordinates.

The way top management allocates rewards and status is a fourth mechanism for influencing culture. Leaders can quickly communicate their priorities by consistently linking pay raises, promotions, and the lack of pay increases and promotions to particular behaviors. For instance, General Foods found that the changing environment of the 1980s rendered its historical emphasis on cost control and earnings less effective. To redirect the efforts of managers toward diversification and sales growth, top management revised the compensation system to link bonuses to sales volume rather than only to increased earnings and began rewarding new-product development more generously.[72]

The fifth mechanism identified by Schein involves the procedures through which an organization recruits, selects, and promotes employees and the ways it dismisses them. An organization's culture can be perpetuated by hiring and promoting individuals whose values are similar to the firm's. By contrast, an organization attempting to alter its culture can accelerate that change by hiring employees whose beliefs and behaviors more closely fit the organization's changing value system.

In addition to these five primary embedding mechanisms, Schein identifies several "secondary reinforcement mechanisms."[73] These include the organization's structure, its operating systems and procedures, the design of its physical space, various stories or legends that are perpetuated about important events and people, and formal statements of organizational philosophy. These mechanisms are labeled *secondary* because they work only if they are consistent with the five primary mechanisms. The primary embedding mechanisms and secondary reinforcement mechanisms are summarized in Table 9.1 on page 250.

As an example of the secondary mechanisms, the belief that open communication and close working relationships are important is reflected in the open designs of the headquarters of companies such as Levi Strauss in California and Nike in Oregon.[74]

Schein emphasizes the critical linkage between leadership and organizational culture by stating that "the unique and essential function of leadership is the manipulation of culture."[75] Culture is created by the actions of leaders; it is institutionalized by leaders; and when it becomes dysfunctional, leadership is

Table 9.1   **Mechanisms for Embedding and Reinforcing Organizational Culture**

Primary Embedding Mechanisms

1. What leaders pay attention to, measure, and control
2. Leader reactions to critical incidents and organizational crises
3. Deliberate role modeling, teaching, and coaching
4. Criteria for allocation of rewards and status
5. Criteria for recruitment, selection, promotion, retirement, and excommunication

Secondary Articulation and Reinforcement Mechanisms

1. Organization design and structure
2. Organizational systems and procedures
3. Design of physical space, facades, buildings
4. Stories about important events and people
5. Formal statements of organizational philosophy, creeds, charters

Source: E. H. Schein, *Organizational Culture and Leadership* (San Francisco: Jossey-Bass, 1985), Chap. 10.

required to change it. What a CEO needs most, according to Schein, is an understanding of how culture can help or hinder the organization in attaining its mission and the skills to make the appropriate changes.[76]

SUMMARY

Top-level managers have a number of means to encourage organizational members to put their full efforts into strategy implementation: strategic leadership, power, and organizational culture. In today's dynamic and turbulent world, the importance of strategic leadership cannot be overemphasized. The firm's leaders must articulate the organization's mission and goals and then inspire, motivate, and support the firm's members as they work together to implement the organization's strategies.

The CEO, simply by virtue of the office, possesses the potential to influence the behavior of the organization's employees. This source of influence is termed *formal authority*. Through it, the CEO can control resources and rewards. Additionally, each CEO has a distinctive leadership style that sets the tone for the firm's members. Some leaders use a transactional style, exchanging rewards for employees' work efforts. This style can be effective in firms that are already performing well and do not anticipate significant environmental change, because it encourages employees to continue to engage in high performance.

In companies that are experiencing competitive difficulties or are undergoing environmental change, a transformational leadership style is preferable. A transformational leader inspires involvement in a mission, giving followers a "vision" of a higher order and motivating them to stretch their abilities. Such leadership is thought to make significant changes in organizational performance.

Because no single CEO, regardless of how talented he or she may be, can lead a complex organization single-handedly, most companies emphasize top management teams. Led by the CEO, such teams of executives are able to enhance the organization's coordinative activities, creativity, information flows, and strategy implementation.

In influencing the behavior of others, CEOs and other top managers have available, in addition to their formal authority and leadership style, various other techniques for wielding power. For instance, managers who are perceived as experts in their field often have significant influence over the behavior of others. They can also use their access to important information and control over its distribution to affect behavior. Leaders often use exchange as a power base, doing something for others to create a sense of obligation. Also, a manager can indirectly influence others by modifying the organization's structure, physical layout, or reward system. A manager who possesses charisma can also have a powerful impact upon followers. Finally, managers who deal successfully with critical environmental contingencies can acquire significant power.

Organizational culture refers to the values and patterns of belief and behavior that are accepted and practiced by the members of an organization. A given organization's culture reflects the influence of its founder, its experiences after the departure of its founder, and, at times, the powerful influence of a transformational leader other than the founder.

An organization's culture can facilitate or hinder the firm's strategic actions. Successful strategy implementation requires a "strategically appropriate culture"—one that is appropriate to, and supportive of, the firm's strategy. Moreover, that culture must contain values that can help the firm adapt to environmental change.

A leader can change the organization's culture through such mechanisms as paying systematic attention to certain areas of the business, serving as a deliberate role model, and allocating rewards and status. Leaders can also set an example for the firm's members through the way in which they react to organizational crises and through the processes the organization uses to attract, hire, and promote employees.

TAKE IT TO THE NET

We invite you to visit the Wright page on the Prentice Hall Web site at:

http://www.prenhall.com/wright

for this chapter's World Wide Web exercise.

KEY CONCEPTS

Charisma   A leader's ability to influence the behavior of others through his or her personal magnetism, enthusiasm, strongly held beliefs, and charm.

Control over information   A situation in which a manager has access to important information and controls its distribution to others to influence their behavior.

Critical contingency   An environmental trend or development that has important implications for an organization. Managers who cope successfully with such contingencies acquire significant amounts of power.

Exchange   A situation in which a leader does a favor for someone so that he or she will feel a sense of obligation toward the leader.

Expertise   A manager's ability to influence the behavior of others because they believe that the manager possesses greater expertise or is more knowledgeable about a situation than they are.

Formal authority   The official, institutionalized right of a manager to make decisions affecting the behavior of subordinates.

Indirect influence   The influence on the behavior of others brought about by modifying the situation in which they work.

Leadership   The capacity to secure the cooperation of others in accomplishing a goal.

Leadership style   The characteristic pattern of behavior that a leader exhibits in the process of exercising authority and making decisions.

Organizational culture   The values and patterns of belief and behavior that are accepted and practiced by the members of a particular organization.

Power   The ability, apart from functional authority or control over resources or rewards, to influence the behavior of others.

Strategic leadership   The process of establishing the firm's direction—by developing and communicating a vision of the future—and motivating and inspiring organization members to move in that direction.

Top management team   A team of top-level executives, headed by the CEO.

Transactional leadership   The capacity to motivate followers by exchanging rewards for performance.

Transformational leadership   The capacity to motivate followers by inspiring involvement and participation in a mission.

DISCUSSION QUESTIONS

1. Explain the difference between leadership and management. Give examples of each concept.

2. Delineate the relationship between an organization's reward system and its strategic decisions.

3. Explain transactional leadership, and give examples. Identify the conditions under which it is likely to be effective.

4. Explain transformational leadership, and give examples. Identify the conditions under which it is likely to be effective.

5. What is the role of clear, accurate, and timely information in each of the three stages of the transformational process?

6. Explain the concept of managerial dependency and why it requires the CEO to develop sources of power other than formal authority.

7. Give examples of leaders you have known who wielded power through expertise; through control over information; through exchange; through indirect influence; and through charisma.

8. Think of an organization with which you are quite familiar. Describe its culture. Explain how its culture may have evolved.

9. Give an example of an organization whose culture is appropriate for its strategy. Now, give an example of a firm whose culture has hindered its strategy.

10. Relate a story about an important event or a person that reflects elements of a particular organization's culture.

STRATEGIC MANAGEMENT EXERCISES

1. Assume that you are the CEO of a commercial airline that competes with the low-cost strategy. Describe an appropriate organizational culture for your company.

2. Assume that your airline (Exercise 1) has now changed its strategy from low-cost to low-cost–differentiation. As CEO, what changes might you consider implementing in style of leadership, exercise of power, and organizational culture?

3. Find, in your library, an example of transformational leadership. Explain the situation fully: Who is the leader? What is the organization? Why was transformational leadership necessary? What characteristics and/or behaviors made the manager a transformational leader? What were the results of his or her attempts to transform the organization? (Particularly good sources for this exercise are the *Wall Street Journal*, *Business Week*, and *Fortune*.)

4. Strategies involving mergers and acquisitions are particularly vulnerable to cultural problems. Mergers between two organizations often are easier to accomplish on paper than in reality. Reality may reveal that the cultures of the organization fail to mesh as easily as corporate assets. From library research, identify a firm acquiring another or identify two companies that are currently merging or have engaged in a merger within the past few years. Learn as much as you can about each company's organizational culture. What problems are the two businesses having in combining their cultures? From your research, what other problems can you predict will occur in the future?

NOTES

1. H. Mintzberg, *The Nature of Managerial Work* (New York: Harper & Row, 1973), Chap. 4.

2. J. P. Kotter, *The Leadership Factor* (New York: Free Press, 1988), p. 11.

3. D. C. Hambrick, "Guest Editor's Introduction: Putting Top Managers Back in the Strategy Picture," *Strategic Management Journal* 10 (1989): 6.

4. D. Tosti and S. Jackson, "Alignment: How It Works and Why It Matters," *Training* 31 (April 1994): 58–64; J. P. Kotter, *A Force for Change: How Leadership Differs from Management* (New York: Free Press, 1990), p. 5.

5. D. V. Day and R. G. Lord, "Executive Leadership and Organizational Performance: Suggestions for a New Theory and Methodology," *Journal of Management* 14 (1988): 453–464.

6. G. A. Yukl, *Leadership in Organizations*, 2nd ed. (Englewood Cliffs, N. J.: Prentice Hall, 1989), pp. 263–266; J. Pfeiffer, "The Ambiguity of Leadership," *Academy of Management Review* 2 (1977): 104–112.

7. S. Lahiry, "Building Commitment Through Organizational Culture," *Training & Development* 48 (April 1994): 50–52; J. R. Emshoff, "How to Increase Employee Loyalty While You Downsize," *Business Horizons* 37 (March/April 1994): 49–57; Yukl, *Leadership in Organizations*, p. 15.

8. Yukl, *Leadership in Organizations*, pp. 17–18.

9. G. Trumfio, "Managing from the Trenches," *Sales & Marketing Management* 146 (February 1994): 39; J. A. Parnell, & E. D. Bell, "A Measure of Managerial Propensity for Participative Management," *Administration and Society* 25: 518-530.

10. Day and Lord, "Executive Leadership and Organizational Performance: Suggestions for a New Theory and Methodology," p. 459.

11. This distinction was first made by J. M. Burns, in *Leadership* (New York: Harper & Row, 1978).

12. See D. T. Bastien and T. J. Hostager, "Jazz as a Process of Organizational Innovation," *Communication Research* 15 (1988): 582–602; C. Manz, D. T. Bastien, and T. J. Hostager, "Executive Leadership during Organizational Change: A Bi-Cycle Model," *Human Resource Planning* 14 (1993): 276–287.

13. B. M. Bass and B. J. Avolio, "Transformational Leadership and Organizational Culture," *International Journal of Public Administration* 17 (1994) p. 22.

14. B. M. Bass, "Leadership: Good, Better, Best," *Organizational Dynamics* 13 (Winter 1985): 26–40; N. M. Tichy and D. O. Ulrich, "SMR Forum: The Leadership Challenge—A Call for the Transformational Leader," *Sloan Management Review* 26 (Fall 1984): 59–68.

15. Ibid.

16. N. M. Tichy and M. A. Devanna, *The Transformational Leader* (New York: Wiley, 1986).

17. P. F. Drucker, *Managing in Turbulent Times* (New York: Harper & Row, 1980), p. 44.

18. J. S. Lublin, "More Companies Tap Industry Outsiders for Top Posts to Gain Fresh Perspectives," *Wall Street Journal*, 21 February 1992; J. Cole and P. B. Carroll, "GM's Hughes Division Hires Armstrong from IBM to Become Chairman, Chief," *Wall Street Journal*, 20 February 1992; B. Hager, L. Driscoll, J. Weber, and G. McWilliams, "CEO Wanted. No Insiders, Please," *Business Week*, 12 August 1991, pp. 44–45.

19. Tichy and Devanna, *The Transformational Leader*.

20. A. E. Pearson, "Six Basics for General Managers," *Harvard Business Review* 67, no. 4 (July–August 1989): 96.

21. Ibid., p. 97. Reprinted by permission of the *Harvard Business Review*. Excerpt from "Six Basics for General Managers," by Andrall E. Pearson (July–August 1989). Copyright © 1989 by the President and Fellows of Harvard College; all rights reserved.

22. Ibid., p. 95. Reprinted by permission of the *Harvard Business Review*. Excerpt from "Six Basics for General Managers," by Andrall E. Pearson (July–August 1989). Copyright © 1989 by the President and Fellows of Harvard College; all rights reserved.

23. Ibid. Reprinted by permission of the *Harvard Business Review*. Excerpt from "Six Basics for General Managers," by Andrall E. Pearson (July–August 1989). Copyright © 1989 by the President and Fellows of Harvard College; all rights reserved.

24. A. M. Mohrman Jr., S. A. Mohrman, G. E. Ledford Jr., T. G. Cummings, E. E. Lawler III, and Associates, *Large-Scale Organizational Change* (San Francisco: Jossey-Bass, 1989), p. 106.

25. W. Bennis and B. Nanus, *Leaders: The Strategies for Taking Charge* (New York: Harper & Row, 1985), pp. 27–33, 87–109.

26. S. Feinstein, "Labor Letter," *Wall Street Journal*, 1 May 1990.

27. P. Salz-Trautman, "Germany," *Management Today* (January 1994): 46.

28. D. A. Nadler, "Managing Organizational Change: An Integrative Perspective," *Journal of Applied Behavioral Science* 17 (1981): 294.

29. A. J. Nurick, "The Paradox of Participation: Lessons from the Tennessee Valley Authority," *Human Resource Management* 24 (Fall 1985): 354–355.

30. W. Bennis, *Why Leaders Can't Lead: The Unconscious Conspiracy Continues* (San Francisco: Jossey-Bass, 1989), pp. 140–141.

31. The first two reasons are based on Hambrick, "Guest Editor's Introduction: Putting Top Managers Back in the Strategy Picture," p. 6. The remaining reasons are based on R. A. Eisenstat and S. G. Cohen, "Summary: Top Management Groups," in J. R. Hackman, ed., *Groups That Work (and Those That Don't): Creating Conditions for Effective Teamwork* (San Francisco: Jossey-Bass, 1990), pp. 78–79. See also D. C. Hambrick and P. A. Mason, "Upper Echelons: The Organization as a Reflection of Its Top Managers," *Academy of Management Review* 9 (1984): 193–206.

32. K. A. Bantel and S. E. Jackson, "Top Management and Innovations in Banking: Does the Composition of the Top Team Make a Difference?" *Strategic Management Journal* 10 (1989): 111.

33. K. Kelly, "United Wants the Whole World in Its Hands," *Business Week*, 27 April 1992, pp. 64–68; K. Kelly, "He Gets By with a Lot of Help from His Friends," *Business Week*, 27 April 1992, p. 68.

34. D. J. Yang, "Nordstrom's Gang of Four," *Business Week*, 15 June 1992, pp. 122–123; A. Bennett, "Firms Run by Executive Teams Can Reap Rewards, Incur Risks," *Wall Street Journal*, 5 February 1992.

35. For a discussion of managers' dependence on others for power see D. Krackhardt and J. R. Hanson, "Informal Networks: The Company Behind the Chart," *Harvard Business Review* 71, no. 4 (July–August 1993): 104–111; J. P. Kotter, "Power, Dependence, and Effective Management," *Harvard Business Review* 55, no. 4 (July–August 1977): 125–136.

36. T. A. Stewart, "New Ways to Exercise Power," *Fortune*, 6 November 1989, p. 53.

37. Kotter, "Power, Dependence and Effective Management," p. 128.

38. J. R. P. French Jr., and B. Raven, "The Bases of Social Power," in D. Cartwright, ed., *Studies in Social Power* (Ann Arbor, Mich.: University of Michigan Press, 1959), pp. 150–167.

39. Kotter, "Power, Dependence and Effective Management," p. 130.

40. Yukl, *Leadership in Organizations*, p. 47.

41. A. Pettigrew, "Information Control as a Power Resource," *Sociology* 6 (1972): 187–204.

42. H. Mintzberg, *Power in and Around Organizations* (Englewood Cliffs, N. J.: Prentice Hall, 1983), pp. 121–122.

43. A. Kuhn, *The Study of Society: A Unified Approach* (Homewood, Ill.: Irwin, 1963).

44. Mintzberg, *Power in and Around Organizations*, p. 122.

45. J. Pfeffer, *Managing with Power: Politics and Influence in Organizations* (Boston: Harvard Business School Press, 1992), p. 107.

46. Ibid., pp. 182–185.

47. Bennett, "Firms Run by Executive Teams Can Reap Rewards, Incur Risks," p. 21.

48. D. E. Berlew, "Leadership and Organizational Excitement," in D. A. Kolb, I. M. Rubin, and J. M. McIntyre, eds., *Organizational Psychology: A Book of Readings*, 2nd ed. (Englewood Cliffs, N. J.:

Prentice Hall, 1974); R. J. House, "A 1976 Theory of Charismatic Leadership," in J. G. Hunt and L. L. Larson, eds., *Leadership: The Cutting Edge* (Carbondale, Ill.: Southern Illinois Press, 1977).

49. Yukl, *Leadership in Organizations*, p. 206.

50. P. Salz-Trautman, "Germany," p. 46.

51. Bass, *Leadership and Performance*, pp. 37–39; J. A. Conger and R. Kanungo, "Toward a Behavioral Theory of Charismatic Leadership in Organizational Settings," *Academy of Management Review* 12 (1987): 637–647.

52. D. J. Hickson, C. R. Hinings, C. A. Lee, R. E. Schneck, and J. M. Pennings, "A Strategic Contingencies Theory of Intraorganizational Power," *Administrative Science Quarterly* 16 (1971): 216–229.

53. G. R. Salancik and J. Pfeffer, "Who Gets Power—And How They Hold on to It: A Strategic–Contingency Theory of Intraorganizational Power," *Organizational Dynamics* 5 (Winter 1977): 5; D. C. Hambrick, "Environment, Strategy, and Power within Top Management Teams," *Administrative Science Quarterly* 26 (1981): 253–276.

54. C. D. Pringle, D. F. Jennings, and J. G. Longenecker, *Managing Organizations: Functions and Behaviors* (Columbus, Ohio: Merrill, 1988), p. 594.

55. E. H. Schein, *Organizational Culture and Leadership* (San Francisco: Jossey-Bass, 1985), p. 9.

56. E. H. Schein, "The Role of the Founder in Creating Organizational Culture," *Organizational Dynamics* 12 (Summer 1983): 14.

57. Yukl, *Leadership in Organizations*, pp. 215–216.

58. Ibid., p. 216.

59. For articles on McDonald's culture, see R. Henkoff, "Big Mac Attacks with Pizza," *Fortune*, 26 February 1990, pp. 87–89; R. Gibson and R. Johnson, "Big Mac, Cooling McDonald's Mystique," *Fortune*, 4 July 1988, pp. 112–116.

60. L. Nakarmi and R. Neff, "Samsung's Radical Shakeup," *Business Week*, 28 February 1994, pp. 74–76.

61. K. Kerwin and A. N. Fins, "Disney Is Looking Just a Little Fragilistic," *Business Week*, 25 June 1990, pp. 52–54; B. Dumaine, "Creating a New Company Culture," *Fortune*, 15 January 1990, p. 128.

62. M. A. Verespej, "Masters of Change," *Industry Week*, 7 March 1994, p. 9; J. P. Kotter and J. L. Haskett, *Corporate Culture and Performance* (New York: Free Press, 1992). For an analysis of cultural impact of related diversification or shareholder value, see S. Chatterjee, M. H. Lubatkin, D. M. Schweiger, and Y. Weber, "Cultural Differences and Shareholder Value in Related Mergers: Linking Equity and Human Capital," *Strategic Management Journal* 13 (1992): 319–334.

63. L. Hayes, "Gerstner Is Struggling as He Tries to Change Ingrained IBM Culture," *Wall Street Journal*, 13 May 1994, pp. A1, A8.

64. Pringle et al., *Managing Organizations: Functions and Behaviors*, p. 309.

65. Schein, *Organizational Culture and Leadership*, p. 30.

66. D. Tosti and S. Jackson, "Alignment: How It Works and Why It Matters," *Training* 31 (April 1994): 58–64; T. Brown, "The Rise and Fall of the Intelligent Organization," *Industry Week*, 7 March 1994, pp. 16–21; D. Lawrence Jr., "The New Social Contract Between Employers and Employees," *Employee Benefits Journal* 19, no. 1 (1994): 21–24.

67. This account is largely based on "The Transformation of EDS' Culture," *Open Line EDS* 11 (Spring 1990): 2–6; "Interview," *Open Line EDS* 11 (Spring 1990): 7–9; and, to a lesser extent, on Pringle et al., *Managing Organizations: Functions and Behaviors*, p. 310.

68. "The Transformation of EDS' Culture," p. 2.

69. Bass, *Leadership and Performance*, p. 24.

70. This discussion is based on Schein, *Organizational Culture and Leadership*, pp. 224–237.

71. J. B. Barney, L. Busenitz, J. O. Fiet, and D. Moesel, "The Relationship Between Venture Capitalists and Managers in New Firms: Determinants of Contractural Covenants," *Managerial Finance* 20 (1994): 19–30; Kotter and Heskett, Corporate Culture and Performance, p. 142.

72. "Changing the Culture at General Foods," *Business Week*, 10 February 1986, pp. 52–57.

73. Schein, *Organizational Culture and Leadership*, pp. 237–242.

74. M. Alpert, "Office Buildings for the 1990s," *Fortune*, 18 November 1991, pp. 141–142; T. R. V. Davis, "The Influence of the Physical Environment in Offices," *Academy of Management Review* 9 (1984): 273.

75. Schein, *Organizational Culture and Leadership*, p. 317.

76. Ibid., pp. 316–317, 320.

STRATEGIC MANAGEMENT MODEL

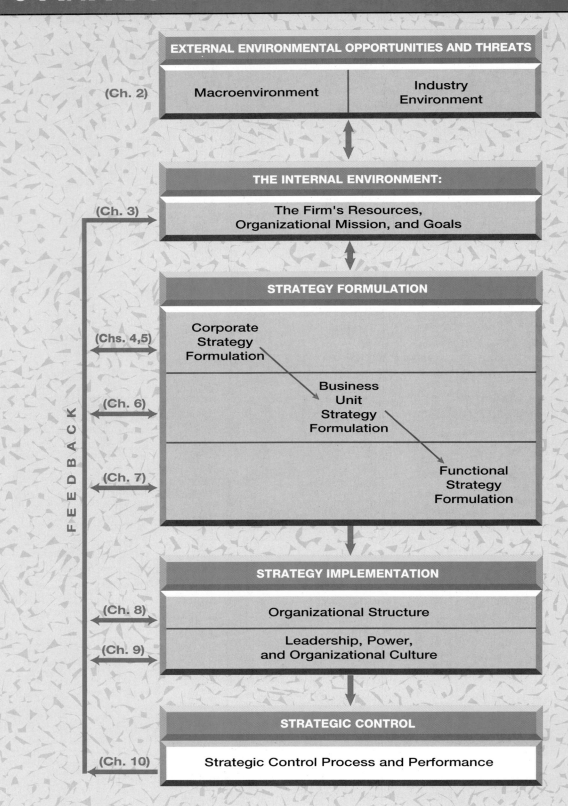

EXTERNAL ENVIRONMENTAL OPPORTUNITIES AND THREATS

(Ch. 2)

| Macroenvironment | Industry Environment |

THE INTERNAL ENVIRONMENT:

(Ch. 3) The Firm's Resources, Organizational Mission, and Goals

STRATEGY FORMULATION

(Chs. 4,5) Corporate Strategy Formulation

(Ch. 6) Business Unit Strategy Formulation

(Ch. 7) Functional Strategy Formulation

STRATEGY IMPLEMENTATION

(Ch. 8) Organizational Structure

(Ch. 9) Leadership, Power, and Organizational Culture

STRATEGIC CONTROL

(Ch. 10) Strategic Control Process and Performance

FEEDBACK

10 Strategic Control Process and Performance

The activities of formulating, implementing, and controlling are closely linked. Chapters 3, 4, 5, 6, and 7 focused on formulating or planning—establishing the organization's mission and goals and developing its corporate-level, business unit, and functional strategies. Then, implementing those strategies was discussed in chapters 8 and 9. We now turn to the task of control.

Strategic control consists of determining the extent to which the organization's strategies are successful in attaining its goals and objectives. If the goals and objectives are not being reached as planned, then the intent of control is to modify the organization's strategies and/or implementation so that the organization's capability to accomplish its goals will be improved.

Control, in the business administration sense, is most often discussed in the context of budgeting. It is important to understand that strategic control is much broader than this traditional usage of the term. In the control of budgeted expenditures, the focus is usually for a time span of a year or less; quantitative measurements are used to determine whether actual expenditures are exceeding planned spending; the emphasis is on internal operations; and corrective action is often taken after the budget period has elapsed. But in strategic control, the focal time period usually ranges anywhere from a few years to more than a decade, and qualitative as well as quantitative measurements are taken. Moreover, both internal operations and the external environment are assessed. The process is ongoing because intermittent corrective actions may be necessary to keep the organization on course. By the end of the focal period, it may be too late. These differences are summarized in Table 10.1.

Table 10.1	Differences Between Strategic Control and Budgetary Control	
	Strategic Control	*Budgetary Control*
	Time period is lengthy—ranging from a few years to more than ten years.	Time period is usually one year or less.
	Measurements are quantitative and qualitative.	Measurements are quantitative.
	Concentration is internal and external.	Concentration is internal.
	Corrective action is ongoing.	Corrective action may be taken after budget period has elapsed.

STRATEGIC CONTROL AND CORPORATE GOVERNANCE

As discussed in chapter 3, corporate governance refers to boards of directors, institutional investors, and blockholders, who monitor firm strategies to ensure managerial responsiveness. How effective these components of corporate governance are with respect to strategic control has been addressed by a number of authors.

Recall that, legally, boards of directors are authorized to represent the interests of the owners. They are also responsible for such aspects of corporate leadership as selecting or replacing the CEO, advising top management, and monitoring executive and firm performance. Although it is common for several top managers, such as the CEO and vice presidents, to also serve as board members, in some situations senior executives have comprised the majority of board membership. Moreover, in many instances CEOs have served as chairs of boards of directors. This lack of separation between top managers and their monitors, the board of directors, has been recognized as problematic. Harvard's Donaldson has suggested that management's role in formulating and implementing strategy "precludes it from also objectively evaluating the strategic path once it is in place."[1] Thus, when senior managers are numerous on the board, there may be a need to reduce their number while adding people from outside the firm to the board. Some authorities have argued that outsiders are further motivated to push for improved firm performance by their desire to build a reputation for effective board membership. Also, select scholars find that, with more outsiders as board members, CEO dismissal becomes more likely if corporate performance is poor.[2] In addition, some experts contend that outsiders are more inclined to exert pressure for corporate restructuring.[3]

This is not to say that insiders are always ineffective board members. An argument has been made that some insiders compete for succession to the position of CEO.[4] Thus, their sensitivity to the appearance of being beholden to the CEO may serve to strengthen their resolve to control strategy formulation and implementation effectively. A concern for legal liability may also encourage insiders to support board control. Indeed, one study finds that insiders are positively associated with board control.[5]

CEO duality may also influence board control. **CEO duality** refers to a CEO also serving as chair of the board. Various studies have shown mixed results regarding the desirability of CEO duality,[6] but one study has indicated that CEO duality may be detrimental.[7] In the context of our discussion, the implication may be that whether insider board members are willing to exert control could depend on whether there is CEO duality. Specifically, when the CEO is also chair of the board, the insider members may be reluctant to disagree with his or her predispositions. That is because the CEO largely determines the future career prospects as well as the monetary and nonmonetary rewards of the firm's senior executives. Additionally, the successive promotions of senior managers to their current position of authority may have been approved by the CEO. Consequently, it may be in the interest of each senior executive to support the decisions of the CEO, particularly in his or her presence. Thus, insider board members may be ineffective monitors of firm strategy when CEO duality exists.

In the absence of CEO duality, however, insiders may contribute to board control, sometimes in subtle and indirect ways so that their potential opposition to the CEO's decisions may escape documentation. For example, insiders with firm-specific knowledge may ostensibly present various sides of issues, while carefully framing the alternatives in favor of one that may be in opposition to the wishes of the CEO. Subtly contributing to effective board control may enhance the reputation of senior executives not only as valuable board members but as enlightened managers. Constructive contributions to board control may also lessen executives' anxiety over potential insider legal liability. Thus, whereas insiders may enhance board control in the absence of CEO duality, they may weaken board control when CEO duality exists. The implication is that strategic control will be enhanced if the chair of the board of directors is an outsider rather than the firm's CEO.

How effective institutional investors and blockholders are with respect to strategic control has also been addressed in a number of studies. Recall that institutional investors include pension and retirement funds, mutual funds, banks, and insurance companies, among other money managers. Blockholders are individuals, groups, or families who are significant shareholders. The premise that institutions and blockholders can effectively exert strategic control is intuitively persuasive. Blockholders as well as institutional investors ordinarily own substantial equity stakes; consequently, it is normally in their best interests to monitor firm strategies.

Although a number of empirical examinations document that institutional investors play effective monitoring roles, the impact of blockholders seems less certain.[8] Apparently, some blockholders are active monitors of firm strategy, whereas others tend to be passive investors. For instance, blockholders who are descendants of a firm's founder may be passive owners, but those whose profession is the management of investments may provide active monitoring.

As is evident from the preceding discussion, boards of directors, institutional investors, and blockholders can exert strategic control by monitoring top executive and firm performance. The CEO, along with senior executives, however, also exert strategic control. In the following paragraphs we discuss the strategic control process in the context of the role top managers should play.

Figure 10.1   **Steps Involved in Strategic Control**

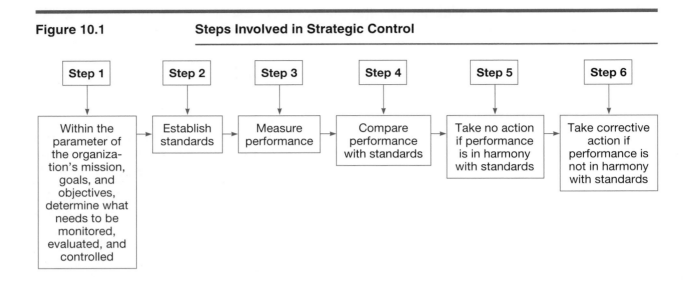

THE STRATEGIC CONTROL PROCESS AND TOP MANAGEMENT

From the perspective of senior executives, the strategic control process consists of several steps. First, top management must decide what elements of the environment and of the organization need to be monitored, evaluated, and controlled. Then, standards must be established with which the actual performance of the organization can be compared. These first two steps will be strongly influenced by the organization's mission, goals, and objectives, which direct management's attention to certain organizational and environmental elements and to the relative importance of particular standards.

Next, management must measure or evaluate the company's actual performance. These evaluations will generally be both quantitative and qualitative. The performance evaluations will then be compared with the previously established standards. If performance is in line with the standards or exceeds them, then no corrective action is necessary. (When performance exceeds standards, management should consider whether the standards are appropriate and whether they should be raised.) However, if performance falls below the standards, then management must take remedial action. These steps are delineated in Figure 10.1.

FOCUS OF STRATEGIC CONTROL

The focus of strategic control is both internal and external. Neither element can be examined in isolation, because it is top management's role to align advantageously the internal operations of the enterprise with its external environment. In fact, strategic control can be visualized as "mediating" the ongoing interactions between environmental variables and the company's internal dimensions. Relying upon quantitative and qualitative performance measures, top management uses strategic control to keep the firm's internal dimensions

Figure 10.2   **Strategic Control as a Mediator**

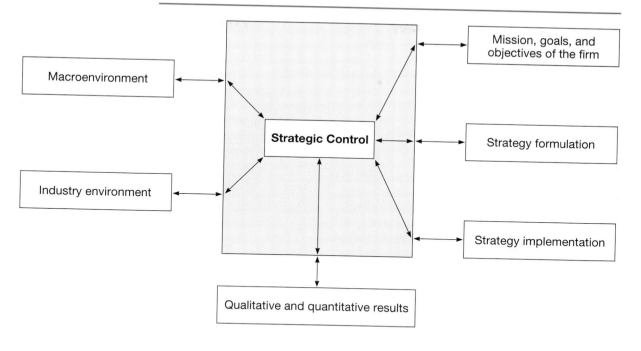

aligned with its external environment. The role of strategic control as a mediator is portrayed diagrammatically in Figure 10.2.

The following sections discuss three key areas that must be monitored and evaluated in the process of strategic control: the macroenvironment, the industry environment, and internal operations.

■ Macroenvironment

The first focus of the strategic control process is usually the organization's macroenvironment. Although individual businesses normally exert little, if any, influence over the forces in the macroenvironment, these forces must be continuously monitored. Changes or shifts in the macroenvironment have strategic ramifications for the company. Consequently, strategic control involves continuously examining the fit between the company and its changing external environment.

In this context, strategic control consists of modifying the company's operations to defend itself better against external threats that may arise and to capitalize on new external opportunities. For instance, during the economic downturn of the early 1990s, several discerning companies prospered by taking advantage of recession-induced opportunities. Campbell Soup, for example, reacted to the trend toward less expensive cook-at-home products by repackaging its high-end Gold Label cream of broccoli soup into the red-and-white can and marketing it as a base for meals that could be prepared at home. In slightly more than a year, consumers bought 55 million cans, making it one of Campbell's best-sellers ever.[9]

Another company that prospered during the economic rough times was Electronic Transaction Corporation. This relatively small business, which verifies checks written by customers, attracted 115 new clients in 1991, among them such retailing giants as Wal-Mart and Kmart.[10]

■ Industry Environment

Strategic control also involves monitoring the industry environment. Again, the purpose is to modify the company's operations so that it can better defend itself against threats and better capitalize on opportunities. It is important to remember in this regard that environmental analysis—both at the macroenvironment and at the industry levels—is not confined to the past or present; top management also needs to estimate future environmental trends.

Take, for instance, the response of one car producer to escalating costs in the automobile industry. BMW, in expanding its manufacturing operations, decided to escape Germany's average 1992 hourly labor cost per car of $24.36 by locating its new plant in South Carolina. (U.S. average hourly labor costs per car were only $15.39; additionally, the average U.S. autoworker received twenty-three annual vacation days and holidays compared to forty-two days in Germany.) BMW hoped that this lowering of production costs would enable it to price its cars more competitively vis-à-vis such Japanese products as Lexus and Infiniti.

Through this decision, BMW is using strategic control to look toward the future. Its U.S. and Japanese competitors are becoming increasingly cost-efficient while continuing to improve product quality. As Nissan, Toyota, and Honda open manufacturing plants in Europe, and GM Europe continues to enjoy considerable success, BMW finds itself challenged on all sides. Hence, it wants to become more globally competitive by producing cars in the United States—the world's largest auto market. By reducing its manufacturing and shipping costs, BMW hopes to remain competitive in the United States as well as in other markets in Latin America.[11]

■ Internal Operations

Strategic control also involves the internal operations of the business through monitoring and evaluating its strategy formulation and implementation. Corrective action may then be necessary. Monitoring and evaluating the company's operations involve viewing its present and future strategic posture. The bases for monitoring and evaluating are the qualitative and quantitative standards established by top management.

Qualitatively, the broad question asked is, How effective is our strategy in accomplishing our mission and goals? Consider the goal of product leadership, for instance. In evaluating its product leadership, an organization compares its products with those of competitors and determines the extent to which it pioneers in the introduction of new products and product improvements.

Note that pioneering is not enough. A company must also follow through. Xerox, for instance, introduced the first commercial fax machine in 1964, but today, its machines account for only 7 percent of U.S. fax sales. Likewise, Raytheon was the first company to market a microwave oven—in 1947—but today, 75 percent of all microwave ovens in U.S. homes are made in the Far East.[12]

In the broad quantitative sense, management will ask, How effective is our strategy in attaining our objectives? (Recall that objectives are specific, quantifiable versions of goals, which, in turn, are desired general ends toward which organizational efforts are directed.) For instance, management can compare the firm's 11.2 percent rate of return on investment over the past year with its stated objective of 10 percent and conclude that its strategy has been effective in that particular respect. Whether evaluating a strategy's effectiveness is undertaken relative to the best in the world, relative to the company's rivals, or relative only to itself, the point of strategic control is to take corrective action if negative gaps exist between intended and actual strategic results.

STRATEGIC CONTROL STANDARDS

Evaluating an enterprise's performance may be accomplished in a number of ways. Management, for instance, often compares current operating results with those from the preceding year. A qualitative judgment may be made about whether the business's products or services are superior to, inferior to, or about the same as last year's. Several quantitative measures may also be used, including return on investment (ROI), return on assets (ROA), return on sales (ROS), and return on equity (ROE).

Confining control standards only to comparisons of current performance versus past performance, however, can be myopic, because it ignores important external variables. For example, assume that a business's ROI has increased from 8 to 10 percent over the past year. Management might consider that a significant improvement. But the meaning of this measure depends upon the industry in which the company operates. In a depressed industry, an ROI of 10 percent may be outstanding, but that same return in a growth industry will be disappointing, because the leading firms may earn 15 to 20 percent. An improvement in a company's ROI is less encouraging, then, if its past performance has been significantly behind that of its major competitors.

Often, strategic control standards are based on the practice of **competitive benchmarking**—the process of measuring a firm's performance against that of the top performers in its industry. After determining the appropriate benchmarks, a firm's managers set goals to meet or exceed the performance of the firm's top competitors. Taken to its logical conclusion, competitive benchmarking—if practiced by all of the firms in an industry—would result in increased industrywide performance. Increasingly, companies may be benchmarking against the best in the world (whether the best is inside or outside of the company's industry).

This section examines a variety of competitive benchmarking standards that can be used for strategic control. These standards can be based on data derived from the PIMS program, published information that is publicly available, ratings of product/service quality, innovation rates, and relative market share standings. Viewed broadly, these standards include both quantitative and qualitative information.

Benchmarking at Xerox and Ford

Benchmarking is a process by which one organization may learn how other firms might perform specific activities more efficiently. The first major adopter of this technique was Xerox, a firm that was shocked in 1979 when Japanese competitor Canon introduced a midsize copier for a retail price that was below Xerox's *production costs*. At first, Xerox managers thought Canon was selling its copier below cost to capture market share, but investigation revealed that Canon was simply far more efficient than Xerox.

As a response, Xerox began a successful turnaround by studying not only how Canon achieved its cost efficiencies, but also how other firms performed certain functions. In one case, for instance, it observed the product shipping process at L. L. Bean (an outdoor clothing manufacturer and catalog retailer). Bean's order-filling system was similar to Xerox's in that both required employees to handle products that varied in shape and size, but Bean could fill orders three times as fast as Xerox. As a result of

imitation, Xerox reduced its order-filling costs by 10 percent.

More recently, Ford learned that its strategic alliance partner, Mazda, was processing accounts payable with fewer than ten employees. Ford, which had 500 accounts-payable processing workers, studied Mazda's system carefully and ultimately reduced its staff by 75 percent. Ford has also learned how to design more exacting tolerances for its parts.

Companies can benchmark virtually any activity, but experts on competitive benchmarking emphasize that an organization must first understand its own processes in detail before studying those of other firms. And it is imperative that the individuals sent to observe those processes in other firms are the people who actually must implement the changes within their own organization. But they are cautioned that any changes they introduce into their own department or division are likely to also affect processes in other parts of the organization.

SOURCES: "Xerox Corp. Unveils Document Fax Centre Pro 735," *Dow Jones Business News*, 1 May 1996; O. Suris and N. M. Christian, "Will Consumers Respond to Ford's Recall Alert?" *Wall Street Journal*, 8 May 1996, pp. B1, B7; P. Eakin, "Quality You Can Bank On," *Quality*, January 1995, pp. 14–20; "Quality and Beyond," *Management Decision*, September 1994, pp. 22–23; T. Sasaki, "What the Japanese Have Learned from Strategic Alliances," *Long Range Planning*, 26, no. 6 (1994): 41–53; J. Carbone, "Benchmarking Corporate Operations—Like Purchasing," *Electronic Business Buyer*, October 1993, pp. 67–70; J. Main, "How to Steal the Best Ideas Around," *Fortune*, 19 October 1992, pp. 102–106.

▪ PIMS Program

A thorough evaluation of a business's performance may take into account the performance of its competitors or the best in the world (even if the best is outside of the industry). For that reason, the PIMS program was developed; the **PIMS (profit impact of market strategy) program** is a database that contains quantitative and qualitative information on the performance of more than 3,000 business units. It helps management of participating companies evaluate the performance of their organizations relative to the performance of other businesses in the same industry or other industries. When a company's results compare unfavorably, strategic control is typically required.

PIMS was developed as a result of General Electric's efforts to evaluate systematically the performance of its business units in the 1960s.[13] Using a program developed by Professor Sidney Schoeffler of Harvard University, GE's top managers and corporate staff began to assess business unit performance in a formal, systematic fashion. Subsequently, other companies were invited to join the project, and in 1975, Professor Schoeffler founded the Strategic Planning Institute to conduct PIMS research.

Each of the participating businesses provides quantitative and qualitative information to the program. Included are data on variables such as market share, product/service quality, new products and services introduced as a percentage of sales, relative prices of products and services, marketing expenses as a percentage of sales, value of plant and equipment relative to sales, and research and development expenses as a percentage of sales. Two profitability measures are used: net operating profit before taxes as a percentage of sales (ROS), and net income before taxes as a percentage of total investment (ROI) or of total assets (ROA).

Each of these variables may be used for strategic control purposes. For instance, if a business's product quality is consistently judged to be below average, then this information can be used to improve quality. Below-average profitability signals management that changes in strategy formulation or implementation may be necessary.

To take full advantage of PIMS, a business needs to be a participating member of the PIMS program. However, all businesses may broadly exert strategic control by comparing their situations with some of the PIMS principles.[14] PIMS, of course, is not the only source of strategic control data. A number of other information bases are discussed in the following section.

▪ Published Information for Strategic Control

Fortune annually publishes the most- and least-admired U.S. corporations with annual sales of at least $500 million in such diverse industries as electronics, pharmaceuticals, retailing, transportation, banking, insurance, metals, food, motor vehicles, and utilities. Corporate dimensions are evaluated along the following eight lines:

- Quality of products/services
- Quality of management
- Innovativeness
- Long-term investment value
- Financial soundness
- Community and environmental responsibility
- Use of corporate assets
- Ability to attract, develop, and keep talented people

The most-admired companies are those that rank high on these variables. Although *Fortune*'s list consists of very large, publicly traded companies, the information in the listing may nevertheless provide valuable guidelines for the strategic control of smaller firms. In addition to *Fortune*, publications such as *Forbes, Industry Week, Business Week,* and *Dun's Business Month* evaluate the performance of companies in various industries.

Which particular measures of comparison to use, of course, must be determined by top management. But a number of competitive benchmarking variables are considered important for strategic control because they significantly affect performance. They are discussed in the following sections.

S T R A T E G I C　　I N S I G H T

Broadening a Myopic Perspective at General Motors

In the 1960s General Motors (GM) developed a quantitative standard for measuring the quality of the automobiles it was manufacturing. On its scale, a score of 100 was perfect; each defect a new car contained lowered its score by one point. So a car with a score of 80 contained 20 defects. GM's management established a score of 60 as "passing."

But when too many cars failed to attain a passing grade, rather than take corrective action and improve the quality of its outputs, management decided to modify the standard. The new standard for perfection was raised from 100 to 145. As a result, a car with 41 defects that would have "failed" under the old standard now had a passing score of 104.

GM and other U. S. automakers, however, became increasingly serious about product quality as pressure from foreign competition steadily increased during the 1970s. But even by 1980, the quality of American-made cars was still suspect. A Detroit consulting firm, Harbour & Associates, reported that GM's 1980 cars averaged 7.4 defects per car, Chrysler's averaged 8.1, and Ford's averaged 6.7. Meanwhile, Japanese-made autos averaged only 2.0 defects.

American manufacturers continued to stress quality improvements throughout the 1980s and into the 1990s, however. By 1992, a GM factory in Oklahoma City produced the most defect-free cars (Buick Centuries and Oldsmobile Cutlasses) of any plant in North America—0.71 defect per car. Second was a Toyota plant in Ontario.

GM increasingly began to realize the role that customer service played in quality considerations. When 1,836 of its new Saturn sedans were recalled because they left the factory with improperly mixed antifreeze that would create holes in the cooling systems, GM took a large step forward in customer service. Rather than recall the cars for free repairs, the usual approach of automakers, GM offered to exchange each car with the defective coolant for a new Saturn.

This service-oriented approach, combined with Saturn's superb quality (it now has the same low defect rate as Honda), resulted in Saturn dealers selling an average of 115 cars per month—twice the sales/dealer rate of second-place Toyota.

SOURCES: R. Blumenstein, N. M. Christian, and O. Suris, "Local GM Labor Dispute Spins Out of Control," *Wall Street Journal*, 13 March 1996, pp. B1, B3; M. Darling, "GM's Saturn: Colossal Blunder?" *Journal of Commerce and Commercial Management*, 6 October 1995, p. 8A; S. Gabriella, "Saturn's Mystique is Endangered As GM Changes the Car and the Organization," *Wall Street Journal*, 27 July 1995, p. B1; M. Keller, *Collision: GM, Toyota, Volkswagen & the Race to the 21st Century* (New York: Doubleday, 1993); N. Templin, "GM's Saturn Subsidiary Is Fighting for Its Future," *Wall Street Journal*, 16 June 1993, p. B4; M. Keller, *Rude Awakening: The Rise, Fall and Struggle for Recovery of General Motors* (New York: Merrow, 1989), pp. 29–30.

■ Product/Service Quality

Interestingly, over the years there has been a positive relationship between the quality of products and services that companies produce and the financial performance of those firms. This relationship is illustrated by the *Fortune* listing just described. Recall that quality has two key aspects—the conformance of a product or service to the internal standards of the firm and the ultimate consumer's perception of the quality of that product or service. It is important to distinguish between these two aspects of quality, because a number of products that have conformed to internal standards have not sold well. So although conformance to standards is a necessary condition for a product's or service's success, it is not sufficient. Ultimately, a firm's outputs must be perceived as superior by the marketplace.[15]

To evaluate product quality, *Fortune* asks some 8,000 executives, outside directors, and financial analysts to judge the outputs of the largest firms in the United States. About 4,000 responses are usually received.[16] According to the results, those firms whose outputs are perceived to possess high quality are also the higher-performing companies.

Taking a different approach, the PIMS program assesses quality through judgments made by both managers and customers.[17] A meeting is held by a team of managers in each of the PIMS participating businesses. These managers identify product/service attributes that they believe influence customer purchases. They then assign a weight to each attribute. Finally, they rate the quality of each attribute of their company's outputs relative to those of the products/services produced by the leading companies. These ratings are augmented by survey results from customers who also rate the quality of the products produced by businesses in various industries. The results of the PIMS program suggest a strong positive correlation between product quality and business performance.

One publication, *Consumer Reports*, may be used by executives as a means for strategic control of output quality. Literally hundreds of products are evaluated by this publication annually. Because the evaluation by *Consumer Reports* is unbiased (it does not accept advertising), it is an excellent source of product quality information for competing businesses. Even if the products of a particular business are not evaluated by this publication, that company can still gain insight on its competitors' product quality.

Specific published information may also exist for select industries. Perhaps the best known is the "Customer Satisfaction Index" released annually by J. D. Power for the automobile industry. A questionnaire survey of 70,000 new-car owners each year examines such variables as satisfaction with eighty-one aspects of vehicle performance; problems reported during the first ninety days of ownership; ratings of dealer service quality; and ratings of the sales, delivery, and condition of new vehicles.[18]

Certainly, it is imperative that an enterprise, regardless of its size, engage in some means of assessing the relative quality of its products and services. If the quality of its outputs compares favorably with that of the competition, then no direct action may be necessary, although emphasizing high quality in future advertising might prove to be advantageous. If the company's outputs do not compare favorably with the competition's, then corrective action is essential.

▪ Innovation

Innovation may be conceptualized, measured, and controlled in different ways. Many researchers have approached this subject by focusing on expenditures for product research and development (R&D) and process R&D.[19] These studies conclude that the more money spent on developing new or improved products and processes, the higher the level of innovation is likely to be.[20] This same approach is taken in the PIMS program.

Some firms plan and control their programs for innovation very carefully. 3M, for instance, has established a standard that 25 percent of each business unit's sales should come from products introduced to the market within the past five years. The standard is taken quite seriously by 3M managers, since "meeting the 25% test is a crucial yardstick at bonus time."[21] Currently, almost a third of 3M's sales come from products introduced within a five-year period.

Not surprisingly, 3M invests between 6 and 7 percent of its sales revenue in R&D, a figure that is double the average of U. S. industry.[22]

Some observers have suggested that the strategic control of innovation must emphasize incremental improvements in products and services rather than sweeping, fundamental innovations.[23] Several attribute the Japanese superiority over U. S. business performance in some industries to the Japanese emphasis on incremental innovations. A continuous series of incremental innovations means that each year the company's outputs improve as a result of small, but numerous and cumulative, innovations.[24]

■ Relative Market Share

A business's size and market share, relative to its largest rivals in the industry, are important in formulating and implementing strategy and in controlling the company's strategic direction. Recall from chapter 6 that both small and large market shares can lead to high performance. In large, leading companies, relative market share and growth in relative market share play important roles in managerial performance evaluations.[25] Managers at all levels in the organization are partially evaluated on their contributions to the company's gains in relative market share. Such gains, of course, also depend upon other strategic variables, such as product quality, innovation, pricing, and industry forces. Thus, changes in relative market share may serve as a strategic control gauge for both internal and external variables.

For instance, several years ago Johnson & Johnson chose to extend its product line of baby shampoo, baby powder, and baby oil to mail-order educational toys. But after a decade, its annual toy sales had still not exceeded $25 million, a very small share of the gigantic toy market. Chairman and CEO Ralph S. Larson made the strategic decision to divest the toy business. As he stated, "If a business doesn't have a reasonable prospect of achieving leadership, we have a responsibility to exit it."[26]

For successful smaller businesses, relative market share serves as a strategic control barometer in another way. The discussion in chapter 6 suggested that some businesses may strategically plan to maintain a low market share. In this event, the strategic control of market share may emphasize variables that do not promote market share growth. Such variables may include policies that encourage high prices and discourage sales events and price discounts. Empirical research has concluded that for certain companies in particular industries, emphasizing increases in relative market share is counterproductive.[27]

Strategic control actions for maintaining a small market share may include limiting the number of product/markets in which the company will compete. A small market share combined with operations in limited product/markets "enables a company to compete in ways that are unavailable to its larger rivals."[28]

EXERTING STRATEGIC CONTROL

Strategic control may be exerted in a number of different ways to ensure that the organization is performing in accordance with its mission, goals, and objectives. Some of the more important ways are presented in this section.

■ Control Through Multilevel Performance Criteria

Strategic control through **multilevel performance criteria** may involve setting performance standards for individuals, functions, products, divisions, or strategic business units. In the first instance, controlling individual performance depends upon what the individual employee does. An office worker's performance might be monitored by measuring the number of orders processed per day; a factory worker's daily production could be evaluated; and a sales representative's monthly sales figures could be appraised. Some jobs, of course, are less subject to quantitative measurement. Examples include a research and development scientist, whose work might not show results for months or years; a corporate planner; and individuals who work in teams.

Control at the functional level may include controlling for the volume of production and defect rates incurred in the manufacturing function. In marketing, performance control might include evaluating sales volume and measuring the level of customer satisfaction through interviews or questionnaire surveys.

At the product, divisional, and strategic business unit levels, strategic control of performance may include evaluating productivity improvements, sales growth, and changes in market share. In a qualitative sense, performance control can also include judging how product, divisional, and strategic business unit executives cooperate with one another to attain synergy for the overall organization.

At all levels, from the individual to the strategic business unit, corrective action should be taken if actual performance is less than the standard that has been established. On the other hand, should performance in some area—such as a function, division, or strategic business unit—be far above the standard, management should attempt to ascertain the reasons for the excellent performance. In some cases, the methods that one unit is using to achieve above-standard performance can be transferred to other organizational units, thereby improving their performance as well.

■ Control Through Performance

Control through performance can take place by monitoring the company's ROI, ROE, or other measures of profitability that were mentioned earlier. These evaluations take the form of comparisons vis-à-vis the performance of others in the marketplace. The PIMS program, of course, evaluates performance in this manner. Growth in relative market share may also be evaluated for strategic control.

In addition to monitoring and evaluating the key areas discussed earlier in the chapter, top management monitors the price of the company's stock. Price fluctuations suggest how investors value the performance of the firm. Management is always very concerned over sharp price changes in the firm's stock. A sudden drop in price will make the firm a more attractive takeover target. Sharp increases may mean that an investor or group of investors is accumulating large blocks of stock to engineer a takeover or a change in top management. Hence, managers continuously monitor price changes in their firm's stock.

■ Control Through Organizational Variables

A final way that strategic control can be exerted is through organizational variables. Control can be effected directly through the formal organization or indirectly through the informal organization.

The Formal Organization

The **formal organization**—the management-specified structure of relationships and procedures used to manage organizational activity—can facilitate or impede the accomplishment of the enterprise's mission, goals, and objectives. As we have already seen, the formal organization determines who reports to whom, how jobs are grouped, and what rules and policies will guide the actions and decisions of employees. Chapter 8 illustrated, for instance, how an organization's structure can become outmoded and no longer appropriate for its mission. At such times, strategic control will dictate a change from, say, a functional structure to a product divisional structure. That change will have to be accompanied by appropriate modifications in organizational reward systems so that the new forms of required behavior will be rewarded and older, less appropriate behaviors will not be.

For example, some organizations that have changed from functional or product divisional structures to matrix structures have experienced considerable difficulty. Such a dramatic change cannot be accomplished overnight, yet some top managers have evidently believed that by drawing a new organization chart and explaining it to their employees, new appropriate behaviors would naturally follow. But they do not. Employees must understand the compelling reasons underlying the change to a matrix structure to divorce them from their old ways of behaving, and they must then be trained extensively in the new types of behaviors that will be required. After this groundwork is laid, the change to the matrix structure must be accompanied by a new organizational reward system that encourages teamwork, frequent reassignment of personnel, greater participation, and open communication. Concomitantly, it should discourage loyalty to a functional area and to one supervisor.

The importance of clearly communicating the organization's values to all employees and establishing a rewards system that reinforces those values cannot be overemphasized. When management overlooks the key role that values and rewards play, or when the relationship among values, communication, and rewards is inconsistent, then informal organizational patterns develop to counterbalance the flaws and inconsistencies.

The Informal Organization

The **informal organization** refers to the interpersonal interactions that naturally evolve when individuals and groups come into contact with one another.[29] These informal relationships can play destructive or constructive roles in helping the organization pursue its mission, goals, and objectives.

When it is obvious to everyone that what is valued by the organization is also what is actually rewarded, then the informal organization tends to promote the attainment of the organization's desired purposes. But when the organization's value system is ambiguous, or when inconsistencies exist between what is valued and what is rewarded, then the informal organization develops its own set of consistent values and rewards. For example, most organizations claim to reward high job performance. If, in fact, employees discern that most of the major promotions and pay raises actually go to individuals who have the greatest seniority, regardless of their level of performance, then this "informal value" is communicated throughout the organization. Managers' exhortations

Downsizing as Strategic Control

One of the most common corrections in strategic control made by corporations during the 1980s and the 1990s has been *downsizing*—an aspect of which involves shrinking an organization's work force to make the firm more competitive. But two studies by consulting firms show that these results are not often attained.

Wyatt Company surveyed 1,005 firms, the majority of which had downsized during the preceding five years. Following the downsizing, only 46 percent of the firms achieved their goals of reducing expenses, only 32 percent increased profits as they had hoped, only 22 percent met their increased productivity goals, only 19 percent improved their competitive advantage as much as they desired, only 13 percent attained their sales goals, and only 9 percent reached their product quality goals.

A Mitchell & Company study of sixteen large firms in various industries revealed that, two years after downsizing, the stock prices of twelve of these sixteen corporations were trading in a range that was 5 to 45 percent below the stocks of comparable firms in their industries. What's wrong? Although the reasons vary from one corporation to another, one common problem seems to be that the changes in the formal organization created by downsizing result in dysfunctional consequences in the informal organization. As one downsizing consultant puts it:

> The numbers might be right, the forecasts might be right and the stock analysts might approve wholeheartedly, but if the human aspects aren't managed well, the effort can go into the tank.

All too often, unfortunately, the human aspects aren't managed too well. For instance, those employees who survive the cuts are often left stunned and wondering whether they'll be next. (They often are next, according to an American Management Association study that shows that companies that downsize once are more likely to downsize again in the future.) Obviously, such emotions are not usually associated with highly motivated, committed employees.

Work force reductions are made in various ways. Some firms simply cut, say, 10 or 15 percent of their employees, "across the board." In such cases, efficient departments lose employees just as do inefficient departments. Other firms attempt to minimize morale problems by offering early retirement to employees who have been with the firm for a certain number of years. Although this technique sounds more rational, these firms are often shocked to find that "a lot of training, experience, and skills [are] going out the door...."

Workers realize that their firms must reduce expenses. However, they resent cost-cutting programs that invariably affect employees first. They recognize that there are many reasons for high costs, and employees are only one of them. Yet they often seem to be the most expendable. But layoffs are no substitute for solving an organization's fundamental problems.

As is evident, downsizing can have detrimental effects on company morale. When Nynex Corporation entered a second round of cuts to trim its work force by 22 percent, managers became particularly bitter. Said one Nynex executive, "Two months ago, I would have said that morale is low and it couldn't go any lower. But I'd have to say it's even lower today."

Not all companies operate this way, of course. Some attempt to retain their human resources even during recessionary periods through such practices as implementing hiring freezes, retraining and deploying older workers, reducing pay temporarily, shortening the workweek, or simply never overstaffing in the first place. Critics charge that effective management at the outset can reduce or eliminate the need for downsizing in the future. In addition, there is increasing evidence to suggest that downsizing can increase costs in the long run.

continued

Downsizing as Strategic Control

SOURCES: A. Markels and M. Murray, "Downsizing to Reduce Costs Hurts Some Firms in Long Run," *Wall Street Journal Interactive Edition*, 14 May 1996; T. Petzinger Jr., "Downsizing Raises Questions about Management Skills," *Wall Street Journal Interactive Edition*, 11 May 1996; J. Nocera, "Living with Layoffs," *Fortune*, 1 April 1996, pp. 69–80; B. Bartosh, "Adventures in Downsizing: A Case Study," *Information Strategy: The Executive's Journal*, Winter 1995, pp. 47–52; G. A. Poole, "The New Idle Rich: How to Do Nothing in the Age of Downsizing," *Forbes*, 4 December 1995, pp. S32–35; D. C. Band and C. M. Tustin, "Strategic Downsizing," *Management Decision*, December 1995, pp. 36–45; "The Pain of Downsizing," *Business Week*, 9 May 1994, pp. 60–68 (source of third quotation); E. Lesly and L. Light, "When Layoffs Alone Don't Turn the Tide," *Business Week*, 7 December 1992, pp. 100–101; E. Faltermayer, "Is This Layoff Necessary?" *Fortune*, 1 June 1992, pp. 71–86 (source of second quotation, p. 72); A. Knox, "The Downside and Dangers of Downsizing," *Washington Post*, 15 March 1992 (source of first quotation).

to perform better will be largely ignored by employees, because they realize that the formally touted value of high performance is vacuous.

The informal organization cannot be directly controlled by management. It can, however, be influenced indirectly by ensuring that the formal organization is consistent in the sense that it clearly communicates its values and then rewards behaviors that are compatible with those values. It may also be influenced through the informal behavior of managers.

For instance, when managers interact with employees during the workday or off-hours, employees learn quickly whether their ideas are solicited, respected, and taken seriously. Informal bonds of mutual trust and respect are translated into loyalty to the organization and to the supervisor.

Managers may also communicate informally simply through their behavior. One manager commented on his CEO's work schedule as follows:

> He was the first one in the office. His car was in the lot by 7:00 every morning, and he never left before 6 P.M. That told people a lot about what he expected from us.[30]

In another case, the owner-manager of an amusement park asks different employees to walk with him through the park during their breaks. As they walk, the manager smiles and greets customers. If there is litter on the grounds, he picks the trash up and deposits it into receptacles. If customers ask questions or appear to need directions, he assists them. The message is very clear. The owner-manager values a clean amusement park and a friendly, courteous, customer-oriented staff.

SUMMARY

Strategic control consists of determining the extent to which the company's strategies are successful in attaining its goals and objectives. If the goals and objectives are not being reached as planned, then the intent of control is to modify the enterprise's strategies and/or implementation so that the organization's ability to accomplish its goals will be improved. In strategic control, the focal time period usually ranges from a few years to more than a decade; qualitative and quantitative measurements are taken; both internal operations and the external environment are assessed; and the process is continuous.

Board of directors, institutional investors, and blockholders monitor firm strategies to insure managerial responsiveness. Moreover, on the basis of the organization's mission, goals, and objectives, top management selects what elements of the environment and of the organization need to be monitored, evaluated, and controlled. Then, standards are established to which the actual performance of the business will be compared. Next, management measures the company's actual performance—both quantitatively and qualitatively. If performance is in line with the standards or exceeds them, then no corrective action is necessary. However, if performance falls below the standards, then management must take remedial action.

The focus of strategic control is both internal and external. Top management's role is to align advantageously the internal operations of the business with its external environment. Hence, strategic control can be visualized as "mediating" the interactions between environmental variables (in both the macroenvironment and the industry environment) and the organization's internal operations.

Evaluating a company's performance may be accomplished in a number of ways. For instance, current operating results can be compared with results from the prior year, both quantitatively and qualitatively. However, management must also evaluate important external variables such as the performance of competitors. Several competitive benchmarks can be used, but chief among them are the focal company's relative product/service quality, its innovative ability to develop new products and services and to improve its production and customer service deliver processes relative to those of its competitors, and its relative market share.

Strategic control can be exerted by top management in a number of different ways. First, management can control performance at several different levels—individual, functional, product, divisional, and strategic business unit. Control can also focus on performance through monitoring key financial ratios and changes in the firm's stock price. Finally, strategic control can be exerted directly through the formal organization by clear communication of the organization's values and a determination that the company's reward system is consistent with those values; and it can be exerted indirectly through the informal organization by appropriate managerial behavior.

TAKE IT TO THE NET

We invite you to visit the Wright page on the Prentice Hall Web site at:

http://www.prenhall.com/wright

for this chapter's World Wide Web exercise.

KEY CONCEPTS

CEO duality   A situation in which the CEO also serves as chair of the board.

Competitive benchmarking   The process of measuring a firm's performance against that of the top performers in its industry.

Formal organization   The management-specified structure of relationships and procedures used to manage organizational activity.

Informal organization   Interpersonal relationships and interactions that naturally evolve when individuals and groups come into contact with one another.

Multilevel performance criteria   Performance standards that are established for each of the following levels: individual employee, function, product line, division, strategic business unit, and organization.

PIMS program   A database, termed the profit impact of market strategy (PIMS), that contains quantitative and qualitative information on the performance of more than 3,000 business units.

Strategic control   Determining the extent to which an organization's strategies are successful in attaining its goals and objectives.

DISCUSSION QUESTIONS

1. Although strategic control and control in the more traditional budgetary sense are similar in some respects, they also differ significantly. Explain their similarities and differences.

2. What roles do the organization's mission, goals, and objectives play in strategic control?

3. Explain how strategic control mediates the interactions between the business's internal dimensions and its external environment.

4. In strategic control, management might compare the organization's performance this year with its performance in previous years. What are the strengths and weaknesses of this one comparison?

5. Explain how competitive benchmarking is used in strategic control. What are some commonly used competitive benchmarks?

6. What is the PIMS program? How can it aid in strategic control?

7. "If a business unit's performance is below standard, corrective action should be taken. If its performance is above standard, no managerial action is necessary." True or false? Why?

8. What is the relationship between strategic control and changes in the firm's stock price?

9. How are organizational values and rewards related to strategic control?

10. Give an example from your own experience of a manager who communicated organizational values through his or her informal behavior.

STRATEGIC MANAGEMENT EXERCISES

1. On the basis of your own perceptions as a consumer, compare the relative quality of two competing products (other than automobiles) or services that you have purchased. How might your perceptions be used by the manufacturers or sellers of these products and services in strategic control?

2. Over the past decade, the U. S.-based automobile companies have attempted to improve the quality of their cars relative to those of Japanese manufacturers. One way U. S. executives can exert strategic control is through comparing the quality of their cars with the quality of Japanese automobiles. Assume that you are a top-level manager with one of the U. S.-based car companies. Refer to a recent *Consumer Reports* issue that evaluates cars. Determine how the quality of the American company's car(s) compares with that of its Japanese rival(s). From your strategic control assessment, would you say that the American car company should take corrective action? Justify your answer.

3. Select a company of your choice. From library research, what source or sources of information can you obtain that may assist the management of that company in making strategic control decisions? Describe the source(s), the information contained, and how the information might be used by management for strategic control.

4. Select an airline company. Conduct library research on your chosen company so that you can elaborate on how strategic control has affected the direction of the company. Recall that strategic control consists of modifying a company's operations to maintain a compatible fit between the company and the changing environment.

NOTES

1. G. Donaldson, "The New Tool for Boards: The Strategic Audit," *Harvard Business Review* 73, no. 4 (1995): 103.

2. See B. Hermalin and M. S. Weisbach, "The Determinants of Board Composition," *Rand Journal of Economics* 19, 4 (1988): 589–605; E. F. Fama and M. C. Jensen, "Separation of Ownership and Control," *Journal of Law and Economics* 26, (1983): 301–325; M. S. Weisbach, "Outside Directors and CEO Turnover," *Journal of Financial Economics* 20 (1988): 431–460.

3. P. A. Gibbs, "Determinants of Corporate Restructuring: The Relative Importance of Corporate Governance, Takeover Threat, and Free Cash Flow," *Strategic Management Journal*, 14 (1993): 51–68.

4. M. S. Mizruchi, "Who Controls Whom? An Examination of the Relation Between Management and Boards of Directors in Large Corporations," *Academy of Management Review* 8 (1983): 426–435.

5. B. K. Boyd, "Board Control and CEO Compensation," *Strategic Management Journal* 15 (1994): 335–344.

6. See J. A. Alexander, M. L. Fennell, and M. T. Halpern, "Leadership Instability in Hospitals: The Influence of Board-CEO Relations and Organization Growth and Decline," *Administrative Science Quarterly* 38 (1993): 74–99; B. R. Baliga, R. C. Moyer, and R. S. Rao, "CEO Duality and Firm Performance: What's the Fuss?" *Strategic Management Journal* 17 (1996): 41–53; S. Finkelstein and R. A. D'Aveni, "CEO Duality as a Double-Edged Sword: How Boards of Directors Balance Entrenchment Avoidance and Unity of Command," *Academy of Management Journal* 37 (1994): 1079–1108.

7. M. Kroll, P. Wright, K. Barksdale, and A. Desai, "The Impact of Board Effectiveness, Large External Shareholders and CEO Rewards Ratio on Acquisition Performance Moderated by CEO Duality," working paper, University of Texas at Tyler.

8. See P. Wright, S. Ferris, A. Sarin, and V. Awasthi, "Impact of Corporate Insider, Blockholder, and Institutional Equity Ownership on Firm Risk Taking," *Academy of Management Journal* 39 (1996): 441–463; J. J. McConnell and H. Servaes, "Additional Evidence on Equity Ownership and Corporate Value," *Journal of Financial Economics* 27 (1990): 595–612.

9. J. Weber, W. Zellner, and Z. Schiller, "Seizing the Dark Day," *Business Week*, 13 January 1992, p. 27.

10. D. J. Yang and G. Smith, "Where Gloom and Doom Equal Boom," *Business Week*, 13 January 1992, p. 28.

11. W. Brown, "BMW to Build Car Assembly Plant in U. S.," *Washington Post*, 24 June 1992; P. Ingrassia and T. Aeppel, "Worried by Japanese, Thriving GM Europe Vows to Get Leaner," *Wall Street Journal*, 27 July 1992.

12. T. A. Stewart, "Lessons from U. S. Business Blunders," *Fortune*, 23 April 1990, p. 128.

13. C. H. Springer, "Strategic Management in General Electric," *Operations Research* 21 (1973): 1177–1182.

14. R. D. Buzzell and B. T. Gale, *The PIMS Principles* (New York: Free Press, 1987).

15. L. Dube, L. M. Renaghan, and J. M. Miller, "Measuring Customer Satisfaction for Strategic Management," *Cornell Hotel and Restaurant Administration Quarterly* (February 1994): 39–47; J. M. Groocock, *The Chain of Quality* (New York: Wiley, 1986).

16. P. Wright, D. Hotard, J. Tanner, and M. Kroll, "Relationships of Select Variables with Business Performance of Diversified Corporations," *American Business Review* 6, no. 1 (January 1988): 71–77.

17. Buzzell and Gale, *The PIMS Principles*, Chap. 6.

18. A. Taylor III, "More Power to J. D. Power," *Fortune*, 18 May 1992, pp. 103–106.

19. Buzzell and Gale, *The PIMS Principles*, Chap. 6; P. Wright, M. Kroll, C. Pringle, and J. Johnson, "Organization Types, Conduct, Profitability, and Risk in the Semiconductor Industry," *Journal of Management Systems* 2, no. 2 (1990): 33–48.

20. P. Fuhrman, "No Need for Valium," *Forbes*, 31 January 1994, pp. 84–85.

21. R. Mitchell, "Masters of Innovation: How 3M Keeps Its New Products Coming," *Business Week*, 10 April 1989, p. 61.

22. K. Kelly, "3M Run Scared? Forget About It," *Business Week*, 16 September 1991, p. 59.

23. R. Simons, "How New Top Managers Use Control Systems as Levers of Strategic Renewal," *Strategic Management Journal 15* (1994): 169–189.

24. O. Port, "Back to Basics," *Business Week*, Special 1989 Bonus Issue, pp. 14–18.

25. Buzzell and Gale, *The PIMS Principles*, Chap. 5.

26. J. Weber and J. Carey, "No Band-Aids for Ralph Larsen," *Business Week*, 28 May 1990, p. 86.

27. W. E. Fruhan Jr., "Pyrrhic Victories in Fights for Market Share,"; and R. G. Hamermesh, M. J. Anderson, and J. E. Harris, "Strategies for Low Market-Share Businesses," in R. G. Hamermesh, ed., *Strategic Management* (New York: Wiley, 1983), pp. 112–125, 126–138.

28. Hamermesh, Anderson, and Harris, "Strategies for Low Market-Share Businesses," p. 135.

29. D. Krackhardt and J. R. Hanson, "Informal Networks: The Company Behind the Chart," *Harvard Business Review* 71, no. 4 (July-August 1993): 104–111.

30. J. Gabarro, "Socialization at the Top—How CEOs and Subordinates Evolve Interpersonal Contacts," *Organizational Dynamics* 7 (Winter 1979): 14.

STRATEGIC MANAGEMENT MODEL

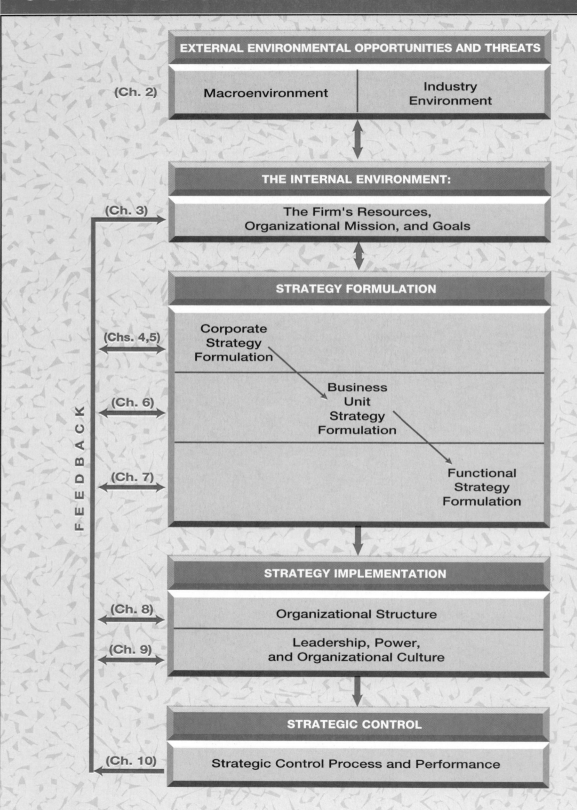

EXTERNAL ENVIRONMENTAL OPPORTUNITIES AND THREATS

(Ch. 2)

Macroenvironment	Industry Environment

THE INTERNAL ENVIRONMENT:

(Ch. 3)

The Firm's Resources, Organizational Mission, and Goals

STRATEGY FORMULATION

(Chs. 4,5)

Corporate Strategy Formulation

(Ch. 6)

Business Unit Strategy Formulation

(Ch. 7)

Functional Strategy Formulation

STRATEGY IMPLEMENTATION

(Ch. 8)

Organizational Structure

(Ch. 9)

Leadership, Power, and Organizational Culture

STRATEGIC CONTROL

(Ch. 10)

Strategic Control Process and Performance

FEEDBACK

11 Strategic Management and the World Marketplace

F ew businesses based in the United States can escape the impact of foreign competition. Besides widely publicized international competition in such industries as automobiles, motorcycles, steel, tires, and watches, American-made goods also compete head to head in their home markets with foreign firms in product lines such as fans, luggage, outerwear, jewelry, musical instruments, dolls, hand tools, consumer electronics, sporting goods, zinc, blouses, suits, semiconductors, and shoes. Among the home bases of the 500 largest industrial corporations in the world, 34 countries are represented, including Zambia and Panama. U.S.-based corporations still dominate the list with 161 companies, followed by Japan with 128 and Britain with 40.[1] In select areas, the United States is no longer at the top. In banking, for instance, the United States places only 4 banks in the world's top 50; Japan accounts for 20, Germany has 8, and 6 are based in France.[2]

Even though a company may choose to operate only within a confined local area, that choice does not necessarily exempt the business from foreign competition. Foreign firms conduct business in virtually every industry represented in the United States. Some American-based businesses, of course, choose to operate in other countries through one or more of the ways that this chapter discusses. But in any case, virtually every top manager must have an understanding of the issues involved in international strategic management.

OVERVIEW OF WORLD OPERATIONS

This chapter focuses primarily on businesses that choose to operate worldwide. This involvement may range from limited activities such as purchasing from foreign sources or exporting to a foreign market to operating throughout the world as if there were no national boundaries. To give you some idea of the magnitude of international trade, we list some selected statistics on U.S. exports and imports in Table 11.1

Ordinarily, international operations evolve gradually. Most enterprises begin their involvement with foreign countries through importing or exporting products. If particular sites overseas possess attractive resources or markets, a business may become further involved through licensing select organizations in those countries to use its technology, production processes, or brand name. Alternatively, the enterprise may enter into partnerships or joint ventures with foreign companies as a means of penetrating certain markets. Gradually, the company may become more deeply involved by initiating direct investments in select countries. Such investments may include the company's starting its own operations abroad or buying portions or all of the ownership of foreign-based organizations. U.S. and foreign direct investments are shown in Table 11.2. Direct investment refers to investors in one country owning at least 10 percent of a private enterprise in another country.

In this chapter, business operations will be considered on three levels: international, multinational, and global. **International businesses** are those that are minimally or moderately involved in foreign operations.[3] They may purchase from foreign companies, export to other nations, enter into licensing agreements with foreign-based organizations, or conduct strategic alliances with foreign firms. **Multinational organizations** are companies that are heavily involved in overseas operations through direct investments abroad. They

---

Table 11.1   **U. S. Exports, Imports, and Balance of Trade (in billions of dollars)**

Year	Exports	Imports	U. S. Balance of Trade
1970	42.7	40.0	+2.7
1975	107.7	98.5	+9.2
1980	220.6	244.9	−24.3
1985	213.1	345.3	−132.2
1990	393.6	495.3	−101.7
1991	421.9	488.1	−66.2
1992	447.5	525.1	−77.6
1993	464.9	574.9	−110.0
1994	512.4	663.8	−151.4

Source: Statistical Abstract of the United States, 1992 (U.S. Department of Commerce, Bureau of the Census), p. 796; C. L. Bach, "U.S. International Transactions, Fourth Quarter and Year 1993," *Survey of Current Business*, March 1994, p. 44; *Statistical Abstract of the United States*, 1995, p. 815.

Table 11.2

U. S. and Foreign Direct Investment (in millions of dollars)

Year	U.S. Direct Investment Abroad	Foreign Direct Investment in the United States	Largest Targets of U.S. Direct Investments (1993)		Largest Foreign Direct Investors in the United States (1993)	
1970	75.5	13.3	1. United Kingdom	96.4	1. Japan	96.2
1975	124.1	27.7	2. Canada	70.4	2. United Kingdom	95.4
1980	215.4	83.0	3. Germany	37.5	3. Netherlands	68.5
1985	230.3	184.6	4. Switzerland	32.9	4. Canada	38.4
1990	430.5	394.9	5. Japan	31.3	5. Germany	34.7
1993	548.6	445.3				

Source: Statistical Abstract of the United States, 1995 (U.S. Department of Commerce, Bureau of the Census), p. 806, 809; C. L. Bach, "U.S. International Transactions, Fourth Quarter and Year 1993," *Survey of Current Business,* March 1994, p. 44.

function on a country-by-country basis, with their subsidiaries operating independently of each other. **Global firms** are also heavily involved in foreign business and have made direct investments overseas, but their subsidiaries operate interdependently.[4] These distinctions are summarized in Table 11.3. Further elaborations on these differing levels of involvement are made in many of the following sections of this chapter. We begin with an examination of the international macroenvironment.

Table 11.3

Various Levels of Operations

Organization	Level of Involvement
Domestic organization	Chooses to operate totally within the confines of the United States.
International organization	Elects minimal or moderate international involvement. May purchase from foreign sources, export to other countries, license operations to foreign firms, or enter into strategic alliances with foreign-based companies.
Multinational organization	Chooses heavy international involvement. Makes direct investments abroad through starting its own operations in other countries or buying part or all of the ownership of foreign-based firms. Subsidiaries operate independently of one another on a country-by-country basis.
Global organization	Elects heavy international involvement. Makes direct investments abroad through starting its own operations in other countries or buying part or all of the ownership of foreign-based firms. Subsidiaries operate interdependently as a single, coordinated system.

MACROENVIRONMENT

As an organization's environment expands from domestic to international, management faces not only a larger number of environmental elements but also far greater environmental complexity. Chapter 2 suggested how certain macroenvironmental forces have strategic implications for top management. This section follows that same format but concentrates upon international forces in the macroenvironment: political-legal forces, economic forces, technological forces, and social forces.

■ Political-Legal Forces

All nations have their own particular laws and regulations that affect business activities. Some countries, for example, have rigid guidelines for hiring and firing employees; some require that a certain percentage of those employed by a foreign-owned business be citizens of the country in which the business operates; and some require that a portion of what is produced within their boundaries be exported to earn foreign exchange. These laws and regulations that are particular to each nation offer opportunities or pose threats to the business interested in operating across national boundaries. At times, the degree of opportunity or threat is influenced by major world political-legal trends.

The years between the end of World War II and the early 1980s can be characterized as a period during which the predominant political-legal trend was for the governments of industrialized countries to exert more influence over business operations. This trend was exhibited by governments in such countries as Great Britain, France, West Germany, Italy, Canada, and Japan. In some cases, governments even owned major manufacturers. For instance, Great Britain owned Jaguar and British Leyland, and West Germany owned Lufthansa. In France, the socialist government of Prime Minister François Mitterrand nationalized some major firms such as ITT-France and Honeywell-Bull in 1981. And Canadian legislation was passed requiring that energy companies operating within the borders of Canada be owned by Canadians.

This same trend also characterized the operations of businesses in less industrialized parts of the world. Communist governments, of course, permitted little, if any, free enterprise, preferring to run their economies through centralized state planning. In developing nations, key industries such as utilities, communications, steel, and raw materials extraction were generally owned by the government.

A second political-legal trend during this time period involved increased trade protection. Many countries increased the protection of their domestic industries through tariffs, import duties, and import restrictions. For example, in Latin American countries, import duties on a variety of products ranged from under 40 percent to more than 100 percent.[5] European and Southeast Asian nations also imposed heavy duties on imports. Even the United States imposed import fees on a variety of products, including food, steel, and cars. Furthermore, the United States convinced Japanese manufacturers to restrict "voluntarily" their exporting of cars to the United States. Likewise, European countries instituted import quotas on selected products such as Japanese stereos and watches.

STRATEGIC INSIGHT

Entering the Japanese Auto Market

Much has been made of the barriers erected by the Japanese government to prevent foreign-made automobiles from being sold in Japan. And, in truth, many barriers exist. But aggressive automakers seem to find ways to compete on Japanese soil.

BMW, for example, viewed Japan as a growth market as early as a decade ago. It was able to enter the market by adapting its models to Japanese regulations and consumer needs, offering extended warranties, investing heavily in service facilities and parts inventories, conducting its own training for Japanese mechanics, and supervising its operations closely. Its commitment was unwavering; analysts estimated that BMW paid almost half a billion dollars alone for choice real estate on which to build showrooms in Tokyo. BMW has more than 125 outlets in Japan.

Other German companies, such as Volkswagen, Mercedes, and Audi, were following suit.

The result? In 1994, about two-thirds of the foreign-made cars registered in Japan were built in Germany. Mercedes and BMW each sold twice as many cars as GM, Ford, and Chrysler combined. Not coincidentally, both German automakers sold through their own dealers, whereas all three American companies continued to rely heavily on importers to sell their cars. It wasn't until late 1992 that some American products began arriving in Japan with steering wheels on the right, as the Japanese prefer.

The Germans' aggressive move into Japan could pay off for years to come. Japan is the world's second-largest automobile market, and Japanese car buyers have exhibited extreme brand loyalty. In fact, some analysts estimate that almost 70 percent of them buy from the same company—and often even from the same salesperson—every time they purchase a new car.

SOURCES: G. F. Adams, "The Impact of Japanese Auto VRAs on the U. S. and Japanese Economies," *Journal of Policy Modeling* (April 1994): pp. 147–164; J. Flint, "Japan and the J-Curve," *Forbes*, 14 March 1994, pp. 40–41; P. D. Ballew and R. H. Schnorbus, "The Impact of the Auto Industry on the Economy," *Chicago Fed Letter*, March 1994, pp. 1–4; W. Spindle, "Have You Driven a Ford Lately—in Japan?" *Business Week*, 21 February 1994, p. 37; "Foreign Car Sales in Japan," *Parade*, 22 March 1992, p. 16; P. Ingrassia, "Detroit's Big Three Are Trying to Conquer a New Market: Japan," *Wall Street Journal*, 19 November 1991; K. L. Miller, "What's This? American Cars Gaining in Japan?" *Business Week*, 22 July 1991, pp. 82–83; T. R. Reid, "U. S. Automakers Grind Gears in Japan," *Washington Post*, 23 September 1990; C. Rapoport, "You Can Make Money in Japan," *Fortune*, 12 February 1990, p. 92; B. Yates, "The Road to Mediocrity," *Washington Post Magazine*, 17 December 1989, p. 35; M. Berger, "How Germany Sells Cars Where Detroit Can't," *Business Week*, 9 September 1985, p. 45.

Protectionist measures not only involved the protection of home industries from foreign imports, but restrictions were also placed on exporting advanced technology to other countries. The United States, for instance, banned the export of certain electronic, nuclear, and defense-related products to many nations.

There were, of course, countervailing trends. To offset the impact of some of the protectionist measures, twenty-three countries entered into the cooperative General Agreement on Tariffs and Trade (GATT) in 1947. GATT has assisted in eradicating or relaxing quota and import license requirements, introducing fairer customs evaluation methods, opposing discriminatory internal taxes, and serving as a mediator between governments on trade issues. GATT membership has now reached ninety-five nations.

By the middle of the 1980s and into the 1990s, however, trends toward the reversal of trade protectionism and strong governmental influence in business operations were becoming evident. In the United States, new economic policies reduced, on the whole, governmental influence in business operations by deregulating certain industries, lowering corporate taxes, granting more generous depreciation allowances, and relaxing rules against mergers and acquisitions. A similar trend was evident in Great Britain. Jaguar, for instance, was sold to individual investors (and later purchased by Ford Motor Company), as was British Telecom. As the trend spread, France's insurance industry and previously nationalized banks and manufacturing businesses were sold to investors.

Furthermore, the countries of Europe banded together to develop a trade-free European Community. Today, Europe is moving gradually, but steadily, toward a single market of 340 million consumers. The European Economic Area, as it is called, is the largest trading bloc on earth, accounting for over 40 percent of the world's gross domestic product (GDP).[6] Meanwhile, across the Atlantic, the United States, Canada, and Mexico proposed a North American Free Trade Agreement to create a $6 trillion tariff-free market within a decade. Parenthetically, some experts have warned that with freer trade and during periods of political instability, Latin American investments in the United States may be increasingly motivated by capital flight.[7]

This trend toward less regulation even extended to the previous communist countries. As the nations of Eastern Europe overturned their governments, they began to permit free-enterprise operations and to invite foreign investment in their economies.[8] As a result of these developments, numerous firms worldwide have found a more receptive political-legal climate.

■ Economic Forces

Common economic indicators such as gross domestic product (GDP) can suggest opportunities for businesses when an economy is expanding or, conversely, can warn of threats when the economy is contracting. But the most challenging international economic variables for strategic planners are interest rates, inflation rates, and currency exchange rates.

For example, the cost of borrowing is very high in a number of Latin American countries, with annual interest rates sometimes exceeding 100 percent. These high interest rates are often accompanied by excessive rates of inflation. In small nations, like Bolivia, annual inflation has been as high as 26,000 percent.[9] But even larger and more industrialized countries, like Brazil, have experienced annual inflation rates of 2,700 percent.[10] Such common decisions as pricing products or estimating costs become almost impossible to make under such conditions. Furthermore, high inflation rates cause the prices of goods and services to rise and, hence, become less competitive in international trade.

Currency exchange rates present challenges because of their dramatic changes over time. For instance, the Mexican peso was devalued by about 75 percent relative to the world's major currencies during the 1980s. U.S. firms operating in Mexico received pesos for their products and services, and their pesos would buy far fewer dollars than before the devaluation. The devaluation, therefore, reduced their profits considerably. By the 1990s, however, wild fluctuations in exchange rates had moderated in other countries and their rate of inflation had declined. The value of the peso had a drop of more than 50 percent relative to the dollar between 1994 and 1995.

▪ Technological Forces

Technology has a major impact on international business operations. For years, manufacturing firms in technologically advanced societies have sought plant location sites in countries with low labor or raw materials costs. Developing nations have generally welcomed such entrants. With them come an influx of financial resources, the opportunity for work force training, and the chance to acquire new technologies. In many cases, this interaction has benefited the developing country. Furthermore, some observers have even predicted that production technologies will be transferred from more advanced countries to such newly industrializing nations as Mexico, Brazil, Spain, Taiwan, Hong Kong, Singapore, and South Korea.[11] In this chapter, the term **technologically advanced nations** is used to refer to the United States, Canada, Japan, Australia, New Zealand, and the major industrial powers of Europe. The term **newly industrializing nations** refers to developing nations that have experienced rapid industrial growth over the past two decades. They were identified earlier in this paragraph. **Developing nations** is the term employed to refer to countries that have not yet experienced significant industrial development and includes any country not grouped under the two other categories.

However, the experiences of other developing nations have been quite disappointing. Although a firm's decision to operate in a foreign country is made for economic reasons, the host country often expects—but does not necessarily get—specific economic and social help in the form of assistance to local entrepreneurs, the establishment of research and development facilities, and the introduction of products relevant to its home market.[12] Such relationships do provide on-the-job training and improve the local economy, but the overall long-term contribution to the host country is questionable in the minds of some leaders of developing nations.[13]

Among the disappointments have been the results of technology transfer from the foreign firm to the host country:

> For example, firms such as Leyland Motors, General Electric, and Daimler-Benz have structured plants in various [developing nations]. The basic problem has continued to be the almost total dependence of the host countries on the multinationals for the provision of parts, motors, and product innovations.[14]

However, technology transfer is not the only source of disappointment for host countries. Their leaders also point to discontent with extractive industries:

> Whatever the raw material, it is argued, the nature of extractive industry constitutes a systematic depletion of the valuable national assets of the host country, while leaving little of enduring value. . . . All the training and technological transfer of this kind are highly specific to the nature of the industry. When bauxite, coal, and other ores are exhausted, the local people's gained knowledge can rarely be transferred to other national undertakings.[15]

Within this context, some of the leaders of developing nations have acquired negative attitudes toward foreign firms. Nevertheless, these countries will continue to need the expertise of the technologically advanced nations.[16] The key is for each party—the company and the host country—to develop an understanding of the wants and needs of the other. In an economic and technological sense, both parties need each other, and both can benefit significantly from a successful relationship.

■ Social Forces

Each of the world's countries has its own distinctive **culture**—that is, its generally accepted values, traditions, and patterns of behavior. Not surprisingly, these cultural differences interfere with the efforts of managers to understand and communicate with those in other societies. The unconscious reference to one's own cultural values—the **self-reference criterion**—has been suggested as the cause of most international business problems. Individuals become so accustomed to their own ways of looking at the world that they believe that any deviation from their perspective is not only wrong but also, perhaps, incomprehensible. But companies that can adjust to the culture of a host country will usually have the competitive edge. For instance, by adapting to local tastes rather than rigidly adhering to those of its U. S. customers, Domino's has found profitable business overseas through selling tuna and sweet corn pizzas in Japan and prawn and pineapple pizzas to Australians.[17]

Culture strongly influences the values that individuals hold. In turn, values influence the goals that individuals and organizations in a particular society set for themselves. The goals of managers in firms from technologically advanced countries, therefore, are likely to clash with the goals of the leaders of developing nations:

> On a macro-level, incongruencies in values have resulted in a major controversy over whether business unit goals should be influenced by market forces or by political priorities. The leaders of the multinationals have argued for market conditions influencing business decisions, whereas the developing nations have primarily sought corporate undertakings which benefit long-term social programs as well as business decisions which boost local employment.[18]

On a micro-level, managers of firms from technologically advanced nations often hold goals that are based on valuing mass production and efficient operations. However, mass production assumes certain worker-machine ratios, and efficient operations require particular worker-machine interfaces. Thus, these managers may demand behavior from local personnel that gives priority to productivity. The local employees, however, may resist these demands because they believe, on the basis of their own values, that business decisions should be secondary to social and religious norms. For instance, in some countries, it is customary to take a nap after lunch. In others, religious requirements call for taking several breaks during the workday to pray.[19]

It is clear that cross-cultural differences in norms and values require modifications in managerial behaviors:

> Doing business abroad often requires a great deal of patience and perseverance. In America, "getting down to business" and being efficient in pursuing and attempting to close sales agreements are considered desirable. . . . The U. S. businessperson is seen as displaying perseverance by quickly moving on to the next potential customer rather than by patiently pursuing an uninterested prospect. . . . Perseverance takes on a different connotation overseas. Whereas the American persists in certain large markets to make sales, successful foreign businesspersons are tenacious with select customers within those markets.[20]

In some countries, making the first business deal may take months or even years. The reason is that until personal friendships and trust develop between the potential buyer and seller, the people of those countries are unwilling to commit themselves to major business transactions.[21] After the first breakthrough, however, business transactions may become routine.

Social norms that are not well understood by outsiders often constrain business transactions. For instance, Japanese business executives expect their clients or suppliers to interact socially with them after working hours. These interactions can consume up to three or four hours an evening, several times a week. Westerners who decline to attend such social gatherings regularly are seriously handicapped in transacting business, because these social settings are requirements for serious business relationships.

Finally, managers of U.S.-based corporations operating abroad should remember that their firms have exceptionally high visibility because of their American origins. Hence, citizens of countries whose culture encourages strong political activism may disrupt the business operations of American corporations to send a political "message" to the U.S. government. For example, only two months after Euro Disneyland opened in France, hundreds of French farmers blocked its entrances with their tractors. The farmers wished to convey their displeasure with cuts in European Community farm subsidies that had been encouraged by the United States.[22]

STRATEGIC INSIGHT

Tips for Doing Business in Asia

- Realize that the Japanese rarely express negative emotions to foreigners. Hence, you can misread their intentions because they may smile even when angry.
- Exchange business cards with your hosts. Bilingual cards are especially appreciated. Show respect by carefully reading each card you receive.
- Control your physical gestures: Don't backslap, pat heads, or cross your legs. Even using your hands may make Japanese executives uncomfortable.
- Avoid jokes and conversation about politics.
- Always eat a bit of whatever food is offered; but never completely clean your plate, or you will be perceived as still being hungry.
- In Hong Kong, to signal your waiter to bring the check, pantomime a writing motion, using both hands. Never curl your index finger at anyone. That gesture is reserved for animals.
- Avoid giving flowers, since the wrong color or type can insult the recipient.

- Do not call on a company without an introduction. In Japan, particularly, meetings are taken very seriously.
- Don't employ the typical American "let's-get-to-the-point" negotiating style. The Japanese, in particular, want to get to know the people they are dealing with before doing business with them.
- Never bring your company's lawyer to a meeting before a deal is closed. Business relationships should be built on trust.
- Never brag—not even about your family. The Japanese, for instance, tend to be humble, even about their children's accomplishments.
- If you receive a compliment from a Chinese executive, deny it politely. Although the Chinese offer frequent compliments, they consider a "thank you" in response to be impolite.
- Never address South Koreans by their given names; that practice is thought to be rude.

SOURCES: A. Rashid, "South Asia: Out of the Shadow," *Far Eastern Economic Review*, 23 December 1993, p. 23; J. T. Yenckel, "Fearless Traveler: Sorting Through the Chaos of Culture," *Washington Post*, 20 October 1991; A. B. Stoddard, "Learning the Cultural Tricks of Foreign Trade," *Washington Business*, 18 June 1990, p. 11; F. H. Katayama, "How to Act Once You Get There," *Fortune, Special Issue: Asia in the 1990s*, Fall 1989, pp. 87–88; T. Holden and S. Woolley, "The Delicate Art of Doing Business in Japan," *Business Week*, 2 October 1989, p. 120.

INDUSTRY ENVIRONMENT

The nature of industry competition in the international arena differs from one country to the next. In some nations, competing successfully may not necessarily depend on such familiar American concepts as bargaining power, the threat of new entrants, or substitute products. Rather, engaging in competition may be possible only if the company is willing to barter by trading the firm's products and services for goods from the host country. A number of Japanese companies, as an example, trade their products for oil in some markets of the Organization of Petroleum Exporting Countries (OPEC).

The industry environment is complicated by the potential for linkages between domestic and international competitive forces. For instance, when a strong overseas competitor enters the domestic market of a firm, the firm's most effective response may be to counter its foreign competitor's move by entering its domestic market:

> Effective counter-competition has a destabilizing impact on the foreign company's cash flows, product-related competitiveness, and decision making about integration. Direct market penetration can drain vital cash flows from the foreign company's domestic operations. This drain can result in lost opportunities, reduced income, and limited production, impairing the competitor's ability to make overseas thrusts.[23]

From a global perspective, industry analysis can be quite challenging. A firm, for instance, may produce its parts in one nation, assemble them in other countries, and sell the final product to another group of nations. As an example, RCA has located its business units in such diverse countries as Taiwan, Japan, Mexico, and Canada. The operations of these business units are coordinated with those of other RCA units located in the United States. Each business unit performs complementary manufacturing or support functions. Hence, one unit may manufacture components; others may perform subassembly work, warehousing, or distribution. Each business unit is an integral link in the overall strategy of RCA's world operations.[24] As might be expected, such industry forces as market position, bargaining power of suppliers and customers, and the threat of new entrants or substitute products have different ramifications for each of RCA's business units, even though, in unison, these units produce television sets.

The world's constantly improving communication networks have, in a sense, "shrunk" some global industries to the extent that a few corporations are able to use one television advertisement to promote their products or services. Cable News Network (CNN), for instance, is beamed into 78 million households in more than a hundred countries, and MTV Network reaches twenty-eight nations. Taking advantage of this "homogeneity," Levi Strauss, for example, produces one advertisement worldwide. It promotes its jeans through ads featuring American rock music and nonspeaking actors. As the director of MTV Europe states: "Eighteen-year-olds in Paris have more in common with 18-year-olds in New York than with their own parents. . . . They buy the same products, go to the same movies, listen to the same music, sip the same colas."[25] However, most firms must still customize the advertisements for their products along particular national or regional boundary lines.

MISSION, GOALS, OBJECTIVES, AND S.W.O.T. ANALYSIS

An organization's mission, the reason for its existence, may be closely intertwined with international operations in several ways. For instance, a firm may need inputs from abroad. Wrigley, the chewing gum manufacturer, would be unable to produce its products without the gum base derived from trees in Southeast Asia. Virtually all of Japan's industries would come to a standstill if imports of raw materials from other nations were halted, since Japan's natural resources are quite limited.

Organizational mission and international involvement are also connected through the economic concept of **comparative advantage**. This concept refers to the idea that certain parts and products may be produced more cheaply or with higher quality in particular countries owing to advantages in labor costs or technology. Also, certain raw materials and natural resources may be extracted more economically in particular locales. For instance, the cost of drilling for oil is significantly lower and its availability is significantly greater in Saudi Arabia than in Europe. Because oil is the basic raw material for producing many chemical products, European chemical firms have sought joint ventures with oil companies in Saudi Arabia. For this reason, Japanese chemical companies are not major world competitors. Japan has no oil, and Japanese chemical firms have, to date, been unsuccessful in arranging joint ventures with firms in oil-producing countries.

Finally, some firms' missions require international connections for prestige reasons. The attempt to surround a perfume product, for instance, with a certain mystique seems to necessitate New York, London, and Paris connections. You may have noticed that the more prestigious brands of cosmetics and perfumes often have "New York, London, and Paris" conspicuously inscribed on their packages.

A firm's goals and objectives may also require global involvement. To reduce costs, for example, a firm may seek production sites in foreign countries. For political-legal reasons, organizations may need to locate manufacturing facilities abroad. For instance, establishing production facilities in selected countries can avoid problems with protectionist trade legislation. Finally, making products in other countries helps management understand the needs of foreign customers. Ford, for example, has twenty plants in Western Europe. Manufacturing there helped Ford engineers design windshield wipers for cars engaged in high-speed driving on the German autobahns.[26]

Remember that a firm's mission is defined within its external environmental opportunities and threats as well as in the context of its internal resource strengths and weaknesses. Top management, then, must evaluate the firm's internal resource strengths and weaknesses and the international environment's opportunities and threats. In the first part of the S.W.O.T. analysis, management can use the following questions as guidelines in evaluating the company's internal strengths and weaknesses:

- Does the firm have a strong market position in the countries in which it operates?
- Does the firm's product/service quality compare favorably with that of its world competitors?
- Does the firm have a technological advantage in the world regions where it operates its major businesses?

- Does the firm have a strong brand reputation in the countries in which it sells its products/services?
- Are the firm's managers and employees more talented than those of its major world competitors?
- Is the firm's financial position strong?
- Is the firm consistently more profitable than its world rivals?
- Are the firm's product and process research and development efforts likely to produce better results than those of its competitors?
- Are the firm's various world operations subject to unionization?

Answers to these questions may serve as a basis for evaluating the firm's strengths and weaknesses.

The following questions may guide management's thinking about the second part of the S.W.O.T. analysis, the opportunities and threats that exist in the firm's external environment:

- What threats and opportunities do political-legal forces present?
- What threats and opportunities are presented by economic forces?
- What threats and opportunities do technological forces present?
- What threats and opportunities are presented by social forces?
- What is the size of the industry(ies)?
- What are the growth rate and potential of the industry(ies)?
- Is the industry(ies) cyclical? If so, can the cyclicality be smoothed out across different world markets?
- Is the industry(ies) subject to fluctuations in demand because of seasonable factors? If so, can these seasonal factors be smoothed out across different world markets?
- How intense in world competition is the industry(ies)?
- What is the median industry(ies) profitability? What is its (their) potential profitability?
- Is the industry(ies) susceptible to unionization?
- What is the rate of innovation in the industry(ies)?

CORPORATE-LEVEL STRATEGIES

In chapters 4 and 5, we saw that firms have available to them several corporate-level strategies: growth, stability, or retrenchment. Using growth strategies, many firms attempt to gain market share to reduce their unit costs of operations. Large increases in sales are sometimes available only through global expansion. Coca-Cola and PepsiCo realized many years ago that significant increases in sales were more likely to be achieved overseas than in the already saturated U. S. marketplace.

Likewise, Caterpillar has become one of the world's leading construction equipment makers because of its global involvement.[27]

> Two-thirds of the total product cost of construction equipment is in heavy components—engines, axles, transmissions, and hydraulics—whose manufacturing costs are capital intensive and highly sensitive to economies of scale. Caterpillar turned its network of sales in different countries into a cost advantage by designing product lines that use identical components and investing heavily in a few

large-scale, state-of-the-art component manufacturing facilities to fill worldwide demand.[28]

Corporate growth strategies may include strategic alliances, license agreements, or direct investments. **International strategic alliances** are partnerships of two or more firms from different nations that join together to accomplish specific projects or to cooperate in select areas of business. One of the best-known examples of an international strategic alliance is the automobile production facility in California that is owned jointly by General Motors and Toyota.

An **international license agreement** is the granting of permission by a firm in one country to a company in another nation to use its technology, brand name, production processes, or other operations. A fee is paid to the granting firm by the company being licensed. For example, pharmaceutical firms such as Merck and Upjohn have licensed organizations in other parts of the world to produce and sell their brands of drugs.

International franchising is a special type of licensing in which a local franchisee pays the franchisor, headquartered in another country, for the right to use the franchisor's brand names, promotion, materials, and procedures.[29] Examples may be found in hotels (Hilton), soft-drink bottling (Coca-Cola), and fast-food restaurants (McDonald's).

Direct investments may take place in one of two ways. A firm may engage in internal growth by establishing physical facilities and operations in another country. Many well-known companies, such as IBM and Citicorp, pursue this route. Alternatively, a company may grow externally by merging with or by acquiring all or part of the ownership of a foreign firm. For example, Electrolux of Sweden purchased U.S.-based Poulan/Weedeater.

Stability is a corporate strategy that a firm adopts when its goal is to maintain its current size and scope of operations in the world. Such a strategy obviously would not include engaging in new strategic alliances, license agreements, or direct investments.

When a firm's performance is disappointing, a corporate retrenchment strategy may be necessary. Retrenchment may involve revising products/markets in particular nations, pruning assets and work forces in other locations, selling or spinning off parts of world operations, selling the entire business, or—in the worst-case scenario—liquidating it. Firestone, for instance, attempted to reverse its poor performance in the early 1980s by selling its operations in five foreign countries and by reducing its ownership to a minority position in other foreign subsidiaries. Eventually, however, Firestone was sold to Bridgestone, a Japanese-based competitor.[30] Next we examine level of operations and market share.

LEVEL OF OPERATIONS AND MARKET SHARE

As we saw earlier in this chapter, a business may be involved only in its domestic market or it may compete overseas at one of three levels: international, multinational, or global. Within the domestic, international, or multinational context, an enterprise may compete successfully with a high or low market share. However, firms that choose to compete at the global level usually operate effectively only through maintaining a high market share. The relationship between level of operations and market share is illustrated in Figure 11.1.

Strategic Alliances: A Popular Way to Enter Foreign Markets

Increasingly, American companies are looking to strategic alliances as efficient ways to enter foreign markets. For instance, U.S.-based firms have formed more than 2,400 strategic alliances with European companies since 1980. Such companies as Occidental Petroleum, Atlantic Richfield, Texaco, Xerox, and Coca-Cola have engaged in strategic alliances with firms in China since the mid-1980s.

Why the popularity of strategic alliances? Both partners often hope to achieve several ends: lower the costs (and the risks) of high-technology product development, increase sales so that greater economies of scale may be attained, broaden a firm's product line by joining with a company that makes complementary products, and gain a lookout post so that other competitors' moves may be more easily tracked.

Sony's Venture with Apple Computer

A few years ago, the giant Japanese consumer electronics manufacturer, Sony, grew interested in the personal computer (PC) industry. During this same time, U.S.-based Apple Computer felt the need to expand its product line to include a small laptop computer. But Apple didn't have the required miniaturization skills. Because the PC industry is characterized by frequent product introductions and brief product life cycles, Apple's management believed that the company couldn't wait to develop internally the skills that were needed.

So Apple asked Sony to manufacture the laptop for them. The result was the Macintosh PowerBook 100, which quickly became a best-seller.

The two companies were an ideal match. For some years, Sony had produced some of the floppy disk drives, monitors, and power supplies used in Apple's larger Macintosh computers.

Chrysler's AMC Venture with Beijing Automotive Works

Of course, some strategic alliances end in failure. After four years of on-again and off-again negotiations, American Motors Corporation (AMC), now a subsidiary of Chrysler, and the Chinese-owned Beijing Automotive Works agreed to produce Jeeps jointly. China offered not only a huge market but also low labor costs and an excellent location for exporting to all of Asia.

But problems arose quickly. Most fundamentally, the two partners could never agree on the nature of the Jeep to be produced. And U.S. executives learned too late that they did not have the right to convert their Chinese earnings into dollars—meaning that the venture often did not have enough hard currency to buy parts from Detroit, because most of its output was sold inside China. As the shaky partnership continued, American managers learned that Beijing Automotive Works was hoarding proceeds from Chinese sales at about the same time that China announced a hefty increase in duties on parts kits imported from Detroit. Shortly thereafter, U.S. managers departed from the country, leaving the Chinese to run the assembly line on their own. Although China still holds the controversial most favored nation trade status, Chrysler has made no attempt to reenter the partnership.

SOURCES: S. Weintraub, "Nafta Benefits Flow to Both Sides of Rio Grande," *Wall Street Journal Interactive Edition*, 10 May 1996; R. L. Rose, "For Whirlpool, Asia Is the New Frontier," *Wall Street Journal*, 25 April 1996, pp. B1, B4; "A Simpler Model of International Joint Venture Distributorships: The American-Kuwaiti Experience," *Omega*, October 1995, pp. 525–538; A. Yan and B. Gray, "Bargaining Power, Management Control, and Performance in United States-China Joint Ventures: A Comparative Case Study," *Academy of Management Journal* 37(6), 1994: 1478–1517; S. Wilhelm, "International Ventures Focus on Asia and Russia," *Puget Sound Business Journal*, 12 May 1995, p. 9A; C. Smith, "Investment: Neighbor's Keeper," *Far Eastern Economic Review*, 10 March 1994, p. 56; R. B. Egen, "The Health of Nations," *Journal of Business Strategy*, March-April 1993, pp. 33–37; B. R. Schlender, "Apple's Japanese Ally," *Fortune*, 4 November 1991, pp. 151–152; J. Mann, *Beijing Jeep* (New York: Simon & Schuster, 1990).

Figure 11.1 **Competing Domestically, Internationally, Multinationally, Globally, and Market Share Goals**

LEVEL OF OPERATIONS

		Domestic Organizations	International Organizations	Multinational Organizations	Global Organizations
MARKET SHARE GOALS	**High**	Domestic, high share	International, high share	Multinational, high share	Global, high share
	Low	Domestic, low share	International, low share	Multinational, low share	

Some businesses may be involved only in their domestic market. In certain cases, they may not yet be subject to foreign competitive pressures. Some realty companies that compete only in local towns serve as examples. On a national basis, these companies operate with very small market shares. Other competitors, such as Century 21, sell real estate nationwide and have large market shares.

Moving outside the domestic market, some companies choose to be involved on an international basis. They operate in various countries but limit their involvement to importing, exporting, licensing, or strategic alliances. The act of exporting alone can significantly benefit even a small company. For instance, Vita-Mix Corporation, a small Ohio business ($15 million in annual sales), began exporting its blenders to such countries as Norway and Venezuela. Since that move, Vita-Mix has more than doubled its work force by hiring sixty-three new employees even though it is located in an economically depressed area and its overall market share is tiny.[31]

Still other companies are involved multinationally. They have direct investments in other countries, and their subsidiaries operate independently of one another. As an example, Colgate-Palmolive has attained a large worldwide market share through its decentralized operations in a number of foreign markets.

Finally, some firms are globally involved. They have direct investments abroad and operate their subsidiaries interdependently. Caterpillar is an example of such a firm. Some of its various world subsidiaries produce components in different countries, other subsidiaries assemble these components, and still other units sell the finished products. Caterpillar has achieved its low-cost position by producing its own heavy components for its large global market. If its various subsidiaries operated independently and only produced for their individual regional markets, Caterpillar would be unable to realize economies of scale.

Global firms normally attempt to gain a high market share. Coordinating an interdependent global system is extremely complex, and this complexity—and expense—can be justified only when a high market share is attainable and it is feasible to profitably coordinate the operations of multiple subsidiaries.

BUSINESS UNIT AND FUNCTIONAL STRATEGIES

Business units may adopt any one of a number of generic strategies, as discussed in chapter 6. If low market share is the business unit's goal, then management may choose from among the strategies of niche–low-cost, niche-differentiation, or niche–low-cost/differentiation. These strategies are appropriate

---

S T R A T E G I C   I N S I G H T

Coca-Cola: A Multinational Firm

Almost half of all the soft drinks consumed in the world are made by Coca-Cola. (Its nearest competitor, PepsiCo, has less than one-fourth of the world market.) Its overseas business is quite profitable: About 68 percent of Coca-Cola's sales and 80 percent of its profits come from 170 countries outside the United States.

What's the secret behind Coke's international success? There may be several.

First, the firm's brand name has been well known across the globe since World War II. Second, Coke's management is patient. It spent several million dollars in China and waited fifteen years to make a profit. Third, the firm pays attention to the details. Coke considers no retail outlet too small to sell its products. In Japan, for instance, Coca-Cola has held seminars for owners of mom-and-pop stores on how to compete with larger outlets. Not surprisingly, Coca-Cola–Japan is Coca-Cola's largest profit center, even larger than Coke–U.S.

Fourth, Coca-Cola is consistent, unless the situation requires flexibility. In much of the world, Coke's package, logo, taste, and adver-

tising are the same. But in countries that are unfamiliar with soft drinks, Coke has modified the flavor of its products to conform more closely to local tastes.

Fifth, it enters new markets intelligently. For instance, to cut through red tape and speed up the entry process, Coke often offers bottling franchises to the nation's most powerful companies. Then to control the bottlers, it sometimes buys part of the firm. In the last decade alone, Coke invested more than $1 billion in bottling strategic alliances.

The future looks bright indeed. Although annual sales growth in the United States averages only 2 or 3 percent, yearly sales are increasing in such large markets as Mexico and Brazil by about 25 percent. Coca-Cola recently doubled its capacity in China, where it sells more than 100 million cases annually. The company is now moving aggressively into Vietnam.

Overall, Coca-Cola expects world sales to double between 1990 and the year 2000. According to insiders, Coke's biggest challenge today is keeping up with world demand.

SOURCES: "Russian Coca-Cola Site Opened by Inchape," *Wall Street Journal*, 11 September 1995, p. A8; E. DeMarco, "Troubles Worsen for Coke Joint Venture in India," *Atlanta Business Chronicle*, 7 July 1995, p. 15A; E. Beck, "Where West Faced East, Colas Now War; Coke is Ahead in Eastern Europe; Pepsi Fires Back," *Wall Street Journal*, 7 September 1995, p. A10; G. G. Marcial, "Two Reasons Why Coke Is It: China and Russia," *Business Week*, 7 March 1994, p. 106; K. Barnes, "On the '90s Ho Chi Minh Trail," *Advertising Age*, 7 February 1994, p. 4; "Lowe Gives Diet Coke Everyman Feel in New Ads," *Marketing*, 27 January 1994, p. 1; M. J. McCarthy, "As a Global Marketer, Coke Excels by Being Tough and Consistent," *Wall Street Journal*, 19 December 1989.

for domestic, international, and multinational enterprises. For instance, Rolls-Royce, an international company, uses the niche-differentiation strategy. It maintains a small market share internationally by selling its cars only to very wealthy buyers in particular nations.

On the other hand, if the goal of a business unit is to attain a large market share, it has available the low-cost, differentiation, low-cost–differentiation, or multiple strategies. These strategies may be adopted by domestic, international, multinational, and global companies. McDonald's is an example of an international company that has experienced success with the low-cost–differentiation strategy. Colgate-Palmolive serves as an illustration of a multinational firm that has successfully employed the low-cost–differentiation strategy. Caterpillar operates with success as a global firm using low-cost–differentiation.

No generic strategy can be successfully implemented without careful planning, execution, and coordination of each business unit's functional departments.[32] In formulating functional strategies, managers must be aware that functions are interrelated. Each functional area, in attaining its purpose, must mesh its activities with the activities of the other functional departments. The extent to which all of the business unit's functional tasks mesh smoothly determines the effectiveness of the unit's generic strategy.

For domestic, international, and multinational companies, the coordination of functional strategies may be undertaken independently within each business unit. Hence, international and multinational companies generally coordinate functional strategies on a country-by-country basis. Global firms, however, coordinate functional strategies across the firm's business units located in various countries, because their units' actions are interdependent.

STRATEGY IMPLEMENTATION

Earlier, in chapters 8 and 9, we learned that structure and behavior are key aspects of strategy and implementation. Whatever organizational structure is adopted by a business that operates in two or more countries, the relationship between its headquarters and its subsidiaries may be either bilateral or multilateral.[33] International and multinational firms generally have bilateral, independent relationships between their headquarters and subsidiaries. This type of relationship, in which the headquarters interacts independently with each subsidiary, is depicted in Figure 11.2.

There are advantages to bilateral relationships. Take, for instance, the case of Bausch & Lomb, the maker of such optical products as Ray-Ban sunglasses and contact lenses. Headquarters sets the firm's overall strategic direction and then allows local management to make all other decisions. As a result of recently permitting managers on the scene to determine the design for sunglasses—so that the designs for the European and Asian markets are now quite different—Bausch & Lomb's international sales have increased from one quarter to approximately half of its total revenue, and the firm now controls 40 percent of the world market for sunglasses.

Global firms, on the other hand, usually maintain multilateral, interdependent relationships between their headquarters and subsidiaries. Figure 11.3 portrays this situation in which the operations of the subsidiaries are interdependent. The primary advantage of multinational relationships is that efficiencies

Figure 11.2   **Bilateral Relationships Between Headquarters and Subsidiaries of International or Multinational Organizations**

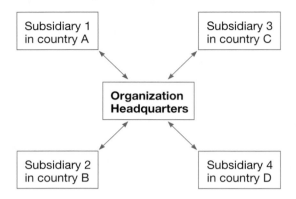

can be gained via specialization of operations in countries that are well-suited to particular operations.

Certainly, operating outside one's own country offers special challenges in areas such as leadership and maintaining a strong organizational culture. Some countries, for instance, resist innovation and radical new approaches to conducting business. Others, however, welcome such change. Swedish companies, for instance, have led the way in employing autonomous work groups that manage themselves.

Recall the dangers of the self-reference criterion. All too often managers believe that the leadership styles and organizational culture that worked in their home country should work elsewhere. But as we have seen, each nation has its own unique culture, norms, traditions, values, and beliefs. Hence, it should be

Figure 11.3   **Multilateral Relationships Between Headquarters and Subsidiaries of a Global Organization**

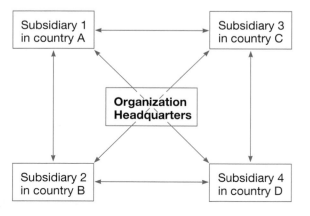

obvious—but often is not—that leadership styles, motivation programs, and organizational values and norms must be tailored to fit the unique culture of each country in which the organization operates.

SUMMARY

This chapter focuses on businesses that choose to operate in the world marketplace. Ordinarily, such operations evolve gradually. Most companies begin their involvement with foreign countries through importing or exporting products. They may become further involved through licensing select organizations in other countries to use their technology, production processes, or brand names. Or they may enter into partnerships or strategic alliances with foreign companies as a means of penetrating certain markets. Still deeper involvement may be achieved by initiating direct investments in particular countries.

There are three levels of foreign business operations: international, in which a domestic company is minimally or moderately involved in foreign operations through importing, exporting, licensing, or conducting strategic alliances; multinational, in which the enterprise makes direct investments abroad and operates each of its foreign subsidiaries independently on a country-by-country basis; and global, in which the firm also makes direct investments abroad but operates its subsidiaries in an interdependent fashion.

Much as a domestic company does, the organization that chooses to engage in world commerce must analyze its macroenvironment and industry environment. The difference, of course, is that as an organization's environment expands from domestic to global, management faces not only a larger number of environmental elements but also far greater environmental complexity.

Within the organization, mission, goals, and objectives may be closely intertwined with world operations. Likewise, corporate-level strategies must take into account unique global considerations.

Enterprises that operate at the international or multinational level may compete successfully with either a high or a low market share, depending upon their particular mission and goals. Global firms, however, must usually maintain a high market share for effective operation.

At the business unit level, the generic strategies of niche–low-cost, niche–differentiation, and niche–low-cost/differentiation are appropriate for international and multinational businesses that desire to maintain a low market share. On the other hand, if the business unit's goal is to attain a high market share, it has available the low-cost, differentiation, low-cost–differentiation, and multiple strategies. These strategies may be adopted by international, multinational, and global companies.

In determining functional strategies, international and multinational businesses coordinate their functional activities on a country-by-country basis. Global firms, however, coordinate functional strategies across the firm's business units located in various countries, since their units' actions are interdependent.

As management implements its strategies, it must take into account the unique culture of each country in which its business operates. The leadership styles, motivation programs, and organizational culture that worked in the United States may need to be tailored to each individual international setting.

TAKE IT TO THE NET

We invite you to visit the Wright page on the Prentice Hall Web site at:

http://www.prenhall.com/wright

for this chapter's World Wide Web exercise.

KEY CONCEPTS

Comparative advantage   The concept that products or parts can be produced less expensively or with higher quality or that natural resources can be extracted more economically in particular geographic locations owing to advantages in labor costs, technology, or availability of such natural resources as minerals and timbers.

Culture   The generally accepted values, traditions, and patterns of behavior of a societal group.

Developing nation   A country that has not yet experienced significant industrial development.

Direct investment   When investors in one country own at least 10 percent of a private enterprise in another country.

Global firm   A firm, heavily involved in the world marketplace through direct investments, that operates its subsidiaries in an interdependent fashion.

International business   A business that is minimally or moderately involved in foreign operations. It may import or export goods, enter into licensing agreements with foreign-based organizations, or conduct strategic alliances with foreign companies.

International franchising   A special type of licensing in which a franchisee pays the franchisor, headquartered in another country, for the right to use the franchisor's brand names, promotion, materials, and procedures.

International license agreement   The granting of permission by an organization in one country to a company in another nation to use its technology, brand name, production processes, or other operations. A fee is paid to the granting organization by the company being licensed.

International strategic alliance   A partnership of two or more organizations from different nations that join together to accomplish specific projects or to cooperate in selected areas of business.

Multinational organization   An organization, heavily involved in overseas operations through direct investments, that functions on a country-by-country basis, with its subsidiaries operating independently of one another.

Newly industrializing nation   A developing nation that has experienced rapid industrial growth over the past two decades. This category includes Mexico, Brazil, Spain, Taiwan, Hong Kong, Singapore, and South Korea.

Self-reference criterion The unconscious reference to one's own cultural values.

Technologically advanced nation A nation that is grouped among the major industrial powers of the world. This category includes the United States, Canada, Japan, Australia, New Zealand, and the industrialized nations of Europe.

DISCUSSION QUESTIONS

1. What businesses can you identify that are not directly affected by foreign competition?

2. Obtain the latest listing of the world's largest industrial corporations. How many U. S.-based firms are on the list? How does this figure compare with a listing from 1960 or 1970?

3. Explain how a domestic company, over time, expands to become a global firm. What are the normal stages in this process?

4. Discuss fully the differences between a multinational enterprise and a global firm.

5. What is the major distinction between an international enterprise and a multinational organization?

6. Forecast what future world political-legal trends might affect global business.

7. How do the goals of a multinational or global organization differ from those of the host country? Why do they differ?

8. Explain how the self-reference criterion can lead to problems for U. S. managers operating abroad.

9. Why might an organization's mission influence management to engage in world operations?

10. Explain the relationship between a business's level of operations and its market share goals.

STRATEGIC MANAGEMENT EXERCISES

1. Select a well-known energy company. From your recollection of current events, what global opportunities and threats does the macroenvironment pose for this company? Identify several specific opportunities and threats for each of the following forces: political-legal, economic, technological, and social.

2. Identify a particular company in a well-defined industry, such as automobiles or computers. From your recollection of current events, analyze that company's industry environment from a world perspective. You may wish to use relevant sections of the "Industry Analysis Worksheet" from Worksheet 2 at the end of chapter 2 to guide your analysis.

3. Acquire the annual report of a firm that operates in more than two countries. Does its annual report specifically identify its mission and goals in global terms? What suggestions would you make to improve this company's mission and goal statements?

4. Using a global firm of your choice, determine what corporate-level and business unit–level strategies it has adopted. Give evidence to support your answers.

5. Assume that you are a member of the top management team of a food-processing company that follows a corporate growth strategy. Your company has decided to expand into both the western and eastern regions of the European continent. Specifically, which countries would you suggest as appropriate for licensing agreements? Why? In which would you prefer to make direct investments? Why?

NOTES

1. "Fortune's Global 500," *Fortune*, 26 July 1994, pp. 188–234.

2. "Global Banking," *The Banker*, February 1994, pp. 49–52; "International Bank Scorecard," *Business Week*, 6 July 1992, p. 63.

3. Some firms initially enter into international business through a strategic alliance. See J. Bleeke and D. Ernst, "Is Your Strategic Alliance Really a Sale?" *Harvard Business Review*, 73 no. 1 (January-February 1995): 97–105. Other firms adopt a different mode of entry. See F. Robles, "International Market Entry Strategies and Performance of United States Catalog Firms," *Journal of Direct Marketing* 8, no. 1 (1994): 59–70.

4. See K. Ohmae, "Putting Global Logic First," *Harvard Business Review* 73 no. 1 (January-February 1995): 119–125. Also see P. Gray, "Productivity Through Globalization," *Information Systems Management* 11, no. 1 (1994): 90–91.

5. *International Financial Statistics Yearbook* (Washington, DC: International Monetary Fund, 1989).

6. C. Rapoport, "Europe Looks Ahead to Hard Choices," *Fortune*, 14 December 1992, p. 145.

7. J. A. King and J. D. Daniels, "Latin American and Caribbean Direct Investments in the U. S.," *Multinational Business Review* 2 (1994): 1–10.

8. F. M. E. Raiszadeh, M. M. Helms, and M. C. Varner, "How Can Eastern Europe Help American Manufacturers?" *The International Executive* 35 (1993): 357–365.

9. *International Financial Statistics Yearbook*, pp. 35–52.

10. C. S. Manegold and M. Kepp, "Elegant Armed Robbery," *Newsweek*, 2 April 1990, p. 30.

11. B. Schofield, "Building-and-Rebuilding—A Global Company," *The McKinsey Quarterly* 2, 1994: 37–45; R. B. Reich, *The Next American Frontier* (New York: Times Books, 1983).

12. A. R. Negandhi, "Multinational Corporations and Host Governments' Relationships: Comparative Study of Conflict and Conflicting Issues," *Human Relations* 33 (1980): 534–535.

13. P. Wright, D. Townsend, J. Kinard, and J. Iverstine, "The Developing World to 1990: Trends and Implications for Multinational Business," *Long Range Planning* 15, no. 4 (July–August 1982): 116–125.

14. Ibid., p. 119. Reprinted from *Long Range Planning*, Vol. 15, P. Wright et al., "The Developing World to 1990: Trends and Implications for Multinational Business," pp. 116–125, Copyright (1982), with permission from Pergamon Press Ltd, Headington Hill Hall, Oxford OX3 OBW, UK.

15. Ibid., p. 119. Reprinted from *Long Range Planning*, Vol. 15, P. Wright et al., "The Developing World to 1990: Trends and Implications for Multinational Business," pp. 116–125, Copyright (1982), with permission from Pergamon Press Ltd, Headington Hill Hall, Oxford OX3 OBW, UK.

16. J. B. Treece and K. L. Miller, "New Worlds to Conquer," *Business Week,* 28 February 1994, pp. 50–52.

17. M. J. Williams, "Rewriting the Export Rules," *Fortune,* 23 April 1990, p. 89.

18. P. Wright, "MNC—Third World Business Unit Performance: Application of Strategic Elements," *Strategic Management Journal* 5 (1984): 232.

19. P. Wright, "Doing Business in Islamic Markets," *Harvard Business Review* 59, no. 1 (January–February 1981): 34–40.

20. P. Wright, "Systematic Approach to Finding Export Opportunities," in D. N. Dickson, ed., *Managing Effectively in the World Marketplace* (New York: Wiley, 1983), pp. 338–339.

21. P. Wright, "Organizational Behavior in Islamic Firms," *Management International Review* 21, no. 2 (1981): 86–94.

22. "No Fun: Tourists Stranded As Farmers Cut Off 'Euro Disneyland' Site," *Harrisonburg* (Va.) *Daily News-Record,* 27 June 1992.

23. C. M. Watson, "Counter-Competition Abroad to Protect Home Markets," in D. N. Dickson, ed., *Managing Effectively in the World Marketplace* (New York: Wiley, 1983), p. 359.

24. P. Wright, "The Strategic Options of Least-Cost, Differentiation, and Niche," *Business Horizons* 29, no. 2 (March–April 1986): 22.

25. K. Wells, "Global Ad Campaigns, After Many Missteps, Finally Pay Dividends," *Wall Street Journal,* 27 August 1992.

26. T. Eiben, "U. S. Exporters on a Global Roll," *Fortune,* 29 June 1992, p. 94.

27. T. Hout, M. Porter, and E. Rudder, "How Global Companies Win Out," in D. N. Dickson, ed., *Managing Effectively in the World Marketplace* (New York: Wiley, 1983), pp. 188–191.

28. Ibid., p. 189.

29. P. Chan and R. Justis, "Franchise Management in East Asia," *Academy of Management Executive* 4 (1990): 75–85.

30. Z. Schiller, "Can Bridgestone Make the Climb?" *Business Week,* 27 February 1989, pp. 78–79; "Survival in the Basic Industries: How Four Companies Hope to Avoid Disaster," *Business Week,* 26 April 1982, pp. 74–76.

31. W. J. Holstein and K. Kelly, "Little Companies, Big Exports," *Business Week,* 13 April 1992, p. 70.

32. B. Parker and M. M. Helms, "Generic Strategies and Firm Performance in a Declining Industry," *Management International Review* 32 (1992): 23–29.

33. Wright, "MNC—Third World Business Unit Performance: Application of Strategic Elements," pp. 231–240.

STRATEGIC MANAGEMENT MODEL

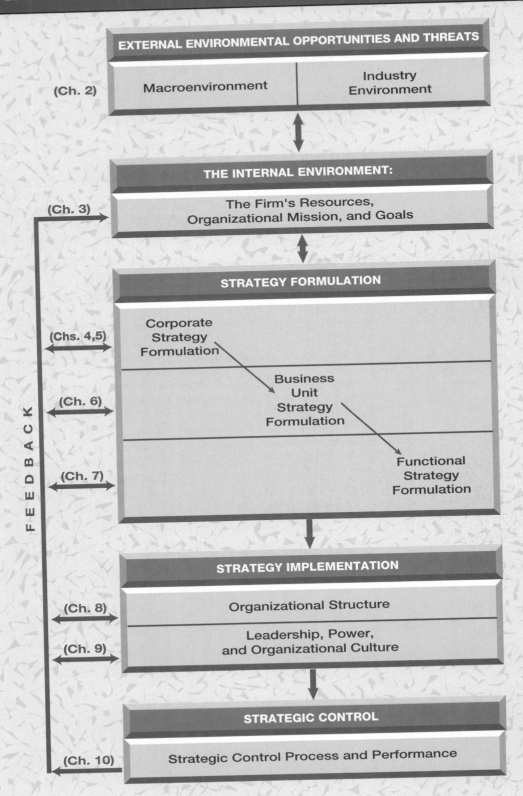

EXTERNAL ENVIRONMENTAL OPPORTUNITIES AND THREATS

(Ch. 2)

Macroenvironment	Industry Environment

THE INTERNAL ENVIRONMENT:

(Ch. 3)

The Firm's Resources, Organizational Mission, and Goals

STRATEGY FORMULATION

(Chs. 4,5)

Corporate Strategy Formulation

(Ch. 6)

Business Unit Strategy Formulation

(Ch. 7)

Functional Strategy Formulation

STRATEGY IMPLEMENTATION

(Ch. 8)

Organizational Structure

(Ch. 9)

Leadership, Power, and Organizational Culture

STRATEGIC CONTROL

(Ch. 10)

Strategic Control Process and Performance

FEEDBACK

12 Strategic Management in Not-for-Profit Organizations

The basic principles of strategic management presented in this book are equally applicable to profit and not-for-profit organizations. It is important, for instance, that all organizations analyze their environment; formulate a mission, goals, and objectives; develop appropriate strategies; implement those strategies; and control their strategic direction. However, in a more specific sense, there are some distinct differences between profit and not-for-profit organizations that have significant strategic implications. This chapter examines those differences.

TYPES OF NOT-FOR-PROFIT ORGANIZATIONS

Although not-for-profit organizations can be categorized in a number of ways, a basic classification consists of two groups: private not-for-profit organizations (which we will refer to as nonprofit organizations) and public not-for-profit organizations (which we will term public organizations). Some significant differences between business organizations and these two types of not-for-profit organizations are illustrated in Table 12.1.

Nonprofit organizations are entities that attempt to contribute to the good of society and are supported by private funds. Examples of such organizations include the following:

- Private educational institutions (e.g., Harvard University, the University of Chicago)
- Charities (e.g., Easter Seal Society, March of Dimes)

Table 12.1   **Some Differences Between Profit and Not-for-Profit Organizations**

	Business Organization	*Nonprofit Organization*	*Public Organization*
Ownership	Private	Private	Public
Funding	Sales of products and services	Membership dues, contributions from private and/or public sources, sale of products and services	Taxes and user fees
Types	Single proprietorship, partnership, corporation	Educational, charitable, social service, health service, foundation, cultural, and religious	Federal government, state government, local government

- Social service organizations (e.g., Alcoholics Anonymous, Girl Scouts of the U. S.A.)
- Health service organizations (e.g., Houston's Methodist Hospital, Johns Hopkins Health System)
- Foundations (e.g., Ford Foundation, Rockefeller Foundation)
- Cultural organizations (e.g., Los Angeles Philharmonic Orchestra, Chicago's Field Museum of Natural History)
- Religious institutions (e.g., St. Patrick's Cathedral, Memphis's Bellevue Baptist Church)

Public organizations are those created, funded, and regulated by the public sector. They are largely synonymous with what we commonly term *government* and include agencies at all levels of government, such as the following:

- Federal government agencies (e.g., Internal Revenue Service, United States Navy, Environmental Protection Agency)
- State government agencies (e.g., University of Kentucky, Texas Department of Corrections, Pennsylvania Turnpike Authority)
- Local government agencies (e.g., Dallas Public Library, Dade County Sheriff's Department, New York City Transit Authority)

In the United States, almost 18.5 million people are employed in public organizations, more than the number employed in manufacturing jobs.[1]

Both nonprofit and public organizations are indispensable to maintaining a civilized society. Many of society's essential needs cannot be provided by for-profit organizations. For instance, most individuals could not afford to pay for private police protection, and each major city has one or more "charity" hospital where the indigent can receive medical care.

The products and services of businesses can be obtained only by those who pay for them, but the outputs of public organizations and those of many nonprofit organizations are available to virtually all members of society. For instance, anyone—even a tourist—can receive the protection of a city's police force; anyone can travel along a toll-free interstate highway; and any child with birth defects is eligible for help from the March of Dimes. Some nonprofit organizations, of course, restrict their goods or services only to those who pay for the cost of providing the outputs. Examples are private universities (which exist to provide the public with an alternative to secular or mass education) and some cultural organizations (which must sell tickets to cover their costs but also usually offer some special annual events that are free to the public at large).

STRATEGIC ISSUES FOR NONPROFIT AND PUBLIC ORGANIZATIONS

This section examines some key strategic management issues in nonprofit and public organizations. First, we look at how environmental analysis may be conducted by these organizations. Then, we determine how they may develop their mission, goals, and objectives. We analyze next how they could formulate, implement, and control their strategies. Finally, we suggest some ways that not-for-profit organizations can increase their strategic management effectiveness.

■ Environmental Analysis

As the environment of not-for-profit organizations becomes increasingly dynamic, strategic management becomes more and more important. For example, nonprofit organizations have recently experienced reductions in federal aid and changes in tax laws that have reduced the incentive for corporations and individuals to make contributions. Simultaneously, competition for financial donations among nonprofits has increased with the rise of organizations dedicated to combating AIDS, Alzheimer's disease, child abuse, and drunk driving.[2]

Likewise, public organizations that once had a near monopoly in certain services, such as the U.S. Postal Service, are experiencing rapid change. Over the past few years, the Postal Service has felt increasing competitive pressure in express mail and the parcel business from such rivals as United Parcel Service and Federal Express. Additionally, in first-class mail, the Postal Service is losing business to a product substitute—the business-owned facsimile (fax) machine. Under such conditions, the necessity of planning well and operating effectively and efficiently becomes clear.

Two of the primary ways in which the environment of not-for-profit organizations differs from the environment of business organizations are in their sources of revenue and in the composition and concerns of their stakeholder groups. The following subsections explore these differences.

Sources of Revenue

Although there are a number of differences between businesses and not-for-profit organizations, perhaps the chief distinction is the source of the organization's revenues. Business income is derived almost exclusively from a single source—the sale of its products and services to individuals or organizations. Not-for-profit organizations, however, may receive revenue from a number of sources: taxes, dues, contributions, and in some instances, sales of their products or services. These differences are illustrated in Figure 12.1.

Figure 12.1   **Sources of Income for Profit and Not-for-Profit Organizations**

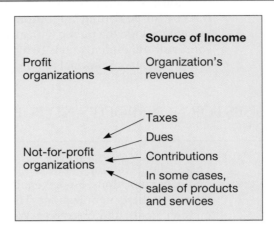

    Some of the contributors of revenue to certain organizations may never use, at least in a direct sense, the organizations' outputs. For instance, consider a family violence center. The center's purpose is to provide a haven for women and their children from abusive spouses, but the center must rely on others, who may never use the center, for financial support. Another example is the local public school system. Public schools have been asked to shoulder increasing responsibilities as society has changed. They are being looked to as sources of prevention training for drug abuse and teenage pregnancy, as locations for after-school care for latchkey children, and as institutions that must increase the quality of education for children. The financial support for pursuing these goals must come from all of the school district's taxpayers—not just the parents of the students who attend the schools. Consequently, some taxpayers may be reluctant to support higher taxes for the public schools.[3]
    Successful businesses know their customers and their needs. They recognize that satisfying their customers' needs is crucial for their existence. But not-for-profit organizations have a less direct relationship with their "customers." Those they serve are not necessarily those who contribute financially to their operations. Hence, their strategic planning must be twofold: planning for serving their clients or customers, and planning for securing the financial funding to provide those services.
    The first type of planning—to serve customers—may sometimes have to be done with little or no input from the customers. For instance, agencies that handle the problems of the mentally ill or those that safeguard children can hardly survey their clients to ascertain their needs. In such cases, agencies often plan their services on the basis of discussions with professionals who have expertise in that particular field and of what similar agencies in other locales have done. The second type of planning—to acquire financial funding—may become quite political. A government agency, for instance, must compete against other agencies for the limited funds available; those that are most successful are often the ones that acquiesce to demands made of them by those who control the funds. Defense Department appropriations, for instance, often depend upon the department's compliance with congressional wishes.

External Constituencies and Stakeholders

Strategic planning in business, as we have seen, involves taking into account the varying goals of the organization's stakeholders (e.g., its owners, employees, customers, creditors). The same is true for not-for-profit organizations, but the stakeholder groups and concerns are significantly different. This difference can best be seen in public organizations.

Although the managers of a government entity may engage in rational strategic planning, these plans may be ignored by political leaders who must respond to public pressure to win reelection. What may be rational in an economic sense may be politically unwise.

> Political leaders have learned that government often works only when a consensus forms to deal with a perceived crisis. The solutions may not conform with any plan, and governmental actions may be taken without regard to rational priorities. Nevertheless, the most important consideration may be that the actions are acceptable to the various constituency groups that are able to affect the decision. Since this occurs at all levels of government on a regular basis, it will be frustrating to managers who want government to function in an orderly manner. Government is not an orderly procedure because there are too many people with a variety of perspectives who are involved in reaching decisions.[4]

This greater number and diversity of stakeholders may result in less managerial autonomy for public agency managers than for managers in business. Because government agencies are "owned" by all citizens, their activities may often be more closely monitored by their constituents. This greater visibility means that managers' decisions are more public.

For example, Los Angeles County's Transportation Commission, a public agency, solicited bids from engineering firms a few years ago to build high-technology electronic trolley cars. Only two builders responded—Idaho-based Morrison Knudsen Corporation and Sumitomo Corporation, headquartered in Tokyo. When word leaked out that the Transportation Commission's construction unit would recommend awarding the contract to Sumitomo, the chairman of Morrison Knudsen attempted to get the decision reversed. Joining with him were various members of the public who strongly argued for a "Made in America" decision, politicians from both California and Los Angeles, and numerous lobbyists, lawyers, and political activists. As a result of the furor, the Transportation Commission reopened the bidding.[5]

In addition to being subject to public visibility, managerial actions are also scrutinized carefully by oversight agencies such as legislative bodies, courts, and executive groups. Hence, although managers of public organizations may not need to concern themselves with such business threats as hostile takeovers, foreign competition, or bankruptcy, they have a complicated environment in which to operate. They must serve customers or clients who may be separate from the organization's sources of funding. But the organization's operations must satisfy both the customers and the funding sources, as well as other constituencies and oversight agencies. This complexity is illustrated in Figure 12.2.

■ Mission, Goals, and Objectives

Not-for-profit organizations need clearly defined missions, goals, and objectives. This section explores this need and examines some reasons why clarity in organizational direction is sometimes lacking.

Figure 12.2   **Stakeholder Constraints on Public Organizations**

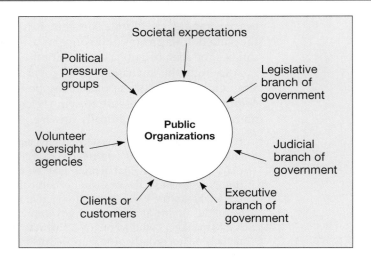

Mission

Certainly, having a well-focused mission and clear goals and objectives is as important to not-for-profit organizations as it is to businesses. Management researcher and consultant Peter F. Drucker points out that "the best nonprofits devote a great deal of thought to defining their organizations' missions."[6]

As an example, consider the Girl Scouts of the U.S.A.[7] In 1976, Frances Hesselbein became national executive director of the organization, which was experiencing several problems. In a diverse society, it was comprised mostly of white, middle-class girls; scout leaders were becoming increasingly difficult to recruit as women entered the work force in growing numbers; the Boy Scouts of America were considering extending membership to girls; and membership in the Girl Scouts had declined steadily for eight years.

Hesselbein's first step was to examine the mission of the Girl Scouts. The organization's management considered these questions: "What is our business?" "Who is the customer?" "What does the customer consider as value?" They decided that the Scouts existed for one major reason: to help girls reach their highest potential. As Hesselbein explained:

> More than any one thing, that made the difference. Because when you are clear about your mission, corporate goals and operating objectives flow from it.[8]

This strong self-identity helped the Scouts reject pressures from women's rights activists to support their causes and from charities to act as door-to-door canvassers. Today, although Hesselbein is no longer president, the organization numbers 2.3 million girls (15 percent of them are from racial minorities); conducts market research to determine the needs of modern girls; awards the most popular proficiency badges for math and computer expertise instead of for good grooming and hosting a party; sports uniforms designed by Halston and Bill Blass; and publishes monographs on such issues as teen pregnancy, drug use, and child abuse.

In the public arena, as Congress attempts to reduce the federal deficit, efforts are being directed toward clarifying the respective missions of the Navy, Army, Air Force, and Marine Corps. For instance, critics have charged for decades that the United States has the only military with four air forces (all four branches of the service have their own airplanes and helicopters). Furthermore, both the Air Force and the Navy have bomber aircraft. As the defense budget shrinks, much thought is being given to reducing this expensive overlap by defining clearly just what the mission of each military branch should be.[9]

Goals and Objectives

Although having a clearly defined mission and goals is essential to an organization's success, many not-for-profit organizations fail in this regard. Businesses, for instance, can easily measure sales, market share, profits, return on

---

STRATEGIC INSIGHT

A Nonprofit Organization's Mission: Howard Hughes Medical Institute

Once a tax shelter created by Howard Hughes, an important, but little known, nonprofit organization is the Howard Hughes Medical Institute. Founded in 1953 by the billionaire aviator-industrialist, the institute states its mission as follows:

• The primary purpose and objective of the Howard Hughes Medical Institute shall be the promotion of human knowledge within the field of the basic sciences (principally the field of medical research and medical education) and the effective application thereof for the benefit of mankind.

The institute is a scientific and philanthropic organization with the principal purpose of conducting biomedical research in five broad areas: genetics, immunology, neuroscience, structural biology, and cell biology and regulation. It accomplishes its scientific mission by funding research through laboratories located in some of the most prestigious academic medical centers, hospitals, universities, and other research institutions in the United States, Canada, Mexico, Australia, and New Zealand. Its philanthropic goals are attained by financially supporting various aspects of science education, from elementary school through postgraduate training.

In 1994, the institute had total assets of $7.8 billion, most of which is invested in equities, private partnerships, and nonequity securities. Earnings from this investment portfolio support the institute's operations. In 1994, the institute funded $280 million in medical research and support services and spent an estimated $50 million on science education. Unlike most foundations, Hughes does not dispense grants. Rather, it hires top researchers who go on working at their own medical schools, universities, or research centers. Without political and money pressures, they are free to set their own agendas.

How effective is Hughes' approach? So far in the 1990s alone, Hughes investigators at various locations have made scientific discoveries that are helping in the fights against colon cancer, cystic fibrosis, atherosclerosis, HIV, immune deficiencies, hypertension, and an inherited form of blindness.

SOURCES: M. B. Regan, "A Research Behemoth Gets Even Bigger," *Business Week*, 21 February 1994, p. 56; *Annual Report of the Howard Hughes Medical Institute 1993* (Bethesda, MD: Howard Hughes Medical Institute); P. Choppin, "Basic Medical Research," *Vital Speeches*, 15 June 1993, pp. 530–533.

investment, and so on. But not-for-profit organizations do not usually have such clear goals.

One of the reasons for this lack of clarity is that many of the goals are value-laden. Some states, for example, held fierce debates over mandatory seat belt laws. Was the goal to protect the lives of automobile drivers and passengers, or was it to protect the rights of those individuals to choose—or not to choose—to buckle up? Is the goal of a prison system rehabilitation of prisoners or punishment?

Second, not-for-profit goals often involve important trade-offs. This situation can be illustrated by the debate surrounding the potential closing of any military base. Its closing will reduce the federal deficit, but it will also harm the economy of the local area. Which is the more important consideration? During the 1992 presidential campaign, economist Herbert Stein emphasized the trade-off dilemma that any president faces: "He has to choose between assisting Russia, assisting urban ghettos in the U. S. and promoting aggregate growth in the American economy."[10] There is simply not sufficient funding available to accomplish all three goals.

Third, goals may often be deliberately vague, broad, and general, such as "protect our environment" or "help the homeless." Broad, general goals are more likely to secure the support of diverse stakeholders and provide inspiration for organization members. Also, vague goals are less likely to invite close scrutiny and debate than specific goals are and, hence, may avoid alienating potential supporters. Universities, for instance, often publicize their goal of offering a high-quality education. Few could argue with such a goal, and it helps skirt such issues as whether research or teaching is more important, how selective the university's admissions policies should be, and how much emphasis will be given to sports programs. Debates on any of these issues are almost certain to alienate some stakeholders, thereby reducing the flow of funds to the university.

Goals in public organizations are often vague because leadership is subject to frequent turnover. Changes in direction, for instance, can occur in a state where a Democrat replaces a Republican governor. Four years later, election results can alter the state's direction yet again. Vague goals, such as "operate the state for the benefit of all of its citizens," therefore, are likely to have more permanency and lend more of an aura of stability than very specific goals will.

Goals may sometimes not reflect the needs of the organization's "customers" as much as they reflect the wishes of the organization's financial donors. Church-affiliated universities, for instance, may make decisions that anger their students but conform to the wishes of the denomination that accounts for much of their financial backing. Some nonprofit organizations, in fact, may be reluctant to turn down substantial funding, even if the donor insists that the funds be used for a purpose outside the basic mission of the organization. Again, vague goals may appear more appropriate in such situations.

The question, of course, is whether these reasons for establishing vague goals are valid. In a number of situations we do not believe that they are. Although formulating goals and objectives is more challenging for not-for-profit organizations than for businesses, having clarity in direction is helpful if organizations are to operate effectively. Perhaps the major reason for our belief is that without clear goals, an organization has no way to measure its progress or its effectiveness.

Both nonprofit and public organizations might bring together their various stakeholders to hammer out a set of specific, measurable objectives. The process will not be smooth, because each stakeholder group may have its own agenda. Even so, without this process, these organizations may be unable to evaluate their performance.

Virtually every organization can define specific goals. Determining goal attainment may be undertaken through setting standards. For instance, the family violence center mentioned earlier could formulate a means of evaluating how effectively it is able to prevent its clients from suffering further abuse and how well it enhances its clients' self-esteem. Moreover, it also may define such performance ratios as expenditures per client day. Because such organizations typically cannot begin to help all of those who need their help, the more tightly they can control their costs, the more clients they can serve. Broad measures of costs per month or per year cannot help control costs as effectively as more specific ratios. Such standards act as a surrogate performance measure when profit figures are not applicable.

■ Strategy Formulation, Implementation, and Control

The processes of formulating, implementing and controlling strategy are often more complicated in not-for-profit organizations than in businesses. Some of those complications are examined next.

Strategy Formulation and Implementation

In general, we can say that most of these not-for-profit organizations attempt to satisfy specific societal needs. For instance, the American Red Cross rushes to aid victims of natural disasters; the Salvation Army ministers to the physical and religious needs of homeless persons. The U.S. Navy keeps the sea lanes of the world open; the Army concentrates on ground defense. Within a state, some universities serve as major research and graduate institutions; others concentrate on teaching undergraduates.

Often, one of the features that distinguishes not-for-profit organizations from businesses is the presence of greater political constraints upon the strategic choices of not-for-profits. In public organizations, for instance, many decisions are subject to the approval of oversight agencies and the legislative and executive branches of government. These strategic decisions become even more politicized by their public visibility in the press. Several years ago, for example, the National Academy of Public Administration complained about the complexity of the controls and rules over managerial decisions in the federal government.[11]

Many functional strategies are also greatly constrained by rules governing such areas as purchasing and personnel. For instance, a General Accounting Office survey of federal government employees revealed that 5.7 percent of those surveyed were "poor performers." Although some of these employees improved their performance, voluntarily quit, or were removed from their jobs, almost 40 percent never improved and were not asked to leave. That group received more than $1 billion in annual salaries.[12] Finally, the frequent turnover of leadership, discussed earlier, may discourage employees from channeling much effort into support of the strategy, since they know that the current strategy may be short-lived.

Even if strategy could be formulated and unfettered by political considerations, implementation of the strategy can be a problem. Public managers have

<table>
<tr><td colspan="2">

Strategies for Churches

</td></tr>
</table>

Internal Growth Strategy

One of the nation's largest churches is Houston's Second Baptist Church. With a Sunday morning attendance of 12,000, the church complex covers thirty-two acres. In 1984, however, the church was simply a conventional church on a large plot of land. Its incoming pastor, H. Edwin Young, was familiar with the demographics of the area: thousands of young families and single people new to Houston. He sold his vision of a growing church to his congregation and persuaded them to pledge over $17 million needed for new physical facilities while the church borrowed over $26 million for additional construction costs.

Pastor Young dispatched church members to study office management techniques at Xerox and IBM and parking and people skills at Disney World. He varied religious services to fit particular needs. In addition to the traditional Sunday morning service, a Sunday evening service caters to a mostly singles crowd; on Wednesday nights, separate services are offered, one traditional and one with religious rock music.

Today, computers regulate mood lighting during church services; shuttle buses bring latecomers in from outlying parking decks; parking attendants empty the church's numerous parking lots every Sunday in half an hour; billboards and television ads invite people to visit this "Fellowship of Excitement"; an information desk is staffed with cheerful attendants; aerobics classes are held daily beginning at 6:00 A.M.; and a restaurant offers two types of menus: "saints" for those who prefer a low-calorie meal, and "sinners," for those who desire richer food.

Turnaround Strategy

The U.S. Catholic Church, like many organizations, is trying to overcome stagnant revenues and steadily rising costs. Taking the lead in this fight is the Archdiocese of Chicago, which has taken the following steps:

- Sold assets of $6.2 million
- Restructured archdiocesan offices and laid off fifty employees to save $1.5 million
- Required all parishes to submit three-year budgets and quarterly financial reports
- Had each parish establish a local advisory council of business leaders
- Devised repayment plans for loans made to the parishes and began charging interest on these loans
- Increased tuition at parish schools
- Raised the assessment each parish pays the archdiocese from 6.5 to 10 percent of its annual revenues.
- Consolidated parishes and schools in the archdiocese
- Encouraged church members to increase their giving
- Began marketing the services of the church to new groups, such as young adults

Although some of the changes have met with resistance, Joseph Cardinal Bernardin maintains that there is little choice. He emphasized that to "fulfill our mission, we have to have the resources."

SOURCES: C. Y. Coleman, "Churches Preach a High-Tech Gospel," *Wall Street Journal*, 6 May 1996, pp. B1, B3; "Religion in America," *American Demographics*, March 1994, pp. 4–6; K. Kelley, "Chicago's Catholic Church: Putting Its House in Order," *Business Week*, 10 June 1991, pp. 60–65 (source of quotation p. 65); R. G. Niebuhr, "Megachurches Strive to Be All Things to All Parishioners," *Wall Street Journal*, 13 May 1991.

weaker authority over their subordinates than business managers do. Such decisions as pay, promotion, termination, and disciplinary action are often subject to rules rather than to managerial discretion. Employees who enthusiastically carry out the strategy of the organization may receive the same rewards as those who ignore the strategy to pursue their own ends. In one of the most flagrant examples of restrictive work rules, New York City public school custodians are required to sweep school floors only every other day and to mop them only three times a year. Furthermore, cafeteria floors need to be mopped only once a week. The average annual salary for such work in 1994 was $60,000.[13] In a similar case, the *Wall Street Journal* reported that restrictive work rules at Philadelphia's International Airport required three employees to change one lightbulb: a building mechanic to remove the light panel, an electrician to insert the new bulb, and a janitor to clean up the area.[14]

Because our political system is designed to ensure frequent turnover through regularly scheduled elections and through limitations on how long individuals can hold some offices, government leaders are encouraged to take a short-range approach to strategic management. Voters in the next election may be more likely to reelect officials who have benefited them during the past several months than those who have an excellent long-range plan but have demonstrated little in the way of immediate results.

Although nonprofit organizations may operate under fewer constraints than public organizations do, implementation of strategy can be constrained by those who oppose the strategy. For instance, public abortion clinics may be picketed by right-to-life advocates. More important, however, may be the constraints imposed by the nature of the work force in many nonprofit organizations. Often, the bulk of the workers are volunteers who receive no pay for their services. As long as the direction of the organization is consistent with their values and beliefs, they will cooperate in implementing strategic decisions. But should the agency's direction deviate from their values, they may quit the organization and even actively oppose its operations.

In fact, many nonprofit organizations develop their organizational culture around a cause. Often, the founder of the organization and the members exhibit the attitudes and behaviors of "true believers" who are willing to work long hours at little or no pay to further their particular beliefs and values. Many environmental groups as well as pro- and antiabortion organizations possess such powerful cultures. Few businesses are able to develop their culture around such powerful and emotional goals.

Another consideration is that businesses often have more attractive financial compensation packages than not-for-profit organizations. Individuals who are motivated by such considerations, therefore, will often seek employment in business organizations. This choice reduces the pool of talented workers from which public and nonprofit organizations can choose. In addition, the trend toward two-income families has certainly diminished the number of volunteers available to nonprofit organizations.

Not-for-profit organizations may also implement their strategies in a more centralized fashion than businesses.[15] As we saw in an earlier chapter, many businesses have responded to increasing environmental change by decentralizing their decision making. Although environments in many cases are equally dynamic for public and nonprofit agencies, the same trend has not occurred there. Because so many differing stakeholder groups must be considered when management implements strategy, often only the top managers are fully aware of how stakeholders' attitudes are changing.[16] For this reason, implementation decisions are made at the top levels of the organization. In addition, under the civil service system in public organizations, which primarily rewards seniority rather than merit, few employees are able to perceive a connection between their job performance and their compensation. Because incentives are not used to channel their behavior into the appropriate areas of strategy implementation, their behavior is instead controlled through an extensive network of rules and procedures, resulting in a bureaucratic configuration in which decision-making authority is centralized.

A further difficulty with implementation of strategy in some not-for-profit organizations is that these institutions are staffed largely by professional people who see themselves as committed to the profession rather than to the particular organization for which they currently work. For instance, physicians are said to be engaged in the practice of medicine (a profession) rather than working for a particular hospital. College professors are often referred to (and view themselves) as professors of physics or history rather than as employees of a specific university. In such cases, they "will probably publish more, spend less time on college committees, devote less time to teaching and students, attend more professional meetings, and be more willing to leave the college"[17] than the individual who identifies more with the organization than the profession. The problem that this perspective poses from the organization's viewpoint is that such persons may have primary loyalty to their profession rather than to the organization that employs them.[18] Therefore, strategic managers may need to persuade these persons to emphasize their responsibilities to the organization as well as to their profession.

Strategic Control

Without clearly stated goals and objectives, strategic control becomes very difficult to achieve. For instance, the quality of education in public schools might be measured in several ways. One way is to determine how well students can solve problems and communicate those solutions, with the measurement taken once at the beginning of a period of time and again at the end of that time period. If the results are less than the school district has set as its goal, then corrective action must be taken. Likewise, a church that did not increase its membership as much as it desired during a particular year would have to take some corrective action, as would a police department that failed to meet its goal of solving 80 percent of the crimes committed during a twelve-month period.

Control is more difficult, obviously, when goals are not clear or when an organization has conflicting goals. Recall the example of the family violence center used earlier. The particular community in which it operates believes that it has been successful because its services are well publicized and fully used. However, it has very nearly gone bankrupt trying to help all who need its services, and its director argues that the center has just begun to scratch the surface!

In some cases, nonprofit organizations have literally had no objectives in certain key areas. The prestigious University of Chicago hospital, for instance, had no budgeting system to track its costs until 1989.[19] Without standards, the hospital's management could not determine the cost of a procedure, such as an appendectomy. Lack of both cost objectives and cost information made the control of costs virtually impossible.

Even under conditions in which the corrective actions that should be taken are clear, control may still not occur. For instance, in business, when a project or program is no longer contributing to a firm's profits, decisions are made either to rejuvenate the program, if appropriate and possible, or to terminate it. Hence, profit serves as a readily acceptable yardstick to help management determine the amount of resources that various programs should receive.[20]

This means of control is not available to not-for-profit organizations. In fact, only rarely are programs terminated, particularly in government. This fact can be demonstrated quickly by virtually any debate on how to reduce the federal deficit. Few individuals want their taxes raised, but any proposal to terminate a program (and, hence, lower expenditures) quickly brings an outcry from those stakeholders who will be adversely affected by the program's demise. As a result, governments at all levels continue to add programs that are needed but rarely end any of their ongoing programs. But strategic control requires that a manager make choices, because it is simply not possible to do everything well.[21] Even when a lack of funding makes it imperative to cut programs, the programs cut are not necessarily the ones least needed; often, the programs eliminated are the ones that are less likely to create a highly vocal protest from their constituents.

STRATEGIC INSIGHT

Strategic Control at the Post Office

The U.S. Postal Service faces increasing competition from air express companies, facsimile machines, long-distance telephone companies, electronic mail, and interactive cable television. While its revenue growth (about $47 billion a year) stagnates, its operating expenses continue to escalate. A 1992 General Accounting Office report revealed that, even though considerable automation of post office operations had occurred, operating expenses were $295 million more than expected. In fact, while the volume of mail delivered declined, the number of work hours increased.

As a result, major attempts at strategic control are under way. The first try, however, failed. Postmaster General Anthony Frank's request for a one-cent increase in first-class postage—which would have raised $800 million annually—was denied by the Postal Service Board of Governors. Although the vote was 6 to 3 in favor of the increase, a unanimous vote is required. Frank responded: "I'm the only CEO of a major corporation in America who doesn't have control over his own prices." Before leaving office, however, he managed to cap labor costs (which amount to 83 percent of operating expenses) and give management more flexibility in hiring temporary workers. He also announced an early-retirement plan designed to trim payrolls, hired a polling company to measure customer satisfaction, and extended window hours.

Frank was succeeded by Marvin Runyon, who continued the strategic control measures by eliminating—through early retirement—25 percent of the Postal Service's managerial positions. He restructured the organization, replacing its seventy-three regional divisions with two functional divisions: one for processing and distributing mail and one for customer services. In total, about 50,000 workers were laid off, and a budget surplus of $500 million was achieved in 1992. Runyon also made good on his promise not to increase postage rates through 1994.

SOURCES: W. Keenan Jr., "Can We Deliver?" *Sales & Marketing Management* (February 1994): 62–67; "General Delivery," *Sales & Marketing Management* (February 1994): 66; S. Barr, "Can the Postal Service Get Lean?" *Folio: The Magazine for Magazine Management*, 1 March 1993, pp. 63–64; W. R. Cummings, "Reinventing the Post Office," *Wall Street Journal*, 11 January 1993; R. Davis, "Postal Chief Wants Service That Delivers," *USA Today*, 10 August 1992; S. Rudavsky, "Postal Service Plans Sweeping Overhaul," *Washington Post*, 7 August 1992; "That Was Then, This Is Now," *Washington Post Magazine*, 14 June 1992, p. 11; M. Lewyn, "Pushing the Envelope at the Post Office," *Business Week*, 25 November 1991, pp. 56–57 (quotation is from p. 56).

Even charitable nonprofit organizations may behave in similar ways. For instance, sometimes the mission of an agency is actually accomplished or its environment changes so that its mission becomes unnecessary. Consider the Mothers' March of Dimes organization, which was originally established to support research that would lead to a cure for polio. With the widespread distribution of the Salk vaccine in the 1950s, polio ceased to be the threat it once was. But the March of Dimes did not go out of existence. Instead, it adopted a new cause—birth defects—in order to sustain itself.

■ Improving Strategic Management

Although some of the difficulties in implementing strategic management concepts in not-for-profit organizations are unlikely to disappear (e.g., the desire of elected officials to be reelected minimizes an emphasis on long-range planning), other problems can be overcome. The concepts of effective strategic management presented in this book are not limited to business institutions. Both nonprofit and public organizations can benefit significantly by analyzing their environmental opportunities and constraints and by formulating a mission and goals that allow them to fulfill the needs of some segment of society. They must then develop a strategy that relates their strengths and weaknesses appropriately to their environment and allows them to create a distinctive competence in their operating arena. An organization structure must be fashioned that enables the agency to deal effectively with its environmental demands; and a culture should be established that enhances—rather than interferes with—its operational effectiveness.

Some not-for-profit organizations are highly effective, of course. But for those that are not, these basic principles of strategic management can be most useful in increasing their ability to carry out their mission. In some of these situations, the culture may be such that improvement is virtually impossible without a major change. Strong transformational leadership may be required, along with a significant modification in policies, so that employees' attitudes and practices can be unfrozen and changed. Top management's commitment to the concept of change must be complete and highly visible. Concurrently, reward systems must be altered to encourage creativity, new ways of doing old things, and service to the agency's clients or customers.

Certainly, such change cannot occur overnight. One authority suggests that top management start gradually to chip away at detrimental cultural aspects and look for special opportunities to implement strategic management principles in narrow, well-defined areas. In this way, management can devote the resources and time that are required for success.[22]

Finally, we would be negligent if we did not emphasize the need for managerial training. In some nonprofit organizations, the top-level managers may be individuals who were sensitive to a particular need in our society and created an organization to serve that need. But even the best of intentions cannot serve society as effectively as good intentions combined with managerial skills. The most socially oriented of programs must, in the long run, use each of its dollars and the time of its employees as effectively and efficiently as it possibly can. Otherwise, all of those who are in need of its services may never receive them or may receive only partial care.

Strategic Alliances for Public Organizations

An increasing number of public organizations are finding that strategic alliances with private industry can improve their operating effectiveness. In some cases, for instance, "privatizing" government functions can reduce costs and improve revenue flows.

Take, for example, Chicago's parking enforcement program. During the 1980s, $420 million of parking ticket fines went unpaid. That's because, after a ticket was written, it took an average of two years for the ticket to be recorded. But, in 1990, Chicago turned the recording process over to Dallas-based Electronic Data Systems (EDS). Now the 14,000 parking tickets written by police officers each day are electronically imaged and stored on optical disks by EDS personnel the very same day. Other parking tickets, written by meter monitors, are entered by the ticket writer directly into hand-held computers and are electronically transferred into EDS's computer. The city is now saving about $5 million a year in administrative expenses, ticket revenues are increasing substantially, and parking meter revenues are significantly higher.

In other developments, such states as California and New York are experimenting with contracting out some welfare functions to private companies. For instance, in New York, a welfare mother costs the state about $23,000 annually. But, in its contract with America Works (a private company), New York pays only $5,300. America Works and other similar firms, such as MAXIMUS and Lockheed IMS, can cut expenses by superior use of computer technology, a lack of restrictive work rules, and little bureaucracy. America Works is not only less expensive for the taxpayers, but it also succeeds at getting almost 70 percent of its clients off the welfare rolls.

Meanwhile, Baltimore has turned over the management of nine inner-city schools to a Minneapolis-based company—Education Alternatives. This company hopes to save money while reducing the student-teacher ratio and increasing the use of technology in these schools. Its profit will come from part of the savings.

Some government agencies are even forming strategic alliances with nonprofit organizations. Florida's prison system, for instance, paroles some of its first offenders into the custody of the Salvation Army. About two-thirds of these parolees become "permanently rehabilitated" (they are not indicted for another crime for at least six years).

As budget deficits mount at the federal, state, and local levels, government officials continue to search for creative ways to lower costs. Strategic alliances with private industry and nonprofit organizations show considerable promise in helping officials attain this goal.

SOURCES: J. Huey, "Finding New Hopes for a New Era," *Fortune*, 25 January 1993, p. 65; J. Mathews, "Taking Welfare Private," *Newsweek*, 29 June 1992, p. 44; A. Kotlowitz, "For-Profit Firms to Manage Public Schools in Baltimore," *Wall Street Journal*, 11 June 1992; P. F. Drucker, "It Profits Us to Strengthen Nonprofits," *Wall Street Journal*, 19 December 1991; R. Henkoff, "Some Hope for Troubled Cities," *Fortune*, 9 September 1991, p. 126.

SUMMARY

Strategic management principles apply equally to businesses and not-for-profit organizations. But these two types of institutions differ in some important ways that have strategic implications.

Perhaps the chief distinction is their source of revenue. Businesses generate income in the form of sales revenue; not-for-profit firms may receive revenue from such diverse sources as taxes, dues, contributions, or even sales. But a business's revenue is derived directly from its customers—those who purchase its products or services. However, a not-for-profit's revenue often comes from individuals who may never even use the outputs of that organization. For instance, a public organization may provide welfare payments to families below the poverty level. However, the sources of those funds are taxes paid by income earners with relatively higher salaries. Similarly, a nonprofit organization such as a privately owned museum may allow the public to view its exhibits for no admission fee. But its revenues may be generated by the interest from an endowment created by a family many decades ago. Therefore, not-for-profit organizations must engage in two types of strategic planning—how to serve their clients or customers, and how to secure the necessary financial funding to provide those services.

A second distinction between businesses and nonprofits is that planning in some not-for-profit firms, particularly public organizations, may be complicated by political considerations, which are not relevant to businesses. The large number and diversity of stakeholders in a government agency means that its managers' decisions are more public than they are in other types of organizations. These decisions must be responsive to the wishes of varying constituencies, requiring management to engage in a difficult balancing act.

Although having a clear mission and goals is essential to an organization's success, many not-for-profit organizations fail in this area. Several reasons account for this shortcoming: Goals tend to be value-laden; they often involve important trade-offs; they may be deliberately vague, broad, and general; leadership is subject to frequent turnover, particularly in public organizations; and the goals may not reflect the needs of the organization's customers as much as they reflect the wishes of the organization's financial supporters. The problem, of course, is that vague goals cannot help management measure an organization's progress or its effectiveness.

Strategy implementation in not-for-profit organizations, particularly public agencies, is often highly visible and political. But even if strategies could be implemented in a rational fashion, public managers would still operate under another unique constraint. They have weaker authority in such areas as pay, promotion, termination, and disciplinary action than business managers have. By the same token, managers in private nonprofit firms must often supervise a work force comprised largely of volunteers, which poses a different set of constraints. Other distinctions exist as well. For instance, research shows that not-for-profit organizations implement their strategies in a more centralized fashion than businesses do, and they are sometimes staffed by professional people who may be more committed to their profession than to the organization for which they currently work.

Strategic control, of course, is difficult to achieve when goals are not clearly defined and measurable. It is made even more difficult by the fact that not-for-profit organizations, unlike businesses, cannot usually terminate programs even if they have outlived their usefulness. Just the threat of program termination quickly brings an outcry from those stakeholders who will be adversely affected by the program's demise, and they often wield sufficient political power to forestall termination indefinitely.

However, both nonprofit and public organizations can benefit significantly by following the principles presented in this book. They, as well as businesses, should analyze their environmental opportunities and constraints and formulate mission and goals that allow them to fulfill the needs of some segment of society. They should then develop a strategy that relates their strengths and weaknesses appropriately to their environment and allows them to create a distinctive competence in their operating arena. To implement their strategy, they must fashion an organization structure that enables them to deal with their environmental demands and a culture that enhances their organizational effectiveness. Cultures and reward systems that are too constraining must be altered to improve the organizations' operating efficiency and their long-term effectiveness.

TAKE IT TO THE NET

We invite you to visit the Wright page on the Prentice Hall Web site at:

http://www.prenhall.com/wright

for this chapter's World Wide Web exercise.

KEY CONCEPTS

Nonprofit organization   A form of not-for-profit organization that is supported by private funds and exists to contribute to the good of society.

Public organization   A form of not-for-profit organization that is created, funded, and regulated by the public sector.

DISCUSSION QUESTIONS

1. Your text states that "nonprofit and public organizations are indispensable to maintaining a civilized society." Explain why.

2. Explain how not-for-profit organizations differ from businesses in the way that they derive their revenue. What are the implications of these differences for strategic management?

3. We have seen that the top managers of public organizations probably have less autonomy than do business CEOs because of the greater number and diversity of stakeholders in public organizations. Explain how multiple stakeholder interests can reduce managerial autonomy.

4. Why do not-for-profit organizations often have vague, general goals rather than clear, specific ones?

5. What are the disadvantages of vague, general goals?

6. Select a not-for-profit organization and describe the specific societal needs that it attempts to satisfy. Does it have any competitors? If so, who are they?

7. How does the implementation of strategy in not-for-profit organizatio differ from that in businesses?

8. Why is strategy implementation more centralized in not-for-profit orga zations than in businesses?

9. From a strategic perspective, what are the difficulties of managing prof sional employees? Volunteer employees?

10. Why do public organizations have more difficulty terminating progra than businesses have?

STRATEGIC MANAGEMENT EXERCISES

1. Assume that you have the resources and backing to found a university. Formulate a mission statement for your university. Now, develop a set of goals for the university. How would you ensure that the needs of your university's "customers" are met through the goals that you have devised? (Note that customers would include employers of the university's graduates, graduate schools that accept your graduates, students, parents who pay tuition, etc.)

2. Use your own university to answer the following questions: What is your university's mission? What are it major goals? Base your answers on written documents, if they exist; otherwise, you will need to derive your answers from interviews and observation. After gathering information on your university, determine how it might formulate and implement appropriate strategies to serve its constituents and stakeholders better. Give specific examples.

3. The United Way of America is supposed to provide financial support for a wide variety of charitable causes. But in the early 1990s, news reports revealed that much abuse and fraud had taken place in its headquarters' organization. From library research of this scandal, suggest how the use of strategic control techniques might have prevented these problems from ever occurring at the United Way of America.

NOTES

1. B. Vobejda, "In Job Strength, Manufacturing Eclipsed by Public Sector," *Washington Post*, 18 August 1992.

2. The demand for business executives to support nonprofits not only has increased for financial help but also for serving as consultants or board members. See W. G. Bowen, "When A Business Leader Joins a Nonprofit Board," *Harvard Business Review* 72, 1 (September-October 1994): 38–43; J. A. Bryne, "Profiting from the Nonprofits," *Business Week*, 26 March 1990, p. 67.

3. W. H. Newman and H. W. Wallender, "Managing Not-for-Profit Enterprises," *Academy of Management Review* 3 (1978): 24–31.

4. Reprinted from W. H. Eldridge, "Why Angels Fear to Tread: A Practitioner's Observations and Solutions on Introducing Strategic Management to a Government Culture," in J. Rabin, G. J. Miller, and W. B. Hildreth, eds., *Handbook of Strategic Management* (New York: Dekker, 1989), p. 329, by courtesy of Marcel Dekker Inc.

5. F. Rose, "How a U. S. Company Used Anti-Japan Mood to Help Reverse a Loss," *Wall Street Journal*, 22 April 1992.

6. P. F. Drucker, "What Business Can Learn from Nonprofits," *Harvard Business Review* 67, no. 4 (1989): 89.

7. Bryne, "Profiting from the Nonprofits," pp. 67, 70–74.

8. Ibid., p. 72.

9. J. Lancaster, "Hill Takes Aim on Duplication in Military Services," *Washington Post*, 8 August 1992.

10. P. D. Harvey and J. D. Snyder, "Charities Need a Bottom Line Too," *Harvard Business Review* 65, no. 1 (1987): 14–22.

11. National Academy of Public Administration, *Revitalizing Federal Management* (Washington, D. C.: National Academy of Public Administration, 1986).

12. D. Priest, "Study Ties Job Success to Bosses," *Washington Post*, 9 October 1990.

13. R. Flick, "How Unions Stole the Big Apple," *Reader's Digest*, January 1992, pp. 39–40.

14. "Philly Thinks Private," *Wall Street Journal*, 30 June 1992.

15. P. C. Nutt, "A Strategic Planning Network for Non-Profit Organizations," *Strategic Management Journal* 5 (1984): 58.

16. J. Ruffat, "Strategic Management of Public and Non-Market Corporations," *Long Range Planning* 16, no. 4 (1983): 75.

17. W. G. Bennis, N. Berkowitz, M. Affinito, and M. Malone, "Reference Groups and Loyalties in the Out-Patient Department," *Administrative Science Quarterly* 2 (1958): 484.

18. Newman and Wallender, "Managing Not-for-Profit Enterprises," pp. 24–31.

19. J. F. Siler and T. Peterson, "Hospital, Heal Thyself," *Business Week*, 27 August 1990, p. 68.

20. Eldridge, "Why Angels Fear to Tread: A Practitioner's Observations and Solutions on Introducing Strategic Management to a Government Culture," p. 329.

21. Ibid., p. 330.

22. Ibid., p. 335.

Company Index

Name Index

Subject Index